D0916014

HOLY WAR IN CHINA

Holy War in China

THE MUSLIM REBELLION AND STATE IN CHINESE CENTRAL ASIA, 1864–1877

Hodong Kim

STANFORD UNIVERSITY PRESS
STANFORD, CALIFORNIA 2004

Stanford University Press
Stanford, California

Printed in the United States of America on acid-free, archival-quality paper

Library of Congress Cataloging-in-Publication Data

Kim, Ho-dong, 1954–
Holy war in China : the Muslim rebellion and state in Chinese Central Asia, 1864–1877 / Hodong Kim.
p. cm.
Includes bibliographical references and index.
ISBN 0-8047-4884-5 (alk. paper)
1. Xinjiang Uygur Zizhiqu (China)—History—19th century. 2. Xinjiang Uygur Zizhiqu (China)—Ethnic relations—History—19th century. I. Title: Muslim rebellion and state in Chinese Central Asia, 1864–1877. II. Title.
DS793.S62 K595 2004
951'.6035—dc22 2003019930

Typeset by Integrated Composition Systems in 10/12.5 Sabon

Original Printing 2004

Last figure below indicates year of this printing:
13 12 11 10 09 08 07 06 05 04

Subsidy Assistance for the publication of this book was provided by China Publication Subventions.

To my Parents

Contents

Illustrations

Acknowledgments

The first version of the present work was completed in 1986 when it was submitted to Harvard University as a doctoral dissertation. At that time, I thought that I would not hurry to publish it so that I could have more time to ponder the subject and write a complete revision. For a deeper understanding of the history of modern Central Asia it seemed necessary for me to expand my scope of interest. The focus of my interest shifted to the topics related to the peculiarities of nomadic societies and states, and their interactions with sedentary societies. So the revision of my dissertation could not but be delayed much longer than I had imagined. Had it not been for the encouragement of many scholars and colleagues, I am afraid that it might never have been accomplished. With their warm support I finished this much overdue task. Although this book cannot be said to be a complete revision of my dissertation in terms of structure or basic arguments, its size is considerably expanded, its organization is reshuffled, and more details and new researches have been added.

During these long years of preparation I have enjoyed the encouragement and help of numerous scholars. First, I owe a debt of gratitude to my two mentors, Min Tuki in Seoul and Joseph Fletcher Jr. at Harvard, who led me to the pastures of Chinese and Central Asian history. I deeply mourn their untimely deaths. The members of my doctoral committee—Omeljan Pritsak, Philip Kuhn, and Thomas Barfield—gave me warm advice and thoughtful criticism. In particular, this work would not have been completed were it not for the help of Professor Barfield at Boston University who read the revised version thoroughly and made numerous corrections.

I should like to thank the scholars who have shown great interest in my work and provided me help and encouragement in various ways: Richard Frye, Eden Naby, William Thackston, Sinasi Tekin, Beatrice Manz, Isenbike Togan, Mark Elliot, Dru Gladney, Thomas Höllman, Saguchi Tōru, Haneda Akira, Mano Eiji, Hamada Masami, Hori Sunao, Umemura Hiroshi, Sawada Minoru, Ji Dachun, Dian Weijiang, and Pan Zhiping. I would especially like to express my sincere gratitude to Professor James Millward for reading the entire manuscript and giving me invaluable comments. My special thanks are due as well to the Harvard-Yenching Institute, the Humboldt Foundation, the Widener Library, and the Sakyejul Publishing Company. I also wish to extend my gratitude to Muriel Bell, Carmen Borbón-Wu, and Anne Friedman at Stanford University Press for their help.

I should like to offer thanks to Koh Byungik, emeritus professor and former president of Seoul National University, for his warm and unflagging support. I remain grateful to my colleagues at the Department of Asian History, Seoul National University: Oh Keumsung, Yu Insun, Kim Yongdeok, Lee Sungkyu, Park Hanje, and Kim Hyeongjong. I want to thank Kwon Youngpil, Min Byunghoon, and the members of the Korean Association for Central Asian Studies. I am grateful to Dr. Yi Eunjeong, Mr. Lee Yonggyu, and Mr. Han Seunghyun for their assistance.

Without the moral support of my family certainly this book would not have been published. I would like to thank my wife, Park Chanoak, and my children—Euihyun, Youngshin, and Sunghyun—for their love and perseverance. Finally, I wish to dedicate this book to my parents who have endured the last fifty years praying for me.

Introduction

Chinese Central Asia, the present Xinjiang-Uyghur Autonomous Region, is divided into two unequal parts by the Tianshan range: Eastern Turkestan, which is mostly desert except for a string of oases fed by the snowmelt mountain waters, and Zungharia, which is a grassland steppe in the plains and the mountain valleys. The whole territory is about three times larger than France with a population of over seventeen million at present.[1] Around the middle of the nineteenth century only between one and two million people lived in this region. Several civilizations of Asia met here and left long-lasting imprints upon the history of the area. From the time of antiquity to our day, Indo–Iranian, Chinese, Islamic, and steppe cultures found their way to this area. The fusion and the friction of these different factors brought a variety of changes to the politics, social life, and culture of this region. Because of such contacts, a large portion of the records on Chinese Central Asia were written by its neighboring peoples. From the second half of the past century scholars began to pay serious attention to its history based on these records. There was also a remarkable increase of our knowledge about this region through geographical explorations and archaeological excavations.

Nevertheless, the historical research on Chinese Central Asia remains inadequate compared to the study of other areas. Interest in the period after the Mongol invasion is particularly lacking. We have only meager knowledge of the Chaghatay khanate and its successor state, the Moghul khanate, whose history in the region extends more than four centuries, although recent efforts have begun to unveil the clouded history of the post-Mongol period.[2] This lack of study can be explained in part by the scarcity of source material with which to pursue research. (One exception to this generalization is the period of Qing rule where there have been a number of detailed studies that take advantage of the abundance of Chinese sources.[3]) Another reason for the general lack of interest in the history of the post-Mongol period can be found in the assumption that Chinese Central Asia stopped being a dynamic factor in Eurasian historical context from the late premodern period. The gradually decreasing economic vitality of the "Silk Road" and the Islamization of Central Asia reinforced this trend.[4]

One of most significant but least explored periods in the region's history is the late nineteenth century, which is the focus of this study. The period began with an enormous political upheaval that quickly engulfed all of Xinjiang in 1864. This revolt led to the expulsion of the Qing dynasty from Central Asia and the establishment of an independent Muslim state led by Ya'qūb Beg. Independence ended with Ya'qūb Beg's death and the Chinese reconquest of the region in 1877. This was a unique historical experience for this region. For the first time in their history, the people of the oases of Eastern Turkestan were united in an independent state for which they sought recognition and support from the outside world. In spite of the many catastrophic results that came in the wake of the rebellion and the Qing reconquest, Eastern Turkestan's decade of independence from China caused the local people to reflect anew on their self-identity. The period of autonomy in the nineteenth century then served as a source of inspiration for a new generation of nationalistic leaders in the twentieth century. Another legacy of this period was the awakening of historical consciousness among the region's intellectuals that resulted in an unprecedented flood of writings by local authors. This stood in stark contrast to the preceding centuries in Chinese Central Asia during which only a few histories had been written by local hands.

The Muslim rebellion and the creation of an independent state also had a colossal impact on China. For the first time since the establishment of the Qing dynasty in 1644, a large territory had broken free of China's control. This provoked intense debates over whether the empire should passively accept the loss of Xinjiang or make an all-out effort to reconquer the region in spite of the huge financial burden this would entail. There was historical precedent for abandonment: Eastern Turkestan had slipped from China's grip during both the Han and Tang dynasties, and the Ming dynasty had never seriously attempted its conquest. The Qing, however, as a dynasty of foreign origin, and which had previously devoted much of its frontier military effort to incorporating vast areas of Mongolia, Tibet, and Manchuria, was very concerned that such a loss might further undermine its authority and encourage more popular unrest. The Qing had already been plagued by a series of rebellions in China itself such as those by the Taiping, the Nian, and Muslims in Shanxi-Gansu and in Yunnan, as well as territorial and trade demands from the Western imperial powers. In the end China decided on a policy of reconquest. With its success, the Qing officially incorporated Xinjiang as a province of China and abolished the institutions of indirect rule it had previously employed. Institutional reforms and the massive colonization of the region by Han Chinese immigrants reinforced this administrative change. In this way, the Qing attempted to incorporate Xinjiang as an integral and "indivisible" part of China, a policy that has continued over the past century under successive Chinese governments.

Because of its historical significance, the Muslim rebellion in Eastern

Turkestan has drawn the attention of a number of scholars. The British author, D. C. Boulger, produced the first published history of this period in a book written in 1878, barely a year after the end of the Muslim state.[5] This work is still the only book in English to treat the subject comprehensively, covering the 1864 Muslim rebellion, the creation of the government by Ya'qūb Beg, its foreign relations, and the collapse of the Muslim state. Considering the limited number of sources available to the author at the time, it remains quite an achievement. Despite its many contributions, the book is now badly outdated and marred by numerous factual mistakes, including stereotyped judgments that distort historical reality to a considerable degree.

More recently scholars in countries that have had continuing territorial interests at stake in the region have contributed to our knowledge on this topic. These include works by D. Tikhonov, A. Khodzhaev, and D. A. Isiev in Russia,[6] and those of Burhan Shahidi and Ji Dachun in China.[7] They have all made strenuous efforts to elucidate this poorly known history, particularly by utilizing the many Muslim sources available in their countries. However, they maintain quite irreconcilable positions on how we should interpret the Muslim rebellion itself and the state established by Ya'qūb Beg. The Russians present the uprising as a Uyghur national-liberation movement against an unjustifiable and oppressive Chinese rule. The Chinese argue that it was a peasant uprising whose leadership was then snatched by the reactionary feudal class represented by Ya'qūb Beg. These positions seem to be rooted less in the analysis of the actual events than in the usefulness of their political implications for each side during the Sino–Soviet dispute.

What has been conspicuously lacking in all these studies, even those that have used Muslim sources, is the perspective of the local Xinjiang people who were the main actors in these events. The contemporary British and the Russian commentators certainly provide us with useful insights from their vantage points as outsiders, but their observations often betray a cultural prejudice and a strong sense of their superiority, a blemish typically found in the nineteenth-century Westerners' writings on non-Western societies. While the Chinese were not certainly "outsiders" in the same sense, in the middle of the nineteenth century Xinjiang was not fully incorporated into the Qing imperial system and its relationship to China was problematic. The Muslims in the region of course recognized the political reality of Qing rule, but culturally they identified themselves as a part of the larger Islamic world and not as a part of greater China. Therefore it is not surprising that the 1864 Xinjiang rebellion took a quite different course than those initiated by Han Chinese rebels in China, such as the Taiping and the Nian. Even rebellions launched in Shanxi and Gansu by ethnic Chinese Muslims (variously known in the literature as Tungans, Dungans, or Hui) took quite a different form compared to those of the Muslim Uyghurs in Turkestan. For this reason it is vital that the native Turkestani perspective be presented if we hope to comprehend the reality of this historical event. And in this respect we are fortunate to have at hand a few works produced by local historians who were directly involved in the events they described. Because their works were hard to find and were written in less well-known languages, these sources have been neglected for far too long. It is now time to give them the keen attention they deserve and give weight to the message they hoped to deliver.[8]

One reason for the emergence of so many new local voices was the excitement generated by the rebellion. At least in its initial stage, they saw themselves as engaged in a movement designed to revitalize a living Islamic spirit that would return their land to the *Dār al-Islām* ("Abode of Islam"). To make this a reality the infidel rulers (the Qing) needed to be toppled from power and replaced by Muslim rulers who would employ Islamic law. The Chinese reconquest ended this dream, but not the forces behind it. Local writers after the reconquest were less inclined to view the rebellion as a mistake than to see the era as a sort of exuberant period in which all the formerly divided Muslims had joined together for the victory of Islam. Failure or not, the lasting glow of this endeavor sparked the composition of a series of historical treatises, most of which are at our disposal for study. Some of these have actually been available for a long time because of the efforts of a Russian scholar, N. N. Pantusov (1849–1909), who published them in printed form at the beginning of the twentieth century.

The most important local historical source published is *Tārīkh-i amniyya* by Mullā Mūsa Sayrāmī (1836–1917).[9] He is truly one of the best historians that Central Asia has ever produced and I feel no shame in depending so heavily on his work for the details and the perspective of this study. His work not only covers the entire period from the beginning of the rebellion to the reconquest but also contains remarkably accurate information. The author labored hard to collect so much of this information and he displayed sound historical judgment in his use of it. Sayrāmī continued to revise his work throughout his lifetime and the final version crystallized into *Tārīkh-i ḥamīdī* in 1908.[10] A second important work is *Ghazāt dar mulk-i Chīn* ("Holy War in China") by Mullā Bilāl (written in 1876–77), which also provides the title for this book.[11] The author was a renowned poet in Ili and the work itself is constructed as a long poem interspersed with prose. It contains unique information of great value for the study of the Ili rebellion, especially about the internal situation of the Tungans and the Turkic Muslims called *Taranchi.* In addition to these two, there are other historical works available only in manuscript form. They are preserved in museums and libraries in Russia, China, England, France, Germany, Sweden, and a few other countries. Although some institutions make it difficult for foreign researchers to obtain access to them, most of these sources are accessible and have been utilized by scholars.[12]

It was not only the local Muslim participants who recognized the significance of that period. Several contemporary Westerners who combined courage with curiosity personally dared to venture into this remote region and left vivid descriptions of their visits. Especially important are the reports of Robert B. Shaw who visited Kashgharia several times and personally met Ya'qūb Beg[13] and W. H. Johnson who risked his life crossing over the Pamirs in 1865 and had an interview with Ḥabīb Allāh, the leader of Khotan revolt.[14] Of no little importance are the travelogues of those who visited this region shortly after the collapse of the Muslim state in 1877. Particularly vivid are the descriptions of E. Schuyler, who effectively transmits to us the enormity of destruction that occurred in Zungharia,[15] while M. F. Grenard reveals the mood of the people after the reconquest in the Khotan area.[16]

Many official documents written by the Chinese, British, Russians, and Ottomans also add vital information to our store of knowledge. Chinese sources are abundant, as usual, but most of them are useful only for the beginning and the end of the period.[17] The reason is self-evident: the Qing officials had been completely wiped out during the rebellion and they returned only after the successful conclusion of the reconquest. However, this gap can be filled by two embassy reports, among others, one by a British mission headed by T. D. Forsyth[18] and the other by a Russian mission led by A. N. Kuropatkin.[19] They both contain extremely valuable information about the government of Ya'qūb Beg. These include a number of details on the socioeconomic conditions, the internal administration of the government, and the army that would have been lost had it not been for their keen and systematic observations. Their reports are indispensable companions for anyone who hopes to study the Eastern Turkestan society in the later half of the nineteenth century.

Important information can be culled from the diplomatic documents drawn up by the officials of the British Foreign Ministry, especially those recounting their contacts with the government of Ya'qūb Beg, some of which were never included in any published materials. These documents also contain translations of Russian reports, the originals of which are still difficult for us to gain access to. The Ottoman archives preserve rich materials not only on the diplomatic relation with Kashgharia but on the internal conditions of the Muslim government in its last years and its confrontation with the Qing army. Many of these materials and personal reports of Ottoman officers who had stayed in Kashgharia were put together by Mehmet Ātif in his book.[20]

This work, *Holy War in China*, is a comprehensive survey of the history of Chinese Central Asia during the turbulent decade from 1864 to 1877. It makes use of as many of the existing available published sources and manuscripts as possible. These original sources range over a wide variety of languages—Uyghur, Persian, Ottoman Turkish, Chinese, Russian, English, French, and German—and reflect an amazing number of perspectives and levels of understanding. By combining and analyzing these numerous sources, as well a large number of secondary sources, I hope to provide a sound overall description that can serve as the basis for further analytical studies. While it is not my principal aim to make any definitive historical judgments, at times this was impossible to avoid, so where I have a definitive opinion, I state it. The structure of the book revolves around the following six questions: (1) What were the direct and indirect causes of the rebellion? (2) How did events unfold after the rebellion's initial success? (3) How could Ya'qūb Beg, a stranger from Khoqand, achieve success as a unifying leader and founder of an independent state? (4) How did Ya'qūb Beg run the government and what was the structure of his administration and army? (5) How did the new state reach out to the international community and how did various nations respond to his overtures? (6) Why did the state fall apart so suddenly at Ya'qūb Beg's death to allow China to reoccupy the region almost without a fight?

The answers to these questions form the six chapters of this book. The result may not be completely satisfactory because in some cases the sources are inadequate while in other instances I lacked the necessary historical tools. For this reason the accuracy of some details may still be doubtful and many important aspects are left unattended. Yet, in spite of these shortcomings, I hope my endeavor calls more attention to the historical importance of this period and to the viewpoints so succinctly and ardently put forward by local historians in Chinese Central Asia.

HOLY WAR IN CHINA

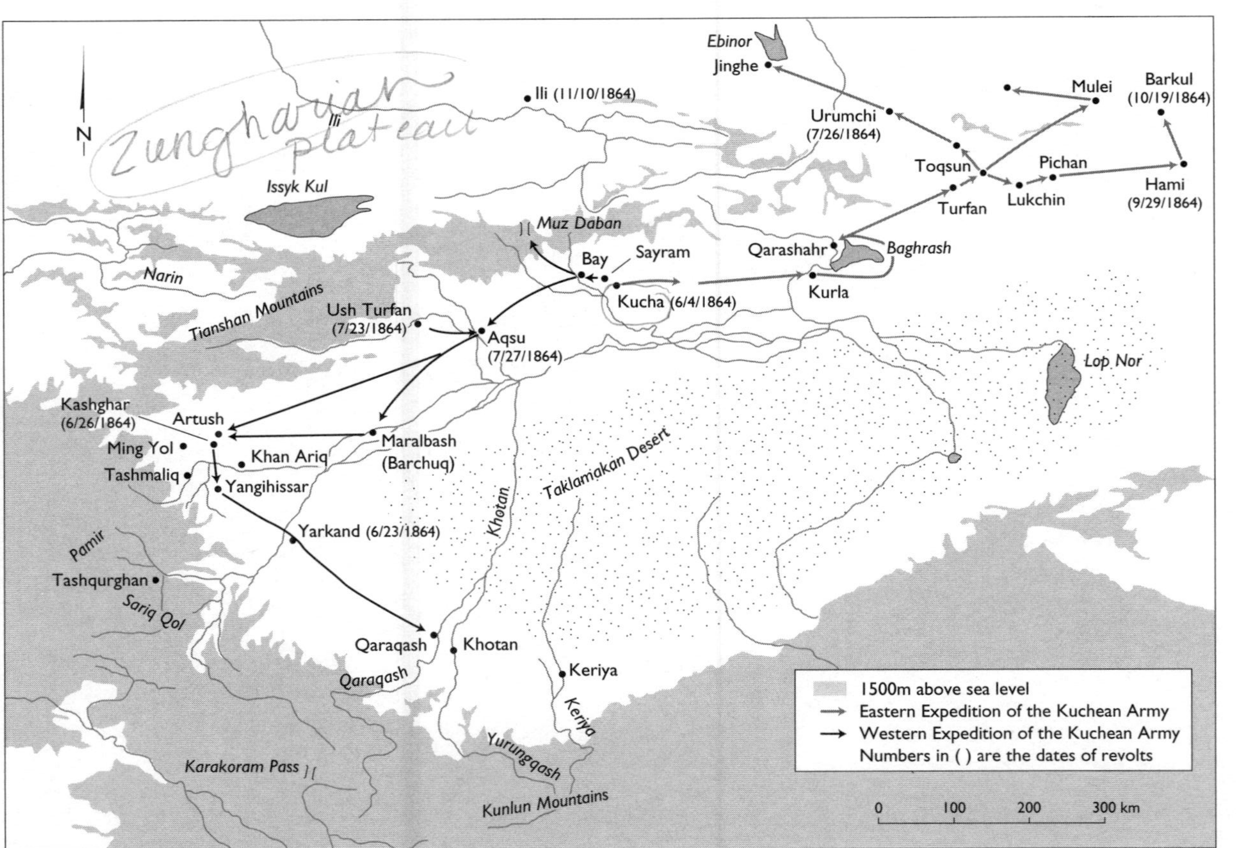

MAP 1. Muslim Revolts and Kuchean Expedition

1 *The Background*

Tungan Revolt in Kucha

THE BEGINNING

It was in Kucha where the banner of the 1864 Muslim rebellion against Qing rule was first raised. At that time Kucha was a small city with less than a thousand households within its walls, although in the past it had been an important center on the Silk Road. During both the Han and Tang dynasties it had served as the "headquarters of the Western Region." The reason for this was strategic. Located in the middle of the northern Tarim Basin, the city served as a key east–west link between China proper and the other Central Asian cities through the Hesi corridor and Uyghuristan (Hami and Turfan). To the north there was a route through the Tianshan mountain region by way of precarious mountain passes and to the south it was but a short distance across the Taklamakan Desert to Khotan.

The city of Kucha was greatly destroyed during the Qing conquest in the middle of the eighteenth century when its population decreased drastically. According to a Chinese record it was "[formerly] a great city with thirty to fifty thousand Muslim households" but had become so debilitated immediately after the conquest that only a thousand families remained in the city.[1] A British mission that visited Kucha in 1873–74 attested to this fact, noting that by their reckoning there were only about 800 households within the city walls, perhaps another 1,200 in the suburbs, and 4,000 households scattered among those villages that fell within the jurisdiction of Kucha. Thus, at the time the rebellion began, the province of Kucha probably had a population of no more than 6,000 households or 42,000 people.[2]

Although Kucha was still considered one of the "Eight Cities of the Southern Circuit" (*Nanlu bacheng*) under the Qing rule, its urban population was much lower than the other prominent cities of Eastern Turkestan such as Khotan (6,000 households), Yarkand (5,000 households) or Kashghar (5,000 households). One reason for the failure of the city to revive after the Qing conquest was the alteration of the overall political situation in Central Asia. Previously China's control of the oasis cities had been threatened by nomadic states based in the Zungharian plateau north of the Tianshan Mountains. When these states were active, Kucha served both as a base of operation for China's attacks on the nomads and as a line of defense to counter nomad attacks against them. After China destroyed the last of these nomadic states in 1757 and took firm control of the steppe region, there was no further need to maintain Kucha as a stronghold. The city's reduced importance is borne out by a document, composed in 1804, stating that it was administered by only a small staff of one imperial agent (*banshi dachen*) supported by twenty petty officials and three hundred soldiers.[3]

Kucha was a seemingly unlikely place for a revolt to start. It was a relatively isolated backwater town that had seen better days and had no history of serious anti-Qing resistance. Yet it was here on June 4th the 1864 Muslim rebellion started. The small number of Qing troops proved insufficient to drive off the furious Muslims who began surging into the city. One reason for the Qing vulnerability to attack was the structure of city itself. Like the other oasis cities around the Tarim Basin, Kucha was encircled by a wall made of "sandy soil mixed with willow twigs" about 1.7–1.8 km in circumference,[4] but its internal structure was different. In Kashghar and Yarkand, the Qing government had constructed separate forts outside the walls, but near the Muslim town, to accommodate its colonial officials and soldiers as well as merchants (mostly non-Turkic and non-Muslim peoples that included a mix of Manchus, Mongols, and Han Chinese).[5] In Kucha they built the fort inside the city itself and then erected new walls designed to separate the living quarters of the local Muslims from the non-Muslim outsiders who served the Qing administration.[6] Thus they were much more vulnerable to attack and had no place to retreat.

Sayrāmī describes the events of that tumultuous night in this way:

> As if it were a celestial calamity or a divine punishment, one night all of a sudden some Tungans were perturbed and set fire to the suburban bazaar (*wayshang bazār*)[7] in the city of Kucha, killing infidels and whomever they caught. At that moment, Allāhyār Khān Beg, son of the governor (*ḥākim*) of Yangihissar, leading some heartbroken Muslims, joined with the Tungans. All the Tungans and Muslims allied together with one mind and set fires to the buildings of the *amban* official. Till dawn they slaughtered many infidels. As soon as it became the daybreak, the [Qing] officials came out [of the fort] with troops to fight. But they could not stand and were defeated. Tungans and Muslims were victorious while the Chinese (*khitaylar*) were vanquished. It happened on the Saturday night, the first day of Muḥarram, 1281, in the *Jawzā* season in the year of Snake.[8]

The Turkic Muslims of Xinjiang referred to Chinese-speaking Muslims living in northwestern provinces by the names of *Tungan* or *Dungan*. In Qing documents these same people were either called *hanhui*, that is, Chinese Muslims, or simply transcribed as *donggan*.[9] The non-Chinese Turkic-speaking Muslims who constituted the overwhelming majority of the population in Eastern Turkestan simply called themselves *musulmān* (Muslim). The common ethnic term of *Uyghur* that is now applied to many Turkic people of this region was not used at the time and is, in fact, a twentieth-century invention.[10]

The exact date of the revolt is somewhat in dispute, but it most probably began during the night of June 3–4, 1864.[11] Sayrāmī names three persons who led the Tungan rebels on that night: Mā Shūr Akhūnd, Mā Lūng Akhūnd, and Shams al-Dīn Khalīfa, all living in Kucha.[12] The first two, with the family name of Ma, were certainly Tungans, and the third was probably a Tungan too because it was not uncommon for them to have Arabic names. Sayrāmī's description makes it clear that the Kuchean revolt was first initiated and led by the Tungans living in that city. Only after they had started the revolt by setting fire to the suburban markets and killing "infidels" were they joined by the Turkic Muslims. These two groups of people, now allied together, stormed into the government buildings and crushed a detachment of the Qing army that came out of the fort to suppress them. The cooperation of the Tungans and the Turks was also found in the memorial of Salingga, the imperial agent residing in Kucha, in which they were called *hanren* and *huimin* respectively.[13]

Other Muslim accounts as well as Chinese sources give us a similar picture on the incident of that night. Ḥājjī Yūsuf, author of *Jamī' al-tavārīkh*, writes that the revolt was started by the initiative of the aforementioned three Tungan leaders. He states that the Tungans, armed with axes, hoes, and clubs, made a sudden assault and then burned official buildings and killed about one thousand Chinese and 150 Qalmaqs (i.e., Mongols).[14] A Qing document confirms this, recording that "Chinese Muslims burnt the city of Kucha" and "all the military and civil officials in Kucha, including Wenyi and Salingga, were killed or wounded and all the official buildings, warehouses, and shops turned into ash."[15] According to another Chinese source, "Ma Long, a native Kuchean Muslim, covertly conspired with outsiders like Dian Manla and Su Manla, and they, leading a group of people, revolted and burnt Kucha."[16] *Xinjiang tuzhi* also writes that

> in the fourth month of the summer a native Muslim in Kucha called Ma Long conspired to rise in revolt. There was a certain Yang Chun from Yumen, one of the insurgent Muslims, who had stealthily infiltrated into Kucha and plotted a revolt with Huang Hezhuo, Dian Manla and Su Manla.[17] On the day of *jihai* [June 3] they burnt the city of Kucha and on the day of *renyin* [June 6] the city fell. Salingga, imperial agent [of Kucha], Wenyi, commandant (*lingdui dachen*) of Yangihissar, and Urenbu, assistant (*bangban dachen*) of Yarkand were killed.[18]

All of our sources share two distinctive characteristics in describing the Kucha revolt: they all stress that it was the Tungans who took the initiative and that they were aided by "outside insurgents" (*waifei*). As we will see, these characteristics were also common to the revolts in other areas of Xinjiang such as Kashghar and Yangihissar where Tungan military commanders were reported to have secretly communicated and conspired with *hanhuis*. In Yarkand the revolt was alleged to have been started as "a commotion of *hanhuis*," while in Urumchi it was two Tungan leaders who initiated the revolt. Indeed, with the exception of Khotan, it appears that it was the Tungans who started the 1864 Muslim rebellion in each of the cities where fighting broke out. The preeminence of the Tungans in the initial stage of the revolt, however, immediately raises some difficult questions. First, why was it not the Turkic Muslims who initiated the revolt? After all, they formed the overwhelming majority of the indigenous population and would seem to have been even more hostile to Qing rule than the Chinese Muslims. Second, who were these so-called "outside insurgents" and what kind of connection existed between them and the rebellious local Tungans?

RUMOR OF MASSACRE

It appears that the Tungans were thrown into panic by a rumor that the Qing government was plotting to exterminate them. This at least was the local native opinion about the cause of the Kucha revolt. Sayrāmī explains it as follows:

> At that time English Christians overpowered the country of Chinese emperor and conquered seventy-two large cities in the region called Būrmā. They even destroyed some of them. At this juncture, a group of people called *Ūsūnggūī Chanmūzā* [i.e., Taipings][19] arose contending sovereignty on the one hand, and the Tungans caused troubles on the other. In the end when the Great Khan (*Ulūgh Khān*) heard the news that Tungans, not being able to stay at Chingchūfū [i.e., Jinjibao], consulted with each other and moved to the west in order to take the nearby areas, he sent the following edict to the chiefs of the provinces in this direction. "Several Tungans defied the submission, so we gave them advice and promise. However, because they were worried and afraid of their crime and unruly behavior, they could not stay and went to the west. If they go to that region, it is possible that the Tungans in that area will become friendly with them and the common people will become disorderly. As soon as you read this edict, exterminate the Tungans in city and, then, report the result to me, the Great Khan!" In this way, he sent the edict to the General of Ili. The General was also startled at this and, after consultations, said, "Tungans are the people of a large number, and their nature and behavior are different [from us]. If they got a scent of [our weakness], we would become like evening and they would become like morning. There is still a long distance for the Tungans to come from the inland (*ichkiri*), so if we invite the Tungans living here and, giving them advice with friendly words, conclude an agreement, then would they not be calmed down and devote themselves to their own livelihood?" . . . However, they did not become calm. Every night they did not go to sleep, spending nights in holy tombs (*mazār*). They vowed

and vowed, and even those who had not performed an ablution once a month now did it several times a day. Their sorrow and anxiety grew deeper day by day. The [Ili] General, having found out such activities of these Tungans, became very anxious. Then he ignored the agreement and, executing the emperor (*khān*)'s edict, sent letters to the ambans in every city: "On such and such time of such and such day, massacre the Tungan people!"[20]

He continues that the contents of this letter was revealed accidentally to a Tungan scribe (*siyāh*) working at a postal station (*örtäng*).[21] This man reported it to his father named Sō Dālūya who was an officer in Urumchi. Sō Dālūya then proceeded to spread this news to the Tungan chiefs in every city, which ignited the revolt in Kucha.[22] Sayrāmī's assertion that the imperial order of Tungan massacre was the immediate cause of the revolt is also corroborated by a similar statement in *Ẓafar-nāma*, composed by Muḥammad 'Alī Khān Kashmīrī in 1867–68 just a few years after the revolt.[23]

Does their claim that the Muslim rebellion was touched off by the rumor of a planned Tungan massacre have any grounding in reality? The edict of Tongzhi Emperor himself, dated September 25, 1864, is noteworthy in its assertion that the belief in such a rumor was widespread.

The present disturbance by Muslim insurgents in all parts of Xinjiang is agitated by absurd stories fabricated by cunning people who fled from the interior region. It seems to me that they were worried good Muslims (*lianghui*) might not trust their words, so they, after having circulated a rumor that the Muslims would be massacred, scared them and made them join.[24]

It may be impossible for us to find out whether such a rumor was really "fabricated" or had any factual basis. Although the emperor would have hardly ordered such a massacre if he considered its inevitable and disastrous consequences, it may be too rash for us to conclude that the rumor was as completely "fabricated by cunning people who fled from the interior region" as the emperor thought. Even if the emperor had not considered such a plan, local Qing officials, worried about the loyalty of their Tungan troops, had previously considered ways they could be purged from positions of power. One thing that both sides agreed on was that it was "the rumor of massacre" itself, whatever its merit, that was a direct cause of the Muslim revolt in Xinjiang.

Several sources allow us to conjecture how such a rumor came to be disseminated, especially when we examine the cause of Muslim revolt at Lintong in Shanxi which had started in June, 1862 and spread all over Shanxi and Gansu provinces. In that spring the Taiping army began to pour into the Shanxi area, and the Han Chinese organized militia units (*tuanlian*) at the suggestion of government officials in order to repel the rebels. Then these Han militias started to slaughter the Muslims who, they feared, might ally with the Taipings. In Guanzhong area a large number of Muslims were massacred as shown by the expressions like "*jiaohui*" (extirpation of Muslims), "*miehui*" (extermination of Muslims) or "*shalu jingjin*" (massacre and cleansing). In Gansu the situation was not much different either. Officials in Pingliang, having mobilized militias, "searched and annihilated insurgents in the city." In 1864 an official in Suzhou secretly invited militia leaders to conspire in "the massacre of Muslims" (*tuhui*), but the Muslims discovered the plot and captured the city.[25]

Then, the question is how the news of these terrible incidents in Shanxi and Gansu was transmitted to the Tungans in Xinjiang. Emperor Tongzhi's edict leads us to believe that it was the "outside insurgents" from the interior of China who disseminated the news and instigated their fellows in Xinjiang to rise. We have a few more reports that support this suspicion. As mentioned earlier, "a certain Yang Chun from Yumen" plotted together with local Tungans and caused the Kucha revolt. Another inland Tungan, named Tuo Ming came to Urumchi and hid himself at the house of Sō Dālūya, and they became the leaders of the revolt there.[26] We do not know whether their arrival and activities were conducted as a part of a systematic anti-Qing movement. The portrayal of Tuo Ming in a Qing document is less that of a committed rebel than of a troublemaking "tinker-peddler" type common in rural China.[27] He "practiced sorcery and fortune-telling" and "divination" while "wandering around the Jinji[bao], Henan and Gansu areas, and got acquainted with various Muslim leaders."[28]

There is no doubt that the outsiders' propaganda was effective in creating an impending sense of crisis among the Tungans in Xinjiang, but what is no less important is the social context that rendered them so susceptible to that propaganda. After the revolt in Kucha and Urumchi, the other cities rose against the Qing even without involvement of outsiders. In most areas the revolts were not carefully premeditated by any leading group and the leaders were chosen only after the revolt had succeeded. Why did they rise against the Qing even without the involvement of the outsiders? Since it was the Tungans who first raised the banner of the revolt in many cities, let us examine the direct cause that turned them against the Qing.

We do not know exactly how many Tungans were living in Xinjiang at that time. According to Ch. Ch. Valikhanov who visited Kashgharia in 1858–59 and left detailed records on its social and economic conditions on the eve of the rebellion, most of the Tungans there came from Shanxi, Gansu, and Sichuan and they were running restaurants or engaged in the transportation of tea by their own wagons.[29] A considerable number of soldiers in the Green Battalions (*luying*) stationed in Xinjiang were also Tungans from the Shanxi and Gansu areas. Based on Chinese sources, the total number of soldiers in these units is estimated at about 4,000–6,000,[30] but the actual number must have far exceeded this range. Estimated numbers only in *Nanlu* ("Southern Circuit," Kashgharia) reached almost 11,000.[31] Many more Tungans, however, were living in the Ili and Urumchi areas which were closer to China proper and had extensive cultivated areas.[32] One source estimates that there were 60,000 Tungans around the Kulja region in the Ili valley alone.[33] According to Sayrāmī, as quoted above, the Ili General is reputed to have said that "Tungans are the people of a large number," and it was certainly not an exaggeration.

Qing officials in Xinjiang were well aware of the existence of the large number of Tungans and that some of them served as soldiers. They were naturally worried about catastrophic repercussions of the revolts of Shanxi and Gansu. It is not surprising that as a preventive measure they gave an order to disarm the Tungan soldiers and to execute suspicious persons. Several sources suggest that a larger scale of killings actually took place in Qarashahr[34] and in Kashghar.[35] Thus the situation in Xinjiang immediately before the rebellion was most favorable to the outside instigators. The rumor of a Tungan massacre was not only imported from the outside but also produced and confirmed in Xinjiang by actual incidents. Without any involvement of organized rebel groups the rumor was rapidly disseminated by travelers, merchants, and messengers over the entire region. Thus we can say that the instantaneous and massive uprising of the Tungans was the result of combined factors: the massacre in Shanxi and Gansu, the propaganda of the Tungans from inland China, the excessive measures implemented by local Qing officials that included actual massacres, and the rising awareness of crisis among the Tungans in Xinjiang.

However, it was not the Tungans alone who rose up against the Qing rule. As soon as the revolts broke out, almost simultaneously the Turkic Muslims joined with them and the hegemony of the rebellion passed into the hands of these Turks. With their participation virtually the entire Muslim population in Xinjiang now stood against the Qing rule. The 1864 rebellion, started as a Tungan revolt, became the Muslim rebellion. But for what reasons did the Turkic Muslims join a Tungan revolt so readily and then so quickly come to dominate it? To answer this question, we have to go back a century in time to discover how and why the Turkic population had become so alienated from Qing rule.

The Limit of Qing Domination

CONQUEST

The Qing annexation of Eastern Turkestan and Zungharia was an important historical event in several respects. First of all, along with the incorporation of Mongolia and Tibet, it almost doubled the territory of China. Unlike the Chinese expansions in the Han and the Tang times, the conquest of this region in the eighteenth century resulted in its permanent incorporation into China and, ultimately opened the way to Sinicization.[36] Furthermore, because the Qing military success came at the expense of the destruction of the Zunghar, the so-called "last nomadic empire,"[37] this event shook "the entire system of the international relation found there at the center of which lay the Oyirat state from the middle of the seventeenth century."[38] The Qing conquest of this region was one of the high points in the process of the Sino–Russian expansion into Inner Asia that had started a century or two earlier and was to be completed in the latter half of the nineteenth century when the Inner Asian frontiers were finally closed. And it was the event heralding the final victory of sedentary states in the long history of confrontations with nomadic peoples. It is not necessary for us to explain the process of the Qing conquest of Xinjiang since there are already detailed studies on this topic. A brief summary is sufficient here.

The death of the last effective Zunghar ruler, Galdan Tsering (r. 1727–45), instantly touched off thirteen years of succession struggles that finally led to the destruction of the state. Initially Galdan Tsering's second son succeeded to the throne, but he was killed by his eldest brother who then proclaimed himself ruler. However, he did not receive wide support from the nobility, and power devolved to another imperial family member, Dawachi, who secured the khanship in 1753. Fighting broke out soon between Dawachi and his former ally, Amursana, who, after being beaten by Dawachi, fled to China to seek its assistance. In the spring of 1755 Emperor Qianlong sent an expeditionary army of fifty thousand and took Ili in June after encountering little resistance. However, at the completion of the expedition, Amursana, who had expected to become the sole ruler of the Zunghars, was dissatisfied with the decision of the Qing court to make him only one of four khans. He revolted and although he gained the victory in the initial clash with the Qing, he was later defeated (1757) and fled into Russian territory where he died. When more than a decade of political turbulence ended with the final conquest of Zungharia by the Qing, the Zunghar population was almost wiped out. According to a Chinese report, almost forty percent of the population had died from smallpox, thirty percent were killed by the Qing troops, and twenty percent had fled into the Qazaq and the Russian territory.[39]

The Qing troops also encountered stiff resistance from the local oasis population in the Tarim Basin led by a family of Naqshbandī Sufis known as Makhdūmzādas, the descendants of a famous Central Asian Sufi, Makhdūm-i A'ẓam (1461–1542), "Great Master."[40] Although he never set foot in Eastern Turkestan, his second son Muḥammad Isḥāq Walī (d. 1599) came to this region and stayed several years, trying to draw important political figures to his order.[41] His descendants and followers eventually succeeded in establishing their influence upon the secular rulers of the region and later became known as the Isḥāqīs or the *Qara Taghliqs* ("Black Mountaineers"). Another line of Makhdūmzādas descended from the eldest son of Makhdūm-i A'ẓam, Muḥammad Amīn (also known as Īshān-i Kalān: d. 1597/98), came to Eastern Turkestan a generation after the Isḥaqīs had established themselves there. Under the leadership of Khwāja Yūsuf (d. 1652/53) and Khwāja Hidāyat Allāh (commonly known as Khwāja Āfāq: d. 1693/94), son and grandson of Muḥammad Amīn respectively, this branch of the family established a foothold in Yarkand and became known as the Āfāqīs or the *Aq Taghliqs* ("White Mountaineers").[42] They were received coldly by the Isḥāqīs who perceived them as rivals. This was the beginning of a long history of enmity, conspiracies, and assassinations between the two families.[43]

Around the middle of the seventeenth century when the political power of the Moghul khans was declining and torn by internal power struggles in the court, the two khwāja families became entangled in partisan fighting. These conflicts resulted in the expulsion of Khwāja Āfāq who reportedly sought help from the Zunghar ruler, Galdan Boshughtu Khan (d. 1696). Such an incident induced a Zunghar invasion of Kashgharia (ca. 1680) and the establishment of colonial rule with Āfāqī khwājas acting as the nominal rulers of Kashgharia.[44] After a while, however, they allied with family members of the former Moghul khans and by taking advantage of the confusion toward the end of Galdan's reign, expelled the Zunghars from their land and gained independence.[45] However, as soon as Tsewang Rabtan (d. 1727) secured power among the Zunghar nomads, he struck back and reimposed colonial rule over Kashgharia. This time, Āfāqī khwājas were taken prisoners and held hostage in Ili while Isḥāqī khwājas were made rulers of Kashgharian cities. Zunghar rule was not seriously challenged for about a half century until Galdan Tsering's death set off new disturbances in Zungharia. The Isḥāqī khwājas threw off the Zunghar yoke in western Kashgharia and seemed to gain their independence.

When the Qing took Ili and eliminated Dawachi, they did not want to leave Kashgharia outside their imperial control. Taking advantage of the mutual conflicts between the two khwāja families, the court decided to release two Āfāqī khwāja brothers, Burhān al-Dīn and Khwāja-i Jahān who had been held hostage in Ili by the Zunghars, with a view to use them as figureheads. The allied force of the Āfāqī khwājas and their followers, the troops sent by Amursana, a small Qing detachment, and a number of local leaders who saw a better prospect in siding with China, marched to Kashghar and Yarkand. At the end of 1755 they soundly defeated the Isḥāqī khwājas and the Qing empire incorporated this region into its dominion.

However, the khwājas, especially Khwāja-i Jahān, intended to be independent rulers and found continuous Qing intervention irksome. The collision between Qing and the khwājas became inevitable when a Manchu general was killed in Kucha in 1757. The next year about ten thousand Qing troops started the western march from Turfan. They encountered strong resistance at first in Yarkand and Kashghar, which the two khwāja brothers were holding, but after a substantial reinforcement, the Qing army under the command of Jaohui took the two cities during the summer of 1759. The khwāja brothers fled to Badakhshan, where they were killed by Sulṭān Shāh, the ruler of the region, and their heads were delivered to the Qing.[46] Thus the conquest was completed and the newly acquired territory, the north and the south of Tianshan mountains, began to be called *Xinjiang*, that is "New Dominion."

The situation in Eastern Turkestan after this Qing conquest was quite different from that in Zungharia, where due to the brutal military operations of the Qing army nomadic populations were virtually exterminated. According to a Qing official census, the population of Kashgharia, to the west of Kucha, was counted 230,000. This probably reflects only those who were registered for taxation, so the actual number must have been much larger than that. This assumption can be corroborated through a report by Qing generals that the number of inhabitants of three cities in the extreme west—Kashghar, Yarkand, and Khotan alone—were estimated at 240,000.[47] If we add to this those who were living in Ush, Aqsu, and Kucha, the total number would be about 370,000.[48]

The Qing army did not commit a systematic slaughter of the native people in the Tarim Basin as they had done in Zungharia, even after they had crushed the resistance of the khwāja brothers. However, such a "benevolent" measure did not guarantee the security and tranquility in this region. The slaughter and expulsion of the khwājas only intensified the resentment against the "infidel" rule among the local Muslim population, particularly when it became known that Khwāja Burhān al-Dīn's son, Sarimsaq, was living in Khoqand khanate as a refugee.

The Qing attempted to gain local support by instituting a policy of indirect rule in which most aspects of government would be in the hands of appointed local leaders known as begs. But the local population did not identify with these new officials whom they viewed as collaborators. Begs were viewed with deep suspicion because they, imitating the lifestyle of the "infidels," performed the *koutou* to their superiors and prostrated themselves before the image of the emperor. Many of the third-ranking *ḥākim beg*s who came from Uyghuristan in the east (commonly called *wang beg* by the Muslims) were particular targets of hatred because of their attempts to amass personal fortunes. Lower-level functionaries, known as *darugha*s, angered many local people because they had no fixed income and so frequently resorted to illegal means to gain wealth. Members of *'ulamā*, the loosely organized Islamic clergy, had never wielded strong influence on the people of Eastern Turkestan, particularly when compared to the khwājas, and after the Qing conquest their influence declined even further. Thus there was "no group to bridge the gulf between the indigenous officialdom and the governed."[49] This "gulf" was to be exploited both by the rulers of the Khoqand khanate and by the Āfāqī khwājas, who had different goals but employed the same means, including *jihād* or *ghazāt* (holy war), to exploit the military and ideological weaknesses of the Qing empire in Kashgharia.

With legitimate avenues of influence and protest largely closed to them, the people's political expression could not but take the form of violence. The Qing government seems to have been well aware of the problem and tried to establish a system that would lessen the animosity of the local population in Eastern Turkestan and strengthen its hold over this region. This system was built on the principle of indirect rule based on firm military superiority. To avoid provocation and unnecessary hostility in Eastern Turkestan, the Qing let indigenous Muslims run the civil administration under the close supervision of Qing officials dispatched from Peking. Thus in Kashgharia it was the beg officials who took charge of the civil administration, while in Uyghuristan the job was left to those local notables who had cooperated with the Qing during the conquest. The latter had been rewarded with their own separate domains and the title of *jasaq junwang*. By contrast, except for a small community of Muslims who were administered by local begs, all of Zungharia was put under direct rule of the Ili General. He was supported by a massive military force composed of soldiers drawn from the Manchu and Mongol banners, as well as Chinese battalions stationed there to suppress promptly any Muslim opposition that might arise in Eastern Turkestan. In spite of this carefully structured policy, the weakness of the Qing domination first became manifest in the 1820s and began to crumble in the 1850s, laying the foundation for the success of the 1864 rebellion. Now let us examine the basic features and weakness of the Qing rule in Eastern Turkestan.

DUAL LAYERS OF INDIRECT RULE

For the civil administration of the indigenous Muslim population the Qing dynasty incorporated the stratum of local beg chiefs into its official system. Beg became the synonym of official in Xinjiang, where formerly it had been a general term designating the nobles. During the period of the Moghul khanate (*ca.* 1347–1680) important officials, military as well as civil, were recruited from the nomadic noble families, but, as the ruling group of the khanate gradually adopted a sedentary way of life, these families were transformed into landed aristocrats. The process was almost complete by the time of the Zunghar conquest.[50] The Zunghars supported this class lest the ruling khwāja family gain total domination, and they entrusted the begs with the civil administration. Toward the middle of the eighteenth century their political and economic power grew strong enough to compete with that of the khwājas. For example, while the khwāja brothers, Burhān al-Dīn and Khwāja-i Jahān, opposed submission to the Qing, many of the landed aristocrats allied themselves with the Chinese. To the Peking government the begs appeared to be not only an effective check against the strong khwāja power, but also a convenient tool for the indirect rule of a newly conquered territory. Thus the traditional Chinese policy of "divide and rule" was employed; the court put the begs against the khwājas while the highest ranking begs in Kashgharia were recruited from Uyghuristan, and it supported the Isḥāqī against the Āfāqī khwājas to perpetuate the mutual animosity between the two different khwāja branches.

After the conquest, in order to incorporate indigenous landed aristocrats into its official system, the Qing conducted comprehensive inquiries and found that there had been about fifteen different official titles such as *ḥākim* (governor), *ishikagha* (deputy governor), or *mīrāb* (supervisor of irrigation) distinguished by their functions. When the government picked new officials from "distinguished Muslim families" (*zhuxing huiren*), that is, those who had rendered meritorious service during the conquest,[51] it gave them these titles with beg appended indiscriminately, for example, *ḥākim beg*, *ishikagha beg*, and *mīrāb beg*. Moreover, the ranking system (*pinji*), which was distinctively Chinese in character, was grafted onto it. The begs were given the ranks from the third to the seventh, and entitled to cultivated land, people to work on it (*yanqi*, or *yänchi* in Turkic), and stipends (*yanglian*) in accordance with their ranks. For instance, a third-ranking beg received the land of 200 *batman*[52] and 100 *yänchi*s while a seventh-ranking beg received 30 *batman* of land and 8 *yänchi*s.

According to Saguchi's detailed study on the beg official system during the Qing period there existed about thirty-five different titles of beg, for example: *ḥākim beg* who supervised the overall administration of districts of varying sizes, *ishikagha beg* who were assistants of *ḥākim beg*; *khazānachi beg* who took care of the treasury; *mīrāb beg* who were in charge of maintaining the irrigation system and distributing water; *qāḍī beg* who handled judicial matters, and *shang beg* who supervised storehouses.[53] However, it appears that sometime later begs not only performed the functions ascribed by their titles but also assumed the responsibility for general administration. As a Yarkand tax-register[54] shows, many small townships around the city of Yarkand were administered by begs with the titles of *mīrāb* (supervisor of irrigation), *qara dīvān* (military comptroller), *muḥtasib* (accountant), *ṣadr* (chancellor), *ḍabṭ-i madar* (town guard), and so on. There is no doubt that they performed the general administrative works of the township.

Around 1830, the Qing government decided to transfer many beg officials in cities to villages to tighten its control over those areas. As a result, the begs who were transferred to villages began to take care of general affairs despite the fact that they were still carrying specific functional titles.[55]

In Eastern Turkestan there were about 270 begs and in Zungharia about 20 (for the administration of the Taranchis).[56] Although there was no fixed term of service for a beg, the posts were not hereditary. This was one of the several measures that the government took to prevent unnecessary aggrandizement of the begs' power. Another measure was the so-called *rule of avoidance*, under which, in principle, the begs holding the ranks from the third to the fifth were to serve in cities or towns other than their hometown. However, this rule was not strictly observed except for the third-ranking begs. Many of the third-ranking *ḥākim*s in Kashgharian cities came from the ruling families in Hami and Turfan who had actively supported the Qing conquest of Xinjiang. And to insure the loyalty of the high-ranking begs, the court made the begs of the third and the fourth ranks visit Peking in turn to have an audience with emperor.

In addition to those begs officially incorporated into the imperial officialdom, there was a semi-official group called bashi (head). According to the above-mentioned Yarkand register there were 84 *mingbashi*s (miliarch) and 346 *yüzbashi*s (centurion)[57] in the Yarkand area alone. The former were posted in the suburban districts and large towns (*dazhuang*) while the latter were placed at small towns (*xiaozhuang*). They did not necessarily administer one thousand or one hundred households as the titles suggest. Their chief responsibility was to assist the begs by collecting taxes from the people under their jurisdiction.[58] In addition to the aforementioned two bashi titles, we can find in other materials *kökbashi* (supervisor of agriculture),[59] *elligbashi* (head of fifty) and *onbashi* (head of ten).[60] The existence of various bashis can be also found in a number of edicts (*yarligh*) issued during the Moghul khanate,[61] so it is apparent that this social stratum had existed well before the Qing conquest. Under the Qing rule they were auxiliary functionaries, without the same economic privileges that the beg officials enjoyed. There was an incident illustrating their social position: just before the 1864 rebellion several bashis in Kucha protested to officials (*manṣabdār*) about the excessive taxation, which ended in their imprisonment.[62] In addition to bashis there were other groups of functionaries who performed auxiliary roles such as interpreters (*tungchi*, from Chinese *tongshi*), adjutants (*darugha begi*), stablers (*mīrākhōr begi*), couriers (*chäkchi*), and scribes (*bichikchi*).[63]

It is noteworthy that the Qing government adhered to the principle of indirect rule even in the religious sphere. There were religious leaders belonging to the class of *ʿulamā* (the learned) who, educated and trained in legal matters of religious law, performed judiciary and educational functions. In Islamic countries it was a traditional practice for the secular rulers to entrust matters related to "holy law" to them. This had been the practice earlier in Eastern Turkestan. For example, 'Abd al-Karīm Khān (d. 1591/92) had opened his tribunal court by seating the military chiefs (*amīr*) on one side and the religious leaders (*qāḍī*s and *muftī*s) on the other so that legal matters could be administered depending on whether they were to be judged by religious law (*sharī'ah*) or secular law (*törä*).[64]

The members of the *'ulamā* had a hierarchy among themselves. According to the report of Valikhanov, in the later half of the 1850s, in Kashgharia there were: one *shaykh al-Islām* who headed the *'ulamā*, two *qāḍī kalān* (chief judges), one *qāḍī 'askar* (military judge), one *ra'īs* (police), and several *qāḍī quḍāt*s (high judges), *a'lam*s (scholars), *muftī al-'askar*s (military prosecutors), and ordinary *qāḍī*s and *muftī*s. In addition, there were *imām*s (preachers), *khalīfa*s (deputies), *khaṭīb*s (reciters), and *mullā*s (teachers).[65] The Qing dynasty utilized these religious leaders to deal with the legal matters of the local people, but it did not incorporate all the existing *'ulamā* members into the officialdom. The new beg system included only the *qāḍī beg* who administered litigation and punishment, and the *muḥtasib beg* who taught Islamic scripture and kept an eye on public morals and education.

Through this method of indirect rule, as described above, the Qing dynasty succeeded in winning some of the ruling elite in the conquered region over to its side, but, because of that, the tax-paying commoners, called *alban-kash*, came to have double layers of rulers, local Muslim begs and their Manchu overlords. So while the discontentment of Muslim masses was increasing more and more, the native officials were in no position to resolve grievances and, naturally, could not take a leading role in social and political upheavals. This left only one group of people in the Muslim society of Eastern Turkestan who could speak for the people: Islamic mystics with the honorific title of *khwāja*. Compared to the insignificant respect that ordinary members of the *'ulamā* received from the people of Eastern Turkestan at that time, these people, especially those who belonged to saintly lineages, had tremendous religious charisma.[66]

The most powerful of these lineages were the Makhdūmzādas. As indicated earlier, there were two competing branches of the Makhdūmzādas, the Isḥāqīs and Āfāqīs. In terms of strength and influence, the Āfāqīs were much more powerful than the Isḥāqīs. This was because the Isḥāqīs had remained in Eastern Turkestan and been tainted by their cooperation with the Qing government. The exiled Āfāqīs in Khoqand, by contrast, claimed to represent the aspiration of those Muslims seeking to throw off "unjust infidel rule" by means of a "holy war." Their respective popularity can be gauged by Valikhanov's report that there were only two hundred Isḥāqī followers in the Khoqand khanate compared with more than fifty thousand households of the Āfāqī followers eager to participate in the war against the "infidels" and to donate money to the Āfāqī khwājas. The Āfāqī also had numerous followers among the nomadic Qirghiz and the Uzbeks.[67] With their popular political and financial support, it was the Āfāqī who were to prove the most consistent challengers to Qing rule in Eastern Turkestan.

MILITARY ESTABLISHMENT

To secure its colonial rule in Xinjiang the Qing stationed a large number of troops there. The primacy of military rule in Xinjiang is well attested by the system of the so-called "military bureau" (*junfu*) headed by the General of Ili (*Yili jangjun*). The Qing dynasty divided the whole of Xinjiang into three circuits (*lu*). Zungharia was renamed[68] *Tianshan Beilu* (Northern Circuit of Tianshan) and encompassed the area around Ili and Tarbaghatai. The Qing called Kashgharia *Tianshan Nanlu* (Southern Circuit of Tianshan). It included the "Four Western Cities" of Khotan, Yarkand, Yangihissar, and Kashghar, and the "Four Eastern Cities" of Ush, Aqsu, Kucha, and Qarashahr, which were together known as the "Eight Cities,"[69] equivalent to the Turkic terms such as *Altishahr* (Six Cities) and *Yättishahr* (Seven Cities). There was a third division called *Donglu* (Eastern Circuit) that included Turfan, Hami, Barkul, Qur Qarausu, and Urumchi.

The Qing court made the Ili General the supreme commander of all the military and administrative affairs in Xinjiang. In large cities of Zungharia as well as Eastern Turkestan were placed high military officials, such as councilor (*canzan dachen*), imperial agent (*banshi dachen*), or commandant (*lingdui dachen*). The entire Southern Circuit was under the jurisdiction of councilor in Kashghar (sometimes in Yarkand) and was subject to the General of Ili.[70] The Eastern Circuit was under the command of lieutenant-general (*dutong*) in Urumchi who was also subordinate to the General of Ili in military matters, but reported to the governor of Gansu province in civil administration.[71] In this respect the administrative status of the Eastern Circuit was somewhat different from the other two Circuits. Not only was it geographically closer to inland China than the other territories, but it had also voluntarily submitted to Qing rule before the rest of Xinjiang was incorporated into the empire. For these reasons the Qing simply extended the traditional system of Chinese local administration (*zhouxian*, districts and counties) to some areas, such as Urumchi and Barkul, while they allowed their old political allies in Hami and Turfan to rule as Qing clients with the title of *jasaq junwang*.[72]

These high military posts were almost always monopolized by the Manchu and the Mongol bannermen. According to the study of Wen-djang

Chu, of the 235 high officials who served in Xinjiang from 1760 through 1874 only five of them might have been "possible Chinese," while the rest were clearly Manchus or Mongols.[73] Another more extensive and detailed study on the background of 619 high officials who served in Xinjiang before 1884 provides a similar result: 76.6 percent Manchus, 9.4 percent Mongols, 2.2 percent Hans, and 11.8 percent unknown.[74] This rule of excluding Han officials from Xinjiang was broken only in 1875 by the appointment of Zuo Zongtang to be the supreme commander of the Xinjiang campaign and with the appointment of Liu Jintang to be the first governor of Xinjiang in 1884 when the region's status was changed to that of a Chinese province.

Another peculiarity of Qing military organization in Xinjiang was its two different systems for staffing military garrisons (*fangbing*). The first employed "residence troops" (*zhufang*) who were permanently settled with their families in the places where they served. The second employed "rotation troops" (*huanfang*) who served fixed terms of three to five years and then returned to their homes when replacements arrived. The Northern and the Eastern Circuits were manned by resident garrison troops, while the Southern Circuit depended entirely on rotation troops dispatched from Shanxi, Gansu, or Urumchi. In Kashghar, Yarkand, and Yangihissar, there were only about five hundred Eight Banner soldiers dispatched from Ili.[75]

The total number of the troops stationed in Xinjiang sometimes fluctuated, but during the reign of Qianlong in the mid-eighteenth century they numbered approximately 30,000. Of these more than half (16,300) were assigned to the Northern Circuit, another quarter (7,400) were allocated to the Eastern Circuit, while somewhat fewer troops (5,000–6,000) were assigned to the Southern Circuit.[76] This left the Qing forces very unbalanced geographically, with almost four-fifths of its total force in the Northern and the Eastern Circuits, particularly around Ili and Urumchi. Ethnic Manchus (drawn from the Eight Banners) and the Han Chinese (drawn from the Green Battalions) each constituted two-fifths of the total number of troops, while the remaining fifth had their origins in such tribal groups as the Solons, Sibos, Chahars, and Ölöts (Zunghars). In addition to these forces there were unknown, but not large, numbers of local Muslim troops under Muslim officials in each city.

The reason for this unbalanced distribution of troops among the Northern, Eastern and Southern Circuits stemmed from several factors that Qing took into consideration. First of all, the court attributed great strategic importance to the area in the north of Tianshan because the region had historically been the abode of powerful nomadic states, including the Zunghar state. In addition, it was centrally located as a base of operations. From here the Qing could check the advance of Russia into Central Asia in the west, suppress rebellions by Kashgharian Muslims in the south, and watch over potentially subversive Qalqa Mongols in the northeast. It was also attractive because it provided excellent pasture land to feed the large number of horses needed to support the cavalry. Zungharia was also rich in undeveloped agricultural land that the Qing government used to establish various agricultural colonies. These included *huitun* that were occupied by the Muslims transported from Eastern Turkestan who were known as Taranchis, *bingtun* and *chitun* established by resident Manchu and Mongol garrison soldiers and their families, *hutun* populated by immigrant Han Chinese peasants, and *qiantun* that were used to house exiles.[77]

While the north may have been geographically central in terms of imperial geography, the placement of so many troops there created a strategic weakness in dealing with Kashgharia. In case of a large rebellion or a foreign invasion, the small number of troops scattered across the region would be grossly inadequate and would require substantial reinforcements from Ili, Urumchi, or China proper. But such assistance would take several months to arrive because of the distances involved, particularly since the most trouble usually occurred in westernmost Kashgharia, which was at the farthest end of the Qing imperium. The situation might easily get out of control before help could arrive from Ili. And it took at least six months after the outbreak of an incident was reported to get a more massive reinforcement army dispatched from Lanzhou to arrive in Kashghar.[78]

These defects became apparent in the early nineteenth century. The need to repulse an invasion in 1826 led by Jahāngīr, an anti-Qing khwāja based in Khoqand, forced the court to dispatch almost 36,000 troops as reinforcements from China proper. When the invasion was repulsed, 10,000 soldiers were ordered to stay behind and reinforce the garrisons of the Southern Circuit that had previously numbered only five or six thousand.[79] With each succeeding outbreak of trouble the number of Qing troops assigned to garrison duty in southern Xinjiang rose. After another invasion in 1830, Wei Yuan wrote that the six thousand troops stationed in the "Western Four Cities" were doubled by dispatching three thousand cavalry from Ili and four thousand Green Battalion troops from Shanxi and Gansu. New units of one thousand each were also posted to Aqsu and Ush[80] increasing the total number of troops in Kashgharia (or the Southern Circuit) to 15,000, a figure that remained stable until the end of the 1850s according to Valikhanov's observations.[81] The Ministry of Households (*hubu*) reported to the emperor in 1853 that "the garrison soldiers in the Northern and Southern Circuits are 40,000."[82] So if we add those in the Eastern Circuit, the total number would have reached almost 50,000. Yet despite the increased number of troops, the Qing government remained vulnerable to Muslim revolts and invasions.

The Qing court recognized that it needed more troops in Xinjiang but it could not increase their numbers because of financial limitations. A basic principle of Qing administration held that the government should "spend in accordance with income" (*liangru weichu*), but this was a principle that was almost impossible to realize in practice. Only a few years after the conquest of Xinjiang, a memorial delivered to the Qianlong emperor in 1761 gave an accounting of its cost. Food provisions for the cavalry and the infantry soldiers (numbering 17,000) who had been dispatched to Xinjiang to pursue the conquest and staying there at that time were supplied by the production of the agricultural colonies (*tuntian*) there. Salaries (*yancaiyin*) to the officials and soldiers cost 333,400 *liang*s (taels) of silver, but only 58,000 *liang*s of this was covered by tax income in Xinjiang. This meant, and the memorial confirms, that the remaining deficit of 275,400 *liang*s of silver had to be provided by subsidies (*xiexiang*) from inland provinces.[83] The expenses only multiplied as the number of troops increased. The estimated annual expense of supporting 40,000 troops in Xinjiang was 1,400,000–1,500,000 *liang*s,[84] but the actual expense was apparently much more than that amount. According to Wei Yuan, the annual subsidy to Xinjiang from inland provinces reached almost 1,800,000 *liang*s,[85] and by the 1840s the figure amounted to over 4 million *liang*s.[86] An additional expense was rotating troops in and out of the Southern Circuit. Because they were dispatched from Shanxi and Gansu, the government had to take the responsibility for the cost of their movement, as well as salaries, provisions, equipment, special bonuses, and traveling expenses.[87]

After Jahāngīr's invasion in the 1820s, the Qing government attempted to increase the local share of the region's administrative cost by raising more revenue. Officials searched the region to put more privately cultivated lands and previously hidden fields on the tax rolls. They also developed new agricultural colonies by encouraging immigration of Han Chinese. But all these efforts failed to produce the desired results.[88] It became clear that the tax revenue obtained from Xinjiang's Muslims would never be sufficient to support the military cost of garrisoning the region. The government would have to depend permanently on subsidies drawn from the inland provinces to cover the expenses of its occupation. However, because of the enormous amount of military spending associated with putting down the Taiping rebellion in the 1850s, the annual subsidies for Xinjiang were soon drastically reduced and sometimes even cut off entirely. This circumstance forced the local administration to increase the tax burdens even more on the Muslims in Xinjiang, which in turn inevitably aggravated the population and worsened the region's socioeconomic condition. The khwājas and the rulers of the neighboring khanate of Khoqand fully exploited this weakness of the Qing.

Intervention of Khoqand Khanate

EARLY CONTACTS

The emergence of Khoqand as a strong political power in Central Asia began in the 1740s, only a decade before the Qing conquest of Zungharia and Eastern Turkestan. Although the origin of this state goes back to a legendary figure named Altun Bishik (Golden Cradle) belonging to the Ming tribe of the Uzbeks around the middle of the sixteenth century, his descendants had remained for two centuries merely as tribal chiefs in the Ferghana valley with the title of *bī*.[89] In the 1740s their leader, ʻAbd al-Karīm Bī, built a new fort at a place called Eski Qurghân (Old Fort) and renamed it Khoqand, beginning the real history of the khanate.[90]

The internal situation leading to the strengthening of their political power is not well known, but the rise of Khoqand in the 1740s apparently owed much to overall political changes in Central Asia that weakened Khoqand's rivals. The powerful Ashtarkhanid dynasty of Uzbeks fell victim to Nādir Shāh Afshar when he invaded Bukhara and Samarqand in 1740. While Nādir Shāh's empire eventually stretched from the borders of Ottoman Turkey into Mughal India, and included both Khiva and Bukhara, it collapsed upon his death in 1747.[91] This opened a period in which there was no hegemonic power in Central Asia. The Afghans in the south inherited many of the eastern provinces of Nādir Shāh's realm and, under the leadership of Aḥmad Shāh Durranī, began to play a large role in Central Asian politics. To the west there arose two new Uzbek khanates, Bukhara and Khiva, that were similar in size and power to Khoqand. To the east and north, Khoqand benefited from the weakening of the Zunghar khanate because it was at war with China. These events freed Khoqand from the outside pressure, providing its rulers a breathing space and time to strengthen their power. The fact that ʻAbd al-Karīm Bī had the temerity to kill the envoys sent by the Zunghar ruler Galdan Tsering in 1745 demonstrated his degree of self-confidence.[92]

The conquest of Zungharia and Eastern Turkestan in 1757 brought the Qing into direct contact with the Qazaqs and Qirghiz, as well as with Khoqand. The Qing commanding general, Jaohui, sent an envoy to the leaders of the cities in Ferghana asking them to help the Qing arrest the fleeing khwāja brothers. According to a Chinese source, Ḥājjī Bī, the chief of the Edigene tribe of the Qirghiz in Pamir, and Irdana (or, Erdeni: r. 1751–70), the ruler of Khoqand, sent their emissaries to China with letters, stating that "we, two hundred and ten thousand population to the east of Bukhara, are all subjects [of the emperor]."[93] Although the Qing perceived this as an expression of submission, later developments suggest that Irdana had quite a different purpose in sending an envoy. Apparently he never intended to acknowledge his status as vassal to the Qing; but rather accepted the Qing diplomatic terms only to secure the economic gains they brought, a strategy pursued by most other Central Asian states that maintained similarly nominal tributary relations with China.[94]

Most of Khoqand's early relationships with the Qing in Kashgharia were trade related. In November, 1760, for example, two Khoqand envoys came to Kashghar and requested that their sale of cattle be exempted from taxation. The Qing government allowed the exemption, but restricted the privilege to official envoys and did not extend it to private merchants.[95] The first serious dispute between the two states, and a harbinger of future conflicts, occurred in 1762 when Irdana took the city of Osh away from the control of Ḥājjī Bī by force. Because Osh was a city in the eastern Ferghana near the Kashgharian border, the Qirghiz chief asked the Qing court to put pressure on Irdana to return the city to him. This soon became a test of muscle between Qing and Khoqand. Irdana adamantly refused the Qing demand, in part because the *ishikagha beg* of Kashghar, 'Abd al-Raḥīm, had secretly informed him that the Qing would take no military action against Khoqand. With this knowledge Irdana was able to deal with the Qing court confidently. In a letter sent to the court, he called himself "khan" and demanded that "Kashghar mountain," that is, Terek Daban, be made the boundary between the two states.[96]

Khoqand was not the only Central Asian state causing trouble for China. Aḥmad Shāh Durranī, the ruler of Afghanistan, was attempting to form an alliance of the Muslim Central Asian khanates and the Qazaqs in order to mount a military campaign against the Qing expansion into Central Asia.[97] According to the report of Valikhanov, such Central Asian rulers as Irdana of Khoqand and Tashkent, Fāḍīl Bī of Khojent and Uratepe (Uratyube), and a sultan of the Qazaqs, had earlier sent a letter to Aḥmad Shāh to ask him "to deliver the Muslim world from the attack of non-believers." In the spring of 1763 Afghan troops were deployed in the area between Khoqand and Tashkent, and Aḥmad Shāh dispatched letters to many leaders of Islamic countries urging them to join in the holy war. According to Valikhanov this provoked at least one revolt in 1765 in a small town called Ush within Kashgharia itself where the Muslims had risen with the expectation of receiving support from the wider Muslim world.[98]

This plan for a coordinated attack against Qing territory also appears in Russian records. According to their reports, Irdana had sent a letter to the Qazaq sultan, Ablai, notifying him that Aḥmad Shāh's emissary had arrived in Khoqand with a message indicating that Aḥmad Shāh had agreed to aid Khoqand in case of a Qing attack. A merchant from Khojent who visited Orenburg in January 1764 informed the Russians that Aḥmad Shāh had concentrated one hundred thousand troops [sic!] to the north of Qandahar in case of war against the Qing.[99] The Qing court received a similar report about such military movements in Central Asia, but the Chinese appeared to believe that the Afghans were "going to attack Bukhara."[100] The Chinese belief that they were unlikely to be the true targets of Aḥmad Shāh was solidly grounded. It is true that he had been pursuing an "expansionist policy,"[101] but he had many territorial disputes with Bukhara and few with China. Moving an army to the borders of Bukhara under the guise of a war against the "infidels" would have fallen well within the bounds of treachery common to Central Asian politics at the time. Still one cannot dismiss the possibility of Afghan military aggression against the Qing. Aḥmad Shāh had invaded India 1761 and defeated non-Muslim forces there.[102] And in 1765 Afghan and Bukharan forces raided Badakhshan to take revenge on Sulṭān Shāh for killing the fleeing khwāja brothers.

Although the "united front" of Muslim countries came to naught because of the internal situation in Afghanistan and dissension among Central Asian states, the attitude of Khoqand manifested during that course was enough to show that she would not be satisfied with "vassal" status to the Qing. Irdana's attitude during the Osh incident certainly indicates his consolidation of power in Ferghana. In this regard, it is worthwhile noting that Irdana was the first Khoqand ruler to assume the title of khan. Previous rulers of Khoqand had been simply called *bī*. In the Muslim literature on the Khoqand khanate, Irdana's assumption of the title of khan, even though it may have been temporary, is not mentioned, and ʿĀlim (r. 1799–1809) has been generally regarded as the first Khoqand ruler who assumed that title.[103] However, his letter of 1763 sent to the Qing, as mentioned earlier, leaves no doubt to the fact that he was the first khan of Khoqand. His assumption of this title may have been merely for a diplomatic ostentation of his power and not for the internal politics, but it still can be interpreted as an expression of his sense of self-confidence.

During the reign of Irdana's son, Narbuta (r. 1770–98/99), not only did the Khoqand territory expand to Namangan, Andijan, and Quramma, but the economy of the country also flourished. He struck black copper coins (*fulūs-i siyāh*) and agricultural production increased considerably.[104] Although his relationship with the Qing did not worsen, the Qing court's demand that Khoqand should hand over Sarimsaq, the son of Burhān al-Dīn Khwāja, who was living in Ferghana, remained a diplomatic stumbling block to improved relations throughout his reign.

The Qing fist became aware of the existence of Sarimsaq in 1761, but it was only in 1784 the court realized that he had now become an adult who was engaged in such subversive political actions as sending secret letters to Muslim leaders in Kashgharia and collecting money from the local population.[105] Naturally the Qing court was apprehensive of the future danger

Sarimsaq posed, so it requested Narbuta's help in extraditing him to China. However, it would have been extremely dangerous politically and unacceptable religiously for Narbuta to hand Sarimsaq over to the Chinese. He was both a khwāja with holy lineage and a greatly revered figure among the Muslims in Kashgharia. The Qing first tried to gain Narbuta's cooperation by sending him gifts, but when these failed to change his mind they threatened to ban the entry of Khoqand merchants into Kashgharia. As this threat failed they tried a different tactic in 1797. If Narbuta would agree to keep Sarimsaq under surveillance and prevent him from attempting an invasion or inciting revolts in Kashgharia, then the Chinese would grant him an official title that came with a regular stipend.[106] Narbuta agreed to this plan.

Qing concerns about subversive khwājas were not the only issue straining Khoqand's relations with China. Because of a dispute between China and Russia, the old border market in Kiakhta had remained closed from 1785 until 1792. During this period Khoqand played the role of a profitable middleman, transporting Chinese goods to Ferghana and then to Russia. As this contraband trade flourished, so did the conflicts of interest between Qing and Khoqand. Toward the end of Narbuta's reign the Qing retaliated by imposing various restrictions on Khoqandian traders, including the prohibiting of marriages between Khoqandian merchants and Khashgharian women.[107]

During the reigns of the next two succeeding rulers, 'Ālim Khān (r. 1799–1809) and 'Umar Khan (r. 1809–1822), the Khoqand khanate witnessed the most prosperous period in its history. Its territory was at least doubled, stretching from Uratepe in the southwest and to Tashkent and Turkestan in the northwest.[108] From this newly acquired territory Khoqand could control the flow of international trade between Russia and Central Asia and this brought much economic wealth to the khanate. Trade relations with Kashgharia also flourished under the guise of official "tributary" visits to Kashghar and Peking, as well as through ordinary trade conducted by private merchants. The volume of trade increased significantly during 'Umar's reign, as is evidenced, for example, by the complaint of a Chinese official that one embassy caravan alone carried eighty-eight cart-loads of Chinese goods, including tea, porcelain, and cloth.[109]

With the strengthening of the khanate's political power and the expansion of the trade with Kashgharia, the conflicts of interest between the two countries began to surface more sharply in the reign of 'Ālim Khān. One Khoqandian source, *Tavārīkh-i shahrukhiyya*, demonstrates that 'Ālim Khān was well aware of the weakness of the Qing rule in Eastern Turkestan and the reasons the emperor of China was sending him presents.

Chiefs (*valiyān*) of the "Seven Cities" (*haft kishvar*) of Kashghar[110] who had been loyal and submissive to Chinese emperors from the time of their ancestors, turned their heads, neither considering nor observing that they were subject [to the emperor], away from him and did not put their courteous hand over the chest. Even a tiny bit of our intrepid commands was not disaproved and the suzerainty over the Andijanis [i.e., Khoqandians] in the "Seven Cities" (*haft shahr*) was entrusted to our hands. Besides, the chiefs of every region are sending trustworthy representatives to us as emissaries and enquiring after our well-being with gifts and tributes (*pīsh-kash va tārtūq*).[111]

However, we cannot accept at face value all the claims asserted here. It is unlikely that the Qing would have ever acknowledged a complete renunciation of its suzerainty over the Khoqandians in Kashgharia or authorized local Muslim chiefs' sending tribute to Khoqand's ruler. However, contemporary Qing sources do prove that these claims were not entirely groundless. For example, when 'Ālim Khān requested that the Qing grant full tax exemption on those commodities taken to Kashgharia by Khoqandian merchants, his demand was not rejected outright. Instead he obtained a half exemption for such goods. Perhaps more significant, his demand for this commercial privilege was presented not by his own envoy, but by the governor of Kashghar who argued the case on his behalf. He also sent a letter to the chief of Khoqandian merchants (known as the *huda-i da*[112]) and asked him to send tribute. He even once sent a letter to the Qing court in which he called the Qing emperor his friend (*dust*), a severe breach of protocol when dealing with the ruler of "All under Heaven." This came to light because court officials had a habit of cleaning up such letters to make them conform to Chinese standards by employing less than verbatim translations. When the emperor discovered the discrepancies between the original letters and the Manchu translations prepared by Qing officials, he was furious at the "arrogant" phrases that 'Ālim Khān's had dared use to address him.[113] The letter was therefore rejected on the grounds that it did not observe "the etiquette of submission by outer barbarians."[114]

As the Khoqand-Kashgharian trade expanded, many Khoqandian merchants came to reside in the cities of Kashgharia. In 1813 'Ālim Khān's successor, 'Umar Khān, therefore requested that the Qing government permit him to station an official political agent with the title of *qāḍī beg* to supervise and tax the Khoqandian merchants. This official would replace the semi-official *huda-i da* he had already posted in Kashgharia.[115] This proposal was rejected, but in 1817 he repeated it, and again the Qing denied it. In 1820 'Umar made the request again, but this time he altered the official title from *qāḍī beg* to the perhaps more innocuous sounding *aqsaqal* ("white beard," meaning elder). Although the Qing officials still refused to accept his petition, they later found out that 'Umar had just gone ahead and ignored them by secretly appointing his *aqsaqal* without their permission.[116] This conflict of interest—the Khoqand ruler's desire to increase the khanate's share in the flourishing trade versus China's unwillingness to grant any ignominious concessions to her vassal state—came to open conflict with the invasion of Kashgharia by Jahāngīr.

"HOLY WAR" OF THE KHWĀJAS

The Khwāja leader, Jahāngīr, the son of Sarimsaq and grandson of Burhān al-Dīn, had long been under the surveillance of 'Umar Khan who received a stipend from the Qing for that reason.[117] This was because the Āfāqī khwājas in Khoqand had never given up their claim to Kashgharia nor renounced their intention to wage "holy war" against China. Rather than seeing their influence decline after more than a half century of Qing colonial rule, the khwājas' importance had instead risen as the political and economic conditions worsened in Kashgharia. Many people there viewed themselves as victims forced to live under the unjust and unjustifiable rule of infidels, and they were prepared to respond actively to the call of the khwājas. The nomadic Qirghiz were also willing to participate in the khwājas' cause, although many suspected that they were more interested in booty than politics.

In 1820 Jahāngīr proposed that he and 'Umar Khan should ally to launch a "holy war" against Kashghar, but his proposal was not accepted. So he escaped from the Khan's surveillance that summer and fled to the Qirghiz who inhabited the northern environs of Kashghar. There he obtained the support of the Chong Baghish and Sayaq tribes of the Qirghiz who provided him with three hundred Qirghiz troops. Assisted by the Qirghiz chief Suranchi, Jahāngīr attacked the border of Kashghar but was soundly beaten by the Qing troops and lost most of his men. He retreated back to Khoqand accompanied only by a few dozen survivors.[118] This aborted invasion, however, was only a prelude to a larger one.

Jahāngīr's second invasion plan began, like the first, when he was again able to escape surveillance in 1822. Muḥammad 'Alī (r. 1822–42; also called Madalī) had just succeeded his father to the throne of Khoqand, but he still maintained his father's policy of keeping Jahāngīr under house arrest. In the summer of that year there was an earthquake of an unprecedented scale in Ferghana that created confusion everywhere. Jahāngīr used this confusion to escape into the Alai mountains,[119] where he hid himself among the Qirghiz for two years. In 1825 he was able to mount another invasion of Kashghar with the aid of a couple of hundred Qirghiz troops, but this too ended in failure. To end the threat of these incursions, the Qing government decided to dispatch a small detachment of troops to destroy Jahāngīr and the Qirghiz's base in Narin. Instead the Qirghiz annihilated the Qing soldiers and their victory instantly boosted Jahāngīr's prestige. He quickly sent messengers to Khoqand to inform Muḥammad 'Alī of his intention to invade Kashgharia once more.[120] At the same time, he sent secret emissaries into Kashgharia where they were instructed to contact local Āfāqī supporters and collect money for the war.[121]

By the summer of 1826, Jahāngīr had succeeded in gathering together a considerable number of Qirghiz, Kashgharian, and Khoqandian followers. Many of the Khoqandian officials in this force were led by ʿĪsa Dādkhwāh and his brother Mūsa who had joined him.[122] Jahāngīr then appeared in Artush in July where he started his "holy war" by paying a visit to the holy shrine of Satuq Boghra Khan.[123] On receiving this news, the Qing army was sent to besiege the shrine, at which point most of the Qirghiz who had accompanied him began to disperse. However, fortune again smiled upon Jahāngīr when this Qing force was defeated. The Muslims in the immediate environs then gathered to join his camp along with a large number of Qirghiz belonging to the Chong Baghish tribe. With this group, Jahāngīr marched on Kashghar where he first took the Muslim town and then laid siege to the Manchu fort. At this time local Muslims from Yangihissar, Yarkand, and Khotan joined him and attacked Qing outposts and Chinese merchants. The invasion had now sparked a full-scale rebellion.[124]

Muḥammad ʿAlī had closely watched Jahāngīr's progress from behind the scenes and now realized that the consequences of his success had become too serious to be left unattended. One reason for this, sources explain, was the new Khoqand ruler had taken very harsh measures against many religious leaders in Khoqand and his relationship with Jahāngīr was not very cordial either,[125] so that his victories were worrisome. Of even greater consequence, however, was the threat to the status of Khoqand's Kashgharian trade that was so vital to the economy of the khanate. Win or lose, Muḥammad ʿAlī was worried that Jahāngīr's rising prominence might eclipse his own and he decided to take action. Although Muḥammad ʿAlī publicly advocated the necessity of the holy war, Khoqandian sources frankly reveal that the main, perhaps primary, motivation for his decision was economic. Citing the words of the khan himself, the *Tavārīkh-i shahrukhiyya* enumerated his reasons for taking part in the campaign himself. First it was extremely reckless that "a khwāja of no experience, but only with some disorderly crowd," could aspire to become a ruler. Second, there was a great danger that the enormous treasures amassed by "infidels" might fall into the hands of other people (than himself!). And finally, as a good Muslim ruler he was obligated to engage in holy war against an infidel power.[126]

Muḥammad ʿAlī was given an excellent opportunity to intervene when, according to the *Muntakhab al-tavārīkh,* Jahāngīr realized the difficulty of taking the Manchu fortress (*gulbāgh-i qurghān*) and so sent an emissary to Khoqand asking for support. The Khoqand ruler then decided to go so that he could take possession of treasures (*khazīna yāmbū*) stored in Chinese offices.[127] Muḥammad 'Alī came to Kashghar with about ten thousand troops, and Jahāngīr met him riding on his horse, an intentional gesture designed to show his status as an equal of the Khoqand ruler. His troops replaced those under Jahāngīr and began to assault the fort. This attempt, however, ended in disaster leaving numerous casualties, which gave him no choice but to return to Khoqand. After the retreat of the Khoqandian army, Jahāngīr succeeded in occupying the fort on August 27. The Qing army had exhausted its food supply and could no longer hold out against the besieging Muslims. Yangihissar, Yarkand, and Khotan also fell and Jahāngīr appointed governors for them, but Aqsu repulsed his assault.[128] A Qing expeditionary relief army of over twenty thousand troops, led by General Cangling, finally reached Maralbashi in March of 1827. They delivered a crushing defeat to Jahāngīr's army at Yangabad and then pushed on to Kashghar, which was reconquered by the end of March. After this defeat Jahāngīr attempted to flee through the mountains in the west, but Qing troops soon caught him and he was sent to Peking as a prisoner. There he was executed by being sliced into pieces.[129]

The Qing government now realized how fragile its control of Kashgharia was, so Nayanceng, the governor-general of Zhili, was dispatched to Kashghar as imperial commissioner to diagnose the problem and to repair the colonial system. He set up an extensive reform program for the administration in Kashgharia. Because he thought that the Khoqand khanate and the khwājas sheltered there were the source of China's problems, he stopped all the trade between Khoqand and Kashghar, especially the export of tea and rhubarb. By this means he hoped to compel Khoqand to hand over the Āfāqī khwājas living in Ferghana and "to force the Khoqand rulers to observe the norms of etiquette on whose basis Qing tried to build her relation with other countries and peoples,"[130] that is, the suzerain-vassal relationship. To put additional economic pressure on Khoqand, he expelled the "Andijanis," that is, the Khoqandians, who had been permitted to stay for up to ten years. He sent an envoy to Bukhara to encourage the Bukharan merchants to come to trade and also invited those Qirghiz who had aided Jahāngīr to sell their livestock.[131]

Nayanceng had to redress the internal corruption too. He forbade the practice of selling and buying the beg titles and various unjust official extortions from the local people. Another question to solve was how to strengthen the military defense against external invasions and internal revolts. After the Jahāngīr invasion the number of Qing garrison troops in Kashgharia increased considerably, so it was necessary to provide them with food and salary. What he did was to confiscate the land belonging to the followers of Jahāngīr on the one hand and reclaim uncultivated land by way of irrigation on the other, and then to establish a military colony there.[132]

This was put into practice from 1828 and resulted in a significant increase of the revenue income. However, it did not take long until the Qing realized the economic embargo against Khoqand could not be a fundamental solution to the problem of Kashgharia.

THE 1832 AGREEMENT

The Qing decision to coerce Khoqand using a trade embargo produced negative results because Khoqand's rulers now fully realized how fearful the Qing government was and what important leverage the khwājas provided for putting pressure on China. Thus, although pressed by economic hardships generated by the embargo, Muḥammad 'Alī decided to support Yūsuf Khwāja, the elder brother of the now executed Jahāngīr. According to *Muntakhab al-tavārīkh*, Yūsuf, who had been living in Shahrisabz, came to Khoqand and visited Ḥaqq Qulī Mīngbāshī, the majordomo at that time. Being encouraged to launch a "holy war" on Kashghar, Ḥaqq Quli and other Khoqandian chiefs obtained permission from the khan to that effect. However, unlike the 1826 invasion, it was not the khwājas but the Khoqand khan who took the initiative and who intended to be the paramount leader of the expedition.[133]

A large number of Khoqand troops commanded by the khanate's highest military leaders, including Ḥaqq Quli, Muḥammad Sharīf Qushbegi, and Lashkar Qushbegi, participated in the Kashghar campaign along with a number of Kashgharian émigrés.[134] They easily occupied the Muslim town of Kashghar at the end of September 1830 and laid siege to the Manchu fort where Qing officials and troops were stationed along with Isḥāqī followers who were taking refuge there. While ten thousand Khoqandian troops were assaulting the walls of the fort and ransacking the environs, Yūsuf went down to Yarkand with several thousand people only to fail to take the city.[135] In the meantime about forty thousand Qing troops arrived at the scene and Muḥammad 'Alī, worried about a new aggressive move from Bukhara, recalled Ḥaqq Qulī and Khoqandian army. Yūsuf Khwāja could not stay behind and so he returned to Khoqand at the end of December.[136]

The invasion of Yūsuf demonstrated to the Qing court that their economic embargo was ineffective as a means to stop the Khoqand's interventions in Kashgharia. Khoqand had proved its ability to wreak havoc on China's western region whenever it wanted to do so. In desperation one Qing official claimed,

> If the officials in Kashgharia are, so to speak, shepherds, the Muslims are sheep, Khoqand is a wolf and the Qirghiz, surrounding us, are like dogs. In the sixth [1826] and the tenth [1830] years [of Daoguang] Khoqand invaded the frontier again, and the dogs, following the wolf, also devoured our sheep. Therefore, [even] the barking of the dogs is hard to trust.[137]

The Qing had no sure remedy for dealing with this small but troublesome khanate in Central Asia. Launching a military expedition against Khoqand was not feasible because Kashgharia's problems alone had already stretched China's financial and military resources to their limits.

In 1832 the Qing government recognized its weakness and finally agreed to submit to Khoqand demands, including many important economic privileges, in return for peace. Based on the official document sent by Khoqand to Cangling, the General of Ili (*Jūngtāng Jāngjūng Ambān*), the demands of Khoqand consisted of the following four points:

(1) to pardon and accept the native Kashgharians (*Kashqarning yärliki*) who, having been accused of their anti-Qing and pro-Khoqand activities, were in exile in various parts of the Khoqand khanate;

(2) to return the land, houses, and tea that the Qing confiscated from the Muslims;

(3) to hand over the right to Khoqand to collect the custom duties that commoners and caravan merchants who accompany diplomatic embassy pay when they cross the border and enter Kashgharia; and

(4) to give exemption of custom duties for the commodities that Khoqandians bring into Kashgharia.[138]

Khoqand requested that the Qing send them a letter with a seal through an envoy if the court accepted these requests. Having been informed about this, the emperor Daoguang issued an edict on April 13, 1832 "to do all as requested."[139] Valikhanov also confirms that the two countries negotiated about the following three points:

(1) the dues on the goods brought by foreigners into the "Six Cities," or Altishahr (Ush Turfan, Kashghar, Yangihissar, Aqsu, Yarkand, and Khotan) should be appropriated by Khoqand;

(2) for the collection of these dues, Khoqand should have agents, called *aqsaqals*, in those cities who would be also the representatives of Khoqand rulers; and

(3) all the foreigners coming to the "Six Cities" should be subject to the Khoqandian agents in administrative and police matters.[140]

However, according to a Qing record, the Kashmiri and Badakhshi merchants were excluded from those on whom Khoqand was entitled to levy the custom duties, so probably Khoqand was allowed to collect the duties only from Khoqandian merchants. The same record also shows that the official title of Khoqandian representative residing in Kashgharia was *huda-i da*.[141] However, the title of *aqsaqal* continued to be used because it was more widely known in Central Asia. The status of *aqsaqal* stipulated in this agreement was not much different from the consul of our day. In addition to these privileges, the Qing government appears to have continued to pay an annual subsidy to the khanate. According to a Russian report in 1849, this amounted to 1,000 (or 250 according to others) *yambus*,[142] a fact confirmed in a document sent by Muḥammad 'Alī Khān to the Ottoman sultan in 1837.[143]

This agreement was unprecedented because the Qing had conceded to Khoqand "consular jurisdiction" and the "tariff autonomy" over the foreigners in her own territory. That is why J. Fletcher calls it "China's first 'unequal treaty' settlement."[144] The 1832 concession of Qing therefore represents an important event in the history of the relations between the Qing Empire and the Khoqand Khanate. It not only reveals that the Qing lacked firm control over Kashgharia, but also that it was willing to cede its economic monopoly over the region, at least in terms of international trade. This concession was the culmination of the Khoqand Khanate's ceaseless efforts to extract more trade benefits from China that had first begun around 1800. As a result, after the 1832 agreement, the Khoqandians came to dominate the Kashgharian economy and formed a sort of shadow government that wielded great influence within the region. Khoqand's chief *aqsaqal* resided in Kashghar where he had his own para-governmental functionaries such as a *zakātchi* (tax collector), a *khazānachi* (treasurer), *mīrzābashi* (chief secretary), as well as his own soldiers. He also appointed junior *aqsaqal*s who served in other cities. Initially Khoqand appointed merchants to the post of *aqsaqal* but later filled it with military men.[145] Khoqand also exploited the Qing's weakness by extending its domination over the Qirghiz nomads living along the border regions and encroaching on the Qing frontier lands around the Narin river, Khotan, and Tashqurghan.[146] Valikhanov goes so far as to claim that as much as one-fourth of Kashgharia's total population, or around 145,000 people (including "all the foreigners and *chalghurt*s [i.e., children of mixed blood born between Khoqand men and Kashghar women]"), came under Khoqand's rule.[147] As a result Kashgharia became an awkward bone being gnawed apart in the struggle between the Qing and Khoqand for dominance in the region.

On the Eve of the Rebellion

CONTINUING INVASIONS

After the 1832 agreement the Khoqand khanate reduced its demands on the Qing government for more privileges. Of course, it continued to send envoys to China attempting to expand its rights to collect the custom duties from Badakhshi and Kashmiri merchants in Kashgharia apparently because they were considered "foreigners," but who were excluded in the earlier agreement. Khoqand also continued to pressure the Qing for the right to occupy the Sariqol region in the Pamirs through which important trade routes passed, although this demand was rejected.[148] Nonetheless, Khoqand did not push these demands very far because it did not wish to jeopardize its exisiting relationship with the Qing in any fundamental way. It had no reason to do so because the Qing and Khoqand now had a shared interest in a stable Kashgharia that was best preserved by maintaining a balance of power between them.

This stability, however, did not last long and the political situation began to deteriorate in both countries beginning in the 1840s. China's military defeat in the Opium War (1840–41) and droughts, floods, and famines around the Yangtze and the Yellow rivers in the 1840s seriously undermined the foundation of the empire. These were followed by large-scale rebellions, such as the Taiping (1850–64) and the Nian (1851–68). The Muslim rebellion in Shanxi and Gansu, which broke out in 1862, seriously undermined the Qing government's power to control Xinjiang. In particular it interrupted normal communications and prevented the delivery of regular subsidies from the inner provinces. Even more important, it produced a sense of crisis among the Tungans residing in Xinjiang.

Xinjiang's political turmoil had repercussions in the Khoqand khanate. Muḥammad 'Alī, who had lost his popularity by the persecution of leading figures in the khanate and his too frequent military expeditions, added his notoriety when he married his stepmother against Islamic law. This act offended many religious leaders and allowed Naṣr Allāh, the amir of Bukhara, to use it against the Khoqand khan by issuing a statement (*rivāyat*) in which he condemned Muḥammad 'Alī as an infidel. Furious at the accusation, Muḥammad 'Alī drove his army to Jizzaq but was forced to retreat by the counterattack of the Bukharan army. The Bukharan amir was then able to crush Khoqand's troops at Khojent and entered the capital of the khanate in 1842. After this defeat, Muḥammad 'Alī fled to Marghilan but was taken prisoner and then executed.[149]

The Bukharan amir soon departed from Khojent and left only a small military detachment behind to protect the khanate. Upon discovering this, a Qirghiz chief from Namanghan named Yūsuf invited Shīr 'Alī from Talas, a surviving member of the Khoqand royal family, to march with him and attack the city. After successfully defeating the Bukharan troops there in 1842, he enthroned Shīr 'Alī but kept the real power in his hands with the title of *mingbashi*. The internal situation remained unstable because the new amir had to cope with both a renewed Bukharan attack and a rebellion by the Qipchaqs. Shīr 'Alī managed to retain his hold on the throne for three years (1842–45), but at his death his successor Murād was killed only eleven days after he was made khan. At that time, a Qipchaq party led by Musulmān Quli enthroned a new khan, Khudāyār (r. 1845–58, 1862–63, 1866–75), who was to gain and lose power repeatedly over the next thirty years.[150]

The cause of this incessant political turmoil in the Khoqand khanate has yet to be studied. P. P. Ivanov attributes it to a shortage of cultivated land that caused a sharp conflict between the settled and the nomadic peoples.[151] But it is as equally likely that political factors, such as the invasion by Bukhara and the weakness of royal power itself, might have contributed to the confusion. Whatever the cause, the turmoil weakened Khoqand's control over Kashgharians. This was well illustrated by the invasion of Kashgharia around the end of August 1847 by the so-called "Seven Khwājas" (*haft khwājagān*) who had crossed the Chinese border with a number of Kashgharian emigrants and Qirghiz followers.[152] Although some argue that they were unleashed or actively backed by the khanate,[153] there seems to be no evidence to support this assumption. On the contrary, Valikhanov writes as follows.

Turmoil of Khoqand was reflected in Kashghar too: *aqsaqal*s were constantly replaced, and one of them named ['Abd al-Ghafūr] was summoned to Khoqand and executed. Bands of barbarous Qirghiz invaded the borders where Chinese posts were located, and Khoqandian *aqsaqal*s, saying that they would stop the Qirghiz incursion, received bribes [from the Qing government]. The khwājas, taking advantage of the confusion, collected a small band composed mostly of Kashgharian émigrés and barbarous Qirghiz and approached to Kashghar in the autumn of 1847.[154]

The Muslim town of Kashghar fell into their hands less than a month after they began the invasion and the Manchu forts in Kashghar and Yangihissar were then besieged. However, upon the arrival of a Qing relief force in the beginning of November, the invaders fled back to Khoqand. Throughout the 1850s, invasions of Kashgharia by khwājas from Khoqand became a regular feature of the region's politics. These invasions included those led by Dīvān Quli and Wālī Khān in 1852, by Ḥusayn Īshān Khwāja in 1855, followed by another invasion of Walī Khān in 1857.[155] Compared with the invasions mounted by Yūsuf Khwāja in 1830 at the instigation of the Khoqand khanate, this new series of invasions lacked formal state support.

H. Bellew who visited Kashgharia in the early 1870s and made inquiries about the reason of the Seven Khwājas' incursion wrote that they had taken "advantage of the anarchy on all sides, and the internal strife distracting parties in Khokand, banded together and collecting a small force invaded Káshghar."[156] The Qing court investigation of the invasion of Ḥusayn Īshān Khwāja and Walī Khān in 1855 also concluded that they were not sponsored by the Khoqand khanate.[157] Indeed Walī Khān was not welcome in the khanate and "fled from Khoqand with seven Kashgharian emigrants."[158] That Khoqand did not support their invasion can be seen by Khudāyār Khān's attempt to execute Walī Khān on the grounds that he had massacred innocent Muslims, and he ordered a watch on other khwājas so that they could not freely cross the borders.[159]

Nonetheless, Khoqand did not consider the khwājas' invasions of Kashgharia extremely harmful to her interests. That the Qing had already lost control over Kashgharia could be seen in the case of Nūr Muḥammad Khān, who represented Khoqand as an *aqsaqal* in Kashgharia at the time. When the Seven Khwājas had invaded, it was he who had commanded the army fighting against the Qing. But after the khwājas were expelled, he remained in office there and China was unable to eject him.[160] For this reason Khoqand was not worried that these invasions would cause the Qing to sever relations and thereby inflict economic losses on Khoqand. On the contrary, if the khwājas could succeed in taking some cities and collect treasure in Kashgharia, Khoqand hoped to benefit from their gains. However, "when the power of the khwājas became strengthened and the revolt developed into a popular rebellion, and when the khwājas excluded her intervention, then [Khoqand] endeavored to plant discord and to instigate secession, thus to cause confusion within the army."[161] It appears then that Khoqand was content to let the khwājas cause trouble as long as they remained weak enough to be controlled, so that the khanate took direct action only in extreme cases.

The invasions of the khwājas time and again ended in failure, and it was the Muslims in Kashgharia who received the most devastating blows in retaliation for these repeated incursions. Since there was an insufficient armed force there, the Qing mobilized a number of exiles (*qianfan*, or *chämpän* in Turkic transcription) "marked with a scar on the left cheek,"[162] for the suppression of revolts, but their atrocities antagonized many local people.[163] People were not permitted to assemble in the streets or to visit the shrine of Khwāja Āfāq.[164] The government even banned performing plays or singing songs.[165] The khwājas themselves were also callous about the security of local Muslims and allowed them to be plundered and killed. One of the most notorious cases took place during the invasion of Walī Khān in 1857 when he shocked the Western world by killing the German explorer Adolf Schlagintweit for no apparent reason.[166] Incredible stories are also recorded in Muslim sources, in particular that he killed so many innocent Muslims that four minarets were formed by the piles of human skulls,[167] or that to test the sharpness of a sword he once cut off the head of the artisan who brought him the sword as a gift.[168] These stories illustrate the unscrupulous nature of many of the khwājas' actions, which they justified in the name of "holy war." This arbitrary behavior by the khwājas, as well as the selfish attitude of the Khoqandians, greatly disillusioned the local Kashgharian Muslims.

OMENS

The most serious problem that the Qing officials in Xinjiang faced just before the 1864 Muslim rebellion was a shortage of financial resources. They had previously depended heavily on receiving of large subsidies from other provinces in China, but the events in the 1840s and 1850s, which had driven the Qing dynasty into crisis, greatly reduced the ability of the central government to send such aid. In regard to this Sayrāmī wrote as follows.

> The Chinese emperor (*Khāqān-i Chīn*) could no longer hear the news from the cities which were used to be called *Gūbī*, [i.e., Muslim region].[169] So perhaps he sent edicts saying "I will not send provisions (*kawlan vaẓīfa*)[170] to officials and soldiers working in the region of *Gūbī*. I have taken care of my officials and soldiers by sending *kawlan* from the treasury in this way for years. I have spent much state funds but nothing came from *Gūbī* to the treasury. Abandon *Gūbī* and come back!" However, chiefs of the Chinese here like *Jāngjūng* [Ili General] and *Khān Ambān* [imperial agent in Kashghar] and chiefs of Muslims like provincial governors beginning with Mīrzā Aḥmad Wang Beg, consulted each other and memorialized to the emperor (*Ūlūgh Khān*): "Even though *kawlan* would not come from treasury to the cities here, we will do our effort to dig veins of gold, silver, copper and zinc, and thus take care of the imperial army." . . . As soon as the edict [approving their request] came down, officials in every city collected people and drove them to all the mountains and plains wherever the veins of ore might be discovered. They let mountain slopes be dug up like rat-holes but could not find any vein. . . . Moreover, they introduced several new taxes (*bāj*) under the name of "salt-money" (*tūz pulī*) and extorted money from the people. Every month they imposed money on the head of people and called it *chōqa-bāshī*. In a word, taxes (*albān-yasāq vä jūbālgha*) imposed on people became much more.[171]

In *Tārīkh-i ḥamīdī* (1908) Sayrāmī inserted a number of other stories not included in earlier versions of his *Tārīkh-i amniyya* (1903). One such story is an incident in Aqsu caused by the arbitrary collection of this "salt-money,"[172] a description that supports one recorded in a Qing source down to minor details. As described in this Qing source, beginning during the third month of 1860 the imperial agent of Aqsu, Jinxing, had collected two *tängä*s per month in guise of salt-taxes from every person for the period of three or four months along with similar taxes on Khoqandians.[173] As a result, the Khoqandian *aqsaqal* protested to the General of Ili. After becoming aware of this practice, the emperor ordered an investigation of the matter, saying "it would be a great violation of law if one, under the pretext of the lack of military provisions, suddenly changes regulations and privately collects money and then diverts it to public expense."[174] As a result, seventy-two Chinese and local officials were discharged from the office.[175]

The incident plainly revealed how grave the financial conditions in Xinjiang had become on the eve of the 1864 Muslim rebellion. Because tax receipts were insufficient, government officials also began to sell offices publicly to secure more money. They posted promulgations (*kūngshī khaṭṭ*)[176] in market streets and announced that whoever donated silver to the army would get an official post.[177] Thus the post of Yarkand governor was sold to Rustam Beg of Khotan for 2,000 *yambu*s, and Sā'īd Beg from Kucha bought the Kucha governorship for 1,500 *yambus*.[178] It is hardly surprising that those who bought such posts "at once commenced to recoup his outlay and squeezed the people by severe punishment, fines, and exactions of sorts."[179] So the local Muslims were furious not only at the Qing officials but also with the local high-ranking begs and their assistants. In the contemporary Muslim literature there is clear evidence of an explosion of the fury against these Muslim officials who were accused of "acting like dogs with human faces."[180]

Conditions of the local Muslim population were getting worse because of the malpractices like enforced corvée, sales of offices, and the introduction of new taxes. A French researcher, F. Grenard, who visited Khotan after the fall of Ya'qūb Beg heard grim stories about the period immediately preceding the 1864 rebellion. One of his informants complained that people had led miserable lives under the heavy tax burden imposed by Qing officials and their Muslim begs. Pushed into a corner, they attempted to obtain tax exemptions by bribing the interpreters who worked for officials or sought the protection of Khoqandian *aqsaqal*s. As a last resort some of them just ran away. As a result, the begs demanded that the local *mingbashi*s (who were responsible for the collection of such taxes at village level) cover any deficit caused by people's flight or tax evasion.[181] A Muslim writer in Khotan reports as follows.

> Upon the heads of people several different kinds of taxes (*alvān*) were imposed. One who borrowed ten *tängä* from a Chinese was deprived of his land and livestock and household furniture, but this was not the end of his suffering. Everyday and in every place, they took away fifty or one hundred people on the pretext of some sort of crime and, at night, tied up their arms and legs and threw them into river. They also cut the heels of some people, who pissed blood for several days and finally died.[182]

Under these circumstances the periodic outbursts of rioting in Kashgharia is not at all surprising. One such riot occurred in Kucha in 1857 when Chen Tai and Li Shi (servants of the imperial agent of Kucha, Urcingga) and their interpreter Yūsuf (Yusupi) connived with each other to demand excessive corvée from the local people. Led by Muḥammad 'Alī (Maimaitieli), the inhabitants of three villages including Qonas refused and started rioting.[183] Wishing to avoid a reprimand from the court for this incident, Urcingga (Wuerchinga) executed thirty people without reporting his actions to the General of Ili after interrogating the participants in the riot.[184]

A slightly different version of the same story is also recorded in Sayrāmī's work. According to him, Muḥammad 'Alī Shaykh, Mullā Mūsa Īmām and other community leaders who represented those Kuchean Muslims who could no longer bear the excessive tax burden (*alban-yasaq*) petitioned to officials (*manṣabdār*) for relief. However, since these officials only wanted to quiet the discontent, they did not report the matter to the *amban*. When the local people continued to be restive, these officials reported to the *amban* that "the people denied to obey the great khan (*Ūlūgh Khān*'s) order and rose in revolt." The *amban* responded to this by executing more than ten Muslim leaders including Muḥammad 'Alī Shaykh and Ibrāhīm Arbāb Beg. He also cut off the heels of some people and threw almost forty people, several of them carrying the titles of *kökbashi* and *yüzbashi*, into a prison cell (*dingza*) with their necks shackled by chains (*gull-i janzīr*).[185]

By comparing Sayrāmī's account with the Chinese sources, it appears that the *amban* in question was Urcingga, the imperial agent of Kucha. Similarly the titles borne by the local leaders involved in this incident suggest their social status. A *kökbashi* was an auxiliary functionary who administered agriculture and irrigation while a *yüzbashi* was the person responsible for collecting village taxes. As was noted earlier, the Qing administration held such people responsible when villagers did not pay the full amount of their taxes and required them to make up any deficiency. That was why they had taken on the perilous task of petitioning to the officials for the reduction of tax burden.

The Qing documents record frequent riots and revolts by the local people including one led by a blacksmith named 'Iwaḍ in Kashghar, another in Khan Ariq led by Shāh Mu'mīn (both in 1845), and another in Artush by 'Abd ar-Raḥīm.[186] According to Ḥājjī Yūsuf's report, just on the eve of the Kucha rebellion in 1864, there had already been attempts at revolt by Ibrāhīm Tura, Yolbars Tura, Ṣādiq Beg, Qāsim Beg, Rūza Beg, Bahādur Beg, and others.[187] Epidemics, which broke out continuously in the middle of the nineteenth century worsened the situation. According to one source, numerous lives were lost to epidemics, including cholera outbreaks in Kashghar during 1845, 1847, and 1849; endemic smallpox in Kashghar, Yarkand, and Khotan between 1851–1856; and measles in Yarkand in 1855–56.[188]

These omens appeared to point to an imminent catastrophe for which the Qing troops were hopelessly unprepared. The soldiers stationed in Xinjiang had not received their "salary and provision" (*yansay kawlan*) for a long time and were now on the verge of mass protest.[189] The lack of finances had disastrous effects on the Qing military effectiveness that included slackening discipline, low morale, and deficiencies in the number of Qing garrison troops. The following testimony by one Sibo eyewitness of the 1864 rebellion in Ili proves how ineffective the Qing troops were at that time.

> The Manchus, having lived quietly in cities for a hundred years, lost all their militancy and were physically weakened so much that they could not even pull the bows; the arrows shot by them did not go far and did not penetrate the thickly quilted clothes of the Taranchis. The effeminate Manchu officials neglected teaching soldiers how to use the bows. They dressed fashionably and led a debauched life. In the bat-

> tle with the Taranchis and the Tungans their bulky clothes hampered their movement. . . . On top of these, the soldiers were starving since there was no food in Huiyuan Cheng. The horses of the Manchus were also emaciated from hunger because they could not get fodder. They could not gallop in deep snow. The Taranchis and the Tungans caught the Manchus stuck in snow and killed them.[190]

This Sibo further blames the Manchu officials for the defeat as follows:

> The officials did not care for the soldiers, and the soldiers also held them in contempt. When the rebellion broke out, they did not attempt to lead the army and suppress the rebels bravely. Instead, at the sight of the rebels, they ran away. They worried about preserving their lives in that circumstance, and they did not realize the fact that all in all they would be annihilated and that their wives and daughters would fall in the hands of the rebels. How pitiful all these are![191]

In short, on the eve of the 1864 Kucha revolt, the situation in Xinjiang, and especially in Kashgharia, was extremely unstable and volatile because of the repeated invasions by the khwājas and the maladministration of the Qing government. The local Muslims had been placed under unbearable conditions and their frequent but futile attempts at rebellion had only made their lives more miserable than before. Neither the Qing government nor the Khoqand khanate had the capacity to control the situation. The following description by Sayrāmī aptly depicts the plight of the Muslims at that time.

> Powerless people were driven here and there because of ever increasing taxes, so things came to such a point that fathers could not meet their sons and sons could not see their fathers. At last their patience wore out, and they ran to the doorstep of the Creator and shed tears in drops, nay rather like a flowing river.[192]

So when the Turkic Muslims in Kucha heard the news that the Tungans, provoked by the rumor of imminent massacre, had risen in revolt, they resolutely marched with them to fight against the emperor of China. It was as if the Tungans were the little fuse that had exploded the larger powder keg of Turkic Muslim discontent. And as soon as the news of the revolt spread, Muslims in every city throughout Xinjiang followed in their footsteps and set in motion the great rebellion.

2 *Xinjiang in Revolt*

Spread of Rebellion

KUCHA

The Muslim rebellion in Kucha broke out on the night of June 3–4, 1864 and gained rapid success with the capture of the Manchu fort and the extermination of Qing officials. When this news began to spread, people in the surrounding villages began to swarm into the city, crying for holy war and partaking in looting and seeking revenge. In the midst of this anarchy a struggle for power ensued,[1] because the Tungans were inferior in numbers although it was they who had taken the initiative in the revolt at first. Neither the Tungan *akhūnd*s nor Allāh Yār Beg who had led the Kuchean Muslims into revolt possessed leadership strong enough to stabilize the situation. According to one Muslim report, the city was soon partitioned among the Tungans, the Kuchean Muslims, the Khoqandians, and the Kashgharis[2] and it was imperative for them to look for someone who could calm this chaotic situation. Since they realized that anarchic internal strife could not be beneficial to any party, they began to search for a person with strong leadership and charisma.

At first, they went to Aḥmad Wang Beg, former governor of Kashghar and Yarkand, who was at that time retired in Kucha. The genealogy of his family went back to Aba Bakr, a famous chief of Dughlat tribe, who had ruled an independent kingdom in Kashgharia during 1479–1514. And Aba Bakr's ancestor Khudāīdād was one of the most powerful ministers in the Moghul khanate who put six khans on the throne.[3] However, Aḥmad's great grandfather Mīrzā Hādī[4] had collaborated with the Qing court during the conquest of Xinjiang, and his father Isḥāq rendered a significant service in capturing the rebel khwāja Jahāngīr. In this sense, although Aḥmad Wang Beg belonged to one of the most distinguished families in Xinjiang, his family's reputation was greatly tainted by its active cooperation with the "infidel" rulers. Then why had the Muslims who pledged themselves to the cause of holy war wanted Aḥmad Wang Beg to be their new leader? Was it not contradictory to their cause? To answer these questions we need to look into his activities and reputation more carefully.

First, let us examine the reason why he was discharged from the governorship of Yarkand. In 1852 he accused two Qing *amban*s of Yarkand of wrongdoings, but these two high officials counteracted this accusation by indicting him for the crime of corruption. They contended that he, under the pretext of his visit to Peking and offering of the tributes to the emperor, had requisitioned from the villagers under his jurisdiction one thousand *yambu*s and two thousand lambskins. This case resulted in his dismissal from office when the official investigation of the charges went against him. The investigation concluded that he had made a false charge against the Qing *amban*s because he feared the discovery of the fact that his bodyguards and *akhūnd*s had requisitioned the items in question and he would be punished if this were disclosed.[5]

Later, he was appointed as the governor of Kashghar, a post from which he was also dismissed. Then, in 1860 he was dispatched to Yarkand to conduct the search for those who had helped Walī Khān and to confiscate their properties. However, at this time, he was once more indicted by Qing officials. They insisted on his dismissal from the task on a charge that he took so many retainers with him to make a display of his power that the local Muslims were frightened and took flight.[6] Then again Qing officials, including the councilor of Yarkand, asked permission from the court to arrest and investigate Aḥmad Wang Beg because "he had a secret communication with 'outside barbarians.'"[7] In spite of this request the court took into consideration the meritorious services of Aḥmad's ancestors and did not take any drastic measure to punish him.

The above-mentioned incidents demonstrate the serious conflicts brewing between him and the local Qing officials. In this sense, the assertion by the Qing officials that "he lost the hearts of the Muslims"[8] seems to have been a sort of malicious slander aimed at eliminating him. It would be difficult for us to accept that assertion *bona fide* and to regard him as "a typical high-ranking beg official of a feudal-lord type" arousing "aversion" and "deep hatred" from the local Muslims.[9] As a matter of fact, Sayrāmī did not spare his praise of Aḥmad. He depicted Aḥmad as a devout Muslim who had never dispensed with the daily prayer (*namāz*) and never touched any of the prohibited things such as alcohol or opium. He used to attend his office wearing clothes appropriate for pious Muslims except for two days, the first and the fifteenth, in a month when he dressed himself with the Qing official uniform. And when he handled legal matters, he always asked the legal opinion (*fatva*) from the *'ulamā* and put his utmost effort into conforming to Islamic law. He also practiced asceticism after being initiated into Sufi paths like the Qadiriyya or the Naqshbandiyya. He made large donations on behalf of resting places (*langar*), retreats (*ribāṭ*), colleges (*madrassa*), and mosques (*masjid*). Thus Sayrāmī appraised him highly among the descendants of Khudāīdād by writing that there had been no one like him: "he was noble and impartial, and he was friend of the *'ulamā* and rearer of the people."[10]

Considering these remarks by Sayrāmī, we can understand the reason he incurred such a strong animosity from the Qing officials. Probably it was because of his attitude toward Islamic law and the local Muslims. There is no doubt that the Kuchean Muslims were very well aware of this and, therefore, as soon as the revolt accomplished the initial success, they hurried to him and asked him to be their leader. According to a Muslim source, they urged him to accept their proposal with the following words.

> From the time of your ancestors [your family] has administered the country as "great khan" (*ūlūg khān*). You know very well the principle of government and the administration of justice. If you become like a father and rule over us, big and little peoples, we will obey your orders with all our soul and spirit. We recognize you as our leader in all matters of statecraft and wish you to sit on the throne of khan.[11]

However, Aḥmad's reply to this entreaty was quite unexpected: he first of all pointed out that the Muslims could not match the Chinese in terms of number and then reminded them of the fact that his family had received good graces from Chinese emperors and worked as high officials. And he told them as follows:

> Under any circumstances I will not betray my lord who has given me "salt" (*tūz*). It is mandatory and essential for everybody to keep the "obligation of salt" (*tūz ḥaqqī*). I will not ruin myself by following your words and becoming your chief. Whoever you choose, it is up to you. But my age has already reached seventy and since I have been blessed with enough glory and power, there remains no more wish or craving to me.[12]

As Hamada Masami vividly describes in his article, of the two sharply irreconcilable choices—the "obligation of salt" to one's master who provided provisions and nourishment on the one hand, and the duty of holy war (*jihād*) that every sincere Muslim is supposed to fulfil on the other–Aḥmad selected the first.[13] Thereupon the crowd, being frustrated and feeling betrayed, cried out "Do you still have any lingering hope to your Chinese?," and dragging him out killed him. Although he refused to become the leader of the Muslim revolt in Kucha and was thus slaughtered, according to Sayrāmī the *'ulamā* at that time still considered Aḥmad Wang Beg a "noble martyr" (*shahīd-i i'lā'*) because of this high reputation.[14]

Then, the Muslims went to Rāshidīn Khwāja to ask him to be their leader. We can find no material showing his activities prior to the rebellion, except that he had lived a tranquil life as an ascetic (*darvīsh*) and as a custodian of the shrine of his ancestor Arshad al-Dīn (d. 1364–65). Obviously he had no experience in real politics whatsoever. Then, why did Muslim leaders visit him and ask for his leadership? Although Aḥmad and Rāshidīn had completely different backgrounds, they shared one common characteristic. Both of them belonged to prestigious families and wielded strong charisma among the local Muslims. They took Rāshidīn Khwāja out of his praying house "regardless of his wish" and proclaimed him as khan. They told him that "You [i.e., your family] have been our leader from former times. Now you should be our leader and ascend to the throne and rule over us as our chief." Having said this, they put him on a white carpet following the ceremony in the days of former khans. At the same time they made Tukhta Ishikagha Beg his "minister" (*vizīr*). And they executed eight beg officials beginning with Kucha governor Qurbān Beg and plundered their properties.[15]

From this time Rāshidīn began to be called "Khān Khwāja" which was transcribed as "Huang Hezhuo" in Chinese documents. This title means that he was khan and khwāja at the same time, in other words "priest-king," which shows one of the characteristics of the Kuchean regime, the unity of church and state. His name, Rāshidīn, inscribed on the coins minted by his order also vindicates this point. Rāshidīn actually denotes the first four "right-guided" Caliphs who are called in Arabic *khulāfa al-rāshidīn*. However, we should note that Rāshidīn was probably not his original name.[16] It is rather more likely that his original name was Rashīd al-Dīn (which was pronounced Rashīdīn in Kashgharian dialects) but changed into Rāshidīn to have a more charismatic aura.[17] On the coins that were made by his order was inscribed *Sayyid Ghāzī Rāshidīn Khān*,[18] that is, "Rāshidīn, the king (*khān*), the Prophet's descendant (*sayyid*) and holy warrior (*ghāzī*)"; and on the edicts was affixed his name with a long title of '*Zubda'-i Rasūl Allāh Abū al-Muẓaffar vä al-Manṣūr Sayyid Rāshidīn Khān Ghāzī Khwājam*' ("The Essence of the Allāh's Apostle, the Victorious and Triumphant Leader, Sayyid Rāshidīn Khān Ghāzī Khwājam").[19]

Some Muslim writers argued that Rāshidīn was a key figure of the rebellion from the first, leading, organizing and encouraging other people to participate in the holy war. We can find such claims, for example, in *Rashīd al-Dīn nāma* by Qārī Najm al-Dīn, *Risāla-i maktūb* by Muḥammad Ṣāliḥ Yārkandī, and *Tadhkirat an-najāt* by Dāūd Akhūnd of Kurla.[20] However, their works tend to glorify and exaggerate the role and the virtue of Rāshidīn because they were written in dedication to him and some of them were read by him personally. The last work even completely omits mention of the participation of the Tungans. Therefore, it is hard for us to accept their descriptions of Rāshidīn's role at face value. In fact Rāshidīn Khwāja did not play any significant role in the Kucha revolt in its initial stage. Not only

Sayrāmī's work but also Chinese sources amply prove this point. Only after the Muslim leaders had wiped out the Qing officials and troops from the city, did they ask Aḥmad Wang Beg to become their new leader. But when they failed to obtain his assent, they recognized Rāshidīn as the second best and enthroned him as khan whether he liked it or not. A Muslim work written in 1867–68 entitled *Ẓafar-nāma* also states that he was enthroned "after Kuchean people and the Tungans assembled and rose in revolt."[21]

URUMCHI

After Kucha, it was Urumchi, the capital city of the Eastern Circuit, that next caught the fire of revolt. Before the Qing conquest this area had been inhabited by the nomadic Zunghars, who were almost exterminated by the conquerors. The Qing government, as soon as it had occupied this place, built a fortress below the Hongshanzui (Red Mountain Peak) and, a little later, another one about three kilometers away from there. The former was called Jiu Cheng ("Old City," also called Dihua) where five thousand Chinese army troops were stationed under the control of a marshal (*tidu*), and the latter was called Gongning Cheng where three thousand Manchu and two thousand Chinese soldiers, accompanied by their families, were residing. Besides these, several thousand civilian households from Gansu and criminals exiled from inland China were dispersed around the neighboring areas such as Changji, Manas, Gumadi, Jimsa, and others.[22] What we should not forget is the fact that those non-Manchu Chinese soldiers and peasants were mostly Tungans. So there were a large number of Tungan soldiers and peasants in the vicinity of Urumchi while only a few Turkic Muslims were found,[23] and it is not surprising that the revolt here was also initiated by the Tungans.

The Urumchi revolt began on June 26, 1864, only about three weeks after the Kucha revolt, and its two most prominent leaders, Tuo Ming (alias Tuo Delin) and Suo Huanzhang, were Tungans. A Qing source describes Tuo in the following way.

> In the first year of Tongzhi when Shanxi Muslims rose in revolt, there was a chief of the adherents named Tuo Ming, *ahong* [i.e. *akhūnd*]. He was in dire poverty and had no regular job, but, since he knew a little bit of Chinese writing, he practiced sorcery and fortune-telling, wandering around the Jinji[bao], Henan and Gansu areas, and got acquainted with various Muslim leaders. Taking advantage of the rebellion [in Shanxi], he went out of the Pass by way of Xining and arrived in Urumchi. Living in the house of Suo Huanzhang, lieutenant-colonel (*canjiang*), he deluded many Muslims by practicing divination. More and more people began to follow him.[24]

And as for Suo Huanzhang the same source continues,

Huanzhang was the son of Suo Wen, former marshal (*tidu*) of Ganzhou.[25] While he was brewing rebellion in his mind for a long time, he met Tuo Ming. Then he elevated him to "instructor" (*zhangjiao*) and, making him teach the scripture, attended him as his teacher.[26]

Tuo Ming was a Tungan from Gansu province and known to Muslims by various names of Dāūd Khalīfa, Lawrīnjā (*laorenjia*), or Lawtai (*laotaiye*). The preceding quotation clearly shows the negative perception of the Qing court, which regarded him as a ringleader of the revolt. However, a contemporary Russian source depicts him as a religious leader deeply respected by the Tungans.[27] Suo Huanzhang was not, of course, a man of religion but a military officer. Nonetheless, as his connection with Tuo Ming suggests, he seems to have maintained close contacts with religious leaders in the Xinjiang and Gansu areas and wielded wide influence among the Tungans. This is not surprising in view of the fact that his father, Suo Wen, had been the leader of a religious sect in Salar and maintained contacts with Tungan religious leaders in various regions through his emissaries.[28]

From about 1863 these two Tungan leaders plotted together and began to conceal arms in a mosque. This fact tells us that the situation in Urumchi had deteriorated before the 1864 rebellion. There were several reasons for the worsening situation. First, Pingžui, the commander (*dutong*) in Urumchi, attempted to levy excessive taxes and demands for provisions on the pretext of strengthening defenses, which caused outrage among the people. Second, the hostility between the local Tungan Muslims and the Chinese peasants and soldiers who had immigrated from Shanxi and Henan became acute and it often developed into gang fights, especially in Mulei area. In the midst of this, it was reported that Chinese residents had organized a militia group (*tuanlian*) and were going to attack the Tungans, and a certain Ma Quan, a low-level official in the district of Dihua, rallied Tungans in order to respond to it. As a result, in May of 1864, a fierce clash broke out in Qitai and Ma Quan fled to the Nanshan Mountain with his followers.[29]

Though ominous signs continued to appear from the spring of 1864, the actual storm of revolt did not surface until June 15 when the news of the revolt of Kucha reached Urumchi. Qing officials there immediately dispatched a relief army to Kucha, about 2,100 strong but mostly made of Tungans. They proceeded up to Ushaq Tal where they were soundly defeated by Isḥāq Khwāja who had been sent to Qarashahr by Rāshidīn Khwāja and was marching to the east with his Kuchean army. The remnants of the defeated army came back to Urumchi.[30] On June 23 the Tungans within the city gathered at a mosque at the Southern Gate (Nanguan) and plotted to rise in revolt. This conspiracy was detected and reported to Qing officials, but Suo Huanzhang succeeded in falsifying the report and covering up the truth.[31] On June 26 they were joined by those Tungan soldiers who had fled from

Ushaq Tal and assaulted the Old City of Urumchi. They could easily take it because there remained only a few soldiers inside. Yebcongge, ex-lieutenant-colonel of Urumchi, took refuge in the house of Suo Huanzhang, apparently without any suspicion about him, but he was killed treacherously by Suo. Pingžui, the commander, stayed shut up in the Manchu fort and waited for the arrival of a backup force.[32]

We have previously introduced Sayrāmī's argument that the 1864 Muslim rebellion was touched off when Suo Huanzhang, who became aware of the emperor's edict to the Ili General commanding the massacre of the Tungans, sent letters to Tungan leaders in several areas. In the case of Urumchi his argument is corroborated by a Russian merchant, I. Somov, who visited several years after the rebellion (1872) and asked about its cause. According to his report, they replied that it was the rumor that Chinese emperor issued an order to massacre the Tungans.[33] If it is true, as asserted in the Qing sources, that both Tuo and Suo had previously been conspiring to revolt for one or two years, then they had probably been actively engaged in spreading the rumor of massacre after the outbreak of rebellion in the Shan-Gan area and preparing some measure of self-defense like storing arms. And when they heard the news of Kucha, they instantly took action.

As soon as the Tungans had taken the control of the Old City, they enthroned Tuo Ming as *Qingzhen wang* (King of Islam) and proclaimed the creation of *Qingzhen guo* (Kingdom of Islam).[34] Suo became "commander" (*yanshay* from Chinese *yuanshuai*).[35] They called in Ma Quan, who had fled to Nanshan, and the reinforced Muslim force laid siege to the Manchu fort. They divided the remaining troops into two units and dispatched them to take other cities where a large number of Tungans were living. These cities included Manas, also called Suilai, which fell between July 17 (the Muslim town) and September 16 (the Manchu fort), and Qur Qarausu which fell on September 29.[36] At the same time, because they had had difficulties taking the Manchu fort in Urumchi, they sent an envoy to the Kuchean khwājas seeking their assistance. In a rare case of cooperation between different rebel groups, the commander of the eastern expeditionary army of Kucha, Isḥāq Khwāja, sent 5,000 troops to aid the Tungans and the allied army took the fort on October 3.[37] Pingžui exploded gunpowder and killed himself and his family. After the fall of the Urumchi fort to the allied Muslim force of Urumchi and Kucha, Changji and Qutubi fell one after the other on the 6th and the 20th of October. Jimsa and Gucheng also fell between the end of February and the beginning of March 1865.[38] In this way the Urumchi regime succeeded in taking all of the Eastern Circuit except for Hami, Turfan, and Barkul.

Although we do not have enough source material to reconstruct exactly what happened after that in Urumchi, some sources suggest that a serious power struggle erupted within the leading group of Urumchi. According to one Chinese source, Tuo Ming sent Suo Huanzhang to Turfan, which meant his exclusion from the center of power and reflects the deteriorating relations between these two leaders.[39] In the meantime, Tuo made Ma Sheng, Ma Guan, Ma Tai, and Ma Zhong "generals" (*yuanshuai*) of the regions that came under his control. Moreover, he even appointed the generals of Gansu and Shanxi, though he had no domination over these areas: Ma Si to Suzhou, Ma Duosan to Xining, Ma Yanlong to Hezhou, and Ma Hualong to Ningxia.[40] However, when Ma Sheng soon began to assert hegemony in Urumchi, Tuo let Ma Guan, the commander of Suilai, kill him and his party.[41] According to Somov, there was one called Ma Fupo, with the title of *dayanshay* (marshal), who virtually controlled the whole power so that Dāūd (Tuo Ming) could not make any important decision without his consent.[42] It is not clear whether this Ma Fupo and Ma Guan was one and the same person.

YARKAND

Among the cities to the south of Tianshan it was Yarkand that immediately followed Kucha in revolt. Yarkand was one of the eight cities in the Southern Circuit and in terms of size of the Qing garrison troops it ranked next only to Kashghar. The Muslim town was enclosed by mud walls with five gates whose circumference reached almost 5 km with a height of about 10 m.[43] After the conquest the Qing built a fortress about 400–500 m to the west of the Muslim town that accommodated their officials and troops.[44]

The first report from the Qing side on the Yarkand revolt was a memorial by Ili General who informed the court that "On the 23rd day of the 6th month (July 26), around the hour of *chou* (between 1–3 o'clock in the morning), Chinese Muslims in Yarkand caused a disturbance and burned the gates. It is not still clear whether the councilor and soldiers were injured."[45] However, this became the last report by Qing officials from this city because the communication with Yarkand, located the farthest west, was completely severed. Later it became known that the rebel army killed the councilor of Yarkand along with thirteen Qing and local Muslim officials.[46] Although the report of Ili General was brief, it is sufficient to demonstrate the fact that the Tungans initiated the revolt in Yarkand too.

The British and the Russian embassies that visited this area almost ten years after the incident confirm the Qing report. According to their reports, the Yarkand rebellion was caused by the attempt of the Yarkand *amban* to disarm or kill the Tungan soldiers under his command because he was worried about the repercussions of the Shanxi and Gansu Muslim rebellion to their loyalty. However, his plan was disclosed and enraged Tungan soldiers under the command of Mā Dālūya attacked the Chinese fort around two o'clock in the morning of July 26. They slaughtered two thousand Qing soldiers and their families, but when they faced stiff resistance they withdrew. Next morning when the gates of the Muslim city opened they entered the city and cried for the holy war. At first Muslim leaders hesitated about what to do, but gamblers, ruffians, drunkards, and those who were in debt to Chinese began to participate in raiding and killing. Thus, on that day alone it was reported almost seven thousand Chinese were massacred.[47]

In addition to these reports, extant Muslim sources provide us with more information. According to *Ẓafar-nāma* by Muḥammad Kashmīrī, before the outbreak of the rebellion the amount of taxes imposed on Muslim peasants kept on increasing by manipulative Qing officials, their interpreters, and Muslim begs. For that reason the peasants could not but forsake their native place (*vaṭan*) and, being separated from their families, flee to other places. After the Kucha revolt, the rumor of the order for a Tungan massacre reached Yarkand, and when the Tungans became aware of this order they armed themselves and gathered at a mosque. Thereupon, the Qing officials called in Muslim begs and *akhund*s to dispel their suspicions and concluded a peace agreement (*ṣulḥ*). However, within several days the Tungans became restless again and began to attack the "infidels," and, at this news, the Yarkand people at once rose in revolt.[48] According to an anonymous work entitled *Ghazāt-i Muslimīn*, this incident took place in July 1864 and resulted in the murder of many Chinese merchants (*maymaychī*) and usurers (*giraw-kash*) because they were owed enormous debts by the people of Yarkand, amounting to 25,000 *yambu*s for the previous three years.[49] The Tungans occupied the Muslim town and subsequently assailed the Manchu fort but managed to occupy it for only three days before withdrawing after being counterattacked by Qing forces. At that moment, Tungan leaders felt a strong necessity to find a new leader who could better appeal to the Turkic Muslims. After they came back to the Muslim town, they consulted and installed Ghulām Ḥusayn, a religious man from a noble family in Kabul, as *pādishāh* (king).[50] Then they continued to fight with the Qing army for another two months until invading Muslim troops from Kucha arrived around the end of September and forced them to drop the siège in order to deal with this new threat.

The writer of *Ẓafar-nāma* was very critical of the behavior of those who took command of the revolt. He deplored the situation in this way:

> The Chinese disappeared and Islam became open wide,
> But in cities and countryside the [same] old practices remained.
> All the people were in great joy and said,
> "Now, there will be no more sorrow for us."
> [But] the flame of tyranny did not abate,

And from any grief people were not relieved.[51]

Unlike in Kucha, the Tungans continued to hold their hegemony in the Muslim town of Yarkand after the revolt.[52] They manipulated their puppet ruler, Ghulām Ḥusayn, to provide the *darugha*s and begs with "bills" (*fitik*) so they could be dispatched to the countryside to collect taxes and conscript the people necessary to besiege the Manchu fort that was still in the hands of the Qing.[53] A number of old beg officials who had served the Qing government were incorporated into the new ruling circle, and this disenchanted many Muslims.

The reason the Tungans could retain their hegemony over the Turkic Muslims stemmed primarily from the peculiar composition of population in Yarkand. First of all, the number of Tungans was much larger than that in Kucha. According to Valikhanov, a unit of the Green Battalion numbering almost 2,200 was stationed in Yarkand.[54] Based on a Qing survey, the British embassy of 1873 reported that the number of soldiers was 5,000 and that the number of households in Yarkand was 10,000 (5,000 in the Muslim town and 5,000 around its suburbs including the Manchu fort).[55] At that time most of the soldiers stationed in Kashgharia were the Tungans dispatched from the Shanxi and Gansu areas. Very few Turkic Muslims, except for a few officials and their families, lived in the Manchu fort. Therefore, we can assume that there were quite a large number of Tungans in Yarkand. Moreover, Yarkand was an important center of trade with the Pamir region and beyond, like India and Afghanistan, so a large number of foreign merchants resided there. We have statistics, although a little bit later in Ya'qūb Beg's time, showing that the merchants from Andijan, Badakhshan, Kashmir, including a small number of Indians and Kabulis, reached almost 2,000 households.[56] If we take these facts into consideration, we can understand how the Tungans could maintain their supremacy after the revolt and why they chose a religious person from the other country as their nominal leader.

KASHGHAR

Kashghar was the headquarters of the Qing colonial administration in Kashgharia, or the Southern Circuit, but the size of the city itself was smaller than Yarkand. The circumference of the Muslim town measured only 1.5 km and the population in and around the city was about 5,000 households.[57] The Manchu fort was situated approximately 8 km to the southeast of the town. Valikhanov reports that the number of Qing troops in Kashghar was 5,500 in total.[58]

The revolt in the Kashghar area first broke out at Yangihissar, about 60 km to the south of the city, where there were 2,000 households.[59] Here, only three days after the revolt in Yarkand, "around the hour of *shen* (between

3–5 o'clock in the afternoon) on the 26th day of the sixth month (July 29), Lan Fachun who was the commanding officer of a garrison in Yangihissar secretly communicated with Chinese Muslims, and all of them caused a disturbance simultaneously with the opening of market."[60] On the next day, "Wang Dechun who was sub-lieutenant (*bazong*) in Kashghar [also] secretly communicated with Chinese Muslims and made a tumultuous riot."[61] Although there is no documentary evidence, the two persons named above were, in all probability, commanders of the Tungan garrison units. Chinese sources are silent about why these Tungan officers came to take the initiative in the revolt of Yangihissar, but we have other testimonies that give us the answer.

First, a Muslim historian Ḥājjī Yūsuf asserts that the rebellion in Kashghar was provoked by the governor of the city, Qutluq Beg, who had sent a secret order to suburban villages to kill Tungans which, he claims, was actually carried out.[62] Another source even writes that only 100 out of 4,600 Tungans in Kashghar survived the massacre.[63] It is not easy for us to judge how reliable this claim is. However, the Russian scholar, D. I. Tikhonov, asserts that this is a piece of evidence wiping away any doubt whether there was actually a Tungan massacre.[64] In relation to this we have an interesting report by British R. B. Shaw who visited Kashghar in 1868–69. He transmits the statement of the former Kashghar governor's son named 'Ala Akhūnd who was serving Ya'qūb Beg as *maḥrambashi* (chief attendant).

> The Toongānee soldiers in the Chinese service at Aksoo and Kooché having mutinied, in conjunction with their countrymen further East, the Chinese at Kāshghar were on the alert to disconcert the plans of those Toongānees who formed part of their own garrison. They were all invited to a feast and massacred, and so the Kāshghar Ambān was delivered from that danger.[65]

It is true that the aforementioned materials show a discrepancy about who gave an order to kill Tungans, whether it was Qutluq Beg or Manchu officials, but they all agree about the fact that there was such an order and that the order was actually carried out. Undoubtedly, this massacre was the immediate cause of the revolts in Kashghar and Yangihissar.

It is uncertain, however, what happened right after the revolt initiated by the Tungans at the end of July. They seem to have failed to take either the Manchu fort where Qing garrison troops were holding fast or the Muslim town where Qutluq Beg and other Muslim begs continued to resist. The fact that they could not take the city shows the weakness of the Tungan military power in Kashghar. We cannot ascertain what the reason was for such weakness, but it may have been the result of the decimation of the Tungan population by the massacre or their failure to get support from the Turkic Muslims in the town.

One Muslim author writes that Qutluq Beg, faced with the Tungan assault, had asked for help from the Qirghiz living in Tashmaliq, especially from Ṣiddīq Beg who was the chieftain of the tribe called Turaygir-Qipchaq.[66] However, when Ṣiddīq Beg came, Qutluq Beg became worried that Ṣiddīq might betray him and take the town for himself. So he not only closed the gate firmly but also gave a secret order to arrest him. Responding to this move, Ṣiddīq laid siege to the town and sent his followers to levy supplies from the surrounding villages, which caused instant opposition by the people.[67] Both the Tungans and the Qirghiz failed to take either the Manchu fort or the Muslim town, and their attempt to take control of small villages in the vicinity caused fierce resistance from the Turkic Muslim population there. The statement in a Qing source that "Jin Xiangyin, a Muslim leader in Kashghar, collected a band of followers and, with a Muslim rebel Ṣiddīq of Qirghiz, rose in revolt"[68] suggests that the coalition of these two groups was formed when they were confronted by the difficult situation. To break this deadlock Ṣiddīq Beg and Tungans decided to invite an Āfāqī khwāja from Khoqand, whose influence they could utilize to seize Kashghar.

According to H. Bellew's report, when the subsidy coming from inland China was stopped, Qutluq Beg, by the order of the Qing *amban*, attempted to levy a new tax of 2 percent on every commercial transaction in the town. Enraged people sent a petition to 'Ālim Quli, a strongman in Khoqand, and asked him to redress the problem, but 'Ālim Quli, tied up with internal matters, could not adequately respond to their request. And then, a little later, the Muslim rebellion broke out in Kashghar and several leaders belonging to the Āfāqī faction asked for assistance from Ṣiddīq Beg, who, responding to this, came to the Muslim town. However, driven out by Qutluq Beg and the citizens, Ṣiddīq allied with the Tungans who had been expelled from the Manchu fort and began to lay siege to the Muslim town. He attacked for three months but failed to take it. Then he sent his messenger to 'Ālim Quli and asked him to dispatch a khwāja.[69] Ḥājjī Yūsuf also concurs with Bellew's report but with one important difference. After the revolt twenty-four Khoqandian merchants, in consultation with begs and *akhūnd*s, sent a letter under joint signature and asked for a dispatch of Khoqandian troops to drive away Siddīq Beg and to take Kashghar. In the meantime, Ṣiddīq Beg himself sent two messengers, Jin Laosan and Ma Tuzi, to Khoqand to ask for Buzurg Khwāja.[70]

We cannot say for certain which of the two sources is correct. Ḥājjī Yūsuf's claim that Khoqandian merchants informed Khoqand of the revolt in Kashghar and urged the khanate to take advantage of the situation is quite plausible in terms of the relationship between Khoqand and Kashgharia. However, most other sources agree in that 'Ālim Quli dispatched Buzurg at the request of Ṣiddīq Beg,[71] and it is not difficult for us to guess why Ṣiddīq tried to invite an Āfāqī khwāja to come. He hoped to utilize the khwāja's religious influence so that he could rally the support of Muslims around the surrounding villages and take into possession the Chinese as well as the Muslim towns of Kashghar. Whatever the truth was, 'Ālim Quli in Khoqand accepted the proposal and decided to send Buzurg Khwāja. He also ordered one Khoqandian general to accompany the khwāja, and he was none other than Ya'qūb Beg.

KHOTAN

The Khotan revolt is a peculiar case because it was not initiated by the Tungans as it was in other areas of Xinjiang. Khotan, in a wider sense, consisted of the city of Khotan, which was called Ilchi, and five other adjacent towns: Qaraqash, Yurungqash, Chira, Keriya, and Niya. Altogether they were called the "Six Cities of Khotan" (*Altishahr-i Khotan*).[72] Prior to the Muslim rebellion Ilchi was encircled with low walls,[73] inside and around the vicinity of which about 6,000 households were scattered along the banks of the Khotan river. The Qing had built a fort inside the city wall where 2,000 (or 1,400) troops were stationed. The majority of the population was of course indigenous Turkic Muslims, but due to the city's geographical location in the south a considerable number of merchants from Khoqand, Tibet, Kashmir, Punjab, and Kabul resided in Khotan region.[74] Although there is no material showing the number of the Tungans, we may assume that it was relatively small compared to other cities because Khotan was located in the most distant part of southwest Xinjiang.

As for the cause and the progress of the revolt in Khotan we have only meager Muslim materials and Western reports. We do not even know the exact date of its outbreak. We can barely assume the approximate date by indirect methods. According to a local historian, about a month after the Khotan revolt the battle of Piyalma with the Kuchean army took place.[75] From other sources we know that the battle was in April 1865, which indicates that the Khotan revolt was in March. However, we have other evidence that contradicts this date. After the success of the revolt Ḥabīb Allāh sent his son Ibrāhīm Ṣudūr to Khoqand, and Ibrāhīm, having finished his mission, arrived in Kashghar with several other Khoqandians in February 1865 on his way back to Khotan.[76] This suggests that the Khotan revolt probably happened in 1864. And our guess is corroborated by the assertion of a native historian Muḥammad A'lam. Although he wrote that the outbreak of the revolt in Khotan was on Rabī' I 22, 1280 (September 6, 1863),[77] if we consider the fact that the dates in his work were frequently given as one year earlier, it is highly possible that it is the mistake of Rabī' I 22, 1281, that is, August 25, 1864.

In this respect, the testimony of a British explorer, W. H. Johnson, was not much help either. He visited Khotan and was told the following story by Ḥabīb Allāh himself, the leader of a new Muslim regime. In 1861 Ḥabīb Allāh and his second son went for a pilgrimage to Mecca by way of India and in the first half of 1863 they came back to Khotan via Persia and Turkistan. Later, scarcely had one month passed after his appointment as chief judge before the revolt broke out.[78] This report is extremely valuable because it was based on the statement of Ḥabīb Allāh himself even though we can find no answer to why he took action against the Qing government, not to mention the date of the revolt.

Information about the cause of the revolt is supplied by M. F. Grenard who visited Khotan after the Qing reconquest of this region. According to the accounts of his informant, soon after the news of what had happened in Kucha reached Khotan, Qing officials regarded Ḥabīb Allāh who had just returned from the pilgrimage as a potential rebel leader and ordered him to be arrested. Fearful of being caught, he fled to the place where his eldest son was living. Up to this time he had had no intention of rebelling against the Qing, but soon another incident broke out that changed his mind. A certain Faydā Majdīd, who originally came from Badakhshan, cherished "an evil design" to take advantage of the confusion and, having collected people from Qarghaliq, marched toward Khotan. So Ḥabīb Allāh and his son joined them and succeeded in entering the city. The citizens of Khotan, however, were reluctant to accept a foreigner as their leader and drove out Faydā Majdīd. Consequently Ḥabīb Allāh and his son were able to take power.[79] Another informant of Grenard's stated that the revolt broke out when Qing officials, at the news of the Kucha revolt, became scared and cut off the bridge that connected the town and fort.[80]

Compared to this Western report, the work of Muḥammad A'lam, which was written in Khotan around 1311/1894[81] transmits much more detailed information. Sayrāmī who is usually very helpful to us in reconstructing the 1864 rebellion treats the event in Khotan only briefly. To know what really happened there we cannot but rely on Muḥammad A'lam's work. He first describes the profound discontent of the Khotanese against the Qing rule before the outbreak of the revolt. Many Khotanese forfeited their properties and their heels were cut because of the debt to Chinese merchants, and sometimes they were thrown into a river and drowned. Preposterous taxes were imposed on the commodities of merchants and on their transactions. In the midst of these extreme grievances, one day several drunken local Muslims insulted a Qing official's horse boy and bragged to him that soon they would rise in revolt and certainly take revenge. On being informed of this incident, the Qing authority executed all of them.

People were greatly alarmed and fearful, so they went to a village called Ātā Jūya. They visited Ḥabīb Allāh, a religious man famous at that time for his poor but honest life. They complained about the tyrannical rule (*ẓulm-sitam*) and urged him to lead a holy war (*ghazāt*) saying "if we live, we shall be holy warriors (*ghāzī*); if we die, we shall be martyrs (*shahīd*)." He asked them ten days for deliberation and then, having performed ablution, prayed to holy spirits. One day he saw in his dream the prophet Muḥammad giving him "happy tidings" (*bishārat*), so he decided to take an action.[82] In this way, Muḥammad A'lam explains the Khotan revolt largely from the internal context of Khotan. However, we should not forget another perspective, as suggested by Sayrāmī, that the revolt was caused as a consequence of the rebellion in Kucha.[83]

Ḥabīb Allāh immediately sent his eldest son 'Abd al-Raḥmān to Qaraqash to collect his disciples while he himself, leading 400 people, besieged the Manchu fort (*gulbāgh*) and set fire to a Buddhist temple. A number of Khotanese began to gather at his camp, armed with clubs and spears. Soon the merchants originally from Marghinan, Badakhshan, Kashmir, and Kabul joined under the direction of their *aqsaqal*s; the Tungans also came, led by their *imām*s. At this juncture about 20,000 fresh Muslims came and engaged in the assault on the fort. They were those from Qaraqash conducted by 'Abd al-Raḥmān. On the fourth day finally they succeeded in demolishing the wall with the help of artillery (*zambarak*). The Qing *amban* inside the fort, out of despair, set fire to the explosives and took his own life. In this way the Manchu fort fell to the hands of the Muslims. The number of Chinese who either committed suicide or were killed reached almost 3,700.[84]

Muḥammad A'lam, describing the beginning of the revolt in this way, asserted that it was not Ḥabīb Allāh but his son 'Abd al-Raḥmān who had actually organized people and conducted the revolt. He called the former "His Holiness Ḥājjī" (*Ḥaḍrat-i Ḥājjīm*) while the latter "king" (*pādishāh*). According to him, Ḥabīb Allāh began to be called king only after his son 'Abd al-Raḥmān was killed at the battle against the Kuchean troops at Piyalma, which took place a month after the Khotan revolt.[85] This fact is not recorded in any other material, but his assertion seems to be reliable if we consider his generally accurate and detailed description about the events in Khotan, especially about its initial stage.

The Khotanese thus succeeded in eliminating the Qing power but they had to face serious internal dissension. Immediately after they took the Manchu fort, a certain Fidā'ī Fayḍ Aḥmad Īshān, leading about three hundred adherents, arrived at the city to participate in the "holy war." The title of *īshān* suggests that he was probably a Sufi master. He utilized his religious charisma and, relying on the support of a large number of foreigners (*musāfir*), began to challenge the hegemony of Ḥabīb Allāh and 'Abd al-Raḥmān. However, he was expelled by the Khotanese who opposed the rule of foreigners.[86]

After this incident Ḥabīb Allāh and his son undertook organizing an army with a view to strengthening their base of power. First, infantry troops (*sarbāz*) of 800 were formed and put under the command of Muḥammad 'Alī Khān Kābulī. They were supplied with rifles (*miltiq*) and trained to handle them. A cavalry unit of 1,000 was also organized, headed by Sharbatdār from Khoqand and Ibn Yamīn Aqsaqal from Marghinan who taught them how to ride and to shoot. Messengers were dispatched to villages to levy soldiers. In the Manchu fort Buddhist temples were transformed into mosques and new buildings were constructed.[87]

In spite of all these efforts, internal opposition confronting Ḥabīb Allāh and his son was not quickly subdued. As soon as a new army was organized, they were attacked by 500 Yarkand soldiers led by a son of 'Abd al-Raḥmān, chief of the Yarkand regime, but they were victorious in the battle at Qaraqash. There was another threatening incident. When a religious figure named Zakariya Īshān at the town of Zava assumed the title of *pādishāh* for himself, several important military officers including Ibn Yamīn and Sharbatdār began to be inclined to follow him. His attempt, however, ended in failure. During this turmoil the military force under Ḥabīb Allāh was steadily strengthened and the infantry and the cavalry numbered two thousand and three thousand respectively. They were also equipped with six cannons. After having overcome these challenges, the Muslim government of Khotan seemed to have gained some peace, but it was to be short-lived because they had to face another more formidable enemy from Kucha.

ILI

When the emperor Qianlong vanquished the Zunghars and occupied the Ili valley in the middle of the eighteenth century, he chose this place as the center of Qing rule over Xinjiang. He removed a large number of Manchu and Mongol soldiers from areas like Heilongjiang, Shengjing, Jehol, and Zhangjiakou and stationed them around Ili. They were so-called "resident" Eight Banners who came with their families and settled there permanently. Among them Solons and Sibos belonged to the Manchus, and Chahars, Daghurs, and Oirats were Mongols.[88] In the meantime, not a few Muslim immigrants were living in this area. There were two groups of them. One group was the Taranchis, Turkic Muslims, who had been removed from the Tarim Basin and forced to cultivate the soil as early as from the end of the seventeenth century by the Zunghars. The other group was the Tungans from the Shanxi and Gansu provinces who consisted of merchants, peasants, and soldiers. The Taranchis numbered fifty to sixty thousand and the Tugans about sixty thousand.

The Ili revolt shows a similar pattern to those in the other oases in the sense that it was caused by the repercussion of the Shanxi-Gansu Muslim rebellion on the Tungans in Xinjiang as well as by the aggravation of socioeconomic conditions of the Muslims. Already around the end of 1862 the news of the Muslim rebellion in western China was transmitted to the Tungans in Xinjiang and a rumor was spreading that the Qing government was planning to massacre them. Mullā Bīlāl, an eyewitness of the Ili revolt, wrote in his work *Ghazāt dar mulk-i Chīn*:

> At that time [Emperor] Tōngzhī, the Cursed, was a ruler.
> The paganism is worse than the tyranny.
> This tyrant sent a letter.
> . . . .
> As soon as the letter reached the General [of Ili],
> An enormous stir was created,
> Because its content was as follows:
> "Tungans rebelled against us.
> However many Tungans live in the city of Ili,
> Kill them all and exterminate!"[89]

At that time the Taranchis called the General of Ili Cangcing, who was notorious for his cruel exploitation, by the nickname of "Long Pocket." They invented this nickname because his family name had the same pronunciation of *chang*, which is the Chinese word meaning *long*, and it shows how he amassed wealth by illegal means of exploitation and bribery.[90] In this respect, it is not surprising at all that the Muslims put up flags with a slogan of "people's rise against officials' oppression" (*guanbi minfan*).[91]

The prelude to the rebellion had started on March 17, 1863 when about two hundred Tungans living in a town called Sandaohezi attacked a Chinese garrison at Tarchi. They plundered the armory and killed the soldiers stationed there. Mullā Bīlāl asserted that this incident was triggered by the rumor of a Tungan massacre,[92] but a Qing report alleged that it was "instigated by cunning Muslims who had infiltrated from the inland to Ili."[93] This first revolt was easily put down because of the small number of Muslims involved and they were all killed. In the later half of August, the Tungans began to attack the fort at Qur Qarausu, and the General of Ili dispatched troops to suppress the revolt.[94] The Qing troops, numerically much larger than the Tungans, did not attack them immediately. Instead, they began to negotiate, asking the insurgents to disarm within three days as the terms of capitulation. At this juncture, a large number of Tungans came from Manas and attacked the Qing army, which was completely destroyed. The news of the defeat of the Qing army ignited the full-fledged rebellion in Ili.[95]

The Qing government discharged Cangcing as responsible for the incident and appointed Mingsioi as new General of Ili. He also seems to have attempted to appease the Tungans by negotiation at first. Accompanied by a councilor and a commandant, he visited the Tungan quarters in Ili (Huiyuan Cheng, or Kürä Shahr in Turkic),[96] but they failed to come to an agreement. The Tungans were determined to stand against the Chinese and sought an alliance with the Taranchis. Several Tungan leaders in Kulja (Ningyuan Cheng) led by 'Āshūr Khānjä Akhūn[97] visited 'Abd Rasul[98] who was acting-governor and one of the highest-ranking Taranchi officials at that time. 'Abd Rasul consulted with Nāṣir al-Dīn, *qāḍī kalān* (chief judge) and the leader of *'ulamā*, who gave him a *fatva* (legal opinion) in approval of the holy war.[99] Tungans in Ili and Kulja rose during the night of November 10, and they instantly occupied Kulja. Then they attacked the northern gate of Ili, but with the counterattack of the Qing troops they fled to Kulja. In Kulja the Taranchis and the Tungans massacred the Chinese residents and easily took control of the city.[100]

From the preceding discussion we can confirm the fact that in Ili, as in other areas, the Tungans were very active from the first. They seemed to make an alliance with the Taranchis because a considerable number of Taranchis were living in Ili and its vicinity. The reason the role of Taranchis stands out especially in the work of Mullā Bīlāl is probably because he himself was a Taranchi and naturally more inclined to emphasize the activities of his fellow people. However, as will be explained later, the Tungans, until they were defeated by the Taranchis and departed to Urumchi, maintained their own rulers and had been a powerful group in the course of the rebellion. According to Mullā Bīlāl, 'Abd Rasul sent letters to Muslim leaders in the Ili region urging them to rise against the Qing. Stimulated by him, Mullā Shams al-Dīn Khalīfa and Aḥmad Khān Khwāja led a group of Muslims and attacked Yamatu, located where the rivers Kunges and Qash meet. And other Muslims living in the villages to the south of the Ili river succeeded in assaulting and taking the towns of Khojägir and Zorghan Sumun.[101]

For the Muslims who occupied Kulja the next target was Bayandai (Huining Cheng). Mullā Bīlāl names the twenty-four Muslim leaders who swore their loyalty to 'Abd Rasul and joined the rebellion. From the titles of these people we can confirm the fact that their leaders basically consisted of two groups: one was religious leaders with titles like *qāḍī*, *mullā*, *muftī*, *khalīfa*, or *akhūn*, and the other was beg officials with titles like *khazānachi beg*, *shāng beg*, and so on.[102] In the siege of Bayandai we see the participation of other groups of people: merchants (*jamī'-yi ahlī-yi tujjārlar*) with the title of *shāngyū*,[103] and Tungans led by their own religious leaders like Shājū Akhūn, Khānjä Akhūn, and Yākūr 'Āshūr Jūsän.[104]

Before the outbreak of the revolt, Cangcing, the Ili General, had dismissed and imprisoned Mu'aẓẓam[105] and appointed 'Abd Rasul as acting *ḥākim beg*. The reason was that several beg officials accused Mu'aẓẓam of extorting money from Muslims and illegally forcing them to cultivate his private farm.[106] After the revolt the Qing officials released him so he could collect Sibo soldiers and suppress the Muslims. Upon his release from Ili, Mu'aẓẓam went to Kulja and entered into an alliance with Aḥmad Khān Khwāja. When he realized that the Qing could be no longer be relied on, he resolved to take leadership for himself, and to this end he assassinated Aḥmad Khazānachi Beg who was the right hand of 'Abd Rasul.[107] The all-out war between the two sides was avoided by negotiation. Rebel leaders assembled and decided to enthrone Mu'aẓẓam *khan*. 'Abd Rasul was made *amīr* (general), Nāṣir al-Dīn *qāḍī kalān*, Mullā Shukāt Akhūn *qāḍī aṣghar* (assisting judge), and Mullā Rūzī Akhūn *muftī* (prosecutor).[108] In this way the Taranchis formed an independent government under the leadership of Mu'aẓẓam and their military force reached almost thirty thousand. However, their future was not so bright because of their difficulties taking the fortresses of Bayandai and Ili, as well as serious conflicts among them for hegemony.

Since they could not easily reduce Bayandai, they sent messengers to Urumchi and Kucha to ask for army support, but in vain. While the siege extended over a long period, people began to feel skeptical about Mu'aẓẓam's leadership while 'Abd Rasul popularity grew. Being apprehensive, he killed 'Abd Rasul in the beginning of January 1865, that is, a month before the occupation of Bayandai. He also imprisoned his party, beginning with Nāṣir al-Dīn, whom he later killed too. On February 8, 1865 the Muslims finally succeeded in taking the fortress of Bayandai, and almost twenty thousand people inside the town were slaughtered.[109]

With one party going down, another arose, this time led by a certain Maḥmūd, nicknamed *fuchi* (gunner), who claimed to be a descendant of a *ghūth*, one of the highest saintly titles in Islam. After the fall of Bayandai, the Muslims concentrated their attacks on Ili and Suiding. Fuchi Maḥmūd allied himself with Aḥmad Khān Khwāja and came to achieve high popularity for his bravery at the siege of those two towns as well as for his skill of making a sort of wooden dynamite (*chub fu*). He became the leader of the factions that opposed Mu'aẓẓam. He finally succeeded in killing Mu'aẓẓam, but then he himself was murdered about a month later.[110] After this, Mullā Shūkat Akhūn was selected as a new *sulṭān*, and A'la Khān, who was known by various names such as Obul Ala or Abil Oghul, was made his *amīr*.[111] The siege of Ili was protracted, and the people inside were in miserable condition because of the lack of food. They ate dogs, cats, and bowstrings, and finally even human flesh. On March 8, 1866 the Muslims stormed into the fort, which had lost all power to resist. The Ili General Mingsioi killed himself by explosion but his predecessor Cangcing became a prisoner, and was dragged around the street. According to some reports, almost 12,000 Manchus and Han Chinese were massacred and only 2,000 were left alive.[112] After the fall of Ili, a few other forts among the "Nine Forts of Ili" went over to Muslim hands.

In this way, the Muslims gained control over the entire area of Ili, but internal conflicts did not easily calm down. Following the occupation of Ili in the spring of 1866, a conflict flared up between the two Taranchi leaders. Shūkat Akhūn deprived A'la Khān of his post, but the people favored A'la Khān, who pushed Shūkat Akhūn off to become sultan himself.[113] However, A'la Khān, by killing Tukhta Akhūn whom he appointed as commander, provided his opponents with a pretext to unite against him. The former sultan Mullā Shūkat Akhūn and Aḥmad Khān Khwāja rose against him, but since they could not overcome him they took refuge among the Tungans in Suiding. At first, the Tungans had cooperated with the Taranchis until the Qing rule was overthrown. Once this common aim was achieved fighting between these two groups for the control of the Ili valley was inevitable.

The flight of Aḥmad Khān and Mullā Shūkat touched off an eruption of severe hostilities and fighting between the two groups. Yākūr, also known as Ma I, who was the leader of the Tungans, attempted to take advantage of this opportunity to subjugate the Taranchis. A battle was fought near Kulja in April 1867 in which Yākūr and Aḥmad Khān Khwāja were killed and the Tungans were defeated. Most of them took flight to Urumchi and only three to four thousand Tungans stayed around the forts like Suiding, Guangren, and Zhande. Later the Tungans attempted a counterattack with aid from Urumchi, but, though they initially held an advantage, they were finally defeated and submitted to the Taranchis.[114] In this way by 1866 the Taranchis succeeded in eliminating the Qing as well as the Tungan opposition and took control of the entire Ili valley. The Taranchi regime based in Kulja continued to rule this region until Russia wiped it out in 1871.

In the meantime, in Tarbaghatai to the northeast of Ili there was also a Muslim revolt but an independent government did not form. It was started by a certain Su Yude on January 27, 1865 who, having collected Tungans, made an alliance with the Qazaqs and began to attack the fort. According to a report, one thousand and several hundred Muslims, several thousands of Qazaqs, and several hundreds of "Andijanis" participated in the revolt.[115] One Muslim source reports that the revolt broke out because Qing officials' plan to kill Tungans was revealed.[116] In the fort there were only a small number of soldiers, but about a thousand Chinese mine workers in the surrounding areas came and helped the defense, so the siege was protracted. In the beginning of June, led by a certain lamaist monk, almost two thousand Mongol soldiers arrived to assist the defense. With this additional army the situation turned in favor of the Qing side, but councilor Ulongge continued to be passive and could not utilize the opportunity. Around the end of April

1866, the fort finally fell to the Muslims.[117] Nevertheless, they could not stay there long because they felt threatened by the Mongols in the environs. So they left for Urumchi between June and July, and then this place came to be controlled by the Mongols.[118]

Other cities in eastern Xinjiang also revolted. Led by Ma'ṣūm Khān Khwāja, Turfan rebelled on August 17, 1864.[119] Hami revolted on September 29th. However, because these incidents were not independent, but rather related to the approach of a Kuchean Muslim army, it is better to explain them in the context of the Kuchean expedition.

Kuchean Expeditions

EASTERN EXPEDITION

Immediately after Rāshidīn Khwāja was enthroned in Kucha, he organized two separate expeditionary armies, one for the west and the other for the east.[120] He appointed his cousin Burhān al-Dīn (also known as Khaṭīb Khwāja) as the commander of the western march and sent him off to conquer Aqsu, Kashghar, Yarkand, and Khotan. On the eastern march he appointed Isḥāq Khwāja, the brother of Burhān al-Dīn, to be the commander and sent him in the direction of Bugur and Kurla. The number of soldiers in each army was less than 200 at first,[121] but soon increased by those who joined on the road. According to a Chinese record, one party of 1,200 Turkic Muslims and 300 Tungans went to the east and another party made up of 1,000 Turkic Muslims and 100 Tungans went to the west.[122]

The eastern expedition marched to Bugur, which lies 100 km to the east of Kucha, and then to Kurla, a further 170 km from there. Both cities fell immediately without any resistance on the 11th and the 13th of June.[123] Many Muslims there joined the Kuchean army which swelled almost to 2,000. At Kurla, with a view to take Qarashahr, the army detoured to the south of Lake Baghrash by using a narrow path instead of the main road. When they reached Ushaq Tal, they unexpectedly encountered a body of Qing troops camping there. About 2,000 Kuchean troops attacked and delivered a crushing defeat to the Qing army. After this severe fighting they proceeded toward Qarashahr until they encountered another army at Chughur, and here again the Kuchean army led by Isḥāq was victorious.[124] When they arrived in Qarashahr between late July and early August, the Kuchean army discovered that the city had been attacked by the Qarashahr Tungans on June 14. The Kuchean army took the city after a week of assault.[125]

After a rest in Qarashahr and being joined by the Mongols nomadizing around the area, the Kuchean army resumed the eastern expedition in September.[126] After taking the fort of Toqsun, they went to Turfan and laid siege to the city. Turfan had already revolted at the news of the Kuchean army's approach and now joined in attacking the city. At that moment, a request for assistance came from the Urumchi Tungans who had had a hard time taking the Manchu fort of Urumchi. It has already been explained how the Tungans took the fort with Kuchean assistance and how the Kuchean army under Isḥāq's command raided the cities around Urumchi. After the fall of the Manchu fort in Urumchi, the Kuchean army of 5,000 did not immediately return but kept pillaging towns like Jimsa, Gucheng, Xintan, Fukang, Jibuku, Qarabasun, Manas, and Jinghe where they slaughtered a lot of Chinese. Two months later they came back to Turfan.[127] In the meantime, Isḥāq Khwāja sent another 2,000 troops to Mulei[128] located to the north of the Boghdo Ula Mountains. This army crossed the mountains by way of Chiktim, and then attacked Mulei and another town called Dongcheng (Dūngjīn in Sayrāmī's works) to its west. However, they failed to take it and, due to the cold weather, had to come back to Turfan. Next spring, Isḥāq Khwāja again dispatched an army to Mulei and Dongcheng but this too ended in failure.

The Kuchean Muslims were able to occupy Turfan around March of 1865, after almost seven or eight months of siege. According to Sayrāmī, Isḥāq Khwāja realized the difficulty of taking the fort by military means and employed a deceptive tactic: he promised the Chinese, who were so starved and desperate that they resorted to eating human flesh, that if they evacuated the city he would guarantee their security and allow their peaceful return to China. The Chinese accepted his proposal, but as soon as they came out they were mercilessly slaughtered by him.[129] In early summer of 1865, Isḥāq resumed his eastern march to Hami and Barkul.[130] The Muslims in these cities had already rebelled a year before (Hami on September 29 and Barkul on October 19, 1864),[131] but they had not been able to take the city because of strong defense by a Hami prince, Bashīr, and the Qing troops. The situation, however, began to change with the arrival of Isḥāq in Hami with a large number of soldiers. Facing defeat, Bashīr sought a compromise with Isḥāq and peacefully surrendered the Muslim town of Hami to him on June 16.[132] Isḥāq also succeeded in taking the Manchu fort on June 27. Then he marched to Barkul and took its Muslim town.

While he was continuing severe battles with the Qing troops in the Manchu fort of Barkul, a message came from Kucha that Isḥāq should return to fight a new enemy, Ya'qūb Beg, who had come to Kashghar with Khwāja Buzurg from Khoqand and who now controlled that city as well as Yangihissar. When Isḥāq returned to Kucha, he left only a small number of troops in Hami. Soon antagonisms developed among these troops, the Hami Tungans and a group led by Bashīr. In the summer of 1866, a Qing army came down from Barkul at the request of Bashīr and took the city.[133] Although Isḥāq was summoned nominally in response to a new threat from Ya'qūb Beg, it was in fact provoked by Rāshidīn's growing fear of the enormous popularity of Isḥāq. The rift between Isḥāq and Rāshidīn was not just their individual enmity. A serious conflict was developing within the family of the Kuchean khwājas, that is, Rāshidīn's brothers vs. his cousins, and it seems to have been caused by the contest for a greater share of power as the territory under the Kuchean khwājas became larger. The collapse of solidarity within the Kuchean khwājas delivered a fatal blow to them when they confronted Ya'qūb Beg.

WESTERN EXPEDITION

The western expeditionary army led by Burhān al-Dīn progressed to Qizil, Sayram, and Bai without any serious opposition. People of those places joined their ranks and soon the number of soldiers swelled to 7,000—mostly peasants armed with clubs.[134] Having secured the Muzart Pass (Muz Daban), an important strategic point connecting Kashgharia and the Ili valley, they marched to Qara Yolghun with a view to taking Aqsu. When they reached Yaqa Ariq, a place about 80 km to the west of Kucha, they encountered a sudden storm and, while taking shelter to avoid the rain, they fell asleep. At that moment they were caught by a surprise attack of the Aqsu army led by Sa'īd, the governor of Aqsu. Almost 2,800 were killed and Burhān al-Dīn fled to Kucha.[135]

Rāshidīn was furious at the failure of his cousin and sent another army to Aqsu, this time under the command of his elder brother Jamāl al-Dīn whom he considered well suited to the task. This army, at first numbering 700–800 but later swelling to 2,000, left Kucha and avoided the main route that passed through Bai, Yaka Ariq, Qara Yolghun, and Jam. Instead, they opted for a detour, going north toward Muzart Pass and then coming down to Jam. They poured into Jam where Sa'īd Beg's troops were stationed and defeated them. Aqsu fell quickly thereafter on July 17 (Ṣafar 12).[136] With the fall of the city, the imperial agent Fujuri and other Qing officials killed themselves and their families through explosions.[137] The next target was Ush Turfan, an important city about 100km to the west. Burhān al-Dīn and his son Hām al-Dīn took 600 Kuchean soldiers with four cannons and went to Ush Turfan. The Qing officials and soldiers there also exploded their own gunpowder and killed themselves. The Kuchean army entered the town on July 23.[138]

In Ush Turfan the Kuchean khwājas collected more troops for a march to Kashghar. On October 12, Burhān al-Dīn first dispatched his son Hām al-Dīn with an army of 2,000 and he himself marched leading 1,500 soldiers. On his way Hām al-Dīn captured Aqsu governor Sa'īd Beg. After the fall of Aqsu he fled Kashghar where his elder brother Qutluq Beg was working as governor, but at that moment he was going to Ili to ask for assistance from Qing officials. Hām al-Dīn did not kill him, but he thought to use him to make secret contact with Qutluq Beg. His plan was to defeat the Qirghiz chief, Ṣiddīq, by allying himself with the besieged begs inside the Muslim town of Kashghar. The army left Ush Turfan on October 13 and soon arrived at Üstün Artush, 40 km northeast of Kashghar. Having received this news, Ṣiddīq dispatched a body of troops and soundly defeated the Kucheans who were forced to remain in custody for some time under the tight surveillance of the Qirghiz army. Only after accepting the condition that they would never intervene in the matter of Kashghar, could they return to Ush Tufan at the end of December.[139]

At the beginning of 1865, Rāshidīn resolved to extend his domain west of Ush Turfan and ordered a new western expedition. He dispatched an army of 4,000 to Yarkand under the command of his brother, Naẓīr al-Dīn, and, at the same time, gave an order to Burhān al-Dīn and Hām al-Dīn in Ush Turfan to proceed to Yarkand with 1,500 troops. The two armies met in Aqsu where they levied an additional 1,500 soldiers. With 7,000 troops altogether they marched to Yarkand. At first, they reached Maralbashi and easily overpowered the garrison under the command of Mā Dālūya. About 2,000 of them surrendered and non-Muslims were forced to convert to Islam, who were hence called "new Muslims" (*yangi musulmān* or *naw musulmān*).[140] Then they proceeded to Yarkand.

As mentioned earlier, the Chinese fort of Yarkand was at that time in the hands of the Qing army and the Muslim town was held by the Tungans who set up Ghulām Ḥusayn (according to Sayrāmī, 'Abd al-Raḥmān) as a puppet ruler. The combined Kuchean force from Ush Turfan and Kucha entered the city of Yarkand without serious opposition, and they made an agreement with the local Tungans to drive out Ghulām Ḥusayn and to divide the city between themselves while cooperating on the assault of the Manchu fort.[141] At this juncture Ya'qūb Beg came to take Yarkand with his army. Since his activities are described later in much detail, it is sufficient here to state that he had to go back to Kashghar because of the strong resistance from the Kucheans and the Tungans.

In April the Kuchean khwājas and the Tungans in Yarkand organized another expeditionary army to Khotan. The Khotanese army under 'Abd al-Raḥmān's command faced them at Piyalma, about 60 miles northwest of the city. At the battle the Khotanese gained a victory, but lost their leader 'Abd al-Raḥmān. The enemy withdrew to Yarkand.[142] In the end, the Kucheans not only failed to conquer Khotan but also to take the Chinese fort of Yarkand. They could not even subjugate the Tungans in the Muslim town. So they stopped all operations and turned back to Kucha.[143]

From the failure of the campaign against Kashghar led by Burhān al-Dīn, and Hām al-Dīn, and another failure to conquer Yarkand with a large force of 7,000, we can see the obvious limit of Kuchean regime in terms of its military strength. Although a lot of people participated in the campaign, most of them were peasants who had no military training at all and were armed merely with clubs and sticks, or at best helplessly outworn swords and spears left by the Qing army. Their zeal for the holy war was soaring, but because they lacked the necessary military manpower and equipment, they could not overpower the resistance in large cities like Kashghar or Yarkand. The reason they were able to take cities like Aqsu and Turfan had more to do with the defenders' loss of fighting spirit rather than the military power of the Kucheans. This military weakness was not only the problem of the Kuchean regime and we can find similar phenomena in other Muslim regimes based in Yarkand, Khotan, Urumchi, and Ili. Therefore, it is not surprising that Ya'qūb Beg, although he appeared on the stage relatively late, could easily subdue them and achieve unification because he had a group of professional military people with him.

"Holy War"

RELIGIOUS LEADERS

It is necessary to distinguish two phases in the 1864 Muslim rebellion. The first phase was an instant response to the rumor of the Tungan massacre and to other factors like the increasing tax burdens that have been mentioned. The response was abrupt and almost hysterical. People with varied social and ethnic backgrounds were led by those who had enough passion and courage to impress members of each group and direct their anger against the Qing. However, when the existing political order finally collapsed, they could no longer hold together the many different groups because they lacked both charisma and organization. The second phase of the rebellion was the process of seeking a new leadership that could unify conflicting factions. New leaders were often called in as a compromise among these groups. In some areas these leaders were able to consolidate their power successfully while others failed. It is one of the most distinctive characteristics of the 1864 Muslim rebellion in Xinjiang that these new leaders, whether they had real power or not, were mostly recruited from the religious class. Let us now examine who these religious leaders were and what their source of influence was.

Kuchean Muslims succeeded in wiping out the Qing forces but they were faced with serious difficulties caused by the fighting for hegemony among various rebel groups, not to mention the continuing battles with the Qing troops stationed in neighboring cities. The only way to overcome that situation was to unite under an authority to whom all of them could willingly submit. As explained earlier, the one who they had first called on was Aḥmad Wang Beg. Having served as governor for a long time, he was known to be thoroughly familiar with "the basis of government and the operation of the administration" and, at the same time, he was respected as a devout Muslim who upheld religious laws faithfully. Probably because of this attitude he aroused the distrust and suspicion of Qing officials more than once and was discharged from the office. His career shows that he was widely respected by the Muslims not only as a high official but also as a man of religious sincerity, though he was not a man of religion by profession. That was why the rebel leaders went to him and asked him to be their leader, which, however, he rejected and chose to die.

The next person they visited was Rāshidīn Khwāja. Who was he and on what grounds could he become the leader of the rebel army? He was a descendant of the famous Sufi saint of the late fourteenth century named Arshad al-Dīn, the son of Jalāl al-Dīn (Jamāl al-Dīn in some sources). Jalāl al-Dīn and his son had settled at first in a town called Katak—thus those who followed them were called the Katakīs—lying somewhere near Lop.[144] According to a legendary story, Jalāl al-Dīn had preached his teachings there, but the people of Katak refused to follow him. Their disobedience provoked the fury of God and the entire city was completely covered by sand. Later Jalāl al-Dīn met Tughluq Temür (r. 1347–62), who promised to accept Islam if he became khan. After the death of Jalāl al-Dīn, his son Arshad al-Dīn went to see Tughluq Temür who had already become khan by that time. After reminding the khan of the promise made to his father, Arshad al-Dīn finally succeeded in converting him along with 160,000 Moghul nomads in 1353/54.[145] He later settled in Kucha where the khan gave him a lot of *vaqf* (pious endowment) lands.

Although the influence of the Katakīs had weakened considerably since the end of the sixteenth century because of the successful activities of rival Naqshbandī Sufis,[146] Arshad al-Dīn, together with Satuq Boghra Khan during the Qarakhanid period, became one of the most revered saints among the Muslims in Eastern Turkestan. He was called Allāh's companion (*Walī Allāh*) and his mausoleum in Kucha was considered a sacred place of worship. As a descendant of that holy Sufi and as a guardian of his mausoleum Rāshidīn Khwāja had been "living with prayer (*dū'ā*) and cultivation (*ṭalab*) and, not being mixed with people, treading the path of an ascetic (*darvīsh*)."[147] He commanded respect and submission from a large number of Muslims—both the Turks and the Tungans—who considered themselves his disciples (*murīd*).[148]

The report that there was "a numerous and influential colony of Khoja priests" in the suburb of Kucha[149] suggests the economic strength of the

Katakī khwājas who inherited *vaqf* lands from their ancestors, but the possession of such economic properties does not appear to have been the major source of Rāshdīn's influence. And as the later development in Kucha shows, he did not seem to have any special talent in leadership either. Except for his saintly lineage and his life as a Sufi guarding Arshad al-Dīn's holy tomb, Rāshidīn Khwāja did not have any other source of influence. Therefore, we cannot but conclude that his political power as the leader of the Kuchean regime stemmed from his religious authority.[150] Many Muslims believed that Sufi saints had the faculty of performing miracles (*karāmat*) through their spiritual communication with Allāh, prophets, and saints, and thus giving the holy blessings (*barakat*).[151]

Tuo Ming, the leader of Urumchi revolt, was also a man of religion. In all probability he belonged to the Jahrī branch of the Naqshbandiyya, as asserted by J. Fletcher.[152] Contrary to Rāshidīn, he had directed the rebellion from the beginning and was branded by the Qing authority as the ringleader of the revolt who deluded people. However, Somov, a Russian merchant who visited Manas in 1872, describes him as "a religious man who devoted the whole life to his own God" and adds that he, called "master" (*pīrī*) by the Tungans, "was at first just a mediocre Tungan from a poor and insignificant family but, showing some outstanding qualities by the devout and upright way of life, he gained respect and allegiance of many people."[153] He was also reported to have been "wandering around the Jinji, Henan and Gansu areas, and got acquainted with various Muslim leaders."[154] Here "Jinji" is nothing but the stronghold of Jinjibao where the famous Jahrī leader Ma Hualong had his base. This fact strongly suggests the connections between Tuo Ming and Ma Hualong. After Tuo Ming was enthroned as King of Islam, his appointment of Ma as commander (*yuanshuai*) of the Ningxia region also suggests a possibility that Tuo belonged to the Jahriyya.

The background of Suo Huanzhang, who played a leading role together with Tuo Ming, also confirms our point. Although he was a military officer, he was not unrelated to the movements of the Jahrī sect in the Shanxi and Gansu areas. His father Suo Wen, who had been made lieutenant colonel in Ganzhou as a reward for his service rendered during the Jahāngīr rebellion,[155] was actually the leader of a religious sect in Salar and maintained contacts with Tungan religious leaders in various regions through his emissaries.[156] Moreover, as a Chinese source reveals, some of the future Tungan rebel leaders were employed as officers under him. One such example is Ma Chungliang, alias Ma Si, who led the revolt in Suzhou in 1862 and later was appointed, though fictionally, by Tuo Ming as the commander of that area.[157] In this light, the later execution of Suo Wen by the Qing authority as well as Tuo Ming's visit to his son, Suo Huanzhang, do not seem to have been coincidental at all. This evidence supports the assertion that

Tuo Ming was "a Sufi who had been with the Jahrī leader Ma Hualong in China proper and had been invited to Xinjiang by Suo Huanzhang, one of Ma Hualong's disciples."[158]

In Yarkand, the revolt was initiated and led by the Tungans who, once having occupied the Muslim town, continued to control it and kept fighting with the Qing force in the Manchu fort. However, since the absolute majority of the inhabitants of the city and its environs were Turkic Muslims, the Tungans could not but enthrone a nominal leader who could command the Turkic Muslims' respect. This was why Ghulām Ḥusayn (later replaced by his brother 'Abd al-Raḥmān) became the leader of the Yarkand regime. We do not know much about this person except for the fact he came from a notable family in Kabul. It is interesting to note that Mehmet Emin Bughra, in his work written in the 1940s, added the epithet of Mujaddīdī to his name.[159] J. Fletcher already noticed this remark and assumed that Ghulām Ḥusayn may have been a descendant of Aḥmad Sirhindī (1564–1624) who was a famous Sufi in India and was widely known as Mujaddīdī-yi Alf-i Thānī, that is, the Reformer of the Second Millennium.[160] Probably his descendants formed a Sufi sect called Mujaddīdī in Kabul where they exerted a lot of influence. This family belonged to the Naqshbandiyya and its male members were called by the respected title Ḥaḍrāt-i Ṣāḥib-i Shor Bazār. The leaders of this family are known to have displayed powerful political influence up to the middle of the twentieth century around the Kabul area.[161]

It would not be an exaggeration for Muslim sources to describe Ghulām Ḥusayn and his brother as belonging to "a noble family of Kabul." Thus we can surmise that it was nothing more than their religious charisma stemming from their saintly lineage that the Tungans in Yarkand hoped to utilize. Nonetheless, they did not want their puppet leader to become a real ruler, and probably that was why they chose a person from Kabul, not among the native Sufi masters living in Yarkand, who apparently did not have a strong basis of local support.

The case of Kashghar is a good example of what happened when the Muslims did not have a religious leader. Here, as we explained, the revolt broke out all of a sudden without any premeditated plan. The Muslims did not have a definite leader and could not take either the Muslim town or the Manchu fort. The Qirghiz, led by Ṣiddīq, later joined with the Tungans and attempted to take the city, but their efforts were frustrated by the strong resistance of the Qing forces and the Muslim beg officials.

It is noteworthy that, unlike what happened in other cities, the Muslims in Kashghar, not only in the town but also around the neighboring villages, did not ally with the Qirghiz and even violently resisted. Their opposition, of course, stemmed from the deep animosity of the sedentary Muslims against the nomadic Qirghiz, but the situation might have improved if the

Qirghiz had set up a person with religious charisma who could command the respect of the local Muslims.

Our point is again well illustrated by ʿAbd al-Bāqī Kāshqarī who provides us with a useful account of Ṣiddiq Beg's activities. According to him, when Ṣiddiq Beg was governor of Farrash he had a dispute with some Kashgharian begs. The begs, based on the decision of a religious court, confiscated lands and canals that Ṣiddiq had administered. He was furious and, having rallied Qirghizs and Qipchaqs living around Oy Tagh, came down to Kashghar and besieged the town. Although the siege extended for a long time and the provisions were running out, the begs would not surrender. They sent him a "letter of chastisement" (*siyāsat-nāma*) in which they made it clear that they could not accept his rule because he was neither a *sayyid* (descendant of Muḥammad) nor *pādishāhzāda* (descendant of a king).[162] Even after begs and *akhūnd*s inside the town expelled Qutluq Beg in alliance with Khoqandians, they dispatched envoys to the Khoqand khanate to ask assistance, while still refusing to submit to Ṣiddīq.[163] Ṣiddīq also sent an envoy to the Khoqand khanate asking to send an Āfāqī khwāja. There is no doubt that he took such an action with the intention of appeasing the opposition of the local Kashgharians by using a religious figure. This fact amply proves how important the religious authority of a person with a saintly lineage was in rallying the Muslims.

The case of Khotan also shows the significance of religious leadership. The examination of related Muslim sources on the Khotan revolt convinces us of the fact that it was not Ḥabīb Allāh but his son ʿAbd al-Raḥmān who actually collected fellow Muslims and prepared for an action. In spite of this, the reason Ḥabīb Allāh, sometimes together with his son, was described as the prime mover of the revolt is apparently his religious influence. And for the same reason he was enthroned in old age after the death of ʿAbd al-Raḥmān at the battle of Piyalma. According to Sayrāmī, Ḥabīb Allāh was born into the family that had produced *ʿulamā* for generations and he himself was also *muftī*. He was so strict in adhering to a religiously austere life that he never set his foot on soil without having done ablutions (*ṭahārat*) and neither did he neglect the daily five times of praying (*namāz*) even on his journey. It was reported that he was against those religious leaders who regarded taking gifts and donations as a matter of course and criticized their attitude as a violation of *sharīʿah*. It was with just such religious vigor he had performed the obligatory pilgrimage to Mecca and Medina and stayed in the Holy Land for seven years. It is not difficult for us to imagine the extent of his religious influence after he returned from the pilgrimage.[164] There is no doubt that his influence on the inhabitants of Khotan stemmed from his being a man of religion. The fact that, after the success of the revolt, the serious challenges against his regime also came from the same religious people with the title of *īshān* shows the charismatic influence held by religious figures in general.

Finally, the case of Ili shows the same characteristics. As explained earlier, the two groups of Ili Muslims, that is, the Tungans and the Taranchis, put up their own leaders. Those who had the title of *akhūn* and who took the leadership of the Tungans were apparently of the religious group. It is curious that 'Abd Rasul who acted as a leader of the Taranchis was not a man of religion but a secular official with the title of acting governor. However, we should not forget that, before he took action, he had received from the prominent religious scholar Nāṣir al-Dīn the *fatva* approving the "holy war." Mu'aẓẓam who snatched the leadership from 'Abd Rasul was also an official. His genealogy, however, shows an interesting fact. He was son of Khalīzāda, who was son of Khūsh Naẓar, who was son of Malikzāda, who was son of Aurangzib, who was son of Amīn Khwāja, who was son of Niyāz Khwāja, who was son of Ṣūfī Khwāja. And one of the ancestors of this last person was Khwāja Muḥammad Sharīf who was a famous Sufi master in Kashghar in the later half of the sixteenth century.

Muḥammad Sharīf was born in Sayram and studied thirty years at the Madrassa of Ulugh Beg in Samarqand. But after he attained the illumination through the spirit of Satugh Boghra Khan and Aḥmad Yasavī, he came to Kashghar and became the custodian of Satugh Boghra Khan's shrine.[165] He was also known to be the author of the biography of Satuq Boghra Khan.[166] He and his disciples became very influential in the court of the Moghul khans like 'Abd al-Rashīd (r. 1533/34–1559/60) and 'Abd al-Karīm (r. 1559/60–1590/91). However, the influence declined from the reign of Muḥammad Khan (r. 1590/91–1608/09), who was a staunch ally of the Isḥāqi khwājas,[167] and some of his descendants moved to the east around Turfan. One of them was Amīn Khwāja who had helped the Qing conquest of Eastern Turkestan in the 1750s. A branch of this family moved from Turfan to Ili where they kept the post of governor for generations. In this respect, we can assume that Mu'aẓẓam's assumption of power was partly helped by the religious and the secular influence of his family. Moreover, the fact that Fuchi Maḥmūd who replaced Mu'aẓẓam pretended to be a descendant of a saint and that Mullā Shūkat who eliminated Maḥmūd was also *akhūn* indicates the importance of religious authority in the Ili rebellion.

"HOLY WAR" WITH CHINA

We have explained the background as well as the direct cause of the 1864 Muslim rebellion in Xinjiang, and we also examined its outbreak and progress in several important cities. Then, how can we define this massive movement in a wider perspective? In a sense, it is the culmination of the "holy war" led by the khwājas and the riots of the local Muslims during the preceding decades. There is no doubt that it was also a response to the overall crumbling of the Qing empire in the nineteenth century, and in that respect it is comparable to the Taiping and other rebellions of that period. However, no other region except Eastern Turkestan denied the legitimacy of Qing dominion so persistently. And the ideology of the anti-Qing movement led by the khwājas was that of a "holy war" based on an Islamic worldview to which the Qing could not adequately respond.

Although the 1864 rebellion was undoubtedly based on the Islamic principle of holy war, we should not overlook the difference between such a principle and the preceding invasions and riots that shook the region. Many of those incidents had taken place with the direct participation of the Āfāqī khwājas or with their covert instigation and assistance. Their prime motivation was to recapture the region, which they considered their hereditary domain, and their pursuits were aided by the Khoqand Khanate that hoped to maximize its own economic privileges in this region. While these invasions succeeded in rallying support from the Āfāqī followers and some of the local population, many other people in the region (including the Isḥāqīs and beg officials) adamantly opposed them, as did the Tungans. Moreover, the stage of their action was basically limited to the western part of Kashgharia. From the 1850s on, their incursions became more frequent and were accompanied by imprudent pillages and massacres that only made the conditions in Kashgharia more chaotic. As a result, the local people became gradually disillusioned with their cause.

The 1864 rebellion, by way of contrast, was not led or even instigated by those khwājas. In most cities it was the Tungans who became frightened by the rumor of the Tungan massacre and first raised the banner of anti-Qing rebellion. This is the reason the rebellion was not limited to Kashgharia but extended to all parts of Xinjiang, including Zungharia and Uyghuristan. However, the Turkic Muslims who formed the majority of the population in Eastern Turkestan, and who were strongly represented north of the Tianshans, also participated in the rebellion en masse because they had been suffering from worsening conditions since the 1850s. They soon took the hegemony away from the Tungans except for those few areas in which the Tungans were densely settled. Setting aside the question of which group took control of the situation, it is an irrefutable truth that most of the Muslim population in Xinjiang, regardless of their ethnic or social background, participated in the rebellion. This marked a sharp contrast to the preceding holy wars of the khwājas, and it is one of the most distinctive features of the 1864 Muslim rebellion in Xinjiang.

However, a number of studies have shown a tendency to overemphasize the role of a certain ethnic or social group. For example, scholars who consider the 1864 rebellion a peasant uprising try to stress socioeconomic issues as its most dominant feature,[168] while those who focus on the ethnic conflict between the Uyghurs and the Chinese tend to define the rebellion as an "Uyghur national-liberation movement."[169] Although these theories certainly reflect some truth, they do not represent the historical reality appropriately and their theoretical frames do not conform well to what the Muslims at the time were striving for. Certainly one of the important underlying causes of the rebellion was the aggravation of the socioeconomic conditions of the local people, most of whom were peasants. Yet at the same time there was also massive participation by urban populations, merchant leaders, and local beg officials. Moreover, there is no indication that any of the newly created polities pursued any significant program reflecting the class interests of peasants.

It is difficult for us to accept the claim that it was a Uyghur national-liberation movement either. First of all, there was no concept of Uyghur nationality among the people in Xinjiang at that time and even no expression to designate all the population there.[170] They had only the terms like *Kashgharliq* (Kashgharis), *Khotanliq* (Khotanese), *Kuchaliq* (Kucheans) and so on. When they needed a more general term, they simply used *musulmān* to distinguish themselves from the non-Muslim population. In much contemporary Muslim literature we find frequent mentions of *Khitay* as their enemy. However, for them this term signified the Chinese as non-Muslim people par excellence, not as an ethnic group. We should not forget the fact that the Chinese Muslims in Xinjiang were never called *Khitay* even though they spoke the Chinese language. Nor was the fighting between the Taranchis and the Tungans an ethnic conflict, but rather it was a power struggle in which each group wanted to dominate.

So how should we understand the 1864 rebellion? Instead of making a judgment from our scholastic point of view, it is important, first of all, for us to ask how those Muslims who participated in that movement perceived their actions and how they explained their endeavor. To these questions the contemporary sources give us a strikingly unanimous answer: they were Muslims fighting against the "infidel" rule. This may appear to be too simplistic. However, other than Muslim, what common denominator can we find among the Tungans, Taranchis, Qirghizs, Khoqandians, Kabulis, Kashmiris, and the Turkic populations in Eastern Turkestan? These diverse groups came together under the banner of Islam because they were Muslims. Of course, I do not purport to say that the religion was the prime motive of the 1864 rebellion or that it was a religious war. Religious conflict was only one of the factors that provoked the rebellion. Once the rebellion broke out, however, it was Islam that emerged as the most powerful unifying ideology. The reason why Islam could take such a decisive role in mobilizing the local population can be found in the inherent weakness of the Qing rule in Xinjiang.

Recent studies on the Qing empire tend to emphasize the persistence of the Manchu identity deeply anchored in Inner Asian tradition.[171] The Qing imperial ideology was not built on the traditional concept of the Sinocentric world order but on the principle of the coexistence of multifarious cultural regions, China proper being only one of those, under the aegis of the Manchu emperor. We find a similar approach criticizing the Sinicization theory in the studies of the Qitan Liao and the Mongol Yuan. When the alien dynasties ruled over China with their limited human and cultural resources, the process of Sinicization was in some degree inevitable. However, it does not necessarily mean that they aspired to build a Chinese dynasty. The Manchus shared with the Qitans and the Mongols a similar imperial ideology that transcended the geographical and cultural limits of China.

This ideology of the Qing empire was more or less successful in other Inner Asian zones like Manchuria, Mongolia, or Tibet. The Qing court put its effort into making the tribal and the religious leaders in those areas feel that the emperor was not a Chinese emperor alien to their cultures. Several political devices and symbolic gestures were employed for this purpose, such as the prohibition of Han immigration to these frontier areas, marriage ties with tribal chiefs, audiences with emperor, and hunting expeditions.[172] To the Chinese the emperor was of course *huangdi*, bestowed with the Mandate of Heaven and with all the Confucian virtues. To the Mongols and the Manchus, however, he was *khan* or *khaghan*, inheriting the political charisma of Chinggis Khan; and to the Tibetans *chakravartin*, the secular ruler who turns the wheel of the Buddhist laws.[173]

Then, what was he in the eyes of the Muslims in Xinjiang? In Muslim literature he was also called by the title of *Khāqān-i Chīn* (Khaghan of China) or *Ūlūgh Khān* (Great Khan).[174] In Central Asia the title of khaghan or khan could be assumed only by the Chinggisid, at least theoretically, and undoubtedly it aroused great reverence from the local people in Xinjiang. However, after the Islamization of Eastern Turkestan, which was completed by the end of the fifteenth century with the fall of the Hami kingdom, there emerged a competing source of charisma that gradually overwhelmed the Chinggisid imperial ideology. It was the concept of the sovereignty based on *sharīʿah*, the Islamic law. According to a popular Islamic theory, the region in which Muslims form the majority of the population and where the *sharīʿah* law is put into force is called *Dār al-Islām* (Abode of Islam). Those regions ruled by a political power that neither respects Islamic principles nor has any peace pact with Muslims is called *Dār al-Ḥarb* (Abode of War).[175] At its most expansive level, this theory denies the political legitimacy of the

Dār al-Ḥarb and argues that such a territory should eventually be brought under the authority of Islam, by holy war if necessary.

Before the Qing conquest of Xinjiang in 1750s this religious charisma was wielded by Sufi leaders with saintly lineages and from the end of the sixteenth century it was almost monopolized by the Makhdūmzādas. The solidification of their religious influence was followed by the expansion of their power in the secular realm. Before the conquest of the Zunghars in the 1680s an Isḥāqī leader began to be called by the title of *khwājam pādishāh*,[176] and Khwāja Āfāq who ruled over Kashgharian cities under the Zunghar protection was also addressed by the title of *khān khwāja* even though he was not a Chinggisid. Thus the synthesis of the secular and the religious charismas, which Martin Hartmann called "Heiligenstaat,"[177] formed a new tradition in Eastern Turkestan. The emperor Qianlong succeeded in expelling the khwāja family and incorporating the region into his realm, but he could not take away their religious charisma because he had no other source to replace it. The domination of the Qing emperors who were non-Muslims not only contradicted Islamic principles but also was doomed to face the challenge from the khwājas who retained their religious charisma. The Qing imperial ideology, designed to subsume all different cultural regions, could not be fulfilled in Xinjiang.

The Qing policy of utilizing Muslim beg officials did not help much in resolving this problem. On the contrary, a few examples show that the beg officials themselves keenly felt the ideological contradictions between their loyalty to Islam and to the emperor. In 1776, Sulayman who was *junwang* of Turfan spent 7,000 *liang*s and built a *madrassa*, and he also erected a stone monument with bilingual inscriptions. In Chinese text he expressed deep gratitude to the grace of the emperor calling himself "old subject of the Great Qing emperor." However, in the Turki text he paid tribute only to Allāh and Islam without any mention of the emperor.[178] We see a similar case when Iskandar Beg, Kashghar governor, in 1801–02 sponsored the repair of the mausoleum of Alp Ata, a legendary Sufi saint in Turfan. The text of the tablet written in Turki on the front arch of the building shows only his praise for Allāh and Alp Ata with no mention of the Qing emperor at all.[179] These two examples suggest that even the highest beg officials felt the schism of loyalty between Islam and the Qing emperor. The only justification, though partial, that the Qing rule could be accepted by the local Muslims was that the emperor provided them peace and welfare, which they called the rule of justice (*'adālat*). However, whenever this justice was not realized by the tyranny of officials or the increase of the tax burden, the non-Muslim rule could not be tolerated.

This was what happened in 1864, and, when the Muslims rose against the Qing, they denied the imperial rule not merely because it was unjust but also because such injustice was caused by "infidel" rule. Since the 1864 rebellion in Xinjiang was the movement of the Muslims under the non-Muslim domination, its ideal could be best postulated by holy war (*ghazāt*). In almost every page of this historical drama we can read their fervor to expel the infidels and to establish the kingdom of Islam. Rāshidīn called himself holy warrior (*ghāzī*),[180] Tuo Ming styled himself King of Islam, people in Khotan urged Ḥabīb Allāh to lead holy warriors, and the book recording the Ili rebellion was entitled *Holy War in China*. Holy war was not only their ideal, but it was also their best strategy to mobilize the Muslim masses regardless of origin and class. In this movement most of the Muslims in Xinjiang participated from highly educated intellectuals like Sayrāmī and Mullā Bīlāl down to those who belonged to the lowest social stratum who regularly violated Islamic law like gamblers, drunkards, and opium-smokers. Only a minority found their loyalty to the Qing emperor more important.

However, because all of the non-Muslim population in Xinjiang were regarded as infidels and enemies to be exterminated, putting the rebellion into a religious framework resulted in incredible cruelties whenever the towns held by the Qing force were taken. The massive slaughter committed by the Muslim rebels was one of the tragic aspects of their holy war. And yet in spite of this fervor of holy war, the Muslims failed to create a unified force to realize their dream, because the holy war was after all the ideology best used against the infidels. Once these common enemies disappeared, fighting among fellow Muslims started and here the concept of a religious war could no longer serve as a unifying ideology.

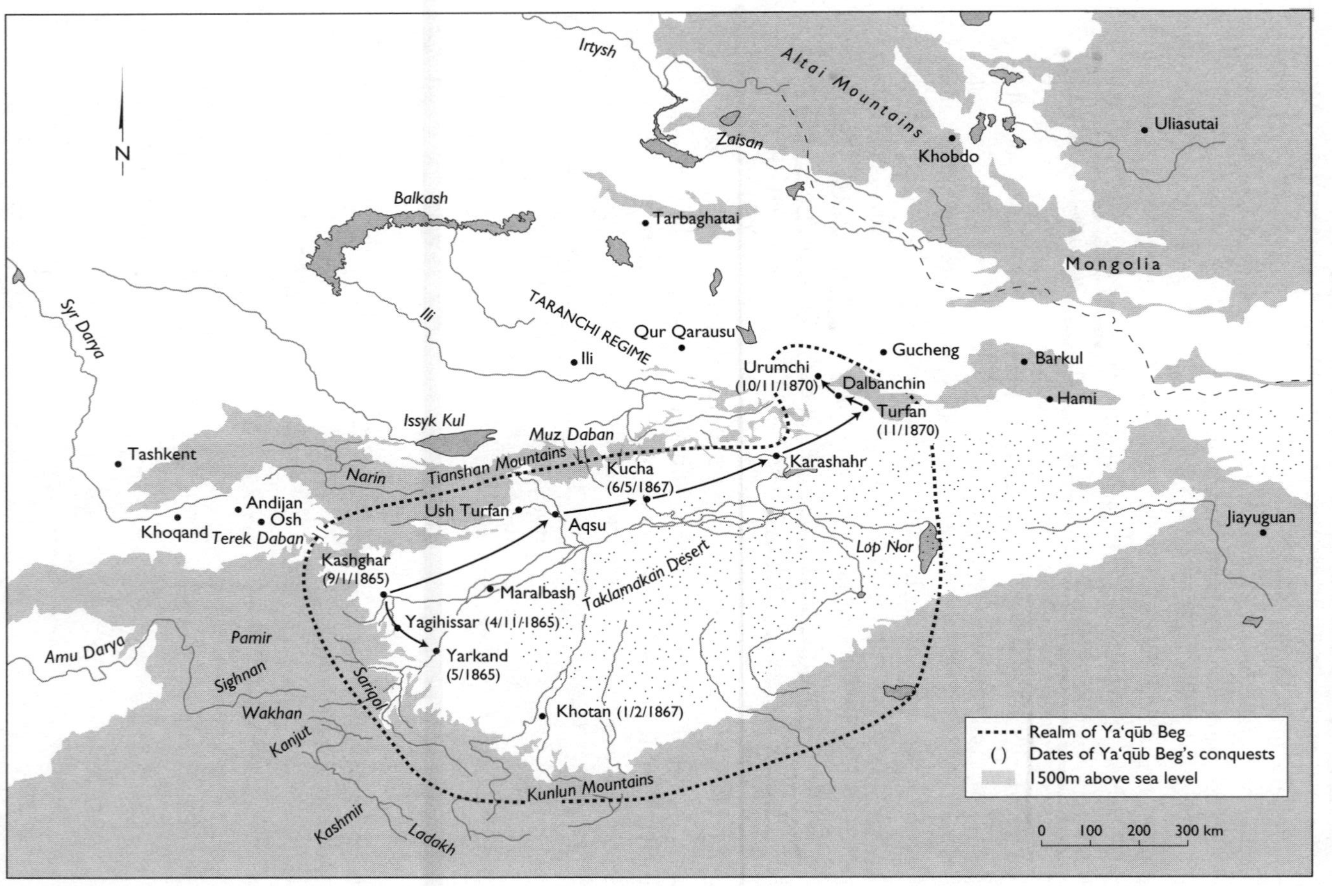

MAP 2. Unification by Ya'qūb Beg and the Realm of the Muslim State

3 *The Emergence of Ya'qūb Beg's Regime*

Ya'qūb Beg

MYTH AND REALITY

It was at the beginning of 1865, a half year after the outbreak of the Muslim rebellion, when Ya'qūb Beg came to Kashghar from Khoqand. Although the Kuchean regime headed by Rāshidīn Khwāja had gained control over the large area from Maralbashi in the west to Turfan in the east, it failed to unify the several different Muslim powers that controlled Kashghar, Yarkand, and Khotan. Moreover, in Kashghar, the Manchu fort was still defended by Qing forces and the Muslim begs occupying the Muslim town continued to offer stubborn resistance. To the north of the Tianshan Mountains there were also independent Muslim powers now freed from Qing rule. It is really surprising then that Ya'qūb Beg, who initially set foot in Kashgharia with only few dozen followers, could have achieved the unification of the entire area south of the Tianshan within a year and a half, and even took control of Urumchi by 1870.

The emergence of Ya'qūb Beg aroused a great deal of interest not only among the Muslims in Central Asia but also among the Western powers. He was known by the epithet Ataliq Ghāzī which reflects his popular image as a *ghāzī* or "holy warrior" striving for Islam while *ataliq* (whose literal meaning is "fatherly") give this title a meaning something like "the great holy warrior." This name fit very well to his image which was nurtured by the Muslims of the time who regarded him a hero fighting against the idolaters in China. The Muslims in Xinjiang had suffered from alien domination since the fall of the Moghul khanate in the 1680s. It was therefore natural that they felt proud of what they accomplished in the 1860s by ending infidel rule and creating the basis for the emergence of a Muslim state. In their eyes Ya'qūb Beg was a hero who brought their holy war to its completion by creating an independent and regionally unified Islamic kingdom. It is not surprising then that Ya'qūb Beg was depicted as a heroic holy warrior in so many of the literary works that described the great events of this

FIGURE 3.1. Portrait of Ya'qūb Beg. Source: *Zapiski Vostochnogo otdeleniia Russkogo arkheologicheskogo obshchestva*, no. 11 (1899), on the page facing p. 87.

period because these works themselves were products of a heightened sense of historical self-consciousness in the region.

Myth-making was not limited to the Muslims. Westerners also made a contribution to it by attributing his seemingly sudden rise and success to his spectacular good luck as embodied in his other title of *badaulat*, signifying "the one with fortune (or blessing)." It is no wonder that he was often called in the Western literature the Fortunate One or the Soldier of Fortune. Because of widespread interest in the region (perhaps the result of the many successful books on the Anglo-Russian "Great Game" rivalry in Central and Inner Asia at the time), the dissemination of this popular image to the wider world was quite rapid. D. C. Boulger's biography of Ya'qūb Beg, *The Life of Yakoob Beg; Athalik Ghazi, and Badaulet; Ameer of Kashgar* published in 1878 right after the collapse of Ya'qūb Beg's state also contributed to disseminating his popular image. Even a novel full of fantasy and historical nonsense was written in French and was translated into Russian.[1]

Although it is true that he became a very popular, almost legendary, figure in his day, his life before he became the ruler of Kashgharia is not well documented. The available sources reveal very little about his early career, but it is at least possible to revise some of the misleading and stereotyped images of Ya'qūb Beg that tend to paint him either as a flawless Muslim hero or as a low born villain who was little better than a bandit. For example, his reputation among the Central Asian Muslims at that time as a holy warrior was partly based on the mistaken information about his "heroic" fighting against the Russians at Aq Masjid in which he took no part. Moreover, after he came to Kashgharia, he fought and slaughtered many more of his own co-religionists than he did infidels. Nor did he refrain from violating religious principles when it was to his political advantage. To conquer Khotan, he swore a false oath of friendship on the Qur'ān with its ruler, Ḥabīb Allāh, who he then imprisoned and murdered. After the Khotanese people discovered his trick and fiercely resisted against him, he had no scruples about giving an order for their massacre. He refused to involve himself in conflicts that were not in his own political interests and did nothing to obstruct Russian attacks on the Central Asian khanates or to prevent the Qing from reconquering the Urumchi area where the Tungans were living.

On the other hand, in a culture where lineage purity and personal honor were of great importance, his enemies spread rumors that Ya'qūb Beg had a disreputable past and had risen to prominence only by his clever manipulation of personal connections. In his time, there was a widespread rumor that he had been a *bacha* (dancing boy) in his youth but, owing to his handsome appearance, he received good graces of high officials and began to climb up the ladder of success.[2] Mīrzā Aḥmad who had known him for a long time in Khoqand also repeated the same claim in his memoir.[3] As E. Schuyler describes in detail, a *bacha* was a beardless youth who performed singing and dancing at teahouses or parties and received pecuniary remuneration. They were also reputed to be willing to provide sexual services to their patrons. At that time having one or two *bacha*s was regarded as a symbol of wealth and status. It was not infrequent that some of the *bacha*s, with the assistance of their patrons, became wealthy men or government officials.[4] The salacious rumor that a powerful ruler like Ya'qūb Beg had been once a *bacha* appealed to many people, including a German scholar Albert von Le Coq who was well known for his archaeological excavations in Kucha and Turfan at the beginning of the last century.

> Although as a youth he had been obliged by poverty to struggle for existence as a public dancer and comedian, he succeeded by bravery, energy, and cunning, after the conquest of the country, in disposing of the Khoja and his adherents, and became the sole ruler of Eastern Turkestan.[5]

Even those accounts that favored Ya'qūb Beg, such as D. C. Boulger's, tend to stress his luck over all other considerations. Boulger wrote that "The Badaulet, or 'the fortunate one,' as he was called, was essentially indebted to good fortune in many crises of his career,"[6] and O. Lattimore called him "Inner Asian adventurer."[7]

However, we should be aware of the problems that these sorts of viewpoints have. They tend to turn the rise of Ya'qūb Beg into an interesting episode of a single individual's success and suppress its historical significance and context. Yet his coming to Kashgharia was not the sudden act of an ambitious adventurer nor can his success be attributed merely to his fortune or bravery. As discussed in Chapter 1, the historical significance of his rise and achievement cannot be understood without considering the changes in the power relations around Xinjiang from the southward expansion of Russia and the weakening of the Qing rule. In addition, it is important to focus on the background and the aim of Ya'qūb Beg's expedition to Kashgharia, how the destruction of the Khoqand khanate changed his position there, and how the weakness of the rebel groups in Xinjiang created an opportunity for him to succeed in ways he could not have originally imagined. Now, bearing in mind these factors, let us trace Ya'qūb Beg's career in Khoqand and his activities in the Tarim Basin after he came to Kashghar at the beginning of 1865.

EARLIER CAREERS

The extant records about the birth of Muḥammad Ya'qūb, widely known as Ya'qūb Beg, are so contradictory that it is difficult to discern reliable information from them. According to Mīrzā Aḥmad, who knew Ya'qūb Beg well before he came to Kashghar and who later became one of his most important officials, Ya'qūb was born to his father's second wife after he had been exiled to Kapa by the order of 'Ālim Khan (r. 1799–1809). Soon after the death of 'Ālim Khan's successor, 'Umar Khan (r. 1809–1822), the family moved back to Piskent (or Pskent), which lay 50km south of Tashkent.[8] If this statement is correct, we can say that Ya'qūb Beg was born before 1822.

Some other sources tend to put his birth much later partly because of Ya'qūb's younger-looking face. For example, Sayrāmī stated that Ya'qūb Beg became the governor of Aq Masjid around 1265 A.H. at the age of 22, which makes the year of his birth 1827–28.[9] A. N. Kuropatkin who led a Russian embassy to Kashgharia in 1876–77 also stated that in 1876 he had "the appearance of a man of about 50 years of age." However, Kuropatkin added that "Those persons who were then about him said that his age was from 58 to 64, notwithstanding that grey hairs had only just begun to make their appearance."[10]

In this sense, the report of a British embassy is more specific on this point. According to it, Ya'qūb Beg's forefathers lived in the mountainous district of Karategin, but later moved to Dehbid, near Samarqand. His father Pur Muḥammad, also known as Muḥammad Laṭīf, was born there. Pur Muḥammad moved from there to Khojent where he finished his education and, then, worked as a *qāḍī* at first in Kuramma, but later in Piskent. He took the sister of Shaykh Niẓām al-Dīn, who also worked as *qāḍī* in the same town, as his second wife and from her got his son Ya'qūb Beg in 1235/1820.[11] Therefore, on the question of his birth, the observation of the British embassy members who personally met him and probably inquired about his age shows the middle value and seems to be more reliable than other sources.

There are some uncertainties about his ethnic background too. His biographer D. C. Boulger argues that he belongs to the Tajik race and that he was a descendant of Amīr Temür based on the British report.[12] However, this claim is self-contradictory because, if he is a Tajik, he cannot be Temür's offspring—unless he claimed this relationship through his maternal side—because Temür was apparently a Turk belonging to the Barlas tribe. Moreover, there is no other report that proves he is descended from Amīr Temür. This claim could be something made up to glorify his genealogy after he became a heroic figure in the same way that Temür had been ascribed to be the descendant of Chinggis Khan.

H. Bellew, one of the members of the British embassy, records his impression of Ya'qūb Beg after he had an audience with him in 1873–74 as follows.

> The face has the general outlines of the Tatar physiognomy, with its asperities softened and rounded by Uzbak blood, and presents a broad full countenance without wrinkle or a seam, and with less of commanding weight than of sensual passion in its expression.[13]

So Bellew suggests that his physiognomy does not show the Tajik feature but rather the mixture of Mongol and Turkic elements. In the official report of the British embassy he was also called "Emir Muhammad Yakúb Khan Uzbak of Káshghar."[14] These reports, however, should not necessarily be interpreted that Ya'qūb Beg was ethnically Uzbek. We should not forget the fact that the concept of ethnicity was not yet crystallized among the people of Central Asia at that time. People were simply called Uzbek or Tajik based on their linguistic as well as tribal affiliations.

R. B. Shaw who met Ya'qūb Beg in 1869 remarked that the language that Ya'qūb Beg used during the interviews was "easy Persian,"[15] which suggests that he might be a Tajik. Especially because many Tajiks were found in Karategin where his ancestors had lived. However, it is quite probable that he knew the Turkic language perfectly well too. We have examples of his edicts written in Persian as well as in Turkic.[16] Without knowing Turkic it would have been impossible for him to keep intimate relations with Qipchaq and Uzbek leaders in the Khoqand khanate. In this sense, it is interesting to note that Mīrzā Aḥmad, in his memoir, called Ya'qūb Beg a "Sart."[17] This was the term employed to designate sedentary peoples in Central Asian towns and villages, including both Tajiks and Uzbeks, without any distinctive tribal affiliation.[18]

Ya'qūb Beg's father, Muḥammad Laṭīf, died soon after he had moved to Piskent and so the boy was then reared by his uncle. When Ya'qūb reached adolescence, he began to frequent tea-houses. Because he had a good-looking face and a talent in singing, he used to be called 'Ya'qūb Bacha,' but it is doubtful that he ever took up dancing as a profession as Kuropatkin asserted.[19] While some *bacha*s do dance and engage in other activities, any handsome beardless youth could be referred to in this way (particularly if he hangs around publicly with older men who are not his relatives), although it sometimes has a disreputable connotation. So he could have been a *bacha*, but not necessarily a dancing boy. Whatever the truth was, he seems to have led a somewhat lax lifestyle, which made his uncle worry about his future. He was sent to Tashkent to learn weaving, but, being bored with the training, Ya'qūb fled back to Piskent. After this incident, by the recommendation of a high official, he obtained a minor official job under a military general named Mingbashi Ghadāī Bāī, and then served under the governor of Khojent, Muḥammad Karīm Kāshka.[20]

In 1842 Naṣr Allāh, the amir of Bukhara, invaded Khoqand and killed Muḥammad 'Alī Khan, alias Madalī Khan. We have mentioned how a Qirghiz chief Yūsuf brought in Shīr 'Alī from Talas and recovered the city of Khoqand from the Bukharans. After Shīr 'Alī's enthronement many Qirghizs and the Qipchaqs began to be involved in Khoqandian politics, which lasted to the end of the khanate. Tribal chiefs manipulated khans at will, and according to the shifts of power among the tribes, khans were dethroned or killed overnight. Shīr 'Alī was merely a nominal ruler since all the power was held by the Qirghiz and the Qipchaq parties. Soon Shīr 'Alī Khan was killed by Murād Khan, son of 'Ālim Khan, and he too was killed by the Qipchaqs led by Musulmān Quli after eleven days in power. They enthroned Khudāyār, son of Shīr 'Alī, in 1845.[21]

It was during this period that Ya'qūb Beg began to climb the ladder of success. When Khudāyār was enthroned in Khoqand by the manipulation of Musulmān Quli, Sarimsaq, another son of Shīr 'Alī, in Tashkent refused to accept his authority. Musulmān Quli, using a trick, invited Sarimsaq to Khoqand and killed him. Musulmān Quli, who now easily secured Tashkent, appointed 'Azīz Bacha as the governor of Tashkent and Nār Muḥammad, another Qipchaq leader, as the governor of Kereuchi (or, Kilauchi). Muḥammad Karīm Kāshka was also lured to Khoqand and killed by Musulmān Quli, then some of those who had been under Kāshka transferred to 'Azīz Bacha. It was at this juncture that Ya'qūb Beg took the service under 'Azīz Bacha in the cavalry (*jigit*). According to the memoir of Mīrzā Aḥmad, it was also around this time Nār Muḥammad married Ya'qūb's sister.[22] A few years later 'Azīz was expelled from the governor's post of Tashkent and Nār Muḥammad replaced him in 1847.[23] Owing to the support of this influential brother-in-law Ya'qūb Beg was appointed beg of Chinaz. Later he was transferred to Aulie Ata and then, when he was about 30 (1849), promoted to beg of Aq Masjid (Qizil Orda in present day) lying on the lower Syr Darya.[24]

The begship of Aq Masjid was one of the most profitable and coveted posts in the khanate because of the valuable custom duties extracted from the caravans passing through there on route to Orenburg or Bukhara. The nomads in the vicinity also paid a tax on their livestock. Ya'qūb Beg appears to have taken full advantage of the situation by amassing a fortune. There was a widespread rumor that he even sold the fishing rights of a lake to Russians in exchange for a rich bribe.[25] This act exceeded the traditional bounds of cupidity and Nār Muḥammad recalled him to demand an explanation. Ya'qūb Beg's defense against the charge of bribery consisted largely of lavishing gifts on his superior and he was allowed to keep his post in spite of the scandal. Ya'qūb Beg was still beg of Aq Masjid in March of 1852 when he and his soldiers were soundly defeated by a much smaller number of Russian troops at Aq Gerik, not far from Fort Aral. Shortly after this event he was recalled to Tashkent.[26] He arrived in April with a large number of valuable presents for Nār Muḥammad.[27] Therefore, the claim that he was still commanding Aq Masjid when it was attacked by a Russian army in 1853 is completely groundless. During this attack, led by General Petrovskii, the garrison's small number of troops put up a heroic resistance against a superior Russian force armed with much strong firepower before being overwhelmed. The belief that it was Ya'qūb Beg who led the defense, although incorrect, was nonetheless fairly widespread at that time.[28]

At this time the internal dissension among the Qipchaq leaders deepened. Musulmān Quli, who held the title of *mingbashi*, was now opposed by a party formed around Ya'qūb Beg's brother-in-law Nār Muḥammad. A clash between Musulmān Quli and Nār Muḥammad led to the flight of the former in 1852, and Utambai, one of Nār Muḥammad's allies, became *ming-*

bashi in September of that year.[29] Ya'qūb Beg had been recalled to Tashkent only months before this incident occurred and subsequently served Nār Muḥammad as a military officer with the title of *baturbashi*[30] or *pānṣad* until even more serious political turmoil erupted.

Taking advantage of the lack of unity among the Qipchaqs, Khudāyār Khan successfully rallied support of the sedentary population and mounted a coup against the nomadic Qipchaqs to end their intervention in the khanate's politics. Nār Muḥammad was taken to Khoqand where he was soon executed,[31] and Musulmān Quli who sought refuge in the mountains was also imprisoned and killed. Numerous Qipchaqs in the cities and the villages of the khanate were massacred. This event, which took place during late 1852 and the first half of 1853, marked the end of the seven-year domination of the Qipchaqs over Khoqandian politics, at least temporarily. Nalivkin claims that Ya'qūb Beg was one of the conspirators allied with Khudāyār in arresting Nār Muḥammad.[32] We cannot verify the authenticity of his remark since no other primary source, to my knowledge, has this story. However, the betrayal of his brother-in-law and political patron would not have been impossible in Khoqandian politics.

From the time of the Qipchaq massacre and the coup by Khudāyār (1852–53) until the arrival of Ṣiddīq Beg's envoy from Kashghar at the end of 1864, the course of Ya'qūb Beg's political life is clouded by uncertainty. The Khoqand khanate was so engulfed in civil war that quick shifts of power made everyone's position precarious and ephemeral. It is not surprising, then, that various sources are full of contradictory remarks about Ya'qūb Beg's career, making it extremely difficult to reconstruct what happened to him during those ten years. By far the most accurate description is found in *Tārīkh-i ṣighārī* by 'Abd Allāh, which is superior to the work of Mīrzā Aḥmad because it has more consistent reports on the political events in the Khoqand khanate and was written in 1874, twenty years earlier than Mīrzā Aḥmad's 1895 account.

'Abd Allāh did not mention what Ya'qūb Beg did during the years between 1853–58 when Khudāyār reigned. H. Bellew reports that he was made *mīr* of Kilauchi,[33] a fact that is not found in 'Abd Allāh's work on which Bellew's description is largely based. Mīrzā Aḥmad says that Ya'qūb Beg was appointed first to "supervisor of the embassy house" and then was made beg of Khojent.[34] We cannot be certain that either of these statements is true because it appears that Mīrzā Aḥmad confuses the events he reported with those that were known to have taken place later in 1862–63 when Ya'qūb Beg was appointed beg of Khojent by 'Ālim Quli.

In 1858 'Ālim Quli, rallying the support of the Qipchaqs, put Mallā Khan on the throne and forced Khudāyār to flee to Bukhara. According to 'Abd Allāh, it was during the reign of Mallā Khan (1858–62) that Ya'qūb

Beg was appointed to *shaghawul*, probably the same "supervisor of embassy house" mentioned by Mīrzā Aḥmad, and was then made beg of Quramma. In 1862 Mallā Khan was assassinated and 'Ālim Quli enthroned Shāh Murād in his stead. When the news of the assassination reached Khudāyār, he marched on Tashkent with the aid of the Bukharans. Qanā'at Shāh, who was the governor of Tashkent at that time, went over to Khudāyār along with Ya'qūb Beg who thereby kept his post at Quramma. This defection proved premature because 'Ālim Quli soon succeeded in regaining his lost territory. Upon the approach of 'Ālim Quli's army to the Tashkent area, Ya'qūb Beg changed sides again, rejoining 'Ālim Quli, who appointed him beg of Khojent.[35]

Khudāyār counterattacked by marching through Khojent, taking the capital of the khanate again. Ya'qūb Beg, whose new post put him in Khudāyār's direct line of attack, was forced to surrender to him in Khojent[36] and from there he was sent to Bukhara under guard. However, Khuādyār was unable to hold Khoqand for long because he was hard pressed by 'Ālim Quli. To relieve this pressure, Khudāyār requested assistance from the amīr of Bukhara, who once more organized an expedition in which Ya'qūb Beg somehow participated. Though the amīr temporarily succeeded in entering the capital of the Khoqand khanate, he realized that he could not remain there and returned to Bukhara. In the midst of this confusion Ya'qūb Beg managed to escape to 'Ālim Quli along with many other able generals such as Mīrzā Aḥmad and 'Abd Allāh who had served Khudāyār. With the situation now completely out of his control, Khudāyār finally retreated to Bukhara, and in July of 1863 Sulṭān Sa'īd was enthroned as khan of Khoqand by 'Ālim Quli. Quramma was again entrusted to Ya'qūb Beg.[37]

Some sources explain the cause of Ya'qūb Beg's exile to Bukhara in different ways. According to Mīrzā Aḥmad, Ya'qūb Beg fled to Bukhara because his conspiracy with Rustam Beg against Khudāyār was prematurely leaked.[38] He also adds that three years later Ya'qūb Beg visited him in Tashkent and that after three more years of unemployment Ya'qūb Beg got the job of *pānṣad* through his good offices to Khudāyār.[39] However, Mīrzā Aḥmad's statement is hard to trust, for he not only skips the four-year reign of Mallā Khan but also gets his chronology confused.[40] Sayrāmī also makes a few errors about Ya'qūb Beg's stays in Bukhara. First he claims that Ya'qūb Beg fled to Bukhara to avoid prison after the bribery scandal erupted when he was the beg of Aq Masjid. He then states that Ya'qūb Beg returned to Khoqand when Mallā Khan was ruling, and became the beg of Khojent. He fell victim to slander by jealous officials who got Mallā Khan to order Ya'qūb's execution, so he was again forced to flee to Bukhara for safety.[41] These remarks by Sayrāmī cannot be sustained. First of all, we know that Ya'qūb Beg was recalled to Tashkent from Aq Masjid by Nār Muḥammad.

So, the story of his flight to Bukhara from Aq Masjid cannot be true. Besides, there is no evidence that Mallā Khan ordered Ya'qūb Beg to be executed. Such a story is found neither in 'Abd Allāh's writing nor in Mīrzā Aḥmad's memoir. At any rate, it is impossible to make a definite judgment on every detail of Ya'qūb Beg's political career during the years of 1853–63 because there are too few sources to compare and countercheck.

In spite of this uncertainty about the details, a close examination of his career leaves no doubt that the two most widespread myths about Ya'qūb Beg have no factual basis. The first myth was that Ya'qūb Beg heroically defended Aq Masjid against the Russian attack in 1853. As we have already observed, there is no doubt that Ya'qūb Beg was not present at Aq Masjid on July 24, 1853 when it was captured after four days' attack by Russian troops under the command of General Petrovskii. Nor was Ya'qūb Beg there earlier on August 1, 1852 when Colonel Blaramberg attacked the fort. His only skirmish with Russians was on March 16, 1852 at Aq Gerik. There, one thousand Khoqand soldiers under Ya'qūb Beg's command were unable to stand against one hundred Russian soldiers equipped with superior firearms. After this defeat Ya'qūb Beg was immediately dismissed from the begship of Aq Masjid and ordered to return to Tashkent.[42]

The second myth was, as Boulger once wrote, that "Alim Kuli recognized in the Kooshbege [i.e., Ya'qūb Beg] a possible rival and successor. Any excuse therefore to keep Yakoob Beg in the background, or indeed to get rid of him altogether, would be very welcome to Alim Kuli."[43] Kuropatkin remarked in the same vein that "This energetic and popular personage and a very formidable rival greatly alarmed Alim Kool, and he had already determined in getting rid of him."[44] But, the fact was that Ya'qūb Beg had never been powerful nor popular enough to threaten 'Ālim Quli. Considering that the highest post that Ya'qūb Beg ever reached was beg of Khojent, and that his status was always precarious and depended on the outcome of the struggle between 'Ālim Quli and Khudāyār, we cannot but be skeptical about the assumption that he was a rival to 'Ālim Quli, an ambitious and powerful king-maker who was backed by a large number of Qipchaqs.

If Ya'qūb Beg did not initially come to Kashgharia expecting to establish an independent Islamic government as a heroic holy warrior or to realize his ambitions as an adventurer, how should we understand his mission to Kashgharia? What we should not forget is that such missions to Kashgharia from Khoqand had been quite common during the previous fifty years because this region had been always important to the economic prosperity of the Khoqand khanate. The series of invasions of Kashgharia by the Makhdūmzāda khwājas had always been organized in such a way that the Khoqand rulers could keep a close eye on them by placing their own confidants among the top leadership positions to ensure that the khwājas would not act against the interests of the khanate. During the invasion of Jahāngīr Khwāja in 1826 ʿĪsa Dādkhwāh (former Andijan governor) was in his suite and in 1830 Yūsuf Khwāja was watched over by Ḥaqq Quli Mingbashi and Lashkar Qushbegi, the khan's brother-in-law.[45]

The 1865 expedition was probably organized along similar lines, and it would not have been to ʿĀlim Quli's interests, or to those of the khanate, to appoint a man he did not trust as a leader of such an important mission. Mīrzā Aḥmad notes that ʿĀlim Quli decided to send Buzurg to Kashgharia rather than Kättä Khān Tura who was shrewder and had a better claim to leadership, because Buzurg was known to be a weakling who could be more easily controlled.[46] In fact, one source reveals that ʿĀlim Quli even made Buzurg take a vow swearing that he would let no one other than Yaʿqūb Beg direct him in deciding important political matters.[47] This act demonstrates that ʿĀlim Quli was determined to maintain control over his mission to Kashgharia, and that Yaʿqūb Beg was his chosen agent for this task. If he had really considered Yaʿqūb Beg a rival, ʿĀlim Quli would have never appointed him as commander. Bellew's observation on this point is quite accurate: ʿĀlim Quli appointed Yaʿqūb Beg to accompany Buzurg "by way of securing his own interests and maintaining the Khokand influence in the Káshghar States."[48]

Pressed hard by the Russians from the north, ʿĀlim Quli could not afford to send a large body of soldiers to Kashghar. Only a small group left Tashkent which, traveling via Khoqand, reached the frontier city of Osh,[49] where its number was increased to a couple of hundred. At the beginning of January 1865, they reached Ming Yol, the last halting place before reaching Kashghar, and there Yaʿqūb Beg began a brilliant new career at the age of forty-five.

First Steps

OCCUPATION OF KASHGHAR

At the time the small Khoqandian expedition entered the city of Kashghar, the Muslim town was in the hands of Ṣiddīq Beg, the Qirghiz chief who had taken it shortly before their arrival. He had invited Buzurg with the expectation that the khwāja's presence might contribute to his earlier efforts to occupy the city. Although the Qirghiz had failed to take the city by direct attack, the siege exhausted the city's provisions and forced the defenders of Kashghar to submit. One eyewitness relates the wretched condition in the town on the eve of surrender.

> First they ate their horses, then the dogs and cats, then their leather boots and straps, the saddles of their horses, and the strings of their bows. At last they would collect

together in parties of five or six, who would go prowling about with ravenous eyes till they saw someone alone, some unfortunate comrade who still retained the flesh on his bones. They would drag him aside and kill him, afterwards dividing the flesh between them, and each carrying off his piece hidden under his robe.[50]

The Qirghiz who entered the city repaid their stubbornness with the same cruelty, pillaging and slaughtering the inhabitants. Qutluq Beg, Kashghar governor, escaped after having paid them 100 *yambus* as a ransom and then went on pilgrimage to Mecca.[51] Now that he was the master of the Muslim town, Ṣiddīq Beg was not happy about having to let Ya'qūb Beg's party into the city. Nevertheless, he had little choice in the matter since Buzurg was very popular among the Kashgharians. His fears were borne out when the inhabitants of Kashghar began to vent their rage against the Qirghiz as soon as Buzurg was settled in the *urda*, the residence of governor.

The Qirghiz were forced to leave the city and Ṣiddīq Beg retreated to Yangihissar which his brother was holding. From there he gathered a large number of Qirghiz and proceeded to march to the shrine of Ḥaḍrāt-i Pādishāh by way of Qizil Tepe. Ya'qūb Beg mobilized his own forces and deployed them against the Qirghiz at the shrine of Sayyid Jalāl al-Dīn Baghdādī.[52] During the ensuing battle Ṣiddīq was defeated and retreated to Tashmaliq, where he reorganized his force and prepared to give another battle. Leading a force of four thousand, Ya'qūb Beg, accompanied by Buzurg, met the Qirghiz there and once again defeated them, forcing Ṣiddīq to flee to the west for refuge in the mountains. Having overcome his first major trial of strength, Ya'qūb Beg returned to Kashghar through Yangihissar where he left 'Azīz Beg to lay siege to the fort because it was still held by the Qing troops.[53]

In February, Ibrāhīm Ṣudūr,[54] son of Ḥabīb Allāh and sent by his father as an envoy to 'Ālim Quli, returned with Nār Muḥammad Parvānachi,[55] Hamdām Pānṣad, and Mīr Baba Hudāīchi[56] whom 'Ālim Quli sent as a return embassy to Khotan. When they came to Kashghar, Ya'qūb Beg offered them an escort for safety because Yarkand was in the hands of the Kuchean khwājas who were fighting with the Tungans there. In fact, under the guise of escorting the embassy he hoped to exploit the situation.[57] He reached Yarkand with about two hundred soldiers at the end of February. According to 'Abd Allāh, his party was led into the city and stayed there for three days. There ensued clashes between them and the Kucheans who had come earlier in Yarkand. They were predominant at first and even succeeded in capturing Burhān al-Dīn, but because of their numerical inferiority they retreated.[58] On this battle R. B. Shaw left us the following description.

They fought from morning prayer time till afternoon prayers (it was Friday), and Yakoob got the worst of it. At first, his onslaught shook the Koochārees, but, his horses getting tired in the wet soil, he took refuge in the city. Here he was enclosed, but with difficulty escaped away to Kāshghar . . . [59]

In the midst of this confusion Ibrāhīm Ṣudūr also fled to Khotan while the rest of the Khoqand embassy was driven back to Kashghar.

After this aborted attempt to take Yarkand, Yaʿqūb Beg concentrated his effort on occupying Yangihissar. After forty days of siege the fort was finally taken on April 11.[60] Yaʿqūb Beg then named ʿAzīz Beg as the governor of Yangihissar,[61] and sent Mīr Baba (who had come from Khoqand as an envoy) to ʿĀlim Quli with presents to inform him of the fall of the fort and the progress of the situation in general. According to Sayrāmī, the presents consisted of "nine Chinese cannons, nine charming Chinese virgins, nine young Chinese boys, several packs of aromatic tea, nine times nine Chinese *yambus*, nine times nine Qalmuq and Qazaq horses, and nine times nine porcelains."[62] The dispatch of the embassy shows that Yaʿqūb Beg was not an independent adventurer but a Khoqand official responsible for his actions to the khanate. Mīr Baba met with ʿĀlim Quli, who was busy defending Tashkent against the Russians, but he had no chance to deliver the presents because ʿĀlim Quli was killed in action soon thereafter.[63]

After Yangihissar fell, the Qirghiz chief Ṣiddīq Beg appeared again at Tashmaliq and took the fort of Farrash. According to ʿAbd Allāh, he had gathered about a thousand people, mostly Qirghiz but also including many Khoqandians fleeing from Khudāyār, including Kichik Khān Tura. Yaʿqūb Beg brought up his army and met them at Farrash. This time they reached a conciliation without fighting, and Ṣiddīq Beg took service under Yaʿqūb Beg as the magistrate of Farrash as well as the commander of Qirghiz soldiers.[64] When Yaʿqūb Beg returned to Kashghar, he faced a challenge from the begs there. Led by Muqarrab Shāh, these people collected troops to oppose Yaʿqūb Beg, but in several battles that took place around Khan Ariq and Qizil Buy they proved to be no match for the Khoqandians. Muqarrab Shāh fled to Yarkand where he allied himself with Jamāl al-Dīn Khwāja from Aqsu, who was preparing a major attack on Kashghar.[65]

Even without a chance to breathe, Yaʿqūb Beg had to face his most difficult test. He fought a pitched battle at the place called Khan Ariq near Kashghar with the Kuchean army. This battle became a decisive event in the process of unification. As explained earlier, Rāshidīn Khwāja, intending to create an Islamic state that embraced the entire Tarim basin, dispatched two separate expeditionary armies. Compared to the eastern expedition, which achieved a great success in taking such important cities as Qarashahr and Turfan, the western expedition did not produce any significant outcome. It could not take any one of the cities like Kashghar, Yarkand, or Khotan. Therefore, the arrival of Yaʿqūb Beg and his sudden success in taking control of Yangihissar and the Muslim town of Kashghar, and even the danger of his taking Yarkand, posed a real threat to the Kucheans.

After the first expedition against Yarkand led by Burhān al-Dīn and his son ended in failure, Rāshidīn Khwāja decided to send another expeditionary army, much larger than the first. This time he entrusted its command to his elder brother Jamāl al-Dīn, who also held the office of Aqsu governor. The troops from Kucha led by A'lam Akhūnd and Ṣādiq Khwāja, and those from Ush Turfan led by Burhān al-Dīn and Hām al-Dīn had come to Aqsu where they joined with Jamāl al-Dīn. According to Sayrāmī, these troops, numbering 26,000, then marched to Yarkand, which easily fell under their control. Collecting more people from Yarkand and its vicinity, they then proceeded to Kashghar by way of small roads to bypass Yangihissar and thereby assault Kashghar by surprise. This army consisted of troops drawn from all the major cities west of Kucha (i.e., Kucha, Shahyar, Aqsu, Ush Turfan, and Yarkand) and also included Tungans who handled the cannons. According to one report, the number of soldiers reached the enormous size of 72,000.[66]

Ya'qūb Beg, by contrast, could muster only a small number of troops. The center was entrusted to Buzurg with 200 Badakhshi soldiers and the right wing was held by Ya'qūb Beg himself together with 1,000 Qirghiz and Qipchaqs, while the left wing was commanded by 'Abd Allāh Pānṣad and Ghāzī Pānṣad with 200 men between them—altogether a force of less than 2,000.[67] The Badakhshi were those whom Jahāndār Shāh, the ruler of Badakhshan, had sent in order to take advantage of the confusion in western Kashgharia. Ya'qūb Beg had incorporated them into his army.[68] Comparing the size of the two armies, Sayrāmī likened Ya'qūb Beg's army to "the Pleiades in the heaven" but the Kuchean army to "the entire stars in the seven spheres."[69] At Khan Ariq the two sides met in a fierce battle. Although Ya'qūb Beg received severe wounds, he survived and emerged as a victor. The large Kuchean army was completely routed and fled back to Aqsu. This battle proved to be the most important of Ya'qūb Beg's career in Eastern Turkestan, for it ultimately led to the fall of the Kuchean regime and opened the way for his conquest of the region.[70]

Considering that the number of the Kuchean troops was at least ten times more than those of Ya'qūb Beg, it may appear hard to understand the outcome of the battle. However, while the defeat was partly the result of the overconfidence by the Kucheans who were depending on their numerical strength, at the same time, we should take note of the different composition of each army. Ya'qūb Beg's army, at least at its core, consisted of fierce nomads—Qipchaqs and Qirghiz—and Badakhshi mountaineers who were full of combat experience, and the Khoqand officials whom we may well consider professional soldiers. On the other hand, the Kuchean army was a mixture of the people from several cities who had received hardly any military training and whose commanders were in most cases religious figures. Sayrāmī deplored the Kuchean army's poor state in this way, "Nothing will be done by the hands of such disorderly troops. Two hundred brave men are better than those of one hundred thousand."[71]

Although equipped with the instruments and armaments of war that had been prepared for two years by the tax and the blood of the Muslims in Aqsu, Yarkand, Ush Turfan, Kucha, and Shahyar, they could not fight even two hours and scattered like dust.[72] Although accounts vary, this battle most likely took place between June and August of 1865.[73] After the battle Yaʿqūb Beg marched back to Kashghar with the Tungans he had taken prisoner. At the news of the Khan Ariq's defeat, Sayyid Aʿlam Akhūnd, who had been left in Yarkand by Jamāl al-Dīn, fled to Aqsu.[74] Yaʿqūb Beg quickly dispatched Mīr Baba, who had just returned from his mission to Khoqand, to Yarkand and, with the aid of Niyāz Beg, the leader of the Yarkand begs, succeeded in taking control of the Muslim town.[75] Yaʿqūb Beg thus took "two games with one arrow, and two big cities by one attack."[76]

After having returned from Khan Ariq, Yaʿqūb Beg concentrated all his efforts on taking the Manchu fort of Kashghar. The Qing troops there had been under siege for almost a year, first by the Qirghiz and then by the army of Yaʿqūb Beg. Provisions had already long run out in the fort, and both famine and disease were prevalent. Having lost all hope of resistance, He Buyun (Hō Dālūya), commander of Chinese garrison troops, entered into secret correspondence with Yaʿqūb Beg, obtaining a guarantee of safety for his family and the soldiers under his command in exchange for their acceptance of Islam. On the first day of September Kuiying, the Kashghar *amban*, and other Qing officials all killed themselves by blowing up the *urda*. The fort was then easily taken, and several days of sacking and plundering followed during which most of the Chinese were killed.[77]

A TURNING POINT

In less than eight months after coming to Kashghar, Yaʿqūb Beg had established a firm footing by occupying two complete cities, Kashghar and Yangihissar, and the Muslim town of Yarkand. However, because the Manchu fort of Yarkand was still in the hands of the Qing army and other Muslim forces were holding Khotan and Kucha, his position was far from secure. Moreover, ʿĀlim Quli's death, news of which Mīr Baba had brought back with him after his aborted mission to Khoqand, made Yaʿqūb Beg realize that he could not go back to Khoqand because Khudāyār (whom he had previously deserted) had taken power there. In fact, he had no reason to do so because he was beginning to see that his future lay in Kashgharia where he might expect to become a ruler in his own right. Accordingly, Yaʿqūb Beg found the existence of Buzurg more and more irksome, particularly as his own popularity had soared after the heroic battle of Khan Ariq while Buzurg was considered politically incompetent.

At this very juncture Ya'qūb Beg met with a significant turning point. Ten days after Ya'qūb Beg and Buzurg occupied the Kashghar fort, news came from Ming Yol that a large body of Khoqandian soldiers was approaching. They were the remnants of 'Ālim Quli's army, mostly Qipchaqs and Qirghizs who had decided to take refuge in Kashghar. After the death of 'Ālim Quli and the fall of Tashkent, Sulṭān Sa'īd Khan had run to Bukhara to ask for help, but he was arrested in Jizzaq by the Bukharans. Those Qipchaqs and Qirghizs who had been engaged in the defense of Tashkent came back to the Ferghana valley. There they enthroned Khudāī Quli Beg, later known as "Belbaghchi (girdle-seller) Khan" because he had been once engaged in selling girdles; and entered Khoqand. Taking advantage of 'Ālim Quli's death, Khudāyār also marched to Khoqand. Those who belonged to 'Ālim Quli's party then fled to Osh, but, when Khudāyār followed at their heels, they moved farther to the east and arrived at Ming Yol. Their numbers reached almost seven thousand,[78] including many former high officials of the Khoqand khanate: Khudāī Quli Khan, Beg Muḥammad Mingbashi, Mīrzā Aḥmad, Muḥammad Naẓar Qushbegi, Muḥammad Yūnus Jān Dādkhwāh, Jāmadār Dādkhwāh, 'Umar Qul Dādkhwāh, and so on. There were also several Makhdūmzādas, such as Kättä Khān Tura, Walī Khān Tura, Ḥākim Khān Tura, and Isrā'īl Khān Tura.[79] Alarmed by the report, Ya'qūb Beg sent the *shaykh al-Islām* of Kashghar, Īshān Maḥmūd Khān, to Ming Yol in order to discover their intention and to persuade them to submit. After some hesitation, they agreed to submit to Ya'qūb Beg and entered Kashghar, welcomed with a feast and robes of honor.

This event was a turning point for Ya'qūb Beg in several respects. In terms of power, even though he succeeded in taking Kashghar and Yangihissar, he had had only a comparatively small number of loyal followers. The Qirghiz detachment under Ṣiddīq could not be relied upon, and the soldiers taken from the Kashgharis and the Yangihissaris were not well disciplined and had doubtful loyalties. Nor was it certain whether the Tungan troops under Hō Dālūya would support Ya'qūb Beg in a crisis even though he was now married to Hō's daughter. Therefore, the incorporation of the seven thousand battle-seasoned troops from his own country was a significant reinforcement. In addition to this military aspect, Ya'qūb Beg's acceptance of them was politically an outward expression that he was no longer subject to the khanate under Khudāyār for those Khoqandian refugees he embraced were all anti-Khudāyārs. At the same time, this act of Ya'qūb Beg signified the abrogation of his commitment to Buzurg, and opened the way for him to be a real ruler.

Before he could become a real ruler, however, he was confronted with two more minor challenges: first, from Walī Khān, and then, from Buzurg. Walī Khān is the one who had invaded Kashghar in 1857 when it was still under the Qing rule and slaughtered so many innocent people. Hardly had a few days passed since the arrival of the Khoqandians, when the followers of Walī Khān began crying "Time! Time! The time of Walī Khān!" in the streets of Kashghar.[80] Ya'qūb Beg easily suppressed them and arrested Walī Khān, sending him to Yangihissar under guard. After this incident Ya'qūb Beg marched with Buzurg to Yarkand where the Tungans had freshly revolted. He laid siege to the city, and as soon as he took it, Beg Muḥammad, along with his Qipchaq followers, allied himself with Buzurg and retired to Kashghar in November. Ya'qūb Beg left Kichik Khān in Yarkand and pursued Buzurg. Ya'qūb Beg attacked the Kashghar fort for almost two months, finally resulting in the expulsion of Beg Muḥammad (who was later killed by Khudāyār Khan in Marghinan) and the arrest of Buzurg whom Ya'qūb Beg sent to Yangihissar. Buzurg was initially replaced by another khwāja, Kättä Khān, who quickly died and Ya'qūb Beg finally assumed the rulership himself in the early spring of 1866.[81]

Conquest of Kashgharia

SEIZURE OF KHOTAN

Ya'qūb Beg had barely suppressed the internal opposition when Yarkand slipped away from his hands again. At the defeat of the Kuchean army at Khan Ariq, Rāshidīn sent Isḥāq to Yarkand, who had returned from Hami to Kucha a year before. Isḥāq left Kucha with three thousand soldiers around the end of December 1865.[82] After ten days' stay in Aqsu he marched to Yarkand, but when he entered the city, the Tungans took Kichik Khān to the fort, whom Ya'qūb Beg had left in Yarkand, and refused to submit to Isḥāq. Isḥāq occupied only the Muslim town while the Tungans were holding the fort.

At this news Ya'qūb Beg did not proceed directly to Yarkand, but rather to Maralbashi, with a view to cutting the communication line between Aqsu and Yarkand. In the middle of July, after a week of siege, he occupied the fort of Maralbashi which the Tungans, already having submitted to Rāshidīn, were defending.[83] He appointed Ḥākim Khān, son of Kättä Khān, as governor of Maralbashi and then headed toward Yarkand for the third, and last, time.

Both parts of the city were held by his enemies: Isḥāq and the Tungans. The Tungans and the Kucheans allied and attempted a surprise attack on Ya'qūb Beg's army at night. It turned into a disaster because Niyāz Beg had warned Ya'qūb Beg of the plot. Yet, Ya'qūb Beg still could not enter the city. When a relief army sent by Rāshidīn from Aqsu and Ush Turfan was unable to pass through Maralbashi, Ya'qūb Beg's strategy proved correct and he was able to come to an agreement with the besieged in Yarkand. Isḥāq and his Kuchean army were allowed to go back to Kucha while the Tungans were incorporated into Yaʿqūb Beg's army. He appointed Muḥammad Yūnus Jān governor of Yarkand.[84] The capture of Yarkand seems to have occurred in early September 1866.[85]

Yaʿqūb Beg's next task was the conquest of Khotan, which he carried out with great notoriety. Khotan maintained more than ten thousand infantry and cavalry troops, including an artillery force, and stood firmly unified behind Ḥabīb Allāh.[86] Yaʿqūb Beg decided to take Khotan not by battle but by trickery. He dispatched his right hand man, ʿAbd Allāh, to inform Ḥabīb Allāh of his intention to pay a visit to the shrine of Imām Jaʿfar Ṣādiq. On December 16, 1866 (the eighth of Barat, 1283), Yaʿqūb Beg proceeded to Yarkand with his troops[87] and from there to Piyalma. Ḥabīb Allāh dispatched one of his sons there,[88] supported by a Khotanese army, to find out Yaʿqūb Beg's real intentions. It is said that Yaʿqūb Beg swore an oath over the Qur'ān and, calling Ḥabīb Allāh "my father (*atam, dadam*)," invited him to meet in a place called Zava for a feast. Ḥabīb Allāh visited Yaʿqūb Beg without suspicion, but he was bound tightly and sent to Yarkand where he was executed.[89] Yaʿqūb Beg then sent a letter to Khotan stamped with Ḥabīb Allāh's seal[90] stating that both leaders would enter the city next morning. Leading figures of Khotan, assuming all was well, came out to welcome them and were arrested immediately by Yaʿqūb Beg. Having entered the city, he secured the treasury first. When the Khotanese realized what had happened, they armed themselves with clubs and began to attack Yaʿqūb Beg's soldiers. Fighting continued several days in and out of the city. At least several thousand Khotanese were killed.[91] According to one source, when the soldiers' hands became blistered because of so much killing, Yaʿqūb Beg was reputed to have ordered butchers to continue the slaughter.[92] This incident took place in January–February of 1867.[93]

These events generated a strong sense of betrayal and animosity in Khotan against Yaʿqūb Beg, who had no scruples about swearing falsely, playing dirty tricks, or slaughtering his enemies. Even after the end of his rule the Khotanese retained their bitterness toward him and his actions. The following lines of a poem disclose the depth of their contempt for this foreign ruler from Andijan.

> From Peking the Chinese came, like the stars in the heaven.
> The Andijanis rose and fled, like the pigs in the forest.
> They came in vain and left in vain, the Andijanis!
> They went away scared and languidly, the Andijanis!
> Everyday they took a virgin, and
> They went hunting for beauties.
> They played with dancing boys (*bacha*),
> which the holy law has forbidden.[94]

Ya'qūb Beg's occupation of the city by trickery and the slaughter of Ḥabīb Allāh along with his sons[95] would have easily revived the sense of martyrdom which had been deeply rooted among the people of Khotan, as it was called the City of Martyrs (*Shahīdān-i Khotan*).[96] Ya'qūb Beg's appointment of Niyāz Beg, a Yarkandi, to the governorship of Khotan seems to have stemmed from his consideration of the general feeling of the Khotanese against the "Andijanis."

COLLAPSE OF THE KUCHEAN REGIME

With the conquest of Khotan, Ya'qūb Beg gained control of the entire area to the west of Maralbashi and he turned his attention to Kucha, the only remaining power in Kashgharia. Many signs of the internal weakness had appeared within the Kucha regime long before Ya'qūb Beg launched his expedition against it. Sayrāmī records revolts in Ush Turfan and Lukchin. For example, in Ush Turfan a number of former begs became more and more irritated with the stern rule, based on the Islamic law, of Muḥammad al-Dīn, his father Burhān al-Dīn, and his brother Hām al-Dīn. These begs, including Tukhta Ḥākim Beg, his brother Aq Beg, Bāī Muḥammad Beg, Qurbān Ghazānachī Beg, and Ismā'īl Bājgīr Beg, gathered at a place called Mazār-i Türk in the village of Gün Chiqan outside Ush Turfan and enthroned a certain Mīrzā Jān Ḥaḍrat. However, the revolt ended in failure, leaving more than two hundred people dead and putting more to flight. Those who were captured were executed, and it was reported that their corpses filled seven wells in the city.[97]

Sayrāmī pointed out as another cause of the revolt the widespread influence of several Sufi paths. At that time, in Ush Turfan, Sufi paths that had "eccentric teachings" such as the Kubrāwiyya, the Isḥāqiyya, Ni'matiyya, Rabūdiyya, and Davāniyya were active.[98] Some followers of these orders were calling their master Allāh Khwājam and, arguing that "Allāh's characteristic is also Khwājam's characteristic," expounded a claim that directly denied the unity of Allāh. Moreover, men and women had meetings at secret places and performed rituals that contradicted religious laws, such as listening to music (*samā'*), dancing (*raqs*), and falling into ecstasy. These orders had many followers all over Kashgharia, especially among the immigrants (*köchmän*)[99] and the foreigners (*bīgāna*). In this way, fanatic devotion to Allāh Khwājam, religious rituals contradictory to *sharī'ah*, and the exclusive secrecy of these groups posed a serious political threat to the Kuchean khwāja rulers.[100]

However, internal dissension among the Kuchean khwājas themselves was much more devastating than anything else. This dissension had developed between Rāshidīn's brothers and their cousins. As mentioned earlier, Rāshidīn recalled Isḥāq from Hami in 1865, with the pretext of the growing danger of Ya'qūb Beg. But Isḥāq was not allowed to lead the expedition against Ya'qūb Beg. Instead, Jamāl al-Dīn, who had already replaced Burhān al-Dīn as the commander of the western march in the summer of 1864, became the commander of the second Kuchean expedition to Yarkand. Isḥāq's army, which numbered almost 16,000, was mostly appropriated by Jamāl al-Dīn. When he marched later to Yarkand after Jamāl al-Dīn's defeat at Khan Ariq, he could collect only 3,000 troops in Kucha. His failure to hold Yarkand was also severely criticized by Rāshidīn and Jamāl al-Dīn, and he even had to hand over a part of his army to Jamāl al-Dīn. Jamāl al-Dīn also clashed with Hām al-Dīn of Ush Turfan. The cause of this dispute was the jurisdiction of Aq Yar which lies halfway between Aqsu and Ush Turfan. It ended finally with the arrest of Hām al-Dīn, who was thrown into prison in Kucha. This took place two months after the revolt of the Ush Turfan begs.[101]

The deepening of the cleavage among the khwājas made it easy for Ya'qūb Beg to subjugate the Kuchean regime. After he heard the news of Hām al-Dīn's imprisonment, he uttered the exclamation "Praise to Allāh! Now, Aqsu and Kucha shall fall in my hand even without fighting."[102] Some of the survivors from the revolt in Ush Turfan volunteered to be guides for Ya'qūb Beg, and several high officials in Aqsu and Kucha also thought it best for their interests to ally themselves with him. Of these 'Abd al-Raḥmān Dādkhwāh and 'Abd Allāh Dīvānbegi in Aqsu, and Tukhta Ishikagha in Kucha, all of whom were at "the rank of *vizīr*," sent secret letters to Ya'qūb Beg, promising their support if he ever marched against Kucha.[103]

Being encouraged by this dissension within the ruling group of Kucha, Ya'qūb Beg resolved to take advantage of the opportunity. He left Kashghar on May 8, 1867 with his troops and marched to Aqsu, through Maralbashi. Upon reaching the Aqsu Darya he easily defeated the Aqsu army under the command of Yaḥya, Jamāl al-Dīn's son. He entered Aqsu in the same month without much resistance. Jamāl al-Dīn was taken prisoner and later sent to Yarkand where he was executed.[104] A detachment went to Ush Turfan to obtain submission from Burhān al-Dīn and his sons. They surrendered without fighting and came to Aqsu to pay homage to Ya'qūb Beg. Ya'qūb Beg marched farther to the east until he met and easily defeated some Kuchean troops at Yaqa Ariq. At the news of this defeat, Rāshidīn called Hām al-Dīn away from Qarashahr, where he had been dispatched to suppress a revolt, and sent him with four thousand soldiers to Yaqa Ariq to oppose Ya'qūb Beg. Instead of fighting, however, Hām al-Dīn defected to Ya'qūb Beg and Kucha fell into his hands on June 5, 1867, barely a month after he departed from Kashghar.[105] Rāshidīn Khwāja seems to have been killed when Kucha was taken, and the other khwājas who attempted resistance were also killed by Ya'qūb Beg. Burhān al-Dīn and his sons, Hām al-Dīn and Maḥmūd al-Dīn, were sent to Kashghar and retired to a secluded life at the *khānaqāh* (prayer house) of Muḥammad Khwāja Ḥaḍrat.[106] Ya'qūb Beg appointed Isḥāq as the governor of Kucha to whose jurisdiction the towns of Shahyar, Bugur, and Kurla belonged.[107]

Thus the Kuchean khwājas' regime ended exactly three years after its creation (1864 June–1867 June). It is worthwhile to listen to the judgment of Sayrāmī on this regime.

In this way, [Kuchean] khwājas reigned for three full years, i.e., 37 months. Their eastern border reached to Barkul, the northern border to Qalmuqistan [i.e., Zungharia], the western border to Yarkand and Maralbashi, and the southern border to Lop and Cherchen. Countless numbers of Chinese (*Bechīn*) infidels were destroyed. . . . Although they took control of the power and authority in this manner, they had never thought to show mercy on any of their brethren, to give abundant gifts to prayers, intellectuals or artisans so that they could transcend worldy matters, to provide charities by building bridges over the river or establishing wells and resting places in the midst of wilderness, to construct mosques and schools and offer them as endowments, or even to build a couple of lodgings for their own use, . . . They did not even bother to know or perform the norms and rules appropriate to monarchs and did not care to learn the details of [necessary] knowledge and practice. Whatever work they undertook, they did it as they pleased and as they wanted. . . . There was no peace to the poor and the common people.[108]

Having completed the unification of Kashgharia, Ya'qūb Beg returned to Kashghar on October 21 and put his energy into rehabilitating the war-stricken country. He also began establishing diplomatic contacts with neighboring countries.

Annexation of Urumchi

FIRST EXPEDITION

During the three years between the conquest of Kashgharia (1867) and the beginning of the first Urumchi expedition (1870) Kashgharia's southern and western borders remained tranquil. While the Khoqand khanate under Khudāyār's rule was not friendly toward the new government in Kashghar, it took no hostile actions against it either. The mountain nomads in the Pamirs along the southwestern and the southern borders of the country were subjugated by an army sent by Ya'qūb Beg, but their chiefs kept their hereditary posts in exchange for tributary payments to him. The northern border was less secure because the Russians refused to acknowledge the legitimacy of Ya'qūb Beg's government and pushed the limits of their frontier to Narin, where they constructed a fort. Ya'qūb Beg, probably remembering the fate of the Khoqand khanate, became extremely alarmed and dispatched his troops near Narin to construct a line of outposts and to watch for further movement by the Russians. After this initial tension, however, the northern border maintained a kind of status quo.

The problem was at the eastern border. After Ya'qūb Beg conquered Kucha and Qarashahr, the limits of his eastern boundary reached Gümüsh, halfway between Qarashahr and Turfan. Turfan was held by the Urumchi Tungans led by Sō Dālūya. When Dāūd (Tuo Ming) sent Sō to Turfan, a reorganization of the leading members seems to have taken place. A Chinese source wrote that Dāūd appointed Ma Sheng, Ma Guan, Ma Tai, and Ma Zhong to be commanders (*yuanshuay*) and that he made Ma Si (Suzhou), Ma Duosan (Xining), Ma Yanlong (Hezhou), and Ma Hualong (Ningxia) commanders in their own territories.[109] Although he had no control over these areas, this indicates that he sought an alliance with the Tungan rebels in Shanxi, Gansu, and Ningxia, and tried to expand his influence to other areas. So there was a danger that the two powers in Xinjiang, Urumchi and Kashghar, would collide against each other sooner or later.

Besides the potential outbreak of war between those two, the area around Turfan and Qarashahr was highly insecure and volatile because of two other factors. The first was the danger posed by the Mongol-speaking Khoshot and Torghut tribes who had taken to raiding their neighbors. The second was the existence of Chinese guerrilla forces who were fighting against the Muslims. After the Qing force was expelled from Eastern Turkestan and Zungharia, the nomadic tribes of the Torghuts and the Khoshots became independent. They raided Ili, Turfan, and Qarashahr which were in a state of confusion because of the rebellion. When Isḥāq Khwāja marched through Turfan and Qarashahr in 1864–65, he had to fight them. These tribes were not submissive to the Ili sultanate either and played a provocative role in the relationship between Russia and the sultanate. Even though by 1867 Ya'qūb Beg had conquered Qarashahr and Ushaq Tal, these nomadic tribes remained a disruptive factor. In the meantime, guerrilla groups, which Chinese sources called *duanlian* (militia), were another independent political power in this border area formed by a considerable number of Chinese who had fled from the Muslims. The largest of these groups was based in Nanshan,[110] almost five thousand strong and led by Xu Xuegong. His irregular forces often raided the garrisons and villages under the administration of the Urumchi government.[111] There were also several other mountain guerillas organized on similar bases.

The first incident on the eastern border was caused by a certain Muẓaffar, Muḥammad 'Alī (Madalī) Khan's son, at the end of 1868. When his father had died in 1842 in Khoqand, he had fled to Kashmir and from there had come to Yarkand after the 1864 rebellion. In the midst of the fighting after the rebellion he went to the Urumchi area to establish his own power base. After collecting a number of Tungans, Mongols, and foreigners (*musā-*

firān), he raided Ya'qūb Beg's eastern domains Kurla and Qarashahr in 1868. Isḥāq Khwāja who was the governor of Kucha under Ya'qūb Beg counterattacked Muẓaffar and easily regained Kurla. Muẓaffar was killed in the battle and there was no further repercussion.[112] But this was only a prologue to larger and fuller border warfare with the Urumchi Tungans.

In the beginning of 1870 a large number of Tungans (twenty thousand according to Sayrāmī) appeared in the Kurla area and the town instantly fell into their hands.[113] Ya'qūb Beg responded by ordering Ḥākim Khān, the governor of Aqsu, to go to Kucha and aid Isḥāq, while he himself left for Aqsu. The Tungans advanced toward Kucha, where they confronted the troops of Isḥāq Khwāja and Ḥākim Khān at a village called Qara Yighach. The Tungans defeated them and entered Kucha without resistance while Isḥāq and Ḥākim Khān fled to Aqsu. After having plundered Kucha for more than a week, the Tungans retired to Turfan in order to avoid a full-scale war with Ya'qūb Beg's main army. On their way to Turfan, the Tungans also took the opportunity to plunder Kurla and Bugur.

Ya'qūb Beg left Kashghar on March 11 and arrived in Aqsu within a week or two with twenty thousand troops. Ya'qūb Beg stayed there ten days, punishing those officials who had failed to defend the frontier against the Tungans. He then marched to Kucha where he dismissed Isḥāq Khwāja from his post as governor of Kucha. After passing through Kurla and Ushaq Tal, he reached Toqsun which the Tungans were defending, but he took the town without much trouble. Ya'qūb Beg's ultimate aim was to take Turfan, which served as one of the main bases of the Tungans, but before he reached the city, the two sides fought two battles at Yamish and Yar. His army won these battles and was soon able to lay siege to Turfan which was too heavily defended to be taken by storm. The siege continued more than a half year and during this period Lukchin, located to the east of Turfan, fell into the hands of Ya'qūb Beg. Finally, in November of 1870, the Tungans of Turfan were terrified by the power of the cannons employed by Ya'qūb Beg and opened the gates to surrender.[114] He appointed Ḥākim Khān Tura as the governor.[115]

After the fall of Turfan, the showdown between Ya'qūb Beg and Dāūd Khalīfa became inevitable. With sixteen thousand infantry and cavalry Ya'qub Beg marched through Dabanchin and arrived at a place called Daqiyanus[116] about ten miles outside of Urumchi, where Dāūd Khalīfa's Tungan army attempted to mount a surprise night attack. However, that night the weather was bitterly cold and heavy snow was falling, which caused them to lose their way and reach Ya'qūb Beg's campsite only at daybreak. In the ensuing battle the Tungans were routed and fled. Ya'qūb Beg pursued them and surrounded the city of Urumchi. Realizing the futility of further resistance, Dāūd surrendered. Thus in late November 1870, Urumchi fell to Ya'qūb Beg. He brought Sō Dālūya from Turfan and made him *dayanshay* (commander-in-general) of the Urumchi region.[117] He also appointed *yanshays* (commanders) for the cities around Urumchi, such as Qutubi, Gumadi, and Manas, which were subject to the *dayanshay* of Urumchi.

Ya'qūb Beg spent the winter of 1870 in Urumchi where Xu Xuegong visited and presented him with gifts. Xu had visited him when Ya'qūb was staying in Turfan and provided him some troops and provisions. His younger brother also participated with fifteen hundred Han Chinese in the assault of Urumchi.[118] According to Sayrāmī, after three months of staying in Urumchi, Ya'qūb Beg returned to Turfan with his army, and after two more months there he arrived in Qarashahr at the beginning of the next spring (around the end of *hamal*, corresponding to March 21–April 20). He imprisoned Khatun Khan who was the leader of Torghut Mongols nomadizing around Qara Modun in the vicinity of Qarashahr and put them under the control of Ḥajjī Mīrzā, the governor of Kurla.[119] In this way, between the winter of 1870 and the spring of 1871, Ya'qūb Beg succeeded in regaining peace on the eastern borders by subjugating the Tungans in Urumchi and the Mongols around Kurla.

SECOND EXPEDITION

Ya'qūb Beg left Qarashahr after a three-month stay, sometime in May–June of 1871. Even before he reached Aqsu on June 8,[120] news arrived of an armed attack on Urumchi by Xu Xuegong and his murder of Sō Dālūya.[121] Ya'qūb Beg ordered Nār Muḥammad from Kucha, Ḥākim Khān from Turfan, and Ḥājjī Mīrzā from Kurla to march on Urumchi and help subjugate Xu. However, when they arrived in Urumchi, the Tungans already raised up Ṭālib Akhūnd, son of Sō Dālūya, to the rank of *dayanshay*,[122] so Ya'qūb Beg ratified his status. The army under Ḥākim Khān's command, assisted by the Tungans, pursued Xu to Nanshan but because he fled to the direction of the Great Nanshan they could not catch him.

When they returned from this unsuccessful chase in the month of *qaws* (November 22–December 21), the situation in Urumchi changed again: the Tungans had betrayed them by making Dāūd Khalīfa their leader and arresting Tālib Akhūnd. They closed the gates and denied entrance to Ya'qūb Beg's army. Intense battles ensued between the two sides. Ya'qūb Beg's army, reinforced by the troops from Aqsu, stormed the city and Dāūd fled to Manas. There Dāūd allied with Xu Xuegong and collected a large number of Tungans. They came back and laid the siege to Urumchi. According to Sayrāmī, there were 20,000 people attacking Urumchi, 16,000 Tungans and 4,000 Chinese militia.[123] The Tungans gained control of the entire surrounding area except for the city of Urumchi, and throughout the winter and spring of 1871–1872 Yaʿqūb Beg's army defended the fort with difficulty.[124]

Yaʿqūb Beg, who had returned to Kashghar that winter, set about organizing another expedition to Urumchi to raise the siege. He made his eldest son, Beg Quli Beg, *amīr-i lashkar* and sent him with seven thousand troops to Urumchi in the spring of 1872. Beg Quli found that the Tungans were defending the fort of Dabanchin under the leadership of Ma Jingui and Xu Xuegong who had come down from Urumchi to assist the defense. After forty days of severe fighting Beg Quli finally took the fort on June 8. Ma Jingui was killed in the battle.[125] He then went to Urumchi where the Tungans were faced with an attack by two armies, that is, the army of Ḥākim Khān inside the city and that of Beg Quli outside. On June 11, after taking many casualties the Tungans surrendered and Xu, who was helping them, fled to Shashanzi.[126]

After two months of resting in Urumchi, Beg Quli proceeded to Gumadi and Manas. Both these cities fell into his hands, and Dāūd died soon after in Manas.[127] Beg Quli made Gänjä Akhūnd, a man of Salar origin, the head of the Urumchi Tungans and then returned to Kashghar in the month of *saritān* (June 22–July 21) of 1873.[128] Yaʿqūb Beg honored Beg Quli's feat by making him *amīr al-umarā*, that is, the commander-in-chief. With the successful completion of the second Urumchi expedition Yaʿqūb Beg added a considerable tract of land to his dominion, which now extended from Pamir in the west to Turfan and Lukchin in the east and from Sarikol and Khotan in the south to Urumchi and Manas to the north.

4 *Muslim State and Its Ruling Structure*

Administration

No serious attempt has been made yet to analyze the basic structure of Ya'qūb Beg's government. The reason it has not received attention, despite the obvious importance of the topic, may be the lack of materials on which one can rely for an appropriate analysis. However, if we cautiously put together scattered information, it is possible to reconstruct basic principles upon which the governmental structure was erected. Our analysis is centered around a few important questions: what was the basis of Ya'qūb Beg's political power?; how did he create the ruling structure to perpetuate his power?; what were the strengths and the weaknesses of his government? The answers to these questions will not only bring out several unexplored aspects about the decade of his rule, but also will expand our perspective in understanding the underlying causes of the destruction of his state. We will be able to see clearly that the Qing reconquest of Xinjiang was not the outcome of a simple military confrontation.

CORE OF POWER

There was hardly anything that we could call the central government in the state of Ya'qūb Beg. This was not because centralized political power was absent but because its structure basically consisted of only a handful of functionaries who were tightly controlled by Ya'qūb Beg. He did not institute a well-defined administrative apparatus, directed by high officials, but decided most of the country's important matters by himself.[1] Therefore, in order to understand the characteristics of the central power, we need to understand Ya'qūb Beg himself.

Based on contemporary Muslim writings, Ya'qūb Beg did not seem to call himself khan. For example, Sayrāmī asserts that he "never called himself *pādishāh*, *sulṭān*, or *khān*. His seal was about the size of a melon seed, and on it was inscribed simply 'Muḥammad Ya'qūb.'"[2] This assertion was confirmed by R. B. Shaw who visited and met Ya'qūb Beg personally. He tells us that he received a passport, dated October 22nd of 1874, upon which

Ya'qūb Beg's seal was affixed in exactly the same form and manner that Sayrāmī describes.[3] Later, Ya'qūb Beg added the title of Badaulat Ghāzī to the seal.[4] However, in British and Ottoman diplomatic documents there are instances in which he was designated as Ya'qub Khān. For example, edicts in the name of the Ottoman sultan issued in 1875 call him "Respectable Ruler of Kashghar Country, Ya'qūb Khān"[5] and "Amīr of Kashghar, His Excellency Ya'qūb Khān."[6] In a British report he was also called "His Highness Atalik Ghazee Yakoob Khan, Ruler of Yarkund."[7] The reason that Britain and Ottoman Turkey addressed him in this way seems to have stemmed from their diplomatic consideration for the ruler of the country with which they maintained friendly relations, even though Ya'qūb Beg did not call himself khan. By contrast, because the Russians were keen not to fully recognize the legitimacy of his government, they addressed him only by the title of "the honourable ruler of Djety-Shahr."[8]

Muslim sources inform us that Ya'qūb Beg commonly used a number of different titles, including *badaulat*, *ataliq ghāzī*, *qushbegi*, and *amīr*, among others. As explained earlier, *badaulat* meant "the fortunate (or blessed) one" and was used as a rather euphemistic appellation. *Ataliq ghāzī,* another very popular title that literally meant "fatherly holy warrior" was translated in contemporary European accounts as "Champion Father" or "Tutor of the Champions." In fact, however, it is more likely that Ya'qūb Beg used this title because *ataliq* was one of the highest ranks in the Bukharan khanate and it had been granted to him by Bukhara in 1868 in recognition of his conquest of Eastern Turkestan. He then embellished it with the honorific *ghāzī* to create a new title meaning the "holy warrior of the *ataliq* (rank)." *Qushbegi* was one of the highest military titles in the Khoqand khanate and Ya'qūb Beg probably received it from 'Ālim Quli when he was dispatched to Kashghar with Buzurg. The title of *amīr* was bestowed on him by the Ottoman sultan 'Abdülazīz in 1873.[9] It was never as popular as *ataliq ghāzī*, but in diplomatic documents he was often addressed by this title. In many cases some of his several titles were used in combination, such as "Badaulat Ataliq Ghāzī, Amīr of Kashghar" or "Ataliq Ghāzī Ya'qūb Beg."

The reason Ya'qūb Beg did not assume the title of khan can be found in a peculiar concept on the political tradition in Central Asia where, except for the descendants of Chinggis Khan or renowned Muslim saints, nobody could use that title. Beside this consideration, his adoption of these titles was relevant to his attitude of stressing hard facts of reality rather than outward embellishments. As a matter of fact, several Europeans who had met Ya'qūb Beg transmitted their strong impression about his candid, serious, and grave manner. H. W. Bellew, who visited Kashghar in 1873 as a member of the British embassy, described him as follows.

Atalik Ghazi has a very remarkable face, and one not easily described. It presents no single feature with undue prominence, and seen in a crowd would pass unnoticed as rather a common sort of face; yet it has peculiar characters and wears an expression which somehow conveys the impression that it is more assumed than natural. . . . The forehead is full and high, and without trace of a frown or wrinkle is displayed to full advantage under a well set turban, the pure white folds of which rest high on the shaven scalp . . . The mouth is large, but not coarse; and the lips are thick and fleshy, but at the same time firmly set. Its expression is one of severity, though now and again in conversation the upper lip is curled for a moment with a very pleasing smile, instantly, however, to resume its apparently studied expression of gravity.[10]

The building Ya'qūb Beg used as his headquarters and residence was called *urda*. This word came from *orda* or *ordu*, which originally meant the tent of nomadic rulers and was used in Central Asia as a general term for the residence of rulers. Ya'qūb Beg's *urda* was constructed on the former site of the Manchu *ambans*' residence that had earlier burned down. It was comprised of four successive rooms: his private space in the rear, an audience hall, a room that contained kitchen, store, and the waiting space for his pages, and finally a room where his royal guards were seated along the wall forming "a long row of solemn looking figures, seated with downcast eyes, motionless and silent."[11] At Ya'qūb Beg's *urda* were found only a small number of officials who performed personal service for him.

The British report listed several offices for this purpose: *zīnbardār* (saddle holder), *dastūrkhwānchi* (banquet master), *yasawul* (aide-de-camp), *mīrākhōr* (stabler), *maḥram* (attendant), *khazānachī* (treasurer), *aftābachī* (cup-bearer), *bekawulbashi* (steward), and so on.[12] These were the offices placed in order to fulfil Ya'qūb Beg's personal needs and had hardly anything to do with the discussion and the decision of important state matters. In the same report we can find almost twenty "principal officers of the state," but some of them such as *ataliq* and *qushbegi* were not actually used as official titles in Kashghar. People were called by those titles simply because they had once carried them in Khoqand. And other official titles concerning civil, military and financial affairs were also very much confused and jumbled so that it is difficult to discover any consistent system to them.

However, the most significant office in the court was that of the *mīrzābashi*, literally meaning "chief secretary," and included the subordinate *mīrzās* under his direction. Scholars have largely overlooked the significance of this office because it was considered just a secretarial post that involved mere paperwork.[13] It is true that in the Khoqand khanate the post was a minor one, and that it had only a slightly higher importance in Bukhara.[14] However, the following description by Sayrāmī shows that *mīrzābashi* under Ya'qūb Beg's rule performed a much more important role.

His Highness Ataliq Ghāzī—Light be upon his grave!—conducted all the affairs of the country for himself. He did not publicly appoint a couple of learned or upright persons to the post of *vizīr*. However, instead of *vizīr*, he decided and carried out all the affairs of state, such as tying and untying of matters or appointment and dismissal of officials, according to the excellent opinions of upright *mīrzā*s, wise *munshī*s[15] and persons with wide experience who were wishing only the best for the well-being of the country and the people. The entire income and expenditure of the state, the number of commanders and soldiers, the counting of horses and armaments, the revenue of the treasury and the workshops,[16] all these were entrusted to *mīrzābashi*s. The *mīrzābashi*s kept all the state affairs in order and reported [to Ataliq Ghāzī]. They assumed the role of supplicant as well as envoy, and through their judgment the agreements could be dissolved. *Mīrzābashi*s' authority was strong and powerful only after Ya'qūb Beg's: the respect and dignity which *mīrzābashi*s received had no limit. Nevertheless, even they were not free from the anger [of Ya'qūb Beg].[17]

A Russian report, although not mentioning the office of *mīrzābashi* specifically, corroborates Sayrāmī's description: "All the arrangements for the administration of the country and all his correspondence, Yakoob Bek carries on through his *chancellerie*, which is composed of four *Mirzas*. These *Mirzas* serve Yakoob Bek both as secretaries and as clerks."[18]

As far as we can gather from various sources, the first *mīrzābashi* appointed by Ya'qūb Beg was Mīrzā Ya'qūb who had come to Kashghar with Ya'qūb Beg and Buzurg. He kept the post for three years and, at his death, was succeeded by Mīrzā Barāt and Mullā 'Īsa Mīrzā. Mullā 'Īsa was soon discharged because of his incompetence and replaced by Mahī al-Dīn Makhdūm b. Ḥājjī 'Alam Akhūnd. He was also known as 'Mīrzā Farsakh' because it was he who put the landmarks in stone along the main road, calculating the distance by *farsakh*.[19] He was said to have known seven different languages and six different calligraphies and was assisted by several *mīrzā*s.[20] Finally he was replaced by Mullā Zayn al-'Ābidīn Makhdūm from Marghinan.[21] However, these names do not represent the full list of *mīrzābashi*s under Ya'qūb Beg, nor do we know their terms of service.

The functions of *mīrzābashi*, as Sayrāmī suggests, were diverse and extensive. He not only gave advice to Ya'qūb Beg in important matters of state but also supervised such financial matters as governmental income and expenses. It was his duty to check and inspect the numbers of officials as well as the state properties. For example, when residents and merchants in Kucha and Kurla who had lost their possessions because of a Tungan attack in 1870 appealed for help, Mullā Zayn al-'Ābidīn Makhdūm was dispatched to examine and recompense their losses.[22] The person who assumed the office of *mīrzābashi* sometimes performed diplomatic missions. R. B. Shaw, when he visited Kashgharia in 1868–69, was welcomed and escorted by a *mīrzābashi* to Kashghar.[23] A. N. Kuropatkin recollects that a *mīrzā* named Makhsum (probably the above-mentioned Mahī al-Dīn Makhdūm) was sent to Tashkent in 1872 as an envoy and that he had "the greatest influence in affairs."[24] The last *mīrzābashi,* Mullā Zayn al-'Ābidīn Makhdūm, was sent by Beg Quli to the Chinese army in Aqsu to open a negotiation where he met a Chinese general called Zūngtūng Dārīn.[25]

It is not difficult to think of the reason Ya'qūb Beg gave such an important role to his *mīrzābashi*s. Many religious and military notables had far better claim to the rulership than Ya'qūb Beg, and he naturally feared that these people might gain great influence in political affairs. What Ya'qūb Beg needed was the people who could efficiently execute his orders with professional skill, yet not threaten his own political status. None of the *mīrzābashi*s under Ya'qūb Beg possessed a high military or religious background, but instead, they had good knowledge about the composition of political documents, revenue accounting, and other practical matters. It was just because they had no such conspicuous backgrounds that their political power depended solely on their loyalty to Ya'qūb Beg. That is why Sayrāmī wrote that "the respect and dignity which *mīrzābashi*s received had no limit. Nevertheless, even they were not yet free from the anger [of Ya'qūb Beg]." He could dismiss them easily whenever he wanted to do so. Although the office of *mīrzābashi* was apparently borrowed from Khoqand, its unique status and the role in Kashgharia was a natural consequence of Ya'qūb Beg's policy for centralization.

LOCAL ADMINISTRATION

First of all, it is necessary for us to define the boundaries of the state under Ya'qūb Beg's rule. According to the British report that was based on an extensive survey over his realm in 1873, his dominion reached to the southwest as far as Shahidullah bordering Ladakh, and to the direction of Sariqol it extended to Aqtash and Sarhadd which adjoins the Pamir and the Wakhan valley.[26] To the west Terek Davan formed the frontier with the neighboring Khoqand, which was by that time already under Russian rule, and to the north it reached as far as Turghat Daban, located several miles north of the Chaqmaq guard post, where it bordered Russia.[27] In the Yulduz steppe to the north of Tianshan nomadic Torghut Mongols recognized Ya'qūb Beg's suzerainty but they were virtually independent. To the east lay Chiktim where the last guard post was established formed frontiers with Hami, and to the northeast his rule extended as far as Manas to the north of Urumchi.[28] Finally, to the south and the southeast, Qarangghu Tagh, Cherchen, and Lop were within his dominion. In this respect, Sayrāmī's observation was relatively accurate:

> The frontiers of the country reached one hundred days' journey from Gumadi in the east to Sariqol in the west, and eighty days' journey from Muzdaban to the north and Qarangghu Tagh to the south. Over thirty-four large and small cities which had governors (*ḥākim*) and belonged to Urumchi and Yättishahr,[29] he was a firm ruler

TABLE 4.1
Local Administrative Units under Ya'qūb Beg

Kuropatkin[a] *(10)*	*Forsyth*[b] *(10)*	*Bellew*[c] *(7)*	*Sayrāmī*[d] *(8)*	*Qing period (8 cities in Nanlu)*
Kashghar	Kashghar	Kashghar (Yangihissar and Maralbashi)	Kashghar (Yangihissar)	Kashghar
Yangihissar	Yangihissar			Yangihissar
Yarkand	Yarkand	Yarkand	Yarkand	Yarkand
Khotan	Khotan	Khotan (Cherchen)	Khotan	Khotan
Ush Turfan	Ush Turfan	Aqsu (Ush Turfan)	Ush Turfan	Ush Turfan
Aqsu	Aqsu		Aqsu	Aqsu (Bai)
Bai			Bai · Sayram	
Kucha	Kucha	Kucha	Kucha	Kucha
Kurla	Kurla	Kurla (Lop and Qarashahr)		Qarashahr
	Qarashahr			
Turfan	Turfan	Turfan	Turfan	

[a] *Kashgaria*, p. 40.
[b] *Report of a Mission to Yarkund*, p. 32.
[c] *Kashmir and Kashghar*, p. 4.
[d] TH/Enver, pp. 575–76; TA/Pantusov, pp. 276–77.

and independent sovereign for fourteen years.[30] In this respect, the territory under Ya'qūb Beg's rule virtually covered the entire Xinjiang except for Hami to the east and Ili to the north.

What kind of local administration did he establish to administer this large realm? Except for a few small areas, sources show that the whole country was divided into a number of *vilāyats* (provinces) for which Ya'qūb Beg appointed governors called *ḥākim* (or *dādkhwāh*).

As we see from Table 4.1, available sources give different numbers of the provinces (in parentheses). It is not clear whether this confusion about the number of provincial units springs from the lack of accuracy of the sources, or from the ambiguity of the provincial system itself. We can find contradictions even in the same source. For example, Sayrāmī writes that after Ya'qūb Beg conquered the western part of the Tarim Basin he "appointed Niyāz Ḥākim Beg to Khotan, Muḥammad Yūnus Jān Shaghāwul to Yarkand, Ālāsh Bī to Kashghar, 'Āmil Khān Tura to Yangihissar, and Ḥākim Khān Tura to Maralbashi. And he made them governors and [the territory under their jurisdiction] their independent fief."[31] And after the occupation of Aqsu, he "made Ḥākim Khān Tura the governor of Aqsu, and bestowed all the attached areas like Bai and Sayram to him as his fief."[32] However, as the table shows, Sayrāmī considers Yangihissar administratively as being attached to Kashghar while he made Bai and Sayram independent from Aqsu.

We cannot exclude the possibility that the number of provinces may have been changed because Ya'qūb Beg's occupation of Eastern Turkestan was achieved not at one time but gradually, and the characteristics of the local administration may have been changed from temporary to a more permanent one as time passed. In the meantime, the British and the Russian embassies visited Kashgharia at different times, one in 1873–74 and the other in 1876–77, which can be the reason for their differences. Nonetheless, we should note the fact that even T. D. Forsyth and H. Bellew who belonged to the same British embassy did not agree with each other.

Considering the fact that one of the distinctive features in central as well as local administration in the khanates of Khoqand and Bukhara was the lack of system and stability and the fact that the mode of Ya'qūb Beg's exercise of power showed a considerable degree of despotic and arbitrary nature, we can acknowledge the high degree of fluidity in the units of local administration, easily being changed according to Ya'qūb Beg's whim. Nevertheless, the territorial boundaries of these provinces were relatively well defined, at least along the main road. For example, R. B. Shaw describes how a younger brother of a Yarkand governor became powerless once he passed beyond his own district; "He could hardly get anything for himself even, so I sent him half a sheep, &c."[33]

Whatever the actual number was, it seems that there were about seven to ten large units of local administration called *vilāyat*. This number, excluding Turfan, shows some resemblance to the Eight Cities of the Southern Circuit (*nanlu bacheng*) as Table 4.1 shows. Although it is not clear whether "the thirty-four large and small cities which had governors (*ḥākim*)" in Sayrāmī's work reflect the situation under Ya'qūb Beg's rule, this number corresponds almost exactly to the 35 *ḥākim beg* established in the Southern Circuit during the Qing period.[34] In fact, we can find in the writings of Sayrāmī and others *ḥākim*s were appointed to places like Maralbashi, Toqsun, Qaraqash, Artush, Guma, and Sariqol, which did not constitute independent provinces.[35] These facts suggest the possibility that Ya'qūb took over the existing Qing local system without much change. These provinces covered the area from Kashghar to Turfan and formed the most essential part of Ya'qūb Beg's state, where the majority of their population was the Turkic Muslim.

Besides this core area, there were other regions that were not incorporated into this provincial system. As explained earlier, after Ya'qūb Beg conquered Urumchi around the end of 1870, he appointed Sō Dālūya (Suo Huanzhang) as *dayanshay* and other leaders as *yanshay* to Qutubi, Manas, Gumadi, and so on. After the murder of Sō, his son succeeded to the post, but, when Beg Quli finished the second expedition in 1871, Ya'qūb made Gänjä Akhūnd, a Salar living in Kashghar, *dayanshay* and dispatched him to Urumchi. The Salars were ethnically Turks and they were living in the present eastern Qinghai province. Some of them were associated with the Jahrī sect of Ma Mingxin and from the later half of the eighteenth century they came to the cities in Kashgharia as merchants.[36] The reason he sent Gänjä Akhūnd may have been Ya'qūb Beg's consideration that through Gänjä Akhūnd he could more easily control the Tungans in Urumchi, many of whom belonged to the same Jahrī sect. In this way, he seems to have acknowledged the peculiarity of the Urumchi area, and the mode of local administration was different from that in the Tarim Basin. In the meantime, the Qirghiz, the Qazaqs, and the Mongols living around the mountain regions of the Tianshan and the Pamir were not directly subject to governors appointed by Ya'qūb Beg but to their own tribal chiefs. Therefore, the rule was rather indirect. Sayrāmī claims that chiefs in Shighnan, Kanjut and Wakhan also acknowledged the suzerainty of Ya'qūb Beg,[37] but such relations do not seem to have been of a permanent character.[38]

Governors exercised full responsibility and authority over the province, at least nominally. According to Sayrāmī, for example, when Ya'qūb Beg made Niyāz Beg the governor of Khotan, he gave that province as his *soyurghal* and entrusted him with the power to administer all the affairs and the right to appoint and dismiss the officials. Yūnus Jān Shaghāwul, governor of Yarkand, was also entrusted with the full power of administration.[39] However, we can find several cases showing that it was Ya'qūb Beg, not the governors, who directly appointed provincial officials in the fields of financial, military, as well as civil administration. This implies the fact that the actual power of governors was rather limited. The principal duties of a governor were to facilitate the collection of taxes, to care for the well-being and the security of his province, and to ensure the border's safety. For these purposes he had the aid of several officials, including a lieutenant governor called *ishikagha* and a number of *yasawul*s and *maḥram*s in his provincial court.

As we have quoted above, when Sayrāmī mentions Ya'qūb Beg's appointment of provincial governors, he uses the expression of *soyurghal*. For example, after he conquered Kashghar and Yangihissar, he "designated governor and [his] *soyurghal* to each area."[40] He also "appointed Niyāz Ḥākim Beg to Khotan, Muḥammad Yūnus Jān Shaghāwul to Yarknd, and . . . , he made them governors and [the territory under their jurisdiction] independent fief (*ḥākim vä soyurghal bi'l-istiqlāl*)."[41] Especially when he appointed Niyāz Beg to Khotan, he writes as follows.

> He appointed Niyāz Ishikagha Beg, a Yarkandi, to the governor of Khotan and fixed it as his independent (*mustaqill*) *soyurghal*. He also let him have the power to take care of the matters of country as he pleased and to have the great authority to select and dismiss officials.[42]

We should remember that the two most fundamental features of the *soyurghal* were (1) tax exemption and administrative immunities, and (2) a perpetual and hereditary right by its owners.[43] In Central Asia these two features had been observed beginning with the early Ashtrakhanids, and then the practice of *soyurghal* began to change gradually so that the first of the two features mentioned above disappeared from the eighteenth century, retaining only the hereditary right. At the same time, the size of *soyurghal* land decreased; *vilāyat* was no more given as *soyurghal*, but *qishlaq* (originally winter camp, but used as a term for village) was usually bestowed. Later, the practice of *soyurghal* changed further that when its original owner died, his descendants could retain the right only with the reconfirmation from the ruler.[44]

In view of the original meaning and its transformation of the term *soyurghal* I cannot agree with the opinion based simply on the terminology found in Muslim sources that Ya'qūb Beg adopted the system of *soyurghal*.[45] Governors under Ya'qūb Beg enjoyed neither the right of exemption nor that of heredity. As will be discussed later in detail, taxes levied by the governors were all sent to Kashghar except for a small amount left for provincial use, and we can hardly find any case of the office of the governorship being inherited. The term *soyurghal* used in Sayrāmī's work seems nothing more than an expression for a favor or grace bestowed by the ruler. We find such a usage even in the chronicle of Shāh Maḥmūd Churās, written in the later half of the seventeenth century: the examples found in his work show that this term was used when a khan entrusted the authority to rule over a certain province to his family members or tribal chiefs. And even when he bestowed a banner (*tugh*) to somebody, it is written that "a banner was given as *soyurghal*."[46]

Therefore, the expression like "independent *soyurghal*" should be understood not in its literal meaning but in the context of the reality under Ya'qūb Beg's rule. And as I pointed out above, Sayrāmī's assertion that a governor received unconditional power to handle important affairs and to appoint or dismiss high officials cannot be accepted as true. When Ya'qūb Beg sent somebody as a governor to a certain province, he frequently named not only a deputy governor (*ishikagha*) but also other high-ranking officials. He held the power in his hands to appoint and discharge commander-in-chief (*amīr-i lashkar*), treasurer (*sarkār*, or *zakātchī*), and even religious offices. Of course, the low-ranking local officials may have been appointed under the direction of governors. In general, however, the local administration with a governor at its head was not part of an integrated vertical hierarchical system because all the officials of whatever level were directly and individually responsible to Ya'qūb Beg alone.

One interesting fact found in the background of the local governors is that most of them were Khoqandians not indigenous Kashgharians. Although it is impossible to make a complete list of the governors because of the lack of information, all the data available to us confirms that fact. The following is the list of governors in each province (the persons in italics were Kashgharians, and the persons with an asterisk are those whose background is unclear).

Kashghar: Aldāsh (or Alāsh)

Yangihissar: *'Azīz Beg*, 'Āmil Khān, Abū al-Qāsim, Mullā Niẓām al-Dīn

Yarkand: Mīr Baba, Qūsh Qipchaq Parvānachi, Muḥammad Yūnus Jān

Khotan: Mīr Baba, *Niyāz Beg*

Ush Turfan: Muḥammad Baba, Isḥāq Jān

Aqsu: *Mīrzā Najm al-Dīn, Ḥākim Khān, *Mullā Jiyān Mīrzābashi, *'Abd al-Raḥmān*

Bai, Sayram: Aḥmad Beg, Muḥammad Amīn

Kucha: *Isḥāq Khwāja*, Nār Muḥammad, 'Āmil Khān

Kurla: Ḥājjī Mīrzā, Niyāz Muḥammad

Turfan: Ḥākim Khān[47]

This list contains twenty-four names in total, but only four were Kashgharian. Even though we do not count two persons with asterisks, eighteen people in the list are non-Kashgharians, mostly from Khoqand. Moreover, of the four Kashgharian governors 'Azīz Beg was executed shortly after he had been appointed governor of Yangihissar, and Isḥāq Khwāja was dismissed from his office after his unsuccessful defense against the Tungan raids in 1869. Only 'Abd al-Raḥmān in Aqsu and Niyāz Beg in Khotan could keep their offices to the end of Ya'qūb Beg's reign. The result undoubtedly shows that the Kashgharians formed a minority among the governors, and that there is no data supporting A. D. Isiev's argument that more than 80 percent of the officials under Ya'qūb Beg's rule were recruited from the Kashgharians.[48] Shinmen Yasushi's detailed study on this topic also confirms our conclusion. According to him, administrators in the center were mostly from Western Turkestan, while the governors and their assistants in the local government show the mixed composition of the Khoqandians and the natives. Important posts in the army were also dominated by non-Kashgharians, and only the judges (*qāḍī*) were mostly recruited from the natives.[49]

A province was divided further into smaller units of townships (*kent*). Each unit, a conglomeration of small villages, had a magistrate (*beg*) as its administrative head who resided in the center of the town. It was not uncommon that bigger towns were called *vilāyat* and the magistrates were called *ḥākim*, probably due to the old custom during the Qing rule or to the flexibility of the nomenclature.[50] In cases where villages were farmed out to military garrisons, those villages seem to have been controlled by the commanders of such garrisons.[51] *Mīrāb* was appointed to supervise the irrigation of several villages and put under the supervision of a beg. He took charge of the distribution of water, the repair of canals, and so on.

The judiciary side was staffed by officials known as *qāḍī*, *muftī*, and *ra'īs* in towns and cities. *Qāḍī* performed the investigation when cases were brought and made his judgments based on the Islamic law. After the judgments were made, the governor enforced them except for the death sentence which needed the confirmation of Ya'qūb Beg. *Muftī* issued *fatva*s (legal opinions) in answer to the questions submitted to him either by *qāḍī*s or private individuals. *Ra'īs* was a member of the religious police, regularly patrolling streets and shops with the assistance of a few *muḥtasibs*. *Ra'īs* usually carried a whip called *dira*, a leather thong fixed to a wooden handle as a symbol of the discipline.[52] Ya'qūb Beg appointed a *qāḍī kalān* (senior justice) and a *qāḍī ra'īs* (police chief) in the capitals of each province and *qāḍī 'askar* (military judge) for the bigger units of the army.[53]

Army

ORGANIZATION AND MANAGEMENT

Initially when Ya'qūb Beg was sent to Kashghar accompanied by Buzurg, he commanded only a small number of followers. This was not too much of a problem, for most of the Āfāqī followers and a number of native Kashgharians looked upon Ya'qūb Beg as an ally in their battles against the Qirghiz under Ṣiddīq Beg who had terrorized the city. They were, however, neither loyal nor well trained, hence Ya'qūb Beg's position in Kashgharia had not been secure until the arrival of reinforcements in the form of a large number of Khoqandian troops who were fleeing from Khudāyār. It was these troops that first gave Ya'qūb Beg a sound base of support in Kashgharia and provided him with the raw material to fashion a true professional army.

The reorganization of the army appears to have taken place in the beginning of 1866 just after Ya'qūb Beg had crushed Buzurg's opposition and was preparing for the final expedition to Yarkand. As Sayrāmī reports, he drew up the registration of the soldiers whom he had put together and divided them into four divisions of cavalry (*yigit*) and one division of infantry (*sarbāz*), each with 3,000 soldiers (see Figure 4.1), bringing the total force of the army to around 15,000. Ya'qūb Beg commanded one cavalry division himself and appointed four generals called *amīr-i lashkar* (or, *lashkarbashi*), to command the others.[54] Other military ranks were also fixed: below *amīr-i*

FIGURE 4.1. Guard of artillery *sarbāz* and group of officers, assembled in the courtyard of Yarkand governor. Source: T. D. Forsyth, *Report of a Mission to Yarkund in 1873* (Calcutta: Foreign Department Press, 1875), photo no. 34.

lashkar came *pānṣadbashi* (head of five hundred), or in short *pānṣad* (eight *pānṣads* were assigned to each division), and then *yüzbashi* (head of one hundred; five *yüzbashis* under one *pānṣad*), followed by *panjāhbashi* (head of fifty) and *dahbashi* (head of ten) (see Figure 4.2). With this reorganized army he successfully accomplished the Yarkand expedition (1866) and, the next year with the same formation, he conquered Aqsu and Kucha (1867).[55]

As his territory expanded, Ya'qūb Beg felt the need to deploy garrison troops in important cities for security. Each garrison was headed by a commander with the title of *amīr-i lashkar* or *pānṣad* depending on the size of the units. For example, after he conquered Yarkand, he made a certain Kepek Qūrbashi the garrison commander of the city, and in the same way, he placed Khālmān Pānṣad in Khotan, Hamdam Pānṣad in Aqsu, Muḥammad Baba Toqsaba in Kucha, Haydar Quli Pānṣad in Turfan, and Tūrdī Quli Dādkhwāh in Urumchi.[56] He also placed small garrisons at the guard-posts (*qarawul*) along the borders of his dominion. Those guard-posts took the form of small forts (*qurghan* or *qurghanchä*). Although various sources disagree on the exact number of Ya'qūb Beg's regular force that received salary and provision from the state, its approximate size seems to have been around between 35,000 and 40,000. Based on *Dāstān-i Muḥammad Yā'qūb* and the report by A. N. Kuropatkin, we can make Table 4.2.

The total number of the two sources cited above does not show much difference, both around 40,000, though there are other sources which give larger numbers.[57] However, one can easily notice the discrepancy of the numbers in each city. Compared to *Dāstān*, Kuropatkin's report shows the

FIGURE 4.2. *Yüzbashi, panjāhbashi, dahbashi,* at attention. Source: T. D. Forsyth, *Report of a Mission to Yarkund in 1873* (Calcutta: Foreign Department Press, 1875), photo no. 67.

heavy concentration of the troops, almost 20,000, in the eastern part of the Tarim Basin (Turfan, Toqsun and Kurla). What we see here is not the normal deployment of the Kashgharian army: the difference in numbers was probably caused by Ya'qūb Beg's transfer of troops during the winter of 1875–76 from the western cities to the eastern border to prepare against the Chinese invasion led by Zuo Zongtang. Then, which period does the number shown in *Dāstān* reflect? The manuscript of this work does not have the date of compilation. However, it seems to indicate the condition after 1870–71 because we find there the mention that 'Abd al-Raḥmān was the governor of Aqsu who was appointed to that post only after the Urumchi expedition.

This regular army was divided into three categories according to their combat functions: *yigit, sarbāz,* and *taifurchi*. The *yigit*, which literally means cavalry, was actually mounted infantry. They could make rapid marches, an average thirty miles a day, but in action "they dismount to fire, their horses being disposed of in rear."[58] The *sarbāz* had no horses but they were better armed and drilled than the *yigits*. The ratio of cavalry and infantry was about three to one. The *taifurchi* formed a division and was stationed in Kashghar. The word *taifur* came from the Chinese word of *dapao*, and it was a large gun, six feet in length and manned by four men. They were recruited mostly from the Chinese and the Tungans who could handle this equipment. There were about 3,000 Tungan *taifurchis* under Mā Dālūya, of Gansu origin, stationed in the Muslim town of Kashghar, and an-

TABLE 4.2
Number of Troops Stationed in Eastern Tukestan Cities

	Dāstān-i Muḥammad Yā'qūb	*Kuropatkin's report*
Kashghar	7,700	4,600–4,800
Yangihissar	1,500	4,000
Yarkand	6,000	
Khotan	12,000	3,000
Maralbashi		400
Ush Turfan	1,500	
Aqsu	6,000	1,200
Bai and Sayram	2,000	400
Kucha	3,000	1,500
Kurla		3,160
Dabanchin		900
Turfan		8,500 (+ 10,000 Tungans)
Toqsun		6,000
Other guard posts		1,500
Total	39,700	35,360 (+ 10,000 Tungans)

other division, about 1,500 Chinese *taifurchi*s under Hō Dālūya, was placed in the fort.[59]

Besides these regular forces, Ya'qūb Beg also had an auxiliary army in case of special needs, consisting of the Tungans in Urumchi and Turfan, and tribal people from the Pamir, especially Qirghiz and Sariqolis. A traveler remarked that in an emergency Ya'qūb Beg could mobilize almost 20,000 among the neighboring Qirghiz.[60] Several thousand of them participated in the first Urumchi expedition.[61] However, it would not be useful to try to determine the exact number because they must have changed from time to time, and these auxiliary armies were neither a permanent nor essential part of the Kashgharian military force.

Ya'qūb Beg took measures to strengthen and expand his army in order to solidify his power basis, but the army itself could be a potential threat to him. He devised measures to eliminate this threat. First of all, he took complete control over the appointment and promotion of army officers. Kuropatkin wrote that "Promotion to *da-bashi* and to *piyand-bashi* was in the hands of the *pansats*. Promotion to *yuz-bashi* and to *pansat* rested with Yakoob Bek, who, at his inspections, could promote a man from the ranks direct to the grade of *pansat*, and in like manner degrade a *pansat* to the ranks."[62] This method was designed not only to check the unnecessary growth of the commanders' power but also to create military elites loyal only to him. Moreover, Ya'qūb Beg tried to preserve his exclusive power by filling the highest military ranks almost completely with non-Kashgharians, especially with the Khoqandians. For example, all four *amīr-i lashkar*s whom Ya'qūb Beg appointed in 1866 were non-Kashgharians: 'Abd Allāh

(Marghilan), Mīrzā Aḥmad (Tashkent), ʿUmar Qul (Qipchaq), and Jāmadār (Afghan). Except for ʿAbd Allāh who had come with Yaʿqūb Beg, the other three arrived later, in September of 1865, with a large anti-Khudāyār group.[63] If we check the background of thirteen *amīr-i lashkar*s who served Yaʿqūb Beg and found in Sayrāmī's work, all of them, except for one, were non-Kashgharian. The case of *pānṣad* was similar.[64] There is no doubt that Yaʿqūb Beg's policy was to give the highest offices of the army to Khoqandians, and thereby exclude Kashgharians. Yaʿqūb Beg, for his part, certainly had sufficient grounds for such a policy. The Kashgharians had supported practically all of his enemies. Ṣiddīq Beg, Muqarrab Shāh Beg, Walī Khān, and Buzurg had all relied on Kashgharian support in their armed attacks on Yaʿqūb Beg.

Another measure that Yaʿqūb Beg took to preserve his power was the policy of checks and balances in dealing with those high-ranking non-Kashgharian military commanders. He knew the Khoqandian politics too well to remain unsuspecting about the loyalty of his Khoqandian officers. In order not to allow them to form a united opposition against him, he filled the highest military posts with people of different backgrounds. The first four *amīr-i lashkar*s are good examples; one Qipchaq, two Sarts from different cities in the Khoqand khanate, and one Afghan. As a way of further strengthening control over the army, he later appointed two of his sons, Beg Quli and Ḥaqq Quli, as *amīr-i lashkar*s. His eldest son was made the commander-in-general after the second Urumchi expedition.

Yaʿqūb Beg also tried to separate the army from the local government so that provincial governors could not have complete control over regional armies and, thus, the regional chiefs of military and civil branches would not form a unified opposition against him. Administratively, garrison commanders were subject to the governors who assumed the military command of the regional armies in case of a military expedition. However, the regional armies were not completely dependent upon the treasury of the governors but were supported by a separate financial channel under the supervision and control of the central government. Nor had the governors the power to dismiss the regional commanders. Thus the relationship between governors and military commanders was not clearly defined and remained ambiguous; only nominally were the latter subject to the former. This phenomenon may be considered an indication of the immaturity of the governmental structure. But it might have been maintained that way on purpose to curb the power of the local governors and to prevent the emergence of close alliances between the regional bureaucratic and military structures.

Yaʿqūb Beg endeavored to eliminate tribal opposition in his army and to reduce the centrifugal force. In this sense, his army was quite different from those in the Bukhara and the Khoqand khanates. The standing armies that both Bukharan and Khoqandian rulers created and tried to maintain were extremely limited in their military strength, whereas the tribal power in the armies like the Qipchaqs and the Qirghizs was in general much stronger. Ya'qūb Beg knew very well the disruptive influence that the tribal armies had produced on the politics of the two khanates. He tried to keep his armed forces predominantly non-tribal. There were auxiliary troops (Qirghiz and Sariqolis) who were collected in case of necessity, but they were marginal in terms of overall military strength of Ya'qūb Beg's army.

The reason the tribal features were not strong in the army of Ya'qūb Beg is easy to explain. The geographical conditions of Eastern Turkestan did not allow the nomadic economy to flourish in any significant degree because waterless deserts that could not support livestock generally surrounded its oases. By contrast, the terrain in Western Turkestan had good pastures not only around the distant mountain slopes and valleys but also in close proximity to cities and towns. The nomads could thereby maintain tribal cohesiveness in the midst of their sedentary neighbors. These strong tribal ties became partly the source of their power and allowed them to intervene in the politics of the khanates.[65] It is interesting to note that a number of tribal names were identified among the town-dwellers in Western Turkestan even in the nineteenth century.[66] On the other hand, in Eastern Turkestan, the nomadic tribes quickly lost their political and social ties once they came down to oases from the mountains in the north. For example, a history of the Moghul khanate written by Shāh Maḥmūd b. Fāḍil Churās in the late seventeenth century shows that approaching the seventeenth century many of the members of the ruling groups who had been identified with tribal names, such as Dūghlāt, Churās, Arlāt, Barlās, gradually lost such identity and began to carry the non-tribal title of *beg*. This tendency was accelerated by the destruction of the Moghul khanate in the 1680s by the Zunghars, and, in *Tadhkira-i 'azīzān* written about a century later by Muḥammad Ṣādiq Kāshgharī, we can hardly find any person identifying himself with tribal name; rather, his name was now tagged with official title or birth place.[67]

In this way, Ya'qūb Beg succeeded in building a powerful army over which he had effective control. The organization of five divisions numbering about 15,000 in 1866 was just the beginning of his ceaseless effort to strengthen his military. He knew that these five divisions were insufficient to effectively ensure the internal and the external security of his dominion, let alone meet the likely challenge of a Chinese invasion. He increased the number to the level of 40,000. How could he manage this huge number of troops? Let us now examine the method of recruitment, the provision and salary, training, armament, and so forth.

MILITARY BUILDUP

At first, Ya'qūb Beg recruited into the army only those who were unemployed or who could "give no account of themselves" while granting exemptions to the peasants (*zamīndār*) from the military obligation.[68] However, not satisfied with the limits of manpower available, he seems to have introduced later "a compulsory system of military service, keeping the voluntary system as but an aid in filling up the ranks of his forces."[69] Males between the ages of fifteen and thirty-five were subject to conscription, but the quota of recruitment does not seem to have been fixed, varying year by year according to the situation. Once conscripted, recruits were assigned to various regional armies, not necessarily in their hometowns, for an indefinite period of service (Figure 4.3). In addition to these local people who were forcibly conscripted, Ya'qūb Beg also attracted many foreigners to his army. His fame was so high at that time in the Islamic world that many foreigners came to Kashgharia in order to try their fortune or to fulfil their desire to fight in the holy war. The Khoqandians formed the majority of the foreign soldiers, but many Afghans and Indians were also found. Since they were usually more skilled and experienced in battle than Kashgharians, once they set foot in Kashgharia, Ya'qūb Beg tried every means to keep them under his service. Many were even forced to marry local women despite the fact they already had wives in their own countries.

Soldiers received their salaries both in cash and in kind. The exact amounts, however, are hard to determine. Kuropatkin writes,

> The payment and victualling of the army in Kashgaria were not regular or subject to any fixed rules. The amount of pay issued to the troops depended on whether they were on the march, or were stationed in barracks in the several towns, or were at the advanced posts, but chiefly on the condition of Yakoob Bek's cash deposits.[70]

Partly for this reason, even the scanty information available exposes wide differences in the amounts of their salary. For example, in 1868–69 R. B. Shaw heard from a certain *yüzbashi* that his pay was 300 *ṭillā*s (about 10 *yambu*) a year, and that a private soldier received 30 *ṭillā*s (about 1 *yambu*) a year. In case of war the rate of pay more than doubled.[71] However, in 1876–77, under favorable circumstances a private soldier received only 3–15 *tängä*s a month (about 0.03–0.16 *yambu* a year), a *dahbashi* 20 *tängä*s (about 0.21 *yambu* a year), a *panjāhbashi* 25 *tängä*s (about 1 *yambu* a year), and a *yüzbashi* 300 *tängä*s (about 3.3 *yambu*s a year).[72] Even considering various factors such as the possible inaccuracy of the figures, we are inclined to believe that there was a significant decrease in the amount of salary that the soldiers received at the end of Ya'qūb Beg's reign. In fact, the situation may have even been worse because the Russian embassy heard complaints from a soldier that he had received only two pieces of cloth and 25 *tängä*s

FIGURE 4.3. Soldiers from Kucha. Source: T. D. Forsyth, *Report of a Mission to Yarkund in 1873* (Calcutta: Foreign Department Press, 1875), photo no. 36.

during his entire five-year period of service.[73] That amount is the equivalent to only a month's pay for a daily laborer at that time.[74] Salary in kind, or more accurately provisions, consisted of (at least in principle) two pieces of bread and a dish of rice (*pilau*) every day plus a fixed amount of tea, flour, groats, and meat every month. Soldiers were also provided with cloth[75] and on the occasion of festivals, they would receive a bonus in cloth or in cash.[76]

Ya'qūb Beg employed three different ways of keeping his troops supplied with provisions. The first was to send the necessary amounts of grain directly to commanders of the regional armies and guard posts under the supervision of financial comptrollers known as *sarkār*. The second was to allot fixed tracts of state land on which hired laborers and/or the soldiers could produce their own food supplies. The final way was to farm out the tax revenue of one or more villages and direct their receipts toward the support of local army units.[77]

Ya'qūb Beg knew well that without renovating the army he would be unable to stand against the eventual Chinese strike. Although by the end of the sixties he had almost 40,000 troops, he realized that for the total military strength the sheer number was not sufficient if it was not backed up by adequate training, organization, armaments, and morale. The Muslims who had joined the ranks of the holy war in the 1864 rebellion may have had soaring enthusiasm but they were not properly equipped and trained. That was the reason the Kuchean army reaching almost 26,000 was soundly defeated at the battle of Khan Ariq by only 2,000 soldiers under Ya'qūb Beg. The arms of the Kuchean army, probably the most powerful in Eastern Turkestan at that time, were mostly taken from the Qing garrisons and those arms were hopelessly dilapidated. Although they used sword (*qilich*), arrows (*oq*), and spear (*näyzä*), sometimes even cannons (*top* or *zambarak*), rifles (*miltiq*), and gunpowder (*dura*), most of the peasant soldiers were simply armed with clubs or sticks (*kältäk*, *chomaq*, *tayaq*).[78]

Therefore, Ya'qūb Beg was keenly aware of the necessity for reinforcing his armaments. By 1870 he seems to have obtained a considerable number of rifles. R. B. Shaw who visited Kashgharia in 1868–69 saw Russian-made rifles. According to his report, there were about 1,000 such rifles and some of them were taken as booty and others were given by envoys from Russia. He also heard that they had begun to make imitations.[79] However, it is hard to believe that the Russians, with whom Ya'qūb Beg had gone to the verge of battle on the border of the Narin river in 1868, would have provided him a large number of rifles. Even though it is true that there were 1,000 rifles, most of these were probably of old style except for a few newer weapons. Our assumption is confirmed by the following remarks by A. N. Kuropatkin.

> Yakoob Bek stood in special need of firearms and cannon. Such of the former as he had were principally flint muskets, got partly from the independent States around, and partly manufactured in the local workshops. Beside flint muskets, Yakoob Bek contrived in the year 1868 to procure a small supply of sporting guns, with one and two barrels. Yakoob Bek's artillery was in a very bad condition.[80]

Ya'qūb Beg could not possibly have equipped his large number of troops by depending on the small flow of generally obsolete weapons that were traded into Eastern Turkestan. Therefore he attempted to open a number of direct channels through which he could purchase modern weapons in quantity. Initially he turned to his neighbor Afghanistan, but, as he was not satisfied with the outcome of the trade,[81] he began to look further afield for help. After opening relations with the Ottoman Empire and England, Ya'qūb Beg put considerable money and effort into negotiating arms purchases from those countries. It is not easy to find out the substance of direct and indirect forms of military aid from Britain, which did not want to make such aid public for fear of diplomatic conflicts with Russia. Nonetheless, it seems to be true that there was actually some military aid from Britain as was strongly suspected by Russians who visited Kashgharia. For example, when R. B. Shaw (1868–69) and T. D. Forsyth (1870, 1872–73) visited this country, they gave Ya'qūb Beg as a gift several hundred breech-loading rifles of the Snider type, muzzle-loading rifles of the Enfield type, and revolvers. According to Reintal', a Russian officer who visited Kashgharia in 1875, a considerable number of percussion rifles were delivered by Britain to Ya'qūb Beg, who built a factory for manufacturing rifles with British help and transformed 4,000 muzzle-loading rifles to breech-loaders. He added that the Kashgharians were capable of producing 16 rifles per week and there were "many English workmen" in Kashgharia. Although this report does not truthfully reflect the situation, and was acknowledged to be "somewhat exaggerated" even by the Russians themselves,[82] we cannot deny the fact that Britain's support helped Ya'qūb Beg's military buildup. However, such support generally took the form of donations through diplomatic channels or from sales by private merchants rather than official support on the governmental level.[83]

Compared to British assistance, it is noteworthy that the support from Ottoman Turkey was not only larger in scale but also proceeded openly and officially. Since the detailed contents of this support will be examined later when we deal with the question of the diplomatic relations with the Ottomans, suffice it to say here that Ya'qūb Beg received 1,200 rifles (200 of a new type and 1,000 of an old type) 6 cannons in 1873, and 2,000 rifles of Enfield type and 6 cannons for mountain terrain in 1875 with a large amount of ammunition and accessories. These were given *gratis* as a reward because Ya'qūb Beg accepted the vassal status of the Ottoman sultan. In addition, he also made his special envoy Sayyid Ya'qūb Khān purchase considerable amounts of armaments in Istanbul and Egypt. According to the report of Kuropatkin, Sayyid Ya'qūb Khān was instructed to buy 12,000 rifles in Istanbul but succeeded in bringing only half of that number to Kashghar and the rest were left because he could not fully meet the expense.[84]

Besides strengthening military armaments Ya'qūb Beg also put a lot of effort into introducing a new organization and training system so as to build a modern army. And he hoped to achieve this aim again through the aid of the Ottomans, and that was the reason he requested the dispatch of a number of Ottoman military officers. He was trying to reform the Kashgharian army based on the model of the Ottoman new military system (*nizām-i cedīd 'askerī*). Although we have almost no information about how he trained his soldiers in the early years, during the 1870s it seems to have been quite strict. According to the testimony of the Russian embassy in 1876, soldiers had to get up five o'clock in the morning and gather in front of their camps, except for Friday when they attended collective prayer at the mosques. They were trained for ten hours a day and the method of training was a mixture of Afghan, Hindu, and Russian styles, with some modifications introduced by Ya'qūb Beg himself. Kuropatkin wrote that "With regard to the infantry, the new training inculcated the manual exercise, especial skill in preserving an unbroken front, and in marching. The cavalry were taught changes of front, to ride past at the walk and at the trot, column of threes and sixes and dismounted exercise."[85] And most of the soldiers, though not all, appear to have put on uniforms.[86]

In this way, Ya'qūb Beg's army seemed to be well ordered and trained at least from its outward appearance, but, looking into it more closely, it turns out to have been a mixture of extremely diverse elements. Based on the observation of T. E. Gordon, it contained not only native Kashgharians and a number of Khoqandians but also Kashmiris, Hindus, Afghans, Kunjuts, Wakhis, Badakhshis, Chinese, Tungans, Mongols, Qirghizs, and so on.[87] Of these various groups in the army, the native Kashgharians were deemed the most lacking in the skills and spirit needed for fighting, while the Chinese and Tungan troops had been recruited mostly from prisoners of war. Those groups considered good in battle, such as the Kashmiris, Hindus and Afghans, were divided into small groups and stationed at different places.[88] Therefore, the group that Ya'qūb Beg most heavily relied on was the Andijanis, those approximately ten thousand Khoqandians whose fate was most closely tied to his own. Because of the great mixture of different ethnic groups even communication within the camps was not easy, which made it difficult to adopt one unified method of training.

In view of these problems, we can understand why Ya'qūb Beg hoped to reorganize the army and to introduce a more systematic way of training. It is curious, however, that he did not put his utmost effort in pursuing the military reform based on the Ottoman new army. This fact is confirmed by the reports of the Ottoman officers who served him and later returned to Istanbul. For example, 'Alī Kāzim, a military engineer with the title of *yüzbashi*, who had been dispatched to Kashghar in 1874, left the following report.

> His Highness Ya'qūb Khān assigned this humble servant to the service of His Eminence Mullā Yūnus, governor of Yarkand. So, in Yarkand which became my post, I worked as an austere military instructor for the purpose of organizing those who had no knowledge whatsoever about the military organization into one artillery battalion and teaching them close-order drills and other skills necessary for artillerymen, so that they could learn the military organization perfectly. This humble servant wished to give additional teachings based on the skills of military engineering which I had learned at the military school of Your Majesty, the Shadow of God, but His Highness Ya'qūb Khān told me that it would be unnecessary. Therefore, following his command that I should train the above-mentioned one battalion and another regiment of 3,000 with the skills of individual (*nefer*), company (*bölük*) and battalion (*tabur*) close-drills, I taught them based on the principle of military organization.[89]

Ya'qūb Beg seemed to have a somewhat reserved attitude toward the Ottoman officers. According to another source, the officers who came in 1875, including Ismā'īl Ḥaqq Efendi, were also assigned to Yarkand and allowed to give only two-hour training sessions a day, and they were forbidden to go alone out of the military camp.[90]

Why did Ya'qūb Beg not fully utilize the Ottoman officers and try to put restrictions to their activities? Mehmet Ātif, the author of *Kāşgar tārīhī* gives us two interesting explanations. The first was Ya'qūb Beg's concern that his special envoy to Istanbul, Sayyid Ya'qūb Khān, might become a future threat to him because of his revered status of *sayyid*, descendant of the Prophet. Therefore, Mehmet Ātif speculated, Ya'qūb Beg did not want any of the Ottoman officers who had maintained close relations with Sayyid Ya'qūb Khān to have strong influence on military matters. His second explanation was more practical: although Ya'qūb Beg wanted to reform his army badly, he was worried that these reforms would provoke internal opposition.[91] An interesting episode recorded in *Kāşgar tārīhī* supports this explanation. Once when Ya'qūb Beg was inspecting the troops being trained by Ismā'īl Ḥaqq Efendi, he expressed his dissatisfaction with the sufficiency of their training. To his criticism Ismā'īl responded as follows.

> The Ottoman sultan commanded us to come here so that we could serve you and do our utmost to educate and reform the army. We are determined to endeavor for Islam with our soul and body, but until this day we have been secluded in the house and could not do anything. If we could not discharge our duty to strengthen Islam, we would rather return to our country.[92]

At this protest Ya'qūb Beg was reported to have said "with tears in his eyes": "I also wish to reform the army as the sultan had done, but it is not time yet to execute it. How much time and effort were spent for the sultan to discard *Yeniçeri* and to build a new army?"[93]

This description seems to be fairly reliable because it was based on the personal accounts of Ismā'īl, and it suggests that Ya'qūb Beg was worried about the strong opposition from the Khoqandians, his principle supporters and main prop of military power, who could regard the all-out military reform as threatening their position. Our assumption becomes more convincing if we consider the fact that, although he relied on a small group of Khoqandian soldiers, he took extreme caution about their possible revolt and so he had to guard his power by extensive intelligence activities.

Nonetheless, he seems to have decided to adopt a more active policy for the reform in his later years. He transferred Ottoman officers like Ismā'īl Ḥaqq Efendi to his capital Kashghar to train the army. He personally participated in the training and showed such an enthusiasm that he said that "If I make a mistake during the training, rebuke me just like others!" He also ordered his army to wear trousers, coat and cap similar to those used in the Ottoman Empire. Later Ismā'īl Ḥaqq Efendi and Zamān Efendi were sent to Aqsu where they trained the troops under the direction of his son

Ḥaqq Quli.[94] Ya'qūb Beg introduced the Ottoman system of military organization into his infantry and cavalry. Though details are not available to us, each division seems to have been reorganized into several battalions (*tabur*) each of which in turn was divided into eight companies (*bölük*) in the case of the infantry, or eight squadrons (*takım*) in the cavalry. According to Kuropatkin's observation, one infantry company consisted of thirty columns and one cavalry company fifteen to sixteen columns. Thus, Ya'qūb Beg changed the principle of military division from the traditional system of ten (*dah*)–fifty (*panjāh*)–one hundred (*yüz*)–five hundred (*pānṣad*) to a new one that he borrowed from the current Ottoman system. However, this new system of division was applied only to a part of the Kashgharian army, and the cavalry continued to maintain the traditional decimal system.[95] We should remember that the Khoqandians formed the majority of the cavalry and it was they who made Ya'qūb Beg grasp the power. This fact suggests that he applied the new system basically to the infantry, which was recruited from the native population; he could not reform the cavalry because of a possible reaction from the Khoqandians.

In this way, Ya'qūb Beg secured an army whose number reached almost forty thousand and took various measures to strengthen his military power, but such a large number of troops could not be maintained without overburdening the Kashgharian economy. In addition to the expenses that were necessary just for the upkeep of the army, the costly expeditions such as those he launched against the Urumchi Tungans exhausted "a lot of governmental treasury."[96] Yet Ya'qūb Beg could neither reduce the number of his troops nor the amount of money spent in arms purchase because he had to be prepared for a future Chinese invasion. The result could be no other means than the increase of tax collection and the reduction of soldiers' salary, which in turn increased the economic burdens of people and lowered the morale of the soldiers. Another point that we should not forget to mention in relation to the weakness of his army is the heterogeneity of its composition. Many of the foreign mercenaries were detained against their will, as evidenced by the bitter complaint of one such soldier: "Our only chance is in some commotion arising, then we should be able to get away."[97] Also many Kashgharians were deeply dissatisfied with the domination of the army by the Khoqandians. Some of them even grumbled that they "were better off under the Chinese."[98]

Society and Religion

SOCIOECONOMIC CONDITIONS

Several decades of political turbulence had a serious impact on the societies of Eastern Turkestan and Zungharia. Many people died in battles while some others fled; the irrigation canals were left unattended for a long time; and trade, internal as well as external, shrank sharply. Yet the degree of the impact was not uniform over all the areas of Xinjiang. Generally speaking, Zungharia and the eastern extreme of Eastern Turkestan (Hami, Turfan, and Qarashahr) were hit harder than Kashgaria. The Ili valley probably fared the worst of all in terms of damage. Many cities and towns turned into complete ruins because of the fighting between the Qing troops and the Muslims, and then, between the Taranchis and the Tungans, which lasted altogether seven years. For instance, E. Schuyler who visited this area in 1873 describes the city of Ili (Huiyuan Cheng) as follows:

> For the whole distance, about ten miles, the road lay through a country which had formerly been well cultivated, but is now a desolated waste. At last we approached the edge of the town, when heaps of ruins presented themselves on every side, and sometimes a whole wall or a roofless house could be seen. Soon the ruins extended on both sides of us as far as we could see, and in front of us up to the very walls of the fortress. . . . Inside of the fortress walls, which were too strong to be destroyed, a similar scene met our view; but here the destruction had been much more complete. The two broad straight avenues were still plainly visible, as they were too wide to be encumbered with ruins; but the other streets were all blocked up by the fallen houses, and their course could scarcely be traced.[99]

On his way to the city of Ili, Schuyler also witnessed a series of other towns in desolation, such as Yarkent, which became "almost indistinguishable," Chimpantsi, where "not a single house was left standing," Khorgos, which "presented nothing but mere mounds," and Alimtu, "another ruined town."[100]

Many people were killed too. One Tungan *aqsaqal* of Suiding told him that "That morning [when Ili fell] there were in it 75,000 people with the army; that evening not a soul was left alive."[101] This may be an overstatement but undoubtedly reflects what actually happened in the city, for the statistics show a drastic reduction of the Ili population. The total population before the rebellion was counted approximately 350,000.[102] The 1876 census done by the Russians shows that the number went down to 131,910 (82,142 settled and 49,768 nomadic population).[103] Even in 1910, more than three decades later, the population of the Ili region had not fully recovered to its former level.[104] From this we can easily imagine the magnitude of the destruction in this region.

Urumchi fared no better than Ili. Many Chinese and Manchus were killed when Urumchi and neighboring areas fell into the hands of the Tungans. Later, during the two years of war (1870–72) with Ya'qūb Beg, numerous Tungans also died. Sayrāmī reports that 15,000 Tungans were killed in Urumchi and 2,000 in Manas when these cities were taken by Beg Quli. Although his estimation that almost 200,000 Tungans perished during this war seems to be much inflated,[105] it is not surprising at all that Zuo Zongtang found only 6,400 households in Urumchi where 23,800 households had been registered before the rebellion.[106] The German archaeologist Le Coq could see the ruins caused by the war between Ya'qūb Beg and the Tungans when he traveled from Turfan to Urumchi in the winter of 1904, almost thirty years after the war.[107]

The conditions in Qarashahr, Turfan, and Hami seem to have been as bad as in Ili or Urumchi. The British mission in 1873–74 reports that the area between Qarashahr and Ushaq Tal was as follows:

> It is about six days' journey in length, and was covered with a succession of Khitay homesteads; but these were all destroyed by the Amír, and the whole way up to Ush Aktal, a distance of fifty miles, is now a mass of ruined farms and deserted homesteads. . . . The population of the division [of Qarashahr] was formerly reckoned at 8,000 houses or 56,000 souls, but now, excepting the Musulman settlement of 300 houses on the river and the new fort built by the Amír, there is hardly anybody in the country.[108]

Because of the destruction of the cultivation and the decreased population, the Qing court, after the reconquest, allowed the area of Qarashahr to be exempted from taxes in 1878.[109] Turfan which had been "one of the most populous and flourishing of all the States of Káshghar" also "suffered frightfully during the late revolution of the Tungani and succeeding conquest by the Amír, and now it is described as a long succession of ruined farmsteads and barely tenanted settlements."[110]

On the other hand, the area to the west of Qarashahr, though not immune from the destruction, was in a better condition than the above-mentioned areas. Although Western visitors could notice somewhat dilapidated conditions in some parts of the cities or in the countryside,[111] the Kashgharian society in general showed enough resilience to recover from whatever destruction had been done. Travelers who traversed this region evidenced how the cultivation and the irrigation were well managed. For example, Shaw did not encounter any ruin of the peasant economy: "As far as the eye could see, there stretched a highly cultivated plain to which orchards and groves of trees surrounding the numerous scattered homesteads gave almost the appearance of wood."[112] The 1873 British mission received the same impression. In Khan Ariq and Qizil Buy near Kashghar, one of its members "carried on a traverse survey wherever he went, which has thrown some light on the intricate maze of rivers and canals which irrigate the villages that are thickly scattered over the whole of the ground visited by him."[113] They witnessed a similar well-cultivated and well-irrigated scene in the Artush and Yarkand areas.[114]

Zuo Zongtang's report which shows the tax collection in grain by the Qing government in 1878, one year after the reconquest, supports our conclusion that Kashgharia was in a far better condition than the other areas of Xinjiang. The amount of grain levied in each city was recorded as follows (unit is *shi*): Zhendi (6,940), Turfan (14,200), Kashghar (60,508), Yangihissar (20,612), Yarkand (79,412), Khotan (36,879), Aqsu (14,230), Ush Turfan (8,378), Kucha (12,849), and Qarashahr (exempted; 6,598 in 1879), which made a total of 254,008 *shi*. Although he did not mention Ili and Urumchi, this amount was, as he pointed out, almost 120,000–130,000 *shi* more than what had been levied prior to the rebellion.[115] These numbers clearly show that the great majority of the revenue came from the area to the west of Qarashahr and suggests that the agricultural production in Kashgharia did not decrease, or it may have even increased, compared to that prior to the rebellion.

One can point out several reasons for such a conspicuous contrast in the socioeconomic conditions between Zungharia and Kashgharia. First of all, more Manchu troops and Chinese colonists were found in Zungharia during the Qing rule, and naturally it took a longer time for the Muslims to take hold of this area than Kashgharia. During the rebellion many Muslims died, and the Manchus and the Chinese were almost exterminated. The two years of protracted warfare between Ya'qūb Beg and the Urumchi Tungans must have devastated the whole area from Turfan up to Manas and killed many Tungans. In the Ili valley disastrous fighting lasted longer than in Urumchi, and the destruction there was almost complete. Compared to these, the revolts in Kashgharia entailed fewer casualties, partly because of the smaller number of the Chinese and the Manchus and partly because of the swift success of the movement. Also, though there was internal fighting between regional Muslim groups, the effects were not so disastrous as in Zungharia, and the conquest of Kashgharian cities by Ya'qūb Beg, once he had consolidated his base in Kashghar and Yangihissar, was swift and usually not followed by massive killings. Khotan was probably the only exception where a large number of people were killed.[116]

EFFORTS FOR RECOVERY

Ya'qūb Beg had to strengthen the economic capability of Eastern Turkestan in order to support at least 40,000 soldiers, but it was not an easy task. Although the Qing court had stationed approximately the same number of troops, these had received large annual subsidies derived from other provinces in China. To maintain the huge number of troops, Ya'qūb Beg had to find sufficient human and financial resources. According to the two Western reports drawn up after extensive research in the country during the seventies, the level of the total population in the region went down compared to that prior to the rebellion. The British report observed that the actual number of the population under Ya'qūb Beg in 1873 was less than 1,015,000 (145,000 households) which was "the revenue reckoning of the

Chinese rulers" before the rebellion, while the Russian mission concluded that the population in 1825 which had reached 1,500,000 decreased to 1,200,000 in 1876.[117] Some sources mention that he ordered a cadastral survey for the Urumchi area.[118] Though we do not know whether similar surveys were done in Kashgharia, it is certain, as Sayrāmī tells, that he tried to eliminate the floating population and to turn them into a working force.

Those who were obstinate and troublesome, villains, unbridled ones, thieves, gamblers, abusers, and pigeoners—all those who were living by ridiculing others, fearing the stern fury of Ataliq Ghāzī, sought the forgiveness from him and, then, settled down to work. If any one was caught fighting and disputing or making a false litigation, he was sent immediately to *yüzbashi*, *pānṣad*, or *jilād* (executioner), and made a soldier.[119]

It was reported that Ya'qūb Beg brought twenty thousand Tungans from Urumchi to Kashgharia when he was returning after the first Urumchi expedition.[120] Those Chinese who survived the rebellion were forced to adopt Islam and employed as soldiers, artisans, or farmers. At the same time, Ya'qūb Beg tried to keep as many foreigners as he could. These foreigners, once they came into Ya'qūb Beg's dominion and served under him, could not return to their countries as freely as they had come. We do not know how many of them were living in Eastern Turkestan during the period of Ya'qūb Beg's rule. According to Valikhanov, in the late 1850s before the rebellion broke out, the total number of foreigners in Altishahr, that is, the western part of Eastern Turkestan, was about 145,000, or approximately one-fourth of the entire native Kashgharian population.[121] This number may have been inflated, but whatever the number of foreigners was before the rebellion, it is likely to have increased after the emergence of Ya'qūb Beg.

Ya'qūb Beg paid special attention to the artisans who could provide him with a variety of military equipment. He mobilized them, as well as unskilled laborers, and built workshops (*ishkhāna*) in large cities like Kashghar, Yarkand, and Khotan. These workshops, run by the state, were of an unprecedented scale, where almost fifty thousand artisans and workers were employed.[122] The craftsmen of precious metals made girdles, quivers, bridles, cruppers, and saddle-girths in gold and silver; the ironsmiths produced rifles, swords, sabers, stirrups, cannons, and arrows; the tailors made embroidered garments and silken cloth; and many other artisans were put together like carpenters, nailers, and metal casters.[123] They were organized along the professions and placed under the masters (*üstäbashi*) who were supervised in their turn by the headmasters (*ishbashi*).[124] One should not regard this system of workshop as a kind of forced labor camp because the participation in the workshops was voluntary at least at its earlier stages. The artisans received a daily wage or monthly salary and provisions for their work.[125] For example, workers at the carpet workshops in Khotan run by the state received 20 *puls* a day, whereas if one provided the government with his products while working in his own house, he was supplied with food gratis and paid 10 *puls*.[126] Ya'qūb Beg's goal of establishing large-scale state workshops lay in organizing the laborers for systematic and effective production.

There were also a large number of miners working on the ores of gold, copper, and iron. In some cases they were self-employed, and in others they had contracts with agents who sold the metals to the government or the market. Extensive gold mines were found in the Khotan region where more than seven thousand miners, mostly drawn from the poor, were working. The government appropriated one-fifth of the original yield of gold, and the miners could sell the rest to licensed dealers under the supervision of government officials. The government further reserved the right to purchase the remaining four-fifths of the yield from the dealers at a rate slightly lower than the market price. To stop illegal hoarding and contraband sales, officials sometimes searched the bodies or the houses of the workers. In case of violations, the punishment was initially lenient, but it appears to have grown harsher toward the end of Ya'qūb Beg's rule.[127] Iron ores were found in the Qizil Tagh,[128] to the northwest of Yarkand, and copper mines in Aqsu, Bai and Kucha. The government practiced no monopoly on this mining, but did keep the smelting furnaces under supervision. The famous jade industry of Khotan was not so active during this period because of the want of Chinese jade cutters.

While Ya'qūb Beg succeeded considerably in remobilizing the people and in organizing the labor force, the condition of internal economy was not much improved. Before the time of Ya'qūb Beg, commercialization and the money economy had been poorly developed, and barter had been a predominant mode of economic transactions in this region. The limited amount of money in circulation and the rapid changes in the comparative value of silver vs. copper money seriously hampered the development of the money economy. To these problems the widespread existence and use of foreign coins, like those of Bukhara and Khoqand, and of counterfeit coins, especially made by the Qirghiz, added to the confusion and distrust of the people for the money. For these reasons daily economic activities remained on the level of exchange.

There is no indication that the situation improved during the period of Ya'qūb Beg. Giving a portion of their products to the government as tax and retaining another for their subsistence, people could turn only a limited amount of their products into the market. The bazaar was the place through which one could get the best view of the commercial activities in Kashgharia at that time.[129] On every market day people from the surrounding villages swarmed into the bazaar; they came with grain, fruits, cotton, poultry, or home-woven cloth, and so on, and bartered those items with whatever they needed for daily life, such as ready-made cloth, hats, boots, belts, and so forth. Money was rarely involved in these transactions. Indigenous Kashgharian merchants had a small amount of capital and little political protection. Even if they made profits, they were afraid of acknowledging their good fortune.[130] Chinese merchants disappeared, but the role and the wealth they had managed to keep were now transferred to the Khoqandians or a few other merchants who enjoyed political protection.

One important event in the field of the internal economy was the introduction of new coins. Even though money was not a predominant medium of economic transactions, its existence was known long before the time of Ya'qūb Beg.[131] After the expulsion of the Qing power from Eastern Turkestan, the old coins continued to be used, while new coins were introduced. Rāshidīn Khwāja established foundries in Aqsu and Kucha where *pul* was stamped, bearing the name of the city, for example, "*ḍarb-i dār al-salṭānat-i Kūchā*" (minted in the kingdom of Kucha), and the name of the ruler, that is, "*Sayyid Ghāzī Rāshidīn Khān.*"[132] But they went out of circulation with the end of the Kuchean regime. It is reported that Ḥabīb Allāh of Khotan also minted *aq tängä* bearing the phrase of *shahāda*, "*lā illāh illā allāh Muḥammad rasūl allāh*" ("There is no god but Allāh, and Muḥammad is His apostle") on one side and "*ḍarb-i Khotan-i laṭīf*" (minted in the city of Khotan) on the other.[133] Unfortunately, no specimen has been known to survive.

Ya'qūb Beg also made new coins, about which Sayrāmī made an interesting remark. According to his assertion, Ya'qūb Beg, before opening formal relations with the Ottoman empire, minted gold coins (*ṭillā*) in the name of Mallā Khan (r. 1858–62) of the Khoqand khanate, and copper coins (*mīs pul*) in imitation of old Qing coins.[134] Another source confirms that Ya'qūb Beg made gold coins in the name of Mallā Bahādur Khān.[135] Throughout the history of the Islamic world, the coinage (*sekke*) and the sermon on the Friday prayer (*khuṭba*) have been the two most important signs showing the locus of sovereignty. From the fact that Ya'qūb Beg ordered *sekke* in the name of Mallā Khan we can learn one important fact. His act apparently signified that while he was not claiming his own independent sovereignty, he was acknowledging only the suzerainty of a Khoqand khan who no longer existed. This allowed him to explicitly deny the authority of the current Khoqand khan, Khudāyār. In this sense, the minting of new coins was tantamount to the proclamation of his virtual independence while avoiding the criticism of being a usurper.

Ya'qūb Beg's policy seeking the legitimate source of his rulership from some other established political power did not change to the end of his reign. Later, he sent his envoy to Istanbul asking Sultan 'Abdülazīz to accept his country as one of the sultan's protectorates and to give a blessing to his rule of Eastern Turkestan. After the envoy returned to Kashghar with the recognition of the sultan, he ordered in the first week of December 1873, the striking of two kinds of new coin—*aq tängä* and *qizil ṭillā*—and praying the Friday sermon all in the name of the sultan.[136] Although we should not ignore the economic considerations behind his decision to make new coins (for example, to inject new blood into the old monetary system so that the economy of the country could gain some stability and vigor, or to provide intermediate monetary units larger than *pul* but smaller than *yambu* to pay his soldiers), it is also important to take into consideration the political motivation, that is, the outward expression of his political legitimacy.

According to various sources, there were several other kinds of coins in use during Ya'qūb Beg's rule. The smallest monetary unit was *pul*. This copper coin had existed well before the Qing conquest and continued in use after that. It was also called by the local people *qara pul* or *khoichan*, from Chinese *heiqian* meaning "the black cash," and in Chinese it was called *dangwu* ("worth five"). Two *puls* made one *darchin* or *dolchan* (both from Chinese *daqian*, "large cash"), which was no other than *dangshi* ("worth ten"). All these were made in copper. Fifty *puls* or twenty-five *darchins* made one *tängä* in silver, equivalent to one *liang*. Before Ya'qūb Beg's time, *tängä* had not been real money, but had existed only as an indicator of monetary value. Two kinds of *tängä* were circulated, one Kashgharian minted by Ya'qūb Beg and the other Khoqandian, two of the former being taken as the same value as one Khoqandian *tängä*. Also a few kinds of *ṭillā* in gold (Kashgharian, Khoqandian, and Bukharan) existed. In addition to these minted coins, there was a silver ingot called *yambu* (from Chinese *yuanbao*) of "the shape of a deep boat with projecting bow and stern."[137] The largest one weighed about 50 *liangs* or 50 *sers*, approximately 2 kg, and there were several other smaller ones of the same shape.

During the years of the rebellion external trade was almost completely cut off. Direct trade with China was nonexistant and only a small amount of Chinese goods were brought into Kashgharia indirectly via Russian territory where the chief emporium was in Vernoe (present Alma-Ata).[138] Naturally tea which had been the foremost import from China was in great scarcity. In 1865 W. H. Johnson witnessed how the people of Khotan dug up the sand-buried old towns and found the tea. He wrote that "The only one [of those towns] that is well known is that in which very large quantities of brick tea are found, and which commands a ready sale in the markets, now that all trade with China is stopped."[139]

The trade of Russia with Eastern Turkestan which was about to flourish could not avoid a serious impact too. In his letter to General Kaufman in 1868, Ya'qūb Beg wrote: "Now, after the destruction of the Chinese power, during six years all has been destroyed that was good and that which commerce had created, so that nothing remains of it all. This was the reason why

your rich merchants were not allowed here, for they could find nothing here but ruins."[140] Although his intention for writing this was to justify his policy not allowing Russian merchants to come to Kashgharia, it certainly reflects the reality. The flow of the Russian goods into Kashgharia through Tokmak in the north or Osh in the west was stopped or greatly impeded during the years of 1864–67. According to one report, during the period of December 1868–December 1869 (13 months) the total amount of the exports and the imports together between the two countries through the Tokmak–Narin route was 274,665 rubles, which suggests that the amount of trade in the year of 1869 would have been at most 250,000 rubles. In 1870 the size of the trade did not show much change, recording 224,025 rubles. But in 1871 the amount almost tripled to 604,710 rubles.[141] The trade via the Tokmak and Narin route took about 85 percent of the entire trade between Russia and Kashgharia, so the increase of the trade volume through this route directly affected the total amount of the trade between the two countries.[142] Probably this rapid increase of the trade volume was one of the reasons Russia pushed Ya'qūb Beg to conclude the commercial treaty of 1872. In the same year the trade went over a million rubles. However, it did not further increase to the end of Ya'qūb Beg's reign.[143]

The Kashgharian trade with India and Kashmir also shows a similar fluctuation to that with Russia; the total volume of Indian–Kashghar trade reached the nadir during the years of 1864–66 and showed a sign of recovery in 1867, recording 227,000 rupees (imports and exports together), but next year the amount was doubled and then continued to grow slowly. Owing to the treaty with the British government in 1874, the trade in 1874 recorded 1,315,000 rupees, but after that year the trade volume did not show any substantial increase.[144]

The cause of such an insignificant change in external trade even after the treaties should be attributed, first of all, to the political uncertainty of the Kashgharian state, its geographical barriers, and to the limited capacity of Kashgharia as a market. But, at the same time, we should not forget another factor, that is, Ya'qūb Beg's cautious attitude toward the expansion of trade with neighboring countries. By concluding commercial treaties with Russia and England he intended to enhance his international political stance and to neutralize the direct threat from Russia rather than to facilitate international trade itself. The fact that even after the conclusion of the treaties many foreign merchants were subjected to various sorts of arbitrary treatments from the government of Kashgharia also supports this point. Ya'qūb Beg may have thought that a drastic increase of the foreign trade, being followed by the influx of foreign goods and merchants, would entail unexpected changes and jeopardize the security of his dominion.

In contrast to his lukewarm attitude toward the expansion of the external trade, Ya'qūb Beg put not a small effort to facilitate internal communication and to enforce security. He put milestones or *tash* (stones) along the main roads to indicate the distance between important cities. As mentioned earlier, Mahī al-Dīn Makhdūm obtained the epithet of 'Mīrzā Farsakh' by his work of erecting such stone posts. Ya'qūb Beg also built numerous halting places (*langar*), small forts (*qurghancha*) along the road, and guard posts (*qarawul*) on the borders to facilitate communication and to ensure security. He himself often supervised and participated in such constructions, being "covered with dust" and even had "his leg hurt by the fall of a stone."[145] The mountain nomads, especially Qirghiz and Sariqolis, who in the time of the Chinese rule often attacked and levied tolls from travelers and merchants, were brought under control. A member of the British embassy described the security of the passage as follows.

> . . . if a man drop his *whip* in the middle of the plain, he will find it there if he looks for it a year afterwards. This is a favourite saying amongst the people of Eastern Turkestan, which I have heard more than once employed to describe the sense of security enjoyed under the present *régime*.[146]

However, we should not forget that the security enforced by the stern rule of Ya'qūb Beg was rather close to "security by terror,"[147] or to the policy of "blood and iron."[148] And to understand the establishment of the internal security we should also take into account the religious policy of Ya'qūb Beg.

REVIVAL OF ISLAMIC SPIRIT

One of the most distinctive changes in social and religious life in Eastern Turkestan during his rule was the strong reaction against the moral laxity, from the Islamic viewpoint, which had pervaded the region during the rule of the infidels. Under the Qing rule people used to drink wine freely and publicly; almost no public entertainment was complete without dancing, and women could walk the streets with unveiled faces. A nineteenth-century observer considered the reason for such a "lack of fanaticism" among the people of Eastern Turkestan to be their unique historical experience, that is, the frequent contacts with the Chinese culture but less frequent interaction with their western neighbors.[149] His viewpoint seems to reflect the general opinion of the contemporary Muslims that the source of the "degeneration" of the Islamic spirit was the Chinese rule.

As soon as the Muslims gained victory over the Qing, their leaders took the measures of purging the infidels and forcing people to observe strictly the *sharī'ah* regulations. In Ush Turfan a severe religious persecution against some Sufi orders, especially the Kubrawiyya, took place, and in Khotan Ḥabīb Allāh enforced almost unprecedentedly rigorous observation of the *sharī'ah*. The leaders in Urumchi even named their newly created government *Qingzhen guo* (Kingdom of Islam). Ya'qūb Beg, who eliminated all these regional powers, was no exception. However, he had not been a revered religious figure and killed many religious leaders, such as Ḥabīb Allāh, Rāshidīn, Jamāl al-Dīn, Walī Khān, Kättä Khān, and Kichik Khān. He also expelled Buzurg with an excuse that Buzurg was making a pilgrimage to Mecca.[150]

These acts certainly provoked fury and anger from many Kashgharians, so Ya'qūb Beg put his utmost effort into refreshing his image as a holy warrior as well as protector of Islam. He could have assumed the title of *khan* or *sulṭān*, but he did not because he wanted to avoid giving the impression of being a usurper. Instead, he preferred the titles like Ataliq Ghāzī or Badaulat because of the religious aura these titles carried. His acknowledgment of the Ottoman sultan as his suzerain was also motivated by a similar desire and his effort was redeemed by the title of *amīr* (or *amīr al-mū'minīn*) bestowed by the sultan.

Ya'qūb Beg put not a small effort for the revival of Islamic spirit to strengthen his legitimacy. He sent a Qur'ān reciter to Mecca in order to set up a hostel (*takiya-khāna*) in the name of Yättishahr.[151] He also ordered the building and repair of many mausoleums, mosques, and praying houses, and to provide *vaqf* funds to religious institutions.[152] He introduced public baths (*ḥammām*) in Kashgharia where they had not existed up to that time. In particular he rebuilt the arch (*gumbad*) of the shrine of Khwāja Āfāq in Kashghar, and ordered builders to put a new praying house and a mosque inside the mausoleum.[153] He regularly paid visits to this shrine which was one of the most celebrated holy places in Eastern Turkestan. He also ordered repairs to the tombs of Bibi Miriyām and Satuq Boghra Khan. It was reported that the number of religious buildings that he constructed or repaired reached almost sixty.[154] Some people even utilized his religious attitude for their own benefit: two shaykhs from Badakhshan, one of them claiming himself "Mahdī of the Last Day," came to Kashgharia and tried to manipulate Ya'qūb Beg. At first, he seems to have been terrified by the warnings of these pretenders and complied with their directions, but later, after consulting with *'ulamā*, ordered them to be put into a pit and be killed by throwing stones.[155]

Ya'qūb Beg not only strictly observed the *sharī'ah* rules himself but also required his subjects to do the same. The following portrayal by Sayrāmī vividly depicts his religious and grave attitude.

> He was the man of medium height and stout build, with upright body like a barley stick, a face of rosy complexion and soft beards. At first, he was temperate and acted with prudence and led his life obeying the regulations of *sharī'ah*. His manners and conduct were almost like those of revered saints or intelligent scholars. His cloth resembled that of noble merchants, and his horses and outfits were not better than those of "captain of fifty" (*panjāhbashi*). When he sat down, he kneeled, like a cam-

el, on a white prayer-carpet or on a mat with his head covered with turban. No one ever saw him loosen his belt binding the loin or sit cross-legged. Neither did he sit on a raised dais or a sofa table: most of the time he just sat in front of his tent, on a mat or low ground. He never set his foot on the soil without performing ablution.[156]

Ya'qūb Beg himself took a transportable tent-mosque, pulled by twenty horses, whenever he traveled. Daily prayers were strictly enforced, and for that purpose he ordered all the *mu'azzin*s of the court and the mosques in towns as well as villages, to start to call for prayer and to end exactly at the same time. It was reported that even each shop had to have one *mu'azzin*. Nobody could walk around the streets or the bazaars without wearing a turban (*dastār*); if somebody was found wearing a fur cap (*tumaq*) or a skull cap (*doppa*), it was instantly torn off and taken away.[157] To enforce the observation of the rules, he placed a number of religious officials in cities and towns as well as in the army.[158] For example, the officials called *qāḍī ra'īs*, aided by several *muḥtasib*s equipped with a whip called *dira*, regularly patrolled the streets and the bazaar.

He examines the weights in the retail shops, and flogs such as have short weights; or in serious cases sends the offenders before the *mufti* for judgment. His own powers do not exceed the summary infliction of 20 to 40 stripes of the dira, and these are freely bestowed on women appearing unveiled in the streets, on gamblers, drunkards, brawlers, and disorderly characters, and such as neglect the stated hours of prayer, and others.[159]

Those who wanted to travel beyond their own districts were required to have passports issued by the local authority. If anyone was found in other districts without a proper passport, he was sent to a police station for inquiry.[160] Fasts and public prayers were enforced while drinking wine, smoking narcotics or tobacco, singing, dancing, and playing music were all prohibited both in public and in private.[161] The following remarks by Kuropatkin seem to depict aptly the social milieu of the time.

He has acted as though he would turn the country into one vast monastery, in which the new monks must, whilst cultivating the soil with the sweat of their brow, give as much as possible—nay, the greater part of their earnings—into the hands of the Government, to devote to warlike impulse.[162]

Taxation

TAXES

The government collected three kinds of regular tax: *'ushr* (or *kharāj*), *ṭanāb*, and *zakāt*. The usage of the two terms—*'ushr* and *kharāj*—was more or less interchangeable in modern Central Asia, both meaning the tax on the grain production. Originally *'ushr* had been the tithe taken from the produce of the land owned by Muslims, whereas *kharāj* was the levy on the land of non-Muslims and, in most cases, it was heavier than *'ushr*. However, the more people converted to Islam, the more the land paying *'ushr* came into being and the less the amount of revenue was collected. Actually the rapid conversion of the people in Khurasan and Transoxiana in the first half of the eighth century owed much to their desire to throw away the burden of *kharāj*. As the revenue income reduced drastically because of the massive conversion of the non-Muslim population to Islam, the Umayyad government tried not to change their tax status accordingly. The inconsistency of these terms in this period did not disappear even after most of the population in Central Asia converted to Islam and *kharāj* lost its ground for existence in principle.[163] *'Ushr* was in theory one tenth of the whole production of all cereal crops and it was usually paid in kind. The reality, however, was different as the British embassy witnessed: "in practice much more is exacted by the Collectors for their own benefit, and whilst at Yangi Hissar we saw Government orders upon certain settlements for the collection of the 'ushr at the rate of three parts in ten."[164]

Ṭanāb was the tax on orchards, meadows, or the fields raising non-cereal crops like cotton, but the term itself was originally a measure of length that differed according to regions and periods. The Qing government had also made a distinction in taxing the land for cereal crops and that for non-cereal crops. For the former the measure was *batman*, the land where one could sow the cereal of 5 *shi* (bushel) 3 *dou* (pint).[165] One tenth of the products from the privately owned lands, or half from the government-owned land, had been taken. As for the land of non-cereal crops, it is not clear whether the measure of *ṭanāb* had been used officially by the Qing government but it was certainly used by Khoqand *aqsaqal*s in Kashgharia when they collected tax from the cotton-fields and the orchards owned by the Khoqandians and the *chalghurt*s, 10 *tängä*s from the orchards and 5 *tängä*s from every *ṭanāb* of the suburban fields and meadows.[166] This kind of tax was called *ṭanābāna* in Khoqand, and when Ya'qūb Beg conquered Kashgharia, he seems to have extended this practice to other land owned by the Kashgharians.

According to Valikhanov, in the late 1850s 1 *ṭanāb* in Kashgharia was 0.375 *desiatina*, that is, 4,050 m^2.[167] But the Forsyth mission reports that in the year of 1873 1 *ṭanāb* equaled 47 yards and that "any space on two sides by a line of that length is called a tanab of land"[168] which would be 1,849 m^2. Shaw also notes that 1 *ṭanāb* was "a square of land whose side is 40 *gaz* in length, each *gaz* being about 3 feet 6 inches," which equals to 1,820 m^2.[169] It is not certain whether the difference between assertions of Valikhanov on the one hand and of the Forsyth mission and Shaw on the other was due to an actual change in the length of a *ṭanāb* or to a mistake of either of the two sides, or to the difference of the area from which they drew the data. In the early seventies the *ṭanāb* tax varied from 1 or 2 to 8 or 10 *tängä*s "according to the nature and value of the crop."[170] At the end of his rule, one had to pay 20 *tängä*s from one *ṭanāb*.[171]

Zakāt (alms), one of the five pillars of Islam, had been originally used either for the common cause or for the needs of the poor. Later, however, it came to mean the custom duty and was used not necessarily for the original purpose of charity. In the late nineteenth-century Kashgharia *zakāt* was 1/40 of all livestock and of merchandise entering the country. Yet prior to the treaties with Russia in 1872 and with England in 1874, from the merchandise of the non-Muslims 5 percent of the *zakāt* tax at the *ad valorem* rate had been taken, and every Hindu merchant had to pay an additional 2 *tängä*s of poll tax (*jizya*) every month, as long as they stayed in the dominion of Ya'qūb Beg. After the treaties, the poll tax on the Hindus was dropped and the rate of 2.5 percent applied to all foreign merchants.

These three regular taxes—*'ushr*, *ṭanāb*, and *zakāt*—were the major items of the governmental income. All these existed before the time of Ya'qūb Beg. When the Zunghars conquered Kashgharia and made its inhabitants their *albatu*, that is, those who had the obligation to pay *alban* (duty), people had to send a certain amount of *alban* to Ili. According to Muslim sources, it comprised three: *jizya*, *bāj* (custom tax), and *kharāj*.[172] The Qing government, after the conquest of Kashgharia, basically preserved the old system of the Zunghars, with some later modifications.[173] The Qing court, being pressed hard by the Khoqand khanate from the late 1820s, gave up the right, on behalf of the khanate, to collect the *zakāt* tax from all the foreign merchants in the western Kashgharian cities, with the exception of the Kashmiris and Badakhshis, as a result of the 1832 agreement.

The rates of the regular taxes were observed only on paper, and people, especially tenant farmers, had to hand over several times more than what they were supposed to. During the Qing rule those who worked on state land (*khaniyya zamīn*) could have only half of the products but there is no doubt that they lost more because of the exploitations by governmental functionaries. Ya'qūb Beg's period was not an exception either. The land that had been in possession of the Qing government and of high beg-officials came into the hands of Ya'qūb Beg, who sold it to private owners or farmed out taxes to governmental officials or military units. Even some hereditary owners and lease-holders had to renew their right by purchase.[174] It is reported that if somebody worked on another's land one-tenth of the product went to the state as *'ushr* and three-fourths of the rest to the landowner.[175] Therefore, what he obtained was 22.5 percent of the original products, of course in principle.

Besides these regular taxes and their abusive practices, peasants also faced several other irregular taxes like *kafsen*, *saman-pul*, *tarāka*, and *qonalgha*. A certain portion of the peasants' products was taken on behalf of begs and *sarkārs* to recompense their non-salary jobs and it was called *kafsen*. Western Turkestan had the same custom.[176] For example, a *mīrāb* also received his share from *aqsaqals* who had to give him 2 percent of the whole output of corn in their villages, of which a half was turned over to the government.[177] Such a share was called *mīrābāna* in the Khoqand khanate.[178] According to Kuropatkin, tax-collectors received two sacks of straw (generally wheat) from every *batman* of grain coming as *kharāj* and it was called *saman-pul*. The form of payment was later changed to cash.[179] This is probably what the Forsyth mission described: "With every 30 [*sic.*, mistake of 3] charaks of grain the Hakim will claim one donkey-load of straw, or an equivalent amounting to 1 tanga 36 pul."[180] There existed the inheritance tax, called *tarāka* (inheritance), also pronounced as *tarika*, by which the state took 2.5 percent from the property of the deceased. Sometimes the rate was doubled.[181] But this tax was often abused to divest the property from those whose forefathers amassed fortunes during the Qing rule by serving as beg officials and who were discontented with the rule of Ya'qūb Beg. Officials went to their houses and estimated the property of inheritors as much higher than its real value. So even though he sold all that he had inherited, he could not pay the tax which was in theory 1/40 of the property.[182] Besides, people frequently had to satisfy the demands, at least in part, of foreign embassies, and sometimes even provide lodging for soldiers, which was called *qonalgha* (quartering).[183]

This situation was aggravated by the fact that governmental officials, including governors, did not have a fixed salary. The revenue that was actually collected by these functionaries must have far exceeded the stipulated amount of the taxes because they had to obtain their shares from the portion of collected taxes that remained for local expenses. To satisfy, more often to maximize, their shares, they usually increased the quota of revenue at each village. The central government seems to have tacitly acknowledged the practice as long as it received the necessary amounts.

Besides the revenue sent to the central government, the governors had to pay a visit twice a year with a huge amount of presents (*tartuq*) to insure their posts. It was called *toqsan* (ninety) because the tribute consisted of the symbolic number of nine or nine times nine.[184] The items of such presents were "a large number of horses, of bales of robes, of carpets, of silken webs, of packages of tea, and of sugar, of plates containing gold and silver money or bars or ingots."[185] For example, Niyāz Beg, the governor of Khotan, once brought to Ya'qūb Beg to regain his favor "seventy camel-loads of presents (or tribute), together with two horse-loads of silver," and a Yarkand governor presented him 100 *yambus* of silver with "thirty horses, mounted by as many slaves." The governor of Guma once gave him "Nine trays of tillahs (400 or 500 each tray), nine trays of yamboos, &c., &c."[186]

Of course this financial burden was not on the governor but on the taxpayers to whom he swiftly turned for recuperation. Sayrāmī deplored that by this kind of extortion Niyāz (Khotan), ʿAbd al-Raḥmān (Aqsu) and Muḥammad Amīn (Bai and Sairam) "brought an enormous ruin" to the country.[187] Yaʿqūb Beg, on his part, bestowed robes of value, girdles and firearms. Generally they, especially the robes, were called *sar-o-pā* (literally head and feet).

COLLECTORS

For the collection of various forms of taxes in the provinces there were officials like *sarkār* (financial supervisor), *zakātchi* (collector of the *zakāt* tax), and *mīrzā*. Shaw defines *sarkār* as "an official (of great or small degree) charged with the duty of collecting and re-distributing or accounting for the revenues in kind, of a large or small district or village under the orders of its governor or head-man; also with all the works of making up or repair of moveable Government property."[188] He says in another place that *sarkār*, which he translates as "comptroller of the household," was "an official in charge of all the royal stores."[189] Although Kuropatkin wrote that *sarkār*s were appointed by the governor and were responsible for furnishing a certain fixed amount of revenue, either in kind or in cash, to the treasury,[190] other sources show that Yaʿqūb Beg himself appointed provincial *sarkār*s. For example, Sayrāmī notes that "Yaʿqūb Beg gave ʿAla al-Dīn Beg as *sarkār* to Muḥammad Baba Toqsaba"[191] who was the governor of Ush Turfan. According to another source, when they collected taxes, they divided the portion that was to go to the central government and the portion that was to go to the governor. In principle, the governor's share from his own province consisted of only a part of the *kharāj* tax (one donkey-load of grain from every three *chäräk*s of *kharāj*), and the rest was either sent to the central government or disposed for the expense of the regional army.[192] From this information we can draw a conclusion that in each province several *sarkār*s existed as officials in charge of collecting, storing, and distributing taxes and that they were headed by one principal *sarkār* whom Yaʿqūb Beg often appointed. Similar offices were found in Bukhara (*dīvān-i sarkār*)[193] and in Khoqand (*sarkār* and *sarkārbashi*).[194]

Zakātchi (or, *ʿāmil al-zakāt*) was an official appointed by Yaʿqūb Beg on the provincial level for the collection of the *zakāt* tax. Sayrāmī recollects that Mīrzā Baba Beg, whom he served for seven years as *mīrzā*, was made the *zakātchi* of Aqsu by Yaʿqūb Beg and took charge of the collection of *zakāt* in the area from Ush Turfan to Kurla. Postal communications were also under his control.[195] Similar offices probably existed in other provinces, but we do not know how many there were, since, if we believe Sayrāmī, Mīrzā Baba Beg alone controlled three different provinces (Ush Turfan, Aqsu, and Kucha). *Zakātchis'* assistants, like Sayrāmī, were called *mīrzā*.[196] They recorded and kept the accounts of the revenue from the villages. Ya'qūb Beg also used *mīrzā*s for collecting details about events and rumors inside the provinces. Thus he kept himself "acquainted with all that is said or done, true or false, and is fully prepared for the discussion of local affairs with the governors, when they annually appear before him."[197] We have no doubt that spies and informants were found at most levels of Kashgharian society. Many visitors actually reported the prevailing mistrust and suspicion in the society at that time.[198]

Each village, called *yaz* or *maḥalla*, was represented by elders selected from the villagers who had various titles, such as *dīvānbegi* (or simply *dīvān*), *aqsaqal*, or *yüzbashi*. They were usually well-to-do and responsible for the collection of taxes. A provincial governor had five to six hundred *dīvān*s if the size of his province was large, or seventy to eighty if it was small. The government chose a rich person (*bai*) from each village every year. It was not uncommon that one was made *dīvānbegi* against his will.[199] For example, it is reported that there were twenty *dīvānbegi*s at the Astin Artush district which contained about twenty small scattered villages.[200] The *dīvānbegi* stood at the lowest echelon of the provincial government[201] and was connected both to the administrative (*ḥākim*, *beg*, and *mīrāb*) and to the financial (*sarkār*, *zakātchi*, and *mīrzā*) officials. It was they who actually performed the work of tax-collection. Government officials assigned them the amount of tax to be collected and, if they were unable to meet this quota, they had to make up the deficit with their own money.[202] The term *dīvānbegi* was attested during the Qing period and Chinese sources transcribed it as *duguan-beg*[203] because *dīvān* was pronounced in many Central Asian dialects as *duwan*. However, the total quota of this office under the Qing rule was only nine and its function was not the same as *dīvānbegi* in Ya'qūb Beg's time. At that time a *yüzbashi* had performed a similar role to that of a *dīvānbegi*. As mentioned earlier, a Yarkand register records 346 *yüzbashi*s in 407 small villages. They were also known as *aqsaqal*, but this term was used more widely in Zungharia than in Kashgharia. The title of *aqsaqal* was also given to the head of each nomadic unit among the Qirghiz, whose function corresponded more or less to *dīvānbegi* in sedentary areas.

Harm done by tax collectors through their oppressive extortion was not limited to the native Kashgharians alone. Foreign merchants also suffered from various hindrances and losses. When Kuropatkin visited Kashgharia in 1876–77, he received complaints from the merchants of Western Turkestan and reported that as many as forty trading agents from Tashkent and Khoqand were going to present him their "collective complaints."[204] Sayrāmī also remarked that when the foreign merchants arrived, their packages were opened for investigation and everything was confiscated by the government. The owner went back "only with string and wrapping cloth."[205]

All these regular and irregular taxes, and their abuses, caused a great suffering to the people of Kashgharia and Zungharia. This kind of situation was commonly found in a society where the government officials had no fixed, or sufficient, salaries and where institutionalized bribery in the form of presents was the primary means to obtain better living conditions and promotions. Most of the regular and the irregular taxes levied in Eastern Turkestan during the reign of Ya'qūb Beg also existed in Western Turkestan to varying degrees. Still, there can be no doubt that the economic condition of the people under his rule, especially approaching the end of his reign, was harsh. People gradually felt disenchanted and betrayed, and many were even hoping for the reconquest by the Chinese. The following episode in *Tārīkh-i ḥamīdī* illustrates well the social milieu at the end of Ya'qūb Beg's rule.

> It is narrated that in the town of Fayzabad in Kashghar someone was sowing the field and shooing birds away. Another person came and asked, "Hey, brother! What are you sowing here?" He replied, "What am I sowing? I am sowing [the seeds of] the Chinese." [At this answer] the one who asked smiled, and, being cheered up, went his way. Less than six months later the Chinese came and camped on that same site.[206]

A conversation of a British doctor, H. Bellew, who visited Kashgharia in 1872 with a young Kashgharian, is another example showing the mood at that time. That young man is recorded to have spoken about the Chinese: "I hate them. But they were not bad rulers. We had everything then. There is nothing now."[207]

5 *Formation of New International Relations*

The Anglo–Russian Rivalry

Since Ivan the Terrible opened the door for the Russian expansion by his conquest of the Kazan and the Astrakhan khanates in 1552 and 1556, Russia's southward expansion was incomparably slower than that of the eastward one. It took only sixty years from the start of the military campaign by Yermak (1579), a Cossack leader, to the arrival of a band of the Cossacks at the Sea of Okhotsk (1639). The rate of the territorial increase was unprecedented in history. Between the middle of the sixteenth and the end of the seventeenth centuries, Russia acquired annually 35,000 square kilometers on average—about the size of modern Netherlands—for one hundred and fifty consecutive years.[1] Of course its largest gain came from Siberia. On the other hand, her southward expansion was blocked for almost three centuries. The attempt by Peter the Great (r. 1689–1725) in 1717 to subjugate Khiva ended in complete disaster when the entire expeditionary force was slaughtered by the Khivans. A decade later, in 1734, a part of the Qazaqs expressed their submission to the Empress Anne (r. 1730–40), but it was nothing but "a bargain with their conscience" to gain material wealth from Russia. Only during the first half of the nineteenth century did Russia gain effective control over the Qazaq steppe and, finally in 1853 did the Russian troops successfully take the town of Aq Masjid on the lower Syr Darya, which marked the beginning of the full-scale and rapid expansion in the direction of Central Asia.

At the bottom of the British Central Asian policy lay the question of the security of their Indian colony. Ever since Emperor Paul's (r. 1796–1801) proposal to Napoleon for the joint expedition to India, the specter of a Russian invasion of India haunted British politicians. But they did not feel much endangered until the early nineteenth century when the Russians crossed the vast tract of the Qazaq steppe and began to overwhelm the Central Asian deserts and oases. From the late 1830s British Russophobia began to build up as Russia actively supported Muḥammad Shāh (r. 1834–48) of Iran in his attack on Herat in 1837. Even though the seven months of siege of Herat ended in failure, this incident made the British reappraise their policy, and these new circumstances played a considerable part in the decision of the British invasion of Afghanistan in 1839. Although Britain's first Afghan War (1839–42) ended in a failure, she continued to be concerned about the Russian activities in the Central Asian field. In the late 1840s and 1850s England went over the Indus line by incorporating Punjab, and penetrated almost a thousand miles into the "debatable land" of former days. On the other hand, with the conquest of Aq Masjid, Russia now formed the Syr Darya line. Thus the intervening areas between the two powers shrunk to "a mere narrow strip of territory, a few hundred miles across, occupied either by tribes torn by internecine war or nationalities in the last stage of decrepitude, and traversed by military routes in all directions."[2]

The Russian occupation of Tashkent in 1865 was enough to revive the specter of the Russian threat to India. Even Henry M. Lawrence, who was one of the staunchest advocates of a policy of "masterly inactivity," felt the pressure to take a more active policy against Russia toward the end of his term as the viceroy of India. It was from Richard S. B. Mayo (viceroy, 1869–72) that Britain decided to surround the northern frontiers of India with "a cordon of friendly independent states."[3] The British government of India decided to include Afghanistan in their sphere of influence[4] and endeavored to exclude the Russian influence from Eastern Turkestan where a new Muslim government had been created by Ya'qūb Beg.

RELATIONS WITH RUSSIA

Around the summer of 1867 when Ya'qūb Beg had conquered all of Kashgharia, it was impossible for him to avoid being entangled in the rivalry between the two great powers in Central Asia. He tried at first to stop all the political as well as commercial contacts with Russia. He may have realized that commercial penetration was often followed by military expansion. Russia could not tolerate Ya'qūb Beg's policy because she had gained important trade privileges (the right to establish a consulate and factories in Kulja and the right for the Russian merchants to visit Eastern Turkestan and to trade) from the Qing government.[5]

The initial response of the Russians to the unfriendly attitude of Ya'qūb Beg was the military threat toward his northwestern border. The earliest rumor about the hostile movement of the Russian army already reached the British in July 1865.[6] But this rumor seems to have been caused by the Russian military activities in 1865, including the takeover of Tashkent in the same month. Two years later, in the later half of 1867, Russia began to move into the valley of Narin. At that time Ya'qūb Beg successfully finished the conquest of Kucha and was staying in Aqsu on his way back to his capital. At the news of the Russian movement he immediately returned to Kashghar on October 1. Alarming information, apparently false, reached him that the Russians had come down to Üstün Artush in the direct vicinity of Kashghar. The Russians built the Narin fort in 1868, and Ya'qūb Beg, in response, sealed the frontier and massed troops along it.[7]

Although this incident did not develop into an armed conflict, the strained relations between the two countries continued. In 1868 a caravan led by a Russian merchant, Khludov, venturing into Kashghar was attacked soon after crossing the border and obliged to return to Vernoe. Then he obtained a letter from the governor of Semirech'e and succeeded in entering Kashghar. E. Schuyler writes that the impression that he produced on Ya'qūb Beg resulted in the dispatch of Mīrzā Muḥammad Shādī to Tashkent.[8] It is obvious that Ya'qūb Beg realized at this time that he could not longer ignore the existence of his strong northern neighbor and that he had to find some way to ease the tension.

Bearing a letter from Ya'qūb Beg for General Kaufman, the Russian governor-general of Turkestan, Shādī Mīrzā arrived at Vernoe in August of 1868 in the company of the Russian merchant Khludov. There he was received by General Kolpakovskii, who informed him that Kaufman had left for St. Petersburg and then complained that the letter he had brought did not observe proper diplomatic usages. Kolpakovskii sent Captain Reintal' to Kashghar with his own letter informing Ya'qūb Beg of Kaufman's absence and demanding the return of some Russian captives and the Qirghiz who had seized them during a recent raid.[9] Ya'qūb Beg captured the Qirghiz responsible but he chose only to return the Russian captives. After this, Mīrzā Shādī was allowed to proceed to St. Petersburg, where he met Kaufman. However, he was not permitted to have any direct communication with the Foreign Ministry and returned to Kashghar in January 1869. Again in the same year there was a widespread rumor in Kashghar that the Russians were instigating Khudāyār Khān of Khoqand to invade Kashgharia. In a secret report, Henry Cayley, who was on special duty in Ladakh, reported news of a possible alliance against Ya'qūb Beg by Khudāyār Khān and Buzurg Khwāja (who had arrived back in Khoqand through Punjab and Ladakh) and about the active Russian support for their cause as well.[10]

In the next spring (1870), due to disturbances along his eastern border, Ya'qūb Beg decided to launch an expedition against the Tungans in Turfan and Urumchi. Ya'qūb Beg's rapid success in this operation of taking Turfan and Urumchi in the same year was alarming to the Russians for their relations with him was far from friendly. They also had poor relations with the Ili sultanate. A. V. Kaul'bars left Vernoe on November 29, 1870 and visited A'la Khān of the Ili sultanate to obtain his permission to establish Russian representatives in Kulja and allow Russian merchants to trade freely in the Ili region, but his mission ended in failure. The Russians were especially anxious about the possibility of a close alliance between the two Muslim governments of A'la Khān and Ya'qūb Beg that might create serious problems among their own Muslim subjects in the border areas and might allow the English to expand their influence into Zungharia. On his way to Kulja in the autumn of 1870, the Russian emissary Borodin actually met Ya'qūb Beg's own envoy who was also heading to Kulja. The Russian had a suspicion that Ya'qūb Beg was attempting to make an alliance with A'la Khān for a joint attack on the Semirech'e region.[11]

Even though the Foreign Ministry in St. Petersburg regarded Ya'qūb Beg's occupation of the Ili valley as improbable,[12] the shadow of such a danger was still strongly felt by Russian generals in Central Asia, especially in view of the weakness of the Ili sultanate.[13] The Russian army took a preemptive measure by blocking the Muzart pass to cut the road from Kashgharia to Kulja. The Russian government eventually reached the conclusion that the hostile powers should be eliminated from Zungharia, and consulted the Chinese government about the recovery of the area by an allied force of the two countries. At first, the War Ministry considered the possibility of taking Kulja and Urumchi at the same time, but when China did not answer the Russian proposal, it was decided to start the expedition alone, limiting it to the Ili valley.[14]

The operation started on June 24, 1871 and ended in ten days with the occupation of Kulja on July 4. It is not clear whether this sweeping campaign was directed against any direct threat from Ya'qūb Beg. As we made clear, Ya'qūb Beg had finished his Urumchi expedition in November of 1870 and he limited his sphere of action to the vicinity of Urumchi. Beg Quli launched the second Urumchi expedition around June of 1871 due to a fresh disturbance. The Russian move seems to have begun approximately at the same time with Beg Quli's advance. We do not know whether the Russian troops were put in motion after Beg Quli's move had been known to the Russians. Whatever the sequence was, it appears that the Russian move was not a response to an active attempt to take Kulja on the part of Ya'qūb Beg, but was rather, as Terent'ev termed it, "a precautionary measure"[15] to a possible complication of matters arising from Ya'qūb Beg's annexation of Urumchi. Whether this threat, which induced the Russians to take such a precautionary measure, was real or not is a matter of dispute.

Up to that point, Russia did not acknowledge Ya'qūb Beg as the legitimate ruler of a new government. The reason was basically twofold: Russia's relations with the Chinese government and the uncertainty about the longevity of Ya'qūb Beg's rule. Because Russia had obtained important commercial privileges in Eastern Turkestan through treaties with China even before the rebellion, she was not in a position to ignore China's claim over this region. Considering the existing diplomatic relations between the two countries, the Russians did not want to risk serious trouble with China by opening relations with a regime that was regarded as illegitimate by the Chinese government and might collapse within a few years.

General Kaufman pushed Ya'qūb Beg hard to respect the privileges that Russia had obtained from China and to surrender the Qirghiz who had raided the border area. But Ya'qūb Beg, for his part, would not submit to these demands while his government remained unrecognized by Russia. Finally, becoming tired of the diplomatic game, Kaufman offered Khudāyār Khān the cooperation of Russia in case he launched a campaign to subjugate Kashghar. Khudāyār, however, did not want "to risk upon one card his peace and, perhaps, his throne," fearing that his troops might desert to Ya'qūb Beg.[16] Instead, he agreed to send his envoy, a certain Sarimsaq Hudāīchi, to persuade Ya'qūb Beg to come to a peaceful understanding with Russia. When this embassy failed to achieve its goal, Kaufman himself sent another non-Russian envoy bearing a letter with stronger words. Ya'qūb Beg responded to this approach by urging the general to send one of his Russian subjects as an envoy. The reason is clear: "Yacoob Beg, although he valued the friendship of Russia, was reluctant to lower his dignity by appearing in the character of supplicant, and at the same time considered the intervention of the Khan of Kokan as an infringement on his independence."[17]

Ya'qūb Beg in this way compelled the Russians to take the first step. Kaufman resolved to send such a mission, headed by a Colonel Kaul'bars, who was a member of his General Staff, to be accompanied by an engineer, a topographer, and a merchant. The party left Kulja early in May 1872 with the goals of concluding a commercial agreement with Ya'qūb Beg and collecting information about the country and its relation with British India. The agreement (for the text of the treaty, see Appendix A) was concluded on June 20 (June 8 in the Julian calendar), 1872, and consisted of five basic points:

1. the right of free trade without prohibition,
2. the right of establishing *caravansarai*s,
3. the right of placing *caravanbashi*s (commercial agents),
4. a custom duty to be exacted at the rate of 2.5 percent *ad valorem*, and
5. the right to traverse the country for transit to other countries.

The content of this treaty was almost exactly the same as the one the Russians previously signed with Bukhara and Khoqand, with one major exception. The Russo–Kashghar agreement acknowledged the *de facto* legitimacy of Ya'qūb Beg's rule whereas the others left their rulers as clients under Russian control. In the text of the agreement, Ya'qūb Beg was addressed by the title of "the honourable ruler of the Djety-Shahr" (*pochtennyi vladetel' Dzhity-shara*). In the translated text, still current among scholars, this title is rendered as "the honourable Chief of Djety-Shahr," which is seriously misleading.[18] There was an enormous difference in political nuance between chief and ruler. By calling him the "ruler," the Russian government tacitly recognized the sovereignty of Ya'qūb Beg over his dominion. This can be seen in the answer that Westman, the Deputy Foreign Minister of Russia, gave to the British when he was asked to clarify the position of his government toward Ya'qūb Beg in view of the visit of Kaul'bars: "Yacoob Beg was at this moment the dominant ruler in that country, and as such, the Imperial Government had treated with him."[19] In exchange for her recognition of Ya'qūb Beg, Russia gained an important diplomatic framework through which she could expand her influence in Kashgharia, primarily economically but politically as well. At the same time, any nonobservance of the agreement by Ya'qūb Beg would give Russia "the pretext of going to war with him."[20] Thus, although with very different intentions in mind, the two countries opened formal diplomatic relations in 1872.

Based on this agreement, a Russian merchant named Somov took a large number of commodities and visited Kashghar, but the result was not satisfactory. Captain Reintal' was dispatched in 1874 to renegotiate with Ya'qūb Beg for the improvement of the conditions of the commercial agreement. When these discussions proved fruitless, the Russians determined to solve the problem by military means around the end of that year by concentrating troops, ammunition, and provisions on the Narin River. The invasion, however, never materialized because the Russians had to deal with a popular revolt in the Khoqand khanate against their puppet ruler, Khudāyār Khan.[21]

The strained relations between Russia and Kashghar continued even after Russia formally annexed the territory of the Khoqand khanate in 1876. Now the borders of the Kashgharian state directly bordered with Russia to the north and the west. In order to tame this new neighbor, General Kaufman dispatched an embassy headed by A. N. Kuropatkin to demand the transfer of several frontier guard posts that Ya'qūb Beg had built. Unable to refuse this adamant demand by Russia, Ya'qūb Beg verbally conceded his willingness to give up the posts of Suyek, Ulughchat, and Maltabar and promised to send his own emissary to General Kaufman for further negotiations.[22]

In summary, after the initial period of hostility and tension between Russia and Kashghar, which almost verged on the outbreak of war, both parties found a *modus vivendi*. Ya'qūb Beg agreed to a commercial treaty and in return the Russian government recognized him as the *de facto* sovereign of Kashgharia and Urumchi. In this way Russia became reconciled to Ya'qūb Beg's growing power and accepted the stability of his regime. On his part, Ya'qūb Beg responded to Russian pressure with caution and tried not to offend his powerful neighbor.

KASHGHARIA AND ENGLAND

The opening of British relations with Kashghar owed much to the efforts of private individuals like R. B. Shaw, G. W. Hayward, and W. H. Johnson.[23] Especially the writings of R. B. Shaw, who visited Kashghar in 1868–69, made a great impact upon the later British policy for Eastern Turkestan. He emphasized the enormous potential of the market there and the danger of losing such a strategically important and commercially fertile ground to Russia. His rosy picture of the wealth and security in Eastern Turkestan under Ya'qūb Beg's rule impressed R. S. B. Mayo who became the new viceroy of India in early 1869.[24] As mentioned earlier, he had set up a new policy in which Afghanistan and Eastern Turkestan were envisioned as independent states friendly to Britain. Ya'qūb Beg, stimulated by the visits of Shaw and Hayward, sent Sayyid Aḥrār as an envoy to Mayo, requesting a British officer to accompany him back to Kashghar. Mayo could not have been more pleased, so he immediately dispatched the first British official envoys, consisting of T. D. Forsyth, G. Henderson, and A. O. Hume, later joined by R. B. Shaw.[25] When they arrived in Yarkand, however, they discovered that Ya'qūb Beg had gone to the eastern frontier where he was engaged in intense fighting with the Tungans. Because of Mayo's stringent instructions that they should not stay in Kashgharia through the winter under any circumstance, the British envoys could not remain long in Yarkand and thus their mission ended in failure.

On returning to Kashghar from the battlefield, Ya'qūb Beg again sent Sayyid Aḥrār to India at the end of 1871 with his letter to the viceroy of India as well as to the Queen of England. The purpose of Sayyid Aḥrār's visit was simply to inform the British government of Ya'qūb Beg's success in his latest campaign against the Urumchi Tungans, and to purchase muskets from the Indian market.[26] The increasing Russian influence over Kashgharia through the 1872 Russo–Kashghar commercial treaty and the untiring effort of Shaw in England in propagating the message of the opening of the future market, "a kind of Eldorado,"[27] provided a new stimulus for accelerating relations between England and Kashghar. In early 1873 "the India Office was bombarded with appeals and deputations from municipal Chambers of Commerce and other bodies, all using Shaw's arguments in favor of a British commercial treaty with the Ataliq Ghazee."[28] The new viceroy, T. G. B. Northbrook, who had succeeded Mayo, also thought that a friendly relationship with Kashghar would be desirable.

In October 1872, Ya'qūb Beg dispatched his special envoy named Sayyid Ya'qūb Khān to the Ottoman sultan, and this envoy, on his way to Istanbul, visited Calcutta in February 1873 and delivered Ya'qūb Beg's letter addressed to the viceroy, dated October 5, 1872 (Sha'bān 1, 1289).[29] In his meeting with the viceroy on March 8, the envoy clearly explained that the primary object of his mission was "to promote and cement a friendly alliance with the British Government in a manner so public as would convince the world of the intimate union between the two Governments, and would serve to deter any other Power from entertaining designs hostile to the peace of his sovereign and dominions."[30] There is no doubt that "any other Power" here primarily denoted Russia. Sayyid Ya'qūb Khān, upon whom Ya'qūb Beg had conferred full power, not only offered an invitation to another British mission to Kashghar to conclude a commercial treaty but also proposed the permanent residence of the representatives of both countries in exchange. As a result, the British mission with three hundred and fifty members headed by T. D. Forsyth was dispatched to the capital of the Kashghar state, joined by Sayyid Ya'qūb Khān on his way back from Istanbul. The party reached Kashghar in early December of 1873. On February 2, 1874, both parties signed the commercial treaty and later, on April 13th of the same year, it was ratified and confirmed by the viceroy of India, Northbrook (for the text of the treaty, see Appendix B).[31]

Though the contents of this treaty were basically the same as those of the Russo–Kashghar treaty of 1872, there is one important difference. In the latter, Russia and Kashghar agreed to appoint respective *caravanbashi*s in each other's territory but they had no other status than that of "commercial agents." By contrast, the Anglo–Kashghar treaty agreed to the appointment of representatives and commercial agents who were also entitled to the formal diplomatic ranks and privileges accorded to ambassadors and consuls respectively. Shaw was appointed "Officer on Special Duty, Kashghar" and served in Kashghar until he returned to India in June 1875.[32]

It was Russian involvement in Kashgharia that had first induced the British to become more involved there themselves. They were always anxious about the security of the India's northern frontier and any possible Russian invasion from that quarter, but they were also keen to exploit an unknown commercial market. Signing the 1874 commercial treaty with Kashghar appeared to be the start of a new and closer relationship. But as G. J. Alder correctly points out, "although the 1873–4 Forsyth mission marks the peak of British influence in Kashghar, it was at the same time an important landmark in the progressive British disillusionment with the commercial capacity of the country."[33] Explorations reported by the mission proved that Russia could not possibly advance into India through the Karakorum Mountains but would have to use the passes in the Pamirs or the Hindu Kush farther west. While Britain could not feel at ease about the possible Russian invasion through the westerly direction, Kashghar no longer held the strategic importance it once had. Similarly the prospect for future trade with Eastern Turkestan was not as promising as it had been portrayed. All in all, British interests in its relationship with Kashghar declined from 1874 onward and became limited to preventing Ya'qūb Beg from being incorporated into Russia's sphere of influence.

Ya'qūb Beg gained much more from his treaty with British India. He not only gained the recognition of his rule from the British government but also rendered his domain safer than before from the Russian threat. Russia could not invade Kashgharia without considering the serious impact such a move would have upon her relation with England. Moreover, as a result of his friendly relation with England, Ya'qūb Beg secured a source for arms purchases. Even though the British Indian government never acted as an official supplier of armaments to Ya'qūb Beg, it granted licenses to private firms to supply arms to Kashghar. In 1875, "as an act of courtesy," the Indian government paid for the carriage of two hundred cases of guns from Bombay to Lahore, destined for Yarkand.[34] However, Ya'qūb Beg did not limit the range of his diplomatic efforts only to his direct neighbors. He also needed the approval of his legitimacy from the wider Muslim world, which led to his approach to the Ottoman Empire.

Diplomacy with the Ottoman Empire[35]

SAYYID YA'QŪB KHĀN

Having taken Aq Masjid in 1853, a frontier town of the Khoqand khanate on the bank of Syr Darya, Russia was about to launch a full-scale operation against Tashkent in 1865. In the face of this threat Khoqand was thrown into great confusion, and the neighboring state of Bukhara took advantage of the opportunity to put Khudāyār Khān, who had been in exile there, on the throne. In order to respond to these threats 'Ālim Quli hurried to send an envoy to Istanbul to ask for assistance in the name of Sayyid Sulṭān Khān whom he had made a nominal ruler. This envoy was none other than Sayyid Ya'qūb Khān (1823–1899) who was to play an important role in future relations between the Ottoman Empire and the Kashghar state. According to Boulger, he was born in Tashkent as a son of Nār Muḥammad Khān who was married to Ya'qūb Beg's sister. So he was Ya'qūb Beg's nephew.[36]

Sayyid Ya'qūb Khān carried the title of *sayyid* which was given only to the descendants of the Prophet Muḥammad and evoked the deep respect of the Muslims. He was also called *qāḍī* because he had received the necessary education to qualify him to make decisions on legal matters. It is reported that he wrote several works but unfortunately these works are not handed down to us.[37] He was also popularly known as Ḥājjī Tura, and Sayrāmī calls him "Īshān Sayyid Qāḍī Turam."[38] The title of *tura* (from Turco-Mongol word *törä* or *törü*, ultimately going back to Torah), which had been given to the Chinggisids alone, was applied to noble religious figures as evidenced by the Makhdūmzādas who carried it. Combining this information, we can conclude that he was not only a very well educated intellectual in Central Asia but also a revered religious figure with noble lineage.

Around the beginning of 1865 he arrived in Istanbul. However, even before he had an audience with the sultan, he received the news of the fall of Tashkent and 'Ālim Quli's death. This rendered his original mission moot, but at this very juncture the amazing news about the activities of Ya'qūb Beg in Kashgharia began to reach Istanbul. On his own initiative, Sayyid Ya'qūb Khān decided to make a new request to the sultan that he bestow an imperial letter (*nāme-i hümāyūn*) and a high Ottoman order (*nişān-i 'alī-yi Osmānī*) upon both Ya'qūb Beg in Kashghar and Khudāyār Khān in Khoqand. In addition, he asked that the Ottomans send samples of percussion-type rifles, magazine-type rifles, and Ottoman army military uniforms representing the ranks from private to general. On September 16, 1868, the Ottoman government responded that it would send the requested rifles and uniforms, but neither the imperial letter nor Ottoman order because the political situation in Central Asia was too unstable.[39] Probably the Porte (Ottoman court) was not certain about the political future of those two rulers and, naturally, worried about creating unnecessary diplomatic friction with Russia.

It is interesting to note that the diplomatic relations between the Ottomans and Kashgharia started with Sayyid Ya'qūb Khān's personal initiative even though his duty as an official envoy of Khoqand had ended with the death of his master, 'Ālim Quli. Why did he volunteer for such a role? The fact that he was Ya'qūb Beg's relative, of course, cannot be discounted. However, we should note that his own explanation for requesting samples of rifles and uniforms was "to strengthen Islam through the improvement of military equipment and organization there [i.e., Central Asia]."[40] In order to cope with the Russian expansion, he felt the need for strengthening the Central Asian states through the introduction of new armaments and the reformation of the military system with the support of the Ottoman Empire. His attitudes in this regard may have been influenced by his three-year stay in Istanbul where he came into contact with members of the Tanzimat reform movement and the ideology of the Young Ottomans who were lobbying for a Pan-Islamic coalition.

In the spring of 1869, Ya'qūb Khān traveled to Kashghar and personally urged Ya'qūb Beg to acknowledge the suzerainty of the Ottoman sultan. However, Ya'qūb Beg was not initially attracted to such a move and was prepared to ignore his advice. But Ya'qūb Khān persisted by explaining, according to Sayrāmī, why he had visited Istanbul and whom he had met there.

After Tashkent had been taken by the Russians, the *'ulamā* and the *sayyids*, declaring that "Now this land has become *ḥarām* [unlawful]," refused to submit to Russia and decided to follow the precedents and laws (*sunnat sharī'at*) of the Prophet—Peace be upon Him! So, emulating the example of the Prophet, they chose to emigrate (*hijrat*). I also made up my mind to emigrate and paid a visit to the two holy cities, after which I stayed some days in Rūm [i.e., the Ottoman empire]. I happened to have discussions with grandees and noble people there, who told me [as follows]. "Although the Ferghana region was occupied by the Russians, some Muslims rose up in the land of [the Chinese] Emperor and achieved the victory and opened Islam. When His Majesty the Caliph heard this news, he issued an edict commanding people to offer a prayer, at the end of five-time prayers at every mosque, for the success of the Muslims in the East who had opened Islam, and before others he himself prayed for [the Muslims] in the East." . . . Ever since the Ottoman empire, that is, Rūm Caliphate and the protector of the Muslims, had been established, whenever the Muslims on the earth raised their heads, the Caliph rejoiced and prayed for their success. And if he heard about their defeats, he grieved and became sorrowful and prayed for their well-being. Whatever news he heard about the uprisings of the Muslims, he let them all be written on the document and be announced. . . . This land of Moghulistan belonged to Your Highness, and it is necessary as well as obligatory for you to inform the Caliph.[41]

Of course, this passage cannot be considered to transmit exactly what Sayyid Ya'qūb Khān said, but it seems to reflect his notions about the desperate situation the Central Asian Muslims faced with the Russian threat as well as about the Pan-Islamic solidarity found in the Ottoman empire.

Compared to the idealistic Sayyid Ya'qūb Khān, however, Ya'qūb Beg was a realistic politician and soldier who had experienced the extremely complicated and unpredictable politics in Khoqand and achieved the unification of Kashgharia, overcoming innumerable obstacles. He was not the kind of person who would blindly devote himself to the idea of Islamic solidarity. As a matter of fact, his record in this area was rather poor. He had refused to assist the Muslims in Khoqand when they rose up against the Russian rule in 1865. Instead he closed the border and strengthened the guard to prevent refugees from entering Kashgharia because he was worried that this might introduce confusion into his realm.[42] British diplomats even suspected that he might take the side of Russia if Britain and the Ottomans fought a war in alliance against Russia.[43] Probably Ya'qūb Beg knew of the diplomatic contacts between Khoqand and the Ottomans during the nineteenth century. However, after he had unified Kashgharia, it was not the Ottomans but Britain and Russia that he first tried to contact, and it was because he thought that these two countries were the most powerful neighboring states that could exert enormous influence on his dominion. Recognition of these two powers was urgent and indispensable for him. Therefore, it is not strange that he did not attempt to contact the Ottomans who were not only far from his country but also insignificant in terms of their influence on international diplomacy.

When such a realistic politician as Ya'qūb Beg decided to take a more active role to contact the Ottomans, it was because he had an expectation that he could gain tangible profits from the relationship. We can understand his decision from two angles. First of all, it was an expectation that his status as a ruler of the state he had just created might have recognition not only from the international community but also in the eyes of the native Kashgharians. Eastern Turkestan had been under the rule of the Qing dynasty during the preceding hundred years, and so there lingered a strong notion that it was a part of Chinese territory even after the Muslim rebellion, the expulsion of the Qing power, and the establishment of his regime. In the meantime, Ya'qūb Beg did not possess a source of indisputable political authority widely accepted in Central Asia and his power was built simply upon sheer military force. Therefore, the recognition by the Ottoman sultan, the nominal leader of global Islamic society at that time, would enhance his political status. He had employed the strategy of using foreign recognition to strengthen his internal status already in 1868–69 when R. B. Shaw visited his country. Even though Shaw repeatedly made it clear that he came as an individual merchant not as an envoy, Ya'qūb Beg deliberately arranged parading him around the country and "assembling several thousands to line the approach" when he visited his *urda*. Shaw was convinced that Ya'qūb Beg was exploiting him "for the benefit of subjects and neighbours as an English envoy."[44]

Another factor causing his change of attitude was the possibility for him to gain material support in the form of military advisors and a supply of armaments. To prepare for the future confrontation with the Qing he needed to equip his army with modern weapons like rifles and cannons. He had made incessant efforts to secure these weapons but without many practical results. It was difficult for him to expect large-scale imports from Britain because they could not openly deliver military equipment for fear of Russian reaction, not to mention the Russians who did not relinquish their hostile attitude toward his state. He had tried other sources like the Afghans or private merchants in India, but the amount of imports was not satisfactory. In this respect the Ottoman empire could be a good alternative source.

However, whatever Ya'qūb Beg's attitude may have been, the relations between the two countries would never have been realized if the Ottoman government had not changed its traditional policy of non-involvement in Central Asia. We know that the Central Asian khanates had repeatedly sent missions to the Porte to ask for moral and material support to stem the Russian expansion: for example, Khiva in 1840 and 1847; Khoqand in 1865; and Bukhara in 1867, 1868, and 1871. However, the Porte never accepted these requests. The basic reasons for the Porte's denial of the entreaties from the Central Asian rulers were the fear of the Russian reaction, the swift success of the Russian operation in the Central Asian field, and the political instability within the khanates.[45] However, with the death of Fuad Paşa in 1869 and of Ali Paşa in 1871 who had both been the grand viziers for a long time and prominent leaders of the Tanzimat reform, a different mood began to set in. The foreign policy shifted toward the direction of opposing the intervention of foreign powers, and the need for Islamic unity began to be stressed. The Ottoman sultan 'Abdülazīz (r. 1861–76), in his later years, viewed favorably the idea of the sultan not only as the head of the Ottoman empire but also as the leader of all the Muslims in other countries.[46] The Young Ottomans had been permitted to return from exile after the death of Ali Paşa and came to have close contacts with the members of the ruling group and propagated the idea of Islamic unity, thus contributing to the formation of public opinion toward that direction. This was the beginning of the so-called Pan-Islamism which reached its climax later during the reign of 'Abdülhamid (r. 1876–1909).[47]

The news of the Muslim uprising and the establishment of independent Muslim governments in the northwestern part of China was received with fervor by those who were aggrieved by the plight of the Muslims all over the world. The Muslims in the Ottoman empire as well as in other countries were amazed by the rapid and enormous success of Ya'qūb Beg. His name and activities were often reported in journals and newspapers in Istanbul. For example, it was reported that 16 million Muslims had risen against the Chinese rule and as a result three leaders were opposed to each other but, after Ya'qūb Beg came from Aq Masjid with 300 soldiers and subjugated them all, he became the ruler of 20 million Muslims.[48] Although the contents of these reports were often distorted and exaggerated, they contributed to furthering the idea of Islamic unity and the sentiments of Pan-Islamism as Namık Kemal vividly testified in 1872: "Twenty years ago, the fact that there were Moslems in Kasgar was not known. Now, public opinion tries to obtain union with them. This inclination resembles an overpowering flood which will not be stopped by any obstacle in its way."[49]

DEVELOPMENT OF RELATIONS

Following the order of Ya'qūb Beg, Sayyid Ya'qūb Khān left Kashghar in October 1872, as an envoy to Istanbul. First, he went to India and met the viceroy in Calcutta where he stayed until next spring. He had contacts with high officials of the Indian government in order to promote friendly relations with Britain. He met the foreign minister of India on February 27, 1873 and explained to him Ya'qūb Beg's concrete proposals for the strengthening of political and economic relations between the two countries. At this meeting he clarified that the aim of his visit to Istanbul was nothing but conveying "a friendly letter and messages on the part of his sovereign" and said that he was going to ask the sultan to accept the country under Ya'qūb Beg's rule as his protectorate. And when he was asked "what course he would pursue if the Sultan refused" to approve Kashghar and the British government having a friendly relation, he answered that, "knowing the helpless condition of Turkey," he felt sure that the request would be refused and, then, Kashghar would do its utmost to promote the diplomatic relations with Britain "without any further reference" to the Ottomans.[50]

We can assume that his answer reflects his frank opinion without any pretension because he knew very well of the repeated refusal of the Ottomans to provide aid to the Central Asian states faced with the Russian threat. On his earlier visit Ya'qūb Khān himself had been denied the imperial letter and the Ottoman order he had asked the sultan to confer on Khudāyār Khān and Ya'qūb Beg. Therefore, it is very possible that he did not expect to achieve a successful result from his new mission. On the other hand, his answer may have been a highly diplomatic tactic because the emphasis on the passive attitude of the Ottomans could induce a more active engagement from Britain. In other words, by pointing out the fact that the Ottoman Empire was not in a position to open diplomatic relations with Kashghar, he was reminding the officials in India of the importance of Britain's role. So he hoped to transmit the willingness of his country to promote the relationship with Britain, without taking into consideration the opinion of the sultan. In fact, when he had an interview with Northbrook on March 8, 1873 he emphasized that point. Ya'qūb Khān made it clear that, although he was carrying a letter of friendship to the sultan, he himself had already explained to Ya'qūb Beg the fact that Britain was geographically closer to Kashgharia and, thus, in a better position than the Ottomans to provide necessary aid. Ya'qūb Khān added that Ya'qūb Beg agreed with his opinion and that one of the aims of his visit to Istanbul was to obtain from the sultan an official approval of Kashgharia's relation with the British government.[51]

Sayyid Ya'qūb Khān appears to have arrived in Istanbul not later than the end of May 1873. There are several documents in the Ottoman archives concerning his first official mission. The first one, dated on May 25, 1873 (Rabī' I 27, 1290) shows that "Ya'qūb Khān who is the ruler (*ḥükümdār*) of Islamic community of a large number of Muslims in the country of Kashgharia" dispatched Sayyid Ya'qūb Khān as his envoy in order to form the "the relation of subordination." It also tells us that the letter that the Kashgharian envoy had brought was translated and presented to the sultan. Sayyid Ya'qūb Khān was allowed to have an audience with the sultan 'Abdülazīz.[52] Other documents witness the positive response, contrary to

Sayyid Ya'qūb Khān's expectation, that the Ottoman government consented to the request from Kashgharia. First of all, on June 16 it was decided that the first-class of the Ottoman order and a sword worth 20,000 *kuruş* should be given to Ya'qūb Beg, "*ḥākim* of Kashghar," and that the second-class Ottoman order and the travel expense of 10,000 *kuruş* should be given to the envoy.[53] On August 2 it was also decided to send an imperial letter as a reply to Ya'qūb Beg's letter.[54] We see another document showing the decision to dispatch rifles, cannons and military instructors, together with two other volunteers.[55]

Although these documents do not provide a detailed list of military aid, a letter sent later by Ya'qūb Beg expressing his thanks to the sultan shows that four instructors, 6 cannons, 1,000 old-type rifles, and 200 new-type rifles were sent.[56] Based on the report of H. Bellew who witnessed Sayyid Ya'qūb Khān and the Ottoman military instructor in Kashghar, among many Turks from Europe were included four military officers and one civilian.[57] From another source we can identify their names. The four officers were Mehmet Yūsuf, Yūsuf Ismā'īl the Circassian, Ismā'īl Ḥaqq Efendi, Zamān Bey from Daghestan, and one civilian was Murād Efendi who retired from the Inner Court.[58]

While Sayyid Ya'qūb Khān was staying in Istanbul in 1873, he seemed to meet intellectuals advocating reforms. As a secret report of N. Ignatiev, Russian ambassador to the Porte in 1864–78, reveals, Sayyid Ya'qūb Khān had a meeting with "the representatives of several of the Asiatic States at the house of Ahmed Vefik Effendi."[59] Ahmet Vefik was not only a renowned writer and scholar but also an important political figure who had served as minister of education and as prime minister. The Young Ottomans like Namık Kemal kept in contact with him.[60] The envoy also met religious leaders of Sufi orders in Istanbul. Especially, he seemed to have an intimate contact with the head of the Uzbek *tekke* of the Naqshbandī branch.[61]

Sayyid Ya'qūb Khān and his company left Istanbul on August 14, 1873 (or just immediately after that date) and arrived in Bombay by way of Egypt. From there they went to a frontier post called Shahidulla under the escort provided by the Indian government, where they were joined by the British embassy under the leadership of T. D. Forsyth.[62] Sayyid Ya'qūb Khān finally reached Kashghar around the end of November. We have several reports, including those of the British embassy members, the letter sent to the sultan by Ya'qūb Beg[63] and another Ottoman source,[64] which allow us to reconstruct Ya'qūb Beg's response to the formal recognition of his state by the Ottoman sultan.

According to the testimony of Bellew, several days after the arrival of the British embassy (December 4), Ya'qūb Beg paid a visit to the mausoleum of Khwāja Āfāq in the suburb of Kashghar, one of the holiest places in this region at that time, and performed the ceremony of wearing the sword and the Ottoman order sent by the sultan and firing a cannon salute one hundred times. There was no pompous parade or ceremony celebrating the occasion, but he simply received congratulations from the soldiers.[65] Soon after this he took the title of *amīr al-mū'minīn* (Commander of the Faithful) and ordered the reading of the Friday prayer and the minting of coins in the name of the sultan,[66] which is tantamount to the official proclamation of his recognition of the Ottoman sultan as suzerain.

However, we should not forget that Ya'qūb Beg's recognition of suzerainty was rather nominal because the Ottomans were not in a position to interfere with the affairs of Kashgharia. In spite of that, the reason the nominal suzerainty was accepted was because it coincided with the interests of the two countries. The sultan hoped to demonstrate his role as the leader of the entire Islamic world by showing his willingness to protect the Central Asian Muslims threatened by the military expansion of the Western infidels, especially the Russians. He might have thought that this new image would enhance his status which had been seriously damaged by the weakening of the empire. The recognition of the sultan's suzerainty was also rewarding to Ya'qūb Beg because it confirmed his status as the ruler of the country not only by his subjects but also among the international community. Moreover, he succeeded in obtaining what he had been pursuing—military equipment.

Diplomatic relations between the two countries further developed on Sayyid Ya'qūb Khān's second visit to Istanbul in 1875.[67] The prime purpose of his visit this time was to transmit Ya'qūb Beg's sincere gratitude for the sultan's favor. The arrival of the envoy from Kashghar was reported on April 23 of 1875 (Rabī' I 27, 1292), and the translation of Ya'qūb Beg's letter was presented to the sultan. The envoy had an audience with him on May 7.[68] In this letter Ya'qūb Beg, first of all, clarified that the bestowal of the sultan's edict and the various gifts was a great honor not only to himself but also to all the inhabitants of Kashgharia and reported how he performed the ceremony to celebrate the occasion. And then he swore that he would never forget the sultan's favor to the end of his life and would perform whatever command he should order. Since the sultan's favor bestowed a new life, he continued, to all the Muslims in Central Asia, all of them turned their soul and body to the sultan. And he expressed his wish that the people in Central Asia could be incorporated into the domain of the Caliph (*dār al-khilāfat*) within a short period of time so that the union of Islam (*ittifāk-i Islām*) should be achieved. Finally, he added that he unfurled the imperial flag (*sancak*) and ordered the Friday prayer to be read and the coins to be struck in the name of the sultan.[69] According to the author of *Kāşgar tārīhī*, Sayyid Ya'qūb Khān presented to the sultan a tablet sent by Ya'qūb Beg, on which the following poem was inscribed in Persian.

'Abdülazīz Khan, with his scepter of upright judgement, has
taken
The imperial domain from all the rulers on the earth.
Its evidence is found in the country of Kashghar,
Since *khuṭba* and *sekke* was done in his name.[70]

In order to strengthen the relationship of the two countries the Ottoman government decided to provide many more arms and presents. From several documents we can draw up the following list: a standard inscribed with *Fātiḥa* (the first chapter of Qur'ān), a dagger with a curved blade, 2,000 rifles, 6 mountain cannons, a clock decorated with imperial insignia (*tuğra*), a ceremonial garment (*ḥallat*), and 500 printed copies of Qur'ān. In addition to these, travel expenses were given to Sayyid Ya'qūb Khān, and the first- and the second-class of the Mecīdī order were bestowed to two sons of Ya'qūb Beg, Beg Quli and Ḥaqq Quli.[71] And an imperial edict dated Rajab 15 (August 17) was handed over. Ya'qūb Beg had requested the designation of Beg Quli, his eldest son, as his heir-apparent, and the sultan, having no reason to object, gave his confirmation on three conditions:

1. *khuṭba* and *sekke* should be continued in the name of the sultan,
2. the shape and the color of the Ottoman flag already bestowed on Ya'qūb Beg should not be changed, and
3. Ya'qūb Beg should not make unnecessary conflict with neighboring countries.

The sultan also bestowed the second rank, in the Ottoman scale of officialdom, upon Beg Quli and the third rank upon Ḥaqq Quli, younger brother of Beg Quli.[72] There is no doubt that this edict reflects the sultan's will to keep Kashgharia as his protectorate although he knew very well that he could not rule it. The development of the relations made possible further military assistance in the form of a three-pound steel cannon, 2,000 Enfield-type rifles, and a considerable amount of ammunition and additional equipment in total weighing 55,800 pounds.[73] It was also decided that three more military officers should be dispatched. These were 'Alī (a specialist in manufacturing armaments), another 'Alī (an artillery officer), and Kāzim Efendi (a military engineer). The whole expense for the transportation to Bombay, more than 50,000 *kuruş*, came from the treasury of the Ottoman government, and the equipment and officers were sent to India in October 1875.[74] Thus, the second mission of Sayyid Ya'qūb Khān succeeded in making the Ottoman government expand her military aid to Kashgharia.

It seems that Sayyid Ya'qūb Khān was ordered to pursue another object, that is, the improvement of relations with Russia. While he was staying in Istanbul, he paid a visit to Ignatiev, Russian ambassador to the Porte, who also made a return visit to him.[75] Ignatiev worked as an ambassador for thirteen years from 1864 to 1877 and, with the full support of the vizier Maḥmūd Nedīm, exerted such powerful influence on Ottoman politics that he earned the title of Sultan Ignatiev.[76] Having sent the military equipment to Kashghar, Sayyid Ya'qūb Khān visited St. Petersburg to obtain the support, or at least neutrality, from the Russian government in case of a war with China.[77] The envoy had an audience with the emperor around September, who told him to meet and discuss the matter with General Kaufman. Sayyid Ya'qūb Khān returned to Kashghar via Tashkent.[78]

The Great Game?

The opening of diplomatic relations between Kashghar and England, Russia and the Ottoman Empire broke with older historical traditions in the region. Before the emergence of Ya'qūb Beg, the political contacts that Eastern Turkestan had had with its neighbors were basically threefold: China in the east, nomadic powers to the north, and Muslim states in the west. The influence from these three directions had been deeply imprinted on various aspects of life in this region, and the political vicissitudes of Eastern Turkestan had been closely associated with the changes of the power balance among these three neighbors. However, during the 1860s and 1870s a new type of unprecedented international relationship began to emerge with the appearance of England and Russia on the scene. This new situation was the result of several important historical developments.

First of all, in the later half of the eighteenth century the last nomadic state, the Zunghar khanate, was crushed by the Qing, thus one of the above three factors disappeared once and for all. Of the two remaining factors, China was predominant and unchallengeable during the period between the 1780s and the 1820s. The situation rapidly changed with the consolidation of Khoqand power, which brought about the balance between China and Khoqand. However, when both countries were almost completely paralyzed by internal disruptions, a situation similar to these power vacuums was created in Xinjiang. The rebellions and the creation of an independent Muslim government stemmed in a sense from this new situation. When Ya'qūb Beg finally unified the whole of Eastern Turkestan, the political map of the surrounding regions was changing once more. While Khoqand power was rapidly receding into oblivion, a new power, Russia, began to draw its long shadow over Eastern Turkestan. At the same time the British who had been lurking behind the great Himalayas became more and more anxious about the Russian advance.

Ya'qūb Beg was keenly aware of these new developments and tried to take advantage of them. He had basically two diplomatic goals: (1) to form an international balance of power around his dominion, and (2) to obtain the acknowledgment of his legitimacy from the neighboring powers. He knew that the most immediate threat was Russia, so he sought to neutralize this threat by concluding a commercial treaty with Russia and enter into diplomatic relations with England as well. While Ya'qūb Beg's diplomatic goal was well defined and adroitly executed, neither England nor Russia ever developed consistent policies in dealing with Kashgharia. Their failure to formulate clearly defined diplomatic goals was primarily caused by the peculiarity of their ways of perceiving the political reality in Eastern Turkestan. Russia was unnecessarily anxious about the potential danger Ya'qūb Beg's state presented to their occupation of Western Turkestan, particularly that Ya'qūb Beg might actively engage himself in supporting anti-Russian movements by Muslims there. If they had read Ya'qūb Beg's mind better, they would have realized that he would not dare to risk such a thing because what Ya'qūb Beg wanted was a *status quo* that preserved his regime and not continuous holy war.

The British diplomatic goal was based largely on the unfounded belief that all of Russia's political and military advances in the region were aimed at laying the groundwork for an invasion of India. Because of Russia's aggressive activities in the Central Asian field, the British could no longer feel comfortable behind the natural mountainous barriers of the Himalayas, the Pamirs, and the Hindukush. The British were also misled by grossly exaggerated estimates of the economic potential of the markets in Eastern Turkestan. For these reasons England decided in the early 1870s that she had to expand her influence on Eastern Turkestan at all costs to prevent the Russians from taking this strategically and commercially important region. However, as the relations with Kashghar became closer and more detailed research was done, British diplomats came to realize that it was practically impossible for the Russian army to move swiftly through the mountains lying to the south of Eastern Turkestan. Around the middle of 1870s, both countries began to see the reality. England lost her earlier fervor and Russia acknowledged Ya'qūb Beg as a *de facto* ruler of the country. Nonetheless, neither country was willing to completely revise its policy because of the commitments that had already been made, even if these commitments had been based on misconceptions. Their moves toward Kashgharia were timid and continually vacillating.

The approach of the Ottoman Empire was not realistic either. Its decision to ally with Kashgharia was in accord with the public opinion in and out of the empire that urged the formation of a common Muslim front against the encroachments of the Western Powers, especially Russia. At the same time, to have Kashghar as one of their protectorates was a comforting balm to the hurt pride of the Ottoman rulers who had for so long been losing pieces of the empire and international diplomatic influence. Hence the

Ottoman alliance with Kashgharia remained basically within the ideological and emotional sphere. In case of war in Eastern Turkestan nobody thought it plausible that the Ottomans would do any good in saving Kashgharia from falling into the hands of either Russia or China. Ya'qūb Beg probably knew that too. It was extremely improbable that Ya'qūb Beg ever considered mounting any holy war against Russia in alliance with the Ottoman Empire. Rather Ya'qūb Beg's goal, which he adroitly exploited, was to use the relationship to improve his domestic political legitimacy and as a way to purchase more armaments.

When one talks about the Anglo–Russian rivalry in Central Asia, the term "Great Game," first coined in the 1830s, has been often used and it certainly reflects a part of the truth.[79] However, we should note that the term easily conjures up the image of Central Asia as a chessboard and of the separate political entities as pawns that were manipulated by England and Russia. In other words, it is supposed that the pawn has no free will and only the players can calculate the next move. Not only is this idea itself hard to accept, but also the reality often betrays this image. There is a conspicuous danger that the rhetoric may lead to the distortion of the reality. Our analysis of the international relations surrounding Kashgharia shows how Ya'qūb Beg shrewdly set one Western power against the other. Whether it was the result of Ya'qūb Beg's adroit foreign policy or of the miscalculation of the situation by the British and the Russians, the fact is that Kashgharia was not a pawn.

One of the biggest misconceptions that both England and Russia held was the belief that it would be almost impossible for the Chinese ever to reconquer their lost territory, even if they were willing to do so. At the news that the Qing armies had advanced into Zungharia and taken the city of Manas in August 1876, diplomats in both countries agreed that their chances of success were low because of the difficulty they would have in defeating the Urumchi Tungans "who, indirectly supported by Yakoob Beg, would finally succeed in repulsing them."[80] Even after the Qing succeeded in reconquering all of Zungharia around the end of 1876, the British and Russians still remained doubtful that the Chinese would be as successful against "the well organized forces of Kashgar" as they had been against "unarmed Tungan masses."[81]

This strategic assessment was the fruit of Ya'qūb Beg's policy of inculcating an image of stability of his country. It is undeniable that Russia and England were confident in Kashgharia's ability to fend off any Qing attacks because they knew that Ya'qūb Beg had tried hard to strengthen his army and that China was in great disarray at that time. Still neither country had committed itself to Kasgharia's military defense. Russia was worried enough to send a mission headed by A. N. Kuropatkin to find out more about Ya'qūb Beg's military strength and about the possibility of a Qing reconquest. But at the same time it also began to allow its merchants to sell grain to the Qing army in Zungharia. England, on the other hand, never expected Kashghar to fall. Therefore the British government put itself up as a mediator to facilitate a diplomatic agreement that would bring peace between China and Kashghar and put pressure upon the Qing government to abandon its military expedition against Ya'qūb Beg.

In the event of a Qing success, however, neither Russia nor England was prepared to risk a greater danger in order to turn the tide of the events. Russia avoided any direct involvement with the Qing military campaign once it began and even supplied it with grain. While England acted as a mediator to aid Kashghar in its dispute with China, she refused to take more radical measures such as those she had taken against Chinese seaports earlier when her own vital economic interests had been jeopardized. The reason for this is simple and clear. The survival of the Kashghar state was not a vital interest to them. The Russians preferred the Chinese takeover but they could live with Ya'qūb Beg because they already had reached a commercial treaty with him, though not quite satisfactory. Britain preferred the survival of his regime in which they had more influence than the Russians. Since the diplomacy of both countries in Eastern Turkestan had been built upon the fear of each other, if the region were retaken by China there would be no harm done to their respective positions because it would still be a buffer state between them, albeit under Chinese control. This final calculation led both countries to preserve their neutrality in the war, leaving the fate of the Muslim state to the contest between China and Kashghar. In the end, the cold reality of international politics was the limit of Ya'qūb Beg's diplomacy in spite of all his efforts and ingenuity.

6 *Collapse of the Muslim State*

Preparation for Reconquest

CLEARING THE ROAD

When Zuo Zongtang came to Shanxi in the middle of 1867, the Muslim rebellion in Shanxi and Gansu showed little sign of subsiding. Except for several big cities where the Qing troops were concentrated, the whole countryside was in the hands of the Tungans, the remnants of the Taiping and the Nian. Conflicting approaches to the suppression of the rebellion among the highest Qing commanders constantly hampered effective operations in the field. Serious lack of provisions and financial resources caused many Qing troops to desert the ranks, and they raided both cities and the countryside, often allied with the Tungans. But the efforts of the Qing government had not been a complete failure. Dorongga, a fierce Manchu general, partly benefited from the lack of unity among the Tungan leaders, and gained considerable success in establishing a Qing foothold in Shanxi until his death in May, 1864.[1]

The Tungan rebels in Shanxi and Gansu were as much in disarray as the Qing troops were. Their army in Shanxi was known as the eighteen great battalions (*shiba daying*) but it was not a centrally coordinated military organization. Because of the lack of research on the structure of the rebel army, it is hard at present for us to say anything certain on this subject. Nonetheless, it appears that each battalion originally sprang from a communal religious group centering around a local mosque, known as *jiaofang*. As many as a half of the eighteen battalion leaders held the religious titles of *akhūn* or *mullā*, which were normally held by the communal leaders of such groups.[2]

The Muslims in Shanxi and Gansu were divided into the so-called four big *menhuans* (path) and three big *jiaopais* (sect). To the former belonged Hufuye (Khufiyya), Jiadilinye (Qādiriyya), Zheherenye (Jahriyya), and Kuburenye (Kubrāwiyya), and to the latter Gedimu (Qadīm), Yiheiwani (Ikhwānī), and Xidaotang (Chinese school). The difference between *men-*

huan and *jiaopi* lies in that the one was established based on Islamic Sufi path while the other was formed regardless of it. The *jiaopai*s possessed their own organizations based on mosques but did not maintain communications with each other, which caused a lack of unity among the rebels. On the other hand, the *menhuan*s had a large number of followers scattered over wide areas under their own leaders. However, it was difficult for them to have close cooperation not only because of difficult communications but also because of the conflicts between the followers of the New Teachings (*xinjiao*) and the Old Teachings (*jiujiao*) and disputes among their numerous subbranches as well.[3] Therefore, although there were four separate rebel centers in Gansu—Ma Hualong in Jinjibao, Ma Zhanao in Hezhou, Ma Guiyuan in Xining, and Ma Wenlu in Suzhou—they failed to achieve unity.

Zuo Zongtang, who had demonstrated his talent as a military commander in the suppression of the Taipings, arrived in Tongguan, Shanxi, in July of 1867.[4] After some preparations, Zuo developed a strategy for recovering the area. The foremost priority was to take the Tungan strongholds around Jinjibao which were defended by Ma Hualong and his followers. In order to achieve this goal, he deemed it necessary first to clear away the Shanxi Tungans occupying Dongzhiyuan in southeastern Gansu. He finished this campaign in April of 1869, reportedly killing twenty to thirty thousand Tungans. Because of the sharp reduction of the soldiers as a result of this defeat, the Shanxi rebels had to reorganize the eighteen battalions into four and retreat to Jinjibao.[5] Bai Yanhu, or Bai Su whose Muslim name was Muḥammad Ayūb, was one of their leaders.[6]

Now the road to Jinjibao was open to the Chinese. After making preparations during the summer, the Qing army started the operation in September. Three Qing army columns approached Jinjibao from different directions: one led by Liu Songshan from the east, another led by Wei Guangdao from the west, and the last led by other generals from the south.[7] This campaign, however, was much harder than Zuo had expected. In order to reach Jinjibao itself, the Qing army had to capture several hundred less fortified points around it. In addition to the Shanxi Tungans who came to Jinjibao, Ma Hualong also called for help from his followers and allies in Gansu. The total number of Tungan battalions increased to fifty.[8] While the Tungans strengthened their defensive position, Zuo Zongtang encountered a number of serious internal troubles. Mutinies occurred in the best forces under his command, and Liu Songshan was killed in a battle in February of 1870. Zuo's military leadership was even seriously questioned at the court.[9]

Internal dissensions and difficulties were not limited only to the Qing army. During the siege of Jinjibao serious conflicts also broke out within the Muslim camp. Against Ma Hualong who sought a peaceful conclusion by way of surrender even at the risk of his own execution, a group led by Bai

Yanhu and Ma's own son insisted on the military showdown. The hard-liners even proposed to make a surprise attack on Peking.[10] A Tungan eyewitness recollects that once they thought to kill Ma Hualong.[11] Therefore, when Ma finally decided to surrender, a large number of Tungans had left Jinjibao under the leadership of Bai and moved to Hezhou where Ma Zhanao had his base. In this way, the Qing army could take Jinjibao after almost a year and half of severe fighting, rather by Ma Hualong's voluntary surrender than its military superiority. They executed Ma Hualong on February 21, 1871.[12]

In March Zuo drove his army to Hezhou and mounted a campaign there in September, but he received a crushing defeat at the battle of Taizisi temple in February 1872. In spite of his impressive victory, Ma Zhanao chose to surrender, which Zuo himself suspected was "a ruse to earn the time to get assisting troops" and was called by one scholar "a mysterious and odd drama."[13] His decision may have been based on his judgment that his victory could not last long and also on his expectation that he might have a good opportunity to take the hegemony of the Muslim community if he surrendered to the Qing voluntarily.[14] In fact, after his surrender Ma Zhanao was not executed like Ma Hualong but was appointed to *tongling*, and his troops formed a branch of the Qing army. Later, his descendants maintained their hegemony over the Muslim community in Gansu for almost 80 years until 1948.[15] Zuo moved his headquarters to Lanzhou in August and concentrated his efforts on recovering Xining and Suzhou, which he took after exhausting battles by the end of 1873. It was at this time that Bai Yanhu earned his epithet *Dahu*, "Big Tiger," for his bravery.

As we have described above, it took almost seven to eight years for Zuo Zongtang to suppress the Muslim rebellion in Shanxi since he had arrived there in 1867. The operation against Jinjibao alone took one and a half years and with the high cost of General Liu Songshan's death. At Taizishi temple he experienced a shameful defeat and only with Ma Zhanao's surrender could he take Hezhou. Also the occupation of Xining and Suzhou took more than a year. It would not be far-fetched to say that his success in quelling the rebellion in Shanxi and Gansu owed more to the dissension among the Muslims than to the superior military power of Zuo Zongtang's army.

DEBATE AND DECISION

In the beginning of 1874, Zuo was prepared to launch a campaign to recover Xinjiang and gave an order to Jin Shun and Zhang Yue to move their troops west. However, an unexpected incident delayed their further march: the Japanese invasion of Taiwan in the spring of 1874 exposed the weakness of the Chinese naval power and alarmed the Qing court. Although the failure to cope with the invasion was partly due to the ill-coordination among the Chinese naval groups, the incident was enough to make the court become "desperately anxious to strengthen the coastal defense."[16] In view of the apparent weakness of the coastal area, the spending of a large amount of revenue for the Xinjiang expedition produced a serious skepticism in the court, for Zuo had already exhausted approximately thirty-two million *liangs* during the campaign in Shanxi and Gansu (1866 September–1874 February).[17] This amount was almost six times larger than the cost of the building of the strategically vital Fuzhou dockyard (about five and a half million *liangs*) that was completed during almost the same period (1866 December–1874 August). And that was one of the most important naval bases at that time which was founded by Zuo himself.[18]

Several officials in Peking raised sincere doubts about the advisability of the Xinjiang campaign. The question of whether the Qing should or could keep Xinjiang under its control was not new. It had been raised as early as 1865 when Li Yunlin, Tarbaghatai councilor, wrote the following memorial:

> The breakdown of the situation in the northwest did not occur all of a sudden. The causes which could not but lead to this collapse are (1) the lack of finance, (2) the lack of soldiers, (3) the inadequacy of personnel management, and (4) the ignorance about what is urgent and what is not. . . . At present, the strategy as for Xinjiang lies in the judgment of whether we should take it or not. Our dynasty had not possessed Xinjiang until the middle of the Qianlong reign. Now the strength of the country has not been fully recovered and both the troops and the treasury are exhausted. If we do not consider nourishing the army and giving a rest to people, but only trying to continue a military campaign for the victory in the far-off land, it would not be a wise strategy for the statecraft. . . .[19]

Several of the highest officials, including Zuo Zongtang and Prince Chun, were fiercely opposed to this suggestion[20] and the question was not raised again until 1874.

The so-called "great policy debate" over the maritime defense (*haifang*) vs. the frontier defense (*saifang*) in 1874–75 is important not only because its outcome determined the fate of the Xinjiang campaign, but also because it revealed the conflicting perceptions of national security among the leading politicians in China at the end of the nineteenth century. The main argument for the maritime defense, advocated especially by Li Hongzhang, was that the threats coming from the coastal area were more serious and urgent than those from the Muslim state established in Xinjiang. While asking the court to "secretly order the commanding general on the western front only to guard the existing border vigilantly and use his soldiers for military colonizing and farming, without taking a rashly aggressive stand," Li proposed to reduce or disband the army in the west and to transfer the savings to maritime defense.[21] Zuo Zongtang responded in his famous memorial of April 12, 1875, that the prime goal of the Western maritime nations was trade profits, not the territory of China or its people. Xinjiang, on the other hand, was essential to the security of Mongolia which, in its turn, was essential to the security of Peking.[22]

This "Domino Theory" strongly appealed to the politicians in Peking because the history of the long struggle between nomadic states in the north and Chinese empires in the south appeared to justify Zuo's point. His view was also supported by two influential Manchu officials in the court, Wenxiang (Grand Secretary of the Military Council) and Prince Chun (father of the newly enthroned Emperor Guangxu).[23] The final decision made later that month approved the Xinjiang campaign and Zuo was appointed as Imperial Commissioner for Military Affairs in Xinjiang. The outcome of this great debate is evidence of how persistent the traditional Chinese view was with regard to the northern and the northwestern frontiers in spite of all the bitter experiences caused by the incursion of the Western powers along the coastal line from the time of the Opium War (1840). I. Hsü remarks that "with the advent of the age of sea power and China's opening to the West in the middle of the nineteenth century, such steppe-oriented strategical thinking was decidedly obsolescent; yet in varying degrees it still prevailed among the historically-minded Chinese scholars and officials."[24] However, we should not forget that the result of such "obsolescent" thinking was the addition of the largest province to China.

Even after receiving court approval for the Xinjiang campaign in 1875, Zuo Zongtang was faced with the difficult problem of financing such a costly undertaking. In the beginning of 1876 he pleaded with the court to approve a foreign loan of ten million *liang*s, which he asked his friend Shen Baozhen, the governor-general of Liangjiang region, to arrange. Quite unexpectedly, Shen objected to the idea of a loan on the ground that interest rates were too high. In March, however, the court decided to allow a half of the sum (five million *liang*s) to be raised by a foreign loan, while making up the rest from the treasury of the Board of Revenue (two million *liang*s) and from the subsidies of various provinces (three million *liang*s).[25]

Although Zuo secured the necessary campaign fund, obtaining provisions was another matter. Jin Liang proposed in 1874 to produce grain on the spot, but Zuo viewed this as impossible to put into practice because the area to the west of Jiayuguan, all the way to Hami, Turfan, and Urumchi, had been severely damaged by war and become desolate. Instead, Zuo sought to purchase the grain from the Russians as well as the local merchants and to transport some from China proper. In 1875 a Russian merchant, I. O. Kamenskii, sold the Chinese five million *jin* (about 670,000 pounds). Such sales of grain to Zuo's army were extremely profitable to

Russian merchants. Flour purchased in Kulja at 10–15 kopeika per *pud* (about 36 pounds) was sold at 8 rubles per *pud* in Gucheng, that is at 60–80 times higher price. Anyhow, Zuo's army bought from Kamenskii alone almost 10,000,000 *jins* of grain during 1876–77 at the price of 400,000 *liangs* of silver.[26]

One Russian scholar argues that the sale of the grain by the Russian merchants from Siberia was done "in spite of" the formal prohibition of the Russian government.[27] However, a report in a Russian newspaper, the *Turkestan Gazette* (1876), clearly demonstrates the involvement of the Russian authorities.

> The Russian traders of Kuldja are well pleased with the report that a Russian detachment will be stationed at Sazanza (North-West of Shiho) for the procession of the caravan of Kamensky who has undertaken to supply the Chinese troops at Guchen with grain. . . . The detachment at Sazanza . . . will most likely put an end to the pillaging [of Chinese marauders] and protect Kamensky's caravans against attacks on the part of the Dungans between Sazanza and Guchen.[28]

After almost a year of preparation, Zuo Zongtang moved his headquarters from Lanzhou to Suzhou in April, 1876. Already in the spring of 1875, the troops under the command of Zhang Yue and Jin Shun left Jiayuguan and secured Hami during the summer. Jin's army had then crossed the Boghdo Ula mountains and reached Barkul. The Qing army also took Gucheng in the same year. Zuo's strategy for the conquest of Xinjiang was clear: first take Zungharia and then Eastern Turkestan. Because he wanted to avoid the direct military confrontation with Ya'qūb Beg's army until he was fully prepared for it, he decided to approach Urumchi from the north (Barkul to Gucheng to Fukang to Manas to Urumchi) not from the south (Hami to Pichan to Turfan to Dabanchin to Urumchi). In April he ordered Liu Jintang's army to leave Suzhou and by the end of July Liu's entire force was assembled in Gucheng. Thus, the total of 82 battalions (each infantry battalion had 500 soldiers, and each cavalry battalion 250), about 30,000–40,000 troops, were placed in Hami (Zhang Yue), Barkul (Jin Shun) and Gucheng (Liu Jintang).[29] Now the Qing expeditionary army was fully posed to launch an attack.

A Swift Collapse

DEATH OF YA'QŪB BEG

Toward the end of 1873 Ḥākim Khān, the governor of Turfan, received alarming news from a frontier post that several tens of thousands of Tungans were approaching led by Dahu and Shuhu. These were none other than those Tungans who were fleeing from Shanxi and Gansu led by Bai

Yanhu, known as Big Tiger, and Yu Xiaohu, or Little Tiger.[30] These people, after leaving Xining in May 1873 before the fall of the city to Zuo Zongtang's army, had poured into the Hami area in August. They temporarily succeeded in taking the Muslim town of Hami in October, but, not being able to stay there because of the pursuing Chinese army, they left toward Turfan.[31] According to Muslim sources, the number of Tungans coming from Hami was in the range of thirteen to thirty-five thousand.[32] Whatever the exact number was, it appears to have been large enough to alarm Ḥākim Khān. According to 'Abd Allāh, Ḥākim Khān reported the news to Beg Quli who had not yet returned to Kashghar after the completion of the second Urumchi expedition and was staying in Toqsun at that time. Beg Quli dispatched someone to Bai Yanhu to discover the Tungans' intentions and their two leaders came to Toqsun to express their desire to submit to Ya'qūb Beg.[33] They were allowed to settle around the areas of Urumchi, Gumadi, Manas, Qutupi, and so forth.[34] After having cleared up the matter, Beg Quli returned to Kashghar in February–March of 1874.[35]

In September–October of 1875 the approach of the Chinese army was reported to Ya'qūb Beg. Upon receiving this news, he entrusted the capital to Beg Quli and personally marched to the eastern frontier. He spent the winter in Aqsu, while dispatching some of his troops to an advanced position on the border. When spring came, he left Aqsu and arrived in Kurla, where he established his headquarters. In response to the advance of Liu Jintang's army to Gucheng in July, he moved again to Toqsun closer to the frontier, and ordered the construction of a fortress there. When he had left Aqsu, he had taken 15,000 troops (12,000 cavalry and 3,000 infantry) with him. Now, with the situation becoming more serious, he ordered 10,000 additional troops (7,000 cavalry and 3,000 infantry) to come from Aqsu commanded by his son Ḥaqq Quli. At the same time, he sent reinforcements composed of several thousands to Urumchi under Mā Dālūya and A'ẓīm Qul Pānṣad. A'ẓīm Qul was given 300–400 soldiers and sent to Gumadi to assist its defense, while the rest of the force remained in Urumchi.[36]

To strengthen the defense of the eastern frontier Ya'qūb Beg also fully utilized the Ottoman officers whom he had taken with him when he came to the East. According to the memoir of 'Alī Kāzim, two Yūsufs who had been training troops in Ush Turfan, and Ismā'īl Ḥaqq who was in Aqsu were ordered to go to the front and to command several units of Ya'qūb Beg's army.[37] His statement concurs with the recollection of Mehmet Yūsuf who asserts that he and two other Ottoman officers accompanied Ya'qūb Beg to Toqsun.[38] Subsequently Ya'qūb Beg called in again 'Alī Kāzim who was in Yarkand at that time. He recruited 300 soldiers from Yarkand, 300 from Aqsu, and another 300 from Bai, altogether 900, and arrived in Kurla. Ya'qūb Beg entrusted him with more troops who had been recruited from

Yangihissar and Kurla. So 'Alī Kāzim took the command of about 1,530 soldiers, backed up by four 3-pound cannons of Krupp manufacture, and stood against the Qing army.

By the end of July 1876 the armies under the command of Liu Jintang and Jin Shun had moved to Fukang. In order to attack Urumchi, they first had to take Gumadi, but the problem was the provision of water needed to traverse the twenty-mile stretch of the desert lying between Fukang and Gumadi. The distance between the two places is about 30 miles. The only source of water was at Huangdian, located off the main road, which was carefully guarded by the Tungans. The Tungan tactic was first to exhaust the Qing troops by thirst and then hit them hard when they approached Gumadi. Liu Jintang responded with a feint operation. Having some of his troops proceed along the main road, he deluded the enemy at Huangdian into thinking that all the Qing troops were marching to Gumadi. This caused them to loosen their defense and he made a successful surprise attack on Huangdian. He thus obtained the needed water and reached Gumadi on August 12. The fort was taken after five days of assault with five to six thousand Muslims dead, including A'ẓīm Qul.[39]

When Liu Jintang and Jin Shun entered the fort of Gumadi, they found a letter sent by Ma Rende, the leader of the Urumchi Tungans, to a Tungan commander at Gumadi requesting reinforcements. After reading the letter, Liu and Jin realized that there could not be many troops there, so they set out for Urumchi on August 18, the day after Gumadi fell. While Jin's army was passing through a place called Qidaowan they had a skirmish with a group of enemy cavalry whom, at least according to Chinese assertions, they easily defeated.[40] According to Sayrāmī the place was called Jīdabān and those Muslims involved were Tungan soldiers led by Mā Dālūya coming to rescue A'ẓīm Qul at Gumadi. They were winning at first, but because Ya'qūb Beg had ordered them not to engage in a battle, they had to retreat. Then Ya'qūb Beg ordered Mā to go back to Kashghar.[41]

Bai Yanhu and Ma Rende who were defending Urumchi realized that their garrison was not large enough to receive the brunt of the Chinese attack and they fled south on August 13, even before the fall of Gumadi. So Urumchi fell to the Qing almost without resistance on the 19th of August. In the meantime, another Qing army column, commanded by Rongquan and assisted by the militia troops of Xu Xuegong and Kong Cai, came down to Manas from the north and took the northern town on August 18. Yu Xiaohu fled to the south, but the Tungans in the southern town offered stiff resistance. Jin Shun came down from Urumchi to give assistance to Xu Xuegong, and Rongquan also came from Tarbaghatai. Without any support from Ya'qūb Beg, they succumbed after two and a half months of siege to the combined Qing army of three columns (Rongquan, Liu Jintang, and Jin

Shun) on November 6. Thus the whole Zungharian campaign, except for the Ili valley, took only three months.[42] Winter was drawing near, and because of the cold and the snow, Zuo Zongtang decided to let his army rest until the next spring.

During the winter Ya'qūb Beg, having ordered the strengthening of the defense of Dabanchin (which lay between Urumchi and Toqsun), moved his headquarters from Toqsun to Kurla, to the west of Qarashahr. Ḥaqq Quli was then stationed at Toqsun, and Ḥākim Khān, with the assistance of Ma Rende, took charge of Turfan's defense. Kuropatkin who met Ya'qūb Beg at Kurla in January of 1877 gives the following account of Ya'qūb Beg's military strength in those areas: 3,160 at Kurla, 900 at Dabanchin, 8,500 in Turfan (with additional 10,000 Tungan levies), and 6,000 at Toqsun. Thus the total was 18,560 (8,160 infantry and 10,400 cavalry) and 10,000 Tungan soldiers.[43] These numbers are more or less similar to Sayrāmī's assertion as mentioned before; Ya'qūb Beg took about 23,000 troops (apparently the Tungans were not counted here) to the eastern frontier. It seems that the total number of Ya'qūb Beg's army in the east, including the Tungan soldiers, was around thirty thousand, which was not much less than the Chinese army of 30,000–40,000.

On April 14, 1877, Liu Jintang let nineteen battalions march from Urumchi to Dabanchin. During the five days of siege and assault by the Qing troops (April 16–20) the Muslim garrison there seems to have offered only passive resistance and finally they fled, leaving about two thousand dead inside the fort. A Muslim captive told the Chinese general that "Andijanis were looking forward to the assistance [from Ya'qūb Beg], but it did not come. As the siege of the Qing army was tightened day by day, people decided to break the siege and flee."[44] After a few days' rest, Liu marched down to Toqsun on the 25th with fourteen battalions. When they arrived there, they found that the fort had already been completely evacuated. Another Muslim captive explained that Ḥaqq Quli and other Muslim leaders at Toqsun, having heard the fall of Dabanchin, all left the fort in hurry.[45]

Approximately at the same time, Xu Zhanbiao and Zhang Yao who had marched from Jimsa and Hami respectively combined their troops and took Chiqtim, Pichan and Lukchin by assault. On April 26th they had a skirmish with the Muslims at a place about three miles to the east of Turfan. But they easily defeated them and entered Turfan on the same day. Ma Rende surrendered, while Ḥākim Khān fled.[46] With the occupation of Turfan and Toqsun the gates to Kashgharia were open wide to the Qing expeditionary army, but before they were able to begin their final move, Ya'qūb Beg suddenly died at Kurla.

There have been several conflicting hypotheses about the cause and the date of his death. The *Times* reported on July 16, 1877 that Ya'qūb Beg died after a short illness, and the Russian *Turkestan Gazette* also reported that he died on May 1 after a fever of seven days' duration.[47] Many Muslims strongly believed that he was poisoned, and this view is still adhered to by several scholars. For example, according to Sayrāmī's version, Ya'qūb Beg became very furious at a certain Kamāl al-Dīn Mīrzā[48] whom he ordered to be flogged by his attendants, but, apparently his fury not being calmed down, he himself began to beat the man. Becoming tired and short of breath, he ordered his servants to bring cold tea. As soon as he drank the tea brought by a certain attendant (*maḥram*), he fell down and his body became hard, its color turning blue, and then beginning to crack. Sayrāmī suspects that the attendant had been previously bribed by Niyāz Beg of Khotan.[49] Other Muslim writers such as Muḥammad A'lam and Ṭālib Akhūnd give quite similar descriptions about the cause of his death, all blaming Niyāz Beg.[50] However, this hypothesis cannot be sustained because Niyāz Beg, the prime suspect, himself denied it in a letter sent to a Chinese general, Zhang Yao, in which he wrote that Ya'qūb Beg had killed himself.[51] There was no reason for him to deny that he poisoned Ya'qūb Beg if he had really done so because that would have guaranteed an ample reward from the Chinese. The rumor that Ḥaqq Quli or Ḥākim Khān might have been involved in the poisoning also has no basis on facts.[52]

Another theory is that Ya'qūb Beg killed himself out of the frustration in the face of the advancing Qing army. This theory, based on military information, was firmly believed by the Chinese generals at that time.[53] Nonetheless, the suicide theory is not convincing because, although the Qing army took Zungharia and the gates of Kashgharia, that is, Turfan and Toqsun, their success was, as will be explained soon, not the result of intensive battles. Ya'qūb Beg sent no backup troops to the Tungans, and, in a sense, he had not yet been defeated by the Chinese. Moreover, he still controlled most of Kashgharia. Why should he have killed himself even before he fought a major battle?

The most plausible explanation seems to be that he died of a stroke, as witnessed by an Ottoman officer, Zamān Khān Efendi. According to his testimony, it was around 5 o'clock in the afternoon of May 28, 1877, when Ya'qūb Beg became so furious at the above-mentioned Kamāl al-Dīn that he beat him to death. He then turned his anger upon Sabīr Akhūnd and began to beat him. "At that moment he received a blow [i.e., shock] which deprived him of his memory and speech."[54] He remained in that condition for several hours and finally died around 2 o'clock in the morning of May 29. The context of the situation—the extreme fury of Ya'qūb Beg, the violent physical exertion, and the sudden attack that resulted in several hours of paralysis—seems to support the theory that he died of some sort of cerebral hemorrhage.[55] Other sources also support this theory of an accidental death.[56]

There are also conflicting opinions on the date of his death: April 28th (Sayrāmī), May 1st (*Turkestan Gazette*), May 29th (Kuropatkin), July (Baranova), and so on.[57] N. M. Przheval'skii, a famous Russian explorer who visited Kurla just before Ya'qūb Beg died had an interview with him on May 9th (April 28th on the Julian calendar) and left May 11th until which Ya'qūb Beg undoubtedly was alive.[58] The dates proposed by Sayrāmī and the *Turkestan Gazette* are thus out of the question. The basis of Baranova's assumption is Sayrāmī's remark that Ya'qūb Beg died two months after the fall of Turfan. However, there seems to be no reason for us to hold only to Sayrāmī's remark as an unmistakable truth and refute all other information that is contradictory to his remark. The Chinese, who must have paid especially close attention to Ya'qūb Beg's moves, asserted that he died around May 22.[59] Other contemporary Muslims who directly or indirectly witnessed the death also concur with the Chinese that Ya'qūb Beg died around the end of May.[60]

FAILED STRATEGY

His sudden death delivered a devastating blow to the defense of the Kashgharian state. Before he died, however, Ya'qūb Beg issued a strange order to his troops not to open fire against the enemy, which produced as much damage as would his own death later. Why did he give such an order which delivered catastrophic results to his state? One of the answers can be his fear of Qing military power. At that time there was a rumor that the Qing army coming to attack Urumchi were almost two hundred thousand, which made Ya'qūb Beg extremely worried. Probably in order to find out the truth, when he was staying in Toqsun he dispatched a certain In'ām Khwāja Īshān to spy on the number of Chinese army, who reported to him: "Chinese are numerous without limit, and one cannot see the beginning and the end of their flags."[61] Although we do not know how much credence Ya'qūb Beg gave to this report, it may have been one of the reasons he chose to take the diplomatic solution rather than the military.

However, his strategy to maintain his realm through diplomatic means did not emerge only when he faced the army of Zuo Zongtang. Already in January of 1871, he sent a letter through a Chinese prisoner to a high Qing official, Cenglu.[62] Although the content of his letter is not known, the embassy sent to Ya'qūb Beg by the Qing in 1871, as mentioned by a Greek traveler, P. Potagos, was probably a response to this gesture.[63] Even before the Qing expeditionary army set foot in Xinjiang, Ya'qūb Beg wanted to send his own envoy directly to Peking. He even made such a suggestion to D. Forsyth in 1873–74, who advised him that such an act might offend the pride of the Chinese government.

There was also a group of Chinese officials who regarded a negotiation with Ya'qūb Beg as desirable. When Forsyth met Li Hongzhang in April, 1876, Li asked him if Ya'qūb Beg could send a letter to the court stating his willingness to submit to China.[64] Also, at the suggestion of Wade and with the good offices of Li Hongzhang, Prince Gong and the Office of Foreign Affairs (*zongli yamen*) sent a letter to Zuo Zongtang asking him to consider the possibility of receiving Ya'qūb Beg's emissary at his headquarters in Suzhou. Zuo replied to the letter:

> I have now issued instructions bringing this subject to the knowledge of all my divisional commanders, directing them that, in the event of a petition being handed in by the Andijani Yakoob, should the tenour of the document approach in some degree what is reasonable and right, they will be at liberty to bring it to my knowledge, forwarding the document itself and the emissary sent with it to Suh-chow, there to await consideration and reply on my part.[65]

Finally, on May 8, 1877, Fraser telegraphed from Peking to London that "The question of an arrangement with the Ameer of Kashghar has been mooted in the Chinese Grand Council. Prince Kung is said to have spoken in favor of termination of hostilities upon a basis of 'uti possidetis,' but without treaty or formal negotiation."[66]

When Ya'qūb Beg faced the advance of the Qing army, he dispatched Sayyid Ya'qūb Khān as his plenipotentiary to London[67] for the negotiation with a Chinese representative, Guo Songdao. At that time Sayyid Ya'qūb Khān was in Istanbul on a diplomatic mission to congratulate Sultan 'Abdülhamid on his ascension to the throne.[68] According to a curious remark in the report dated March 5, 1877 (Ṣafar 19, 1294) by the Ottoman consul in Bombay, who had assisted Sayyid Ya'qūb Khān in his travels then, "according to a rumor, he would rather stay there [i.e., Istanbul] and not come back."[69] It is not possible for us to verify this "rumor," but his report suggests that Sayyid Ya'qūb Khān may have viewed the future of Kashgharia skeptically even at this early date. When Sayyid Ya'qūb Khān met the sultan in the middle of April, he transmitted Ya'qūb Beg's goodwill and oath to remain loyal to the new sultan and delivered his congratulations and presents. We have no information about any of his diplomatic efforts to stop the invasion of the Qing army.[70] It was not until the beginning of June that Sayyid Ya'qūb Khān arrived in London and began his talks with the Chinese with the aid of the British.

The British government, which saw the survival of Ya'qūb Beg's state in Kashgharia as advantageous to her Central Asian diplomacy, was willing to act as a mediator between the two parties. Ya'qūb Beg, in order to save his state, was prepared to "accept any position that China may assign him, anything short of expropriation."[71] In London Sayyid Ya'qūb Khān made it clear in July 1877 that Ya'qūb Beg would acknowledge the suzerainty of

China if he could keep complete control over the country that he was holding at that time. Guo showed a favorable response to this proposition, though disagreeing in some minor points. He sent a letter to Li Hongzhang suggesting that China should not lose a good opportunity to end the campaign to Xinjiang by the good offices of Britain.[72]

However, as the military situation in Eastern Turkestan turned more and more favorable for the Qing side, the attitude of the Peking court hardened accordingly. In contrast to his position in 1876, Prince Gong was now adamantly against any negotiation, declaring that all the decisions were in the hands of Zuo Zongtang. Even Li Hongzhang was of little help, and for Ya'qūb Beg time was running out. At any rate, there is no reason for us to doubt that in 1876–77 Ya'qūb Beg was aware of the British mediation in Peking and London, and that he might have been even optimistic about the outcome of the negotiation. He had reason enough to believe that Sayyid Ya'qūb Khān would achieve some sort of understanding with China. Therefore he probably thought that it would be wise to avoid a direct military confrontation with Zuo's army, or delay it at least until he found out the result of the negotiation in London.

Such a calculation seems to have been the very reason Ya'qūb Beg issued a strict command to his generals and high officials not to open fire against the Qing troops. The existence of such an order is not found in Chinese sources but widely noted in the Muslim sources.[73] Especially Sayrāmī notes that he gave such an order because he hoped to "make peace with the emperor of China and to conclude a treaty in peace."[74] He not only ordered his troops not to fire but also showed outright disapproval with those who disobeyed, even when they opened fire in order to "protect their souls" from attacks by the Chinese troops.[75] One source relates how he punished Mā Dālūya, who had been engaged in the battle with the Chinese at the place called Qidaowan , by placing him for ten days under the sizzling summer heat.[76]

It is highly probable that Ya'qūb Beg was willing to sacrifice all of Zungharia and even the eastern portion of his dominion in order to avoid a battle with the Chinese, considering that such an attitude might help the diplomatic solution. If this was not the case, it is very difficult for us to understand why Bai Yanhu and Ma Rende, with all their garrison troops, evacuated Urumchi without offering any kind of resistance, and why Ḥākim Khān fled Turfan even though he had almost twenty thousand troops and an enormous quantity of provisions there.[77] The Qing army literally walked into Urumchi and Turfan, strategically the most important points on the eastern frontier of the Kashgharian state. When we recall the fact that it took almost a year and half of siege and numerous casualties for Zuo's army to take Jinjibao alone, not to mention their defeat at Hezhou and other exhausting battles in Xining, we cannot simply attribute their quick success in

Xinjiang to any superior military power. As a matter of fact, most of the foreign diplomats at that time regarded the prospect of the Chinese victory over Yaʿqūb Beg's army as quite remote. For example, as we mentioned earlier, at the news of the fall of Manas, both British and Russian diplomats were skeptical that the Qing army would defeat the Urumchi Tungans,[78] and even after the Qing reconquest of Zungharia, they still doubted the prospect of Chinese victory over "the well organized forces of Kashgar."[79]

From our own privileged vantage point, it is not hard to understand Yaʿqūb Beg's strategy. However, for the Muslims who were being threatened by the approach of the Chinese, Yaʿqūb Beg's order and behavior must have appeared most puzzling. People at that time put forward their own speculations about Yaʿqūb Beg's passive attitude toward the Chinese advance. For example, Sayrāmī thought that Yaʿqūb Beg wanted to conclude a peace treaty with the Qing, while another Muslim writer speculated that Yaʿqūb Beg's avoidance of war in Urumchi and Turfan stemmed from his tactical consideration. In other words, he wanted to face the Chinese in an open field where his superior cavalry force could be utilized most effectively.[80] There was a widespread rumor at that time that Zuo Zongtang had sent a letter to Yaʿqūb Beg demanding the extradition of the two "Tigers," that is, Bai Yanhu and Yu Xiaohu, guaranteeing in exchange the recognition of Yaʿqūb Beg's rule.[81] This rumor, even though somewhat distorted, seems to have had at least a factual basis. Chinese records show when Ḥaydar Quli, the commanding general of Dabanchin, was caught by the Qing troops, he asked Liu Jintang to allow him to send a letter persuading Yaʿqūb Beg to deliver Bai Yanhu and to submit to Qing. Ḥaydar Quli remained at Liu's camp but sent his letter to Yaʿqūb Beg through his own men. The records add that there was no reply afterward.[82]

Whatever the truth was, there is one fact that no one can deny: Yaʿqūb Beg's strategy was not fully comprehensible to many of his Muslim subjects and devastated the morale of his army. Soldiers began to desert the ranks and many Kashgharians who had been discontented with his internal policy welcomed the Chinese army. There were many occasions of defections and of secret correspondence with the Qing army.[83] An interesting episode is recorded: on the day when Yaʿqūb Beg died, he is reported to have blamed Niyāz Beg saying "Did you become Khitay's man too? Do you have correspondence with Khitays?"[84] More and more Kashgharians went over to the Qing side, and many Khoqandian soldiers, more loyal to Yaʿqūb Beg, could do nothing caught between the fire of the enemy and the strict order of their ruler. The ground on which Yaʿqūb Beg was standing began to quickly erode: "it was as if one walks to [the edge of] the cliff with his own feet."[85] Yaʿqūb Beg does not seem to have given up his hope for a diplomatic solution to the last minute, but this was a grave mistake. Even if he had not met such a sudden and premature death, his army's serious disarray would have made their battle with the Qing quite difficult.

LAST DAYS

Ya'qūb Beg's death had a devastating effect upon the Muslim defense against the Qing, not because of his death *per se*, but rather because of its suddenness which brought about a series of internal disputes and a succession struggle. The absence of Beg Quli, the heir-apparent, at the scene precipitated the dissension among the Muslim leaders. After the fall of Toqsun and Turfan, the Qing army was fully poised to attack the Muslim troops and even the Muslims themselves were skeptical about the survival of their state. The diplomatic negotiations in London were abruptly suspended on July 16, 1877[86] and Sayyid Ya'qūb Khān at once returned to Istanbul.[87]

At the news of his father's death, Ḥaqq Quli hurried from Qarashahr to Kurla, where he stayed for several days "gaining over the troops by presents of clothes and by disbursing their arrears of pay."[88] However, he did not proclaim himself ruler, probably regarding his brother in Kashghar as the legitimate successor. He appointed Ḥākim Khān as commander-in-chief to look after the defense and set out for Kashghar on June 7th with his father's body and a small number of soldiers. The next day the commanders and governors present in Kurla decided to enthrone Ḥākim Khān as their ruler.[89] As soon as he was proclaimed khan, Ḥākim Khān sent a group of soldiers in pursuit of Ḥaqq Quli and he himself followed their steps. His intention was to secure his rulership by getting rid of Ya'qūb Beg's two sons, and to get hold of the treasury of the deceased ruler in Aqsu. He left behind only a small number of troops for the defense of Kurla, about five thousand Tungans under the command of Bai Yanhu. When the advance guards prior to him arrived in Aqsu, Ḥaqq Quli had already left the city. Soon Ḥaqq Quli was killed around the end of June at the place called Qupruq, fifty miles from Kashghar, by the people sent by Beg Quli who had suspicions about his brother's intention.[90]

The succession struggle quickly evolved into a civil war. A month after the death of Ya'qūb Beg Eastern Turkestan was partitioned into three: (1) Beg Quli in Kashghar who now obtained the allegiance from the governors of Yangihissar and Yarkand, (2) Ḥākim Khān in Aqsu to the east of which came under his rule, and (3) Niyāz Beg in Khotan to which he fled after having accompanied Ḥaqq Quli as far as Aqsu. Although the participants of these three groups did not necessarily show clear-cut distinctions from each other, the background of the three leaders reveals interesting points. First of all, Beg Quli apparently represented the Khoqandian group that had been very influential during the last few decades of the Qing rule and the foremost beneficiaries under Ya'qūb Beg. Ḥākim Khān, who was Kättä Khān's son and one of the last surviving members of the Āfāqī khwājas, emerged after the death of Ya'qūb Beg to claim his family's legacy of leadership that still carried legitimacy and influence in the region. He reportedly sent a letter to Beg Quli, stating, "The khanship was my father's in the first place. Your father, Ya'qūb Khān, usurped it from his hand by force. Now that Ya'qūb Khān is dead, the khanship belongs to me."[91] Niyāz Beg was a representative of the indigenous Kashgharian begs who had accepted Ya'qūb Beg's rule for their survival but became progressively discontented with it. During the last days of Ya'qūb Beg, some of them, when given the chance, went over to the Chinese side. Therefore, their opposition to Beg Quli apparently reflects the growing dissatisfaction of the local Kashgharian begs and the Āfāqī khwājas under the rule of Ya'qūb Beg.

The contest between Beg Quli and Ḥākim Khān first took place in August. The latter advancing from Aqsu camped at a place called Yaidu, while the former stopped at Chul Quduq. These places are located between Maralbashi and Aqsu. They fought twice: Ḥākim Khān prevailed at first, but then suffered a defeat in the second battle. He fled north of Tianshan to the Issiq Kul area, and from there to Marghilan in the Ferghana valley. It is said that five thousand people followed him, but the rest, more than ten thousand troops, were incorporated into Beg Quli's army.[92] The Ottoman officers who had opposed Ḥākim Khān also allied with him. Beg Quli had eliminated one opponent, but the fate of his state was still desperate. On the one hand, several Kuchean begs rose against Beg Quli and seized Kucha, while on the other, Niyāz Beg became independent in Khotan. Beg Quli first resolved to deal with Niyāz. He drove his troops toward Khotan in October, where he met Niyāz's army at Zava. Beg Quli's soldiers easily overcame the enemy and retook Khotan. Niyāz fled to Niya and then to Kurla, where he surrendered to the Qing army.[93]

While the Muslim leaders were busy fighting against each other, the Qing troops completed their preparations for a final offensive against Kashgharia. Liu Jintang, stationed at Toqsun at that time, divided his troops into two columns for an assault on Qarashahr. One column (fourteen battalions) was to follow the Ushaq Tal route along the southern shore of the Baghrash lake in order to surprise Qarashahr from the rear, while the other led by Liu himself was to proceed along the main road. The operation began in early October. When this army approached the vicinity of Qarashahr, the Muslims under Bai Yanhu's command offered little resistance except for flooding the area, apparently intending to denude the country of supplies and thereby delay the Qing march. On October 7th Liu easily entered the city which had been almost completely evacuated and was inundated with "several feet" of water.[94] On the 9th one of Liu's generals took Kurla, which Bai had already abandoned. The city was completely vacant, without a trace of man. Instantly a detachment of twenty-five hundred troops was dispatched to Bugur where they overcame an ineffective resistance by the Muslims.[95]

With the cities in the eastern Kashgharia falling one by one into the enemy's hands, the Muslim leaders at Beg Quli's camp in Khotan saw the prospect of defeating the invading Chinese troops rapidly disappearing. They suggested abandoning Kashghar and then crossing the border to seek safety. People were sent to Kashghar in order to bring out their families, but only Beg Quli's family arrived in Yarkand because the others were taken hostage by Hō Dalūya, a Tungan leader in Kashghar, who now rose against Beg Quli. The Muslim leaders who were waiting in Yarkand ready to cross the border were angry about the outcome and insisted on assaulting Kashghar in order to rescue their families. Forced by this change of circumstance, Beg Quli marched on Kashghar, while dispatching some troops to Kucha to take the city from Qādir Pānṣad and the Kuchean begs who had dissociated themselves from his rule.[96]

Shortly before this, Bai Yanhu and his group had fled from Kurla and come to Kucha which Qādir was holding. Although Qādir offered some resistance, Bai easily defeated him and entered the city. However, he could not stay there long because Liu Jintang's troops were drawing closer in pursuit. The Qing army arrived in the vicinity of Kucha on October 17th. Overpowering the resistance of the Tungans and the Turkic Muslims, they entered the city next day. The cities and the towns lying to the west of Kucha also fell one by one: Qizil on the 20th, Bai on the 21st, Aqsu on 23rd, and Ush Turfan on the 28th of October. Bai Yanhu finally crossed the border and fled to Narin in the Russian territory. About three to four thousand people were reported to have accompanied him.[97]

Beg Quli who came up to Kashghar from Yarkand attacked the city and besieged it for almost a month without any success. When he heard the news that the Chinese army had advanced to Fayzabad, only thirty five miles east of Kashghar, he and his followers hurriedly fled to Ferghana by crossing the Terek Daban. Two of the Ottoman officers were captured by the Qing troops. According the recollection of Mehmet Yūsuf, "the Chinese government was quite fair and just" and after five months of imprisonment he finally obtained "the permission to depart from the Chinese who took good care of him."[98] However, another prisoner of war, ʻAlī Kāzim, left a record full of painful experiences. He writes that, after the departure of Beg Quli, he was taken prisoner by the Qing army with seven other commanding officers and three thousand soldiers. His hands and feet shackled by iron chains, he was taken to a Qing high officer. He was interrogated with questions like "why did you help Yaʻqūb Khān?" and was brutally tortured for thirty-three days. They stripped him naked and pushed skewers beneath his nails. He recalls that he was taken to a Qing commander (*zūngtūng*) five times, his feet and neck shackled by iron chains and his nails driven through with sharp skewers. While he was imprisoned, he witnessed some of Ya'qūb Beg's commanders taken out of the prison and, after being decapitated, their heads were hung on gibbets. He was forced to walk around the markets in the state of being chained, and taken to the place of execution where they let him see the scene of brutal killings. After three months in prison in this way, he and three other Ottoman officers were expelled from Kashgharia.[99]

As soon as Beg Quli had left, about four thousand Chinese troops under the command of Yu Huen and Huang Wanpeng entered the capital on December 18th. With the fall of Kashghar the reconquest of Xinjiang was complete except for the cleaning-up operations in isolated areas. Liu Jintang, who arrived in Yarkand on the 21st of December, dispatched troops to Khotan commanded by Dong Fuxiang while he himself went to Kashghar. He ordered Huang Wanpeng and Yu Huen to pursue Bai Yanhu and Beg Quli. Yu pursued Beg Quli as far as Ming Yol, where a stone monument was erected later. It is inscribed there that he caught Yu Xiaohu (Little Tiger), Ma Yuan (a Urumchi Tungan leader), Jin Xiangyin (a Kashgharian Tungan leader), and his son.[100] Huang, pursuing Bai Yanhu, also approached the Russian border and then returned. The expedition was formally completed with the capture of Khotan on the second day of January 1878.

Later, the refugees who had fled to Western Turkestan made futile attempts to regain their lost dominion. For example, in October 1879, F. Henvey, a British resident official in Ladakh, reported that a group of refugees in Tashkent rallied under the leadership of Ḥākim Khān and ventured an attack on a frontier town of Ming Yol. Some people reportedly witnessed that six carts loaded with dead bodies of Qing soldiers killed in this attack arrived in Kashghar. He also transmits a rumor that Russia provided Beg Quli, Ya'qūb's eldest son, seven thousand Cossack soldiers and expenses to take back Kashgharia. According to his report, Beg Quli also sent a petition to the sultan.[101] His report is confirmed by the petition, preserved in the Ottoman archives, dated December 25, 1879 (Muḥarram 10, 1297) and signed by a certain "Ya'qūb."[102] It explains how the Qing army reconquered the region without fighting because of the discord among the Muslims after Ya'qūb Beg's death, and then reveals the cruelty that the Qing government committed on the Muslims. It also tries to show the abundance of natural resources in Kashgharia and, emphasizing the fact that this region had been a part of the Ottoman empire during the time of Ya'qūb Beg, asked the sultan to help them to recover the independence from the Qing by peaceful means. Although we do not have further information about how the sultan responded to this petition, it is very unlikely that he would have taken any action to accommodate it.

However, the refugees in Tashkent did not seem to abandon their hope completely, as is evidenced by Beg Quli's personal visit to Istanbul around the end of 1880. He presented a long petition dated November 15, 1880, in which he reminded the sultan of his father's incessant efforts to promote the unity of Islam and explained that, in spite of his appointment as the successor, the Muslims did not acknowledge his authority and started a civil war (*muḥārabat-i dāhiliye*) which resulted in the demise of his state. According to his claim, Russia, promising to give him troops, asked several times to attack and retrieve Kashgharia from the Qing. At that time, Russia showed a sharp conflict of interest *vis-à-vis* the Qing in relation to the return of the Kulja region. However, Beg Quli knew that the Russians were just trying to take advantage of him, so he refused their proposal and returned to his father's hometown, Piskent, to live in peace.[103] Then, he heard the news that the Qing dug out Ya'qūb Beg's grave and burned his body and committed tyranny against the Muslims. Leaders in Kashgharia sent him a letter asking to collect people from Khoqand and Tashkent and to liberate the region. Beg Quli decided to recover Kashgharia by attacking the Qing force, armed with the rifles that the sultan had sent earlier and in alliance with 'Abd al-Raḥmān Dādkhwāh who was leading almost ten thousand tents of Qirghiz living in the Alai mountains. Finally, he mentioned that for this venture what he needed was "spiritual assistance" rather than material because he was aware of the enormous distance between the Ottoman empire and his country.[104] The "spiritual assistance" here seems to mean the sultan's endorsement of Beg Quli's status as legitimate leader of the Kashgharians because he was in dispute with Ḥākim Khān over the leadership in their attempt to recover the country. However, we do not know how the sultan responded to Beg Quli's request. He stayed in Göksu Saray where he received a hospitable reception and on November 23, 1881 went to Izmir, whence he returned to Tashkent via India.[105]

All these attempts of the Muslims were being frustrated by internal hegemonic conflicts as well as by international indifference. The Qing empire regained and consolidated its rule over the entire Xinjiang region after a lapse of thirteen years, except for the Ili valley which was still in the hands of Russians.[106] Zuo Zongtang who commanded the whole operation from Suzhou was acclaimed as the most outstanding man in the empire. As a reward for his feat some suggested that he should receive the title of prince (*wang*), but because of the Empress Dowager Cixi's opposition he was made only marquis (*hou*).[107] I. Hsü writes, correctly, that "rare is the historical event that has won the acclaim of traditional Chinese chroniclers, nationalistic writers, and Marxist scholars alike. The Ch'ing recovery of Sinkiang from the Moslem rebels in the 1870s ranks among the few occurrences that enjoy such an unlikely unanimity." The success of this expedition has been largely credited to Zuo's "extraordinary gift as organizer, manipulator, and politician."[108]

It is beyond any doubt that Zuo was an extremely gifted strategist and soldier, as was proven by the suppression of the Taiping rebellion and the Muslim rebellion in Shanxi and Gansu. However, can we attribute the outcome of the Xinjiang expedition solely to the talent of Zuo and the superior power of his army? As would be clear now, there was no major battle between the Qing and the Muslim troops. When the Qing force conquered Zungharia, they met only a slight resistance at Gumadi. Not to mention that Ya'qūb Beg did not actively support the Urumchi Tungans, hoping to make a bargain with the Qing, he even ordered his troops not to engage in the battle. His attitude caused deep suspicion among many Muslims and aggravated their discontent, which caused the sharp fall in the morale of his troops and massive defections to the Chinese. When the Qing troops finally moved down to Kashgharia, Ya'qūb Beg suddenly died in Kurla and the whole Muslim camp became engulfed in internal fighting. It took only seventy days for the Qing army to march from Kurla to Kashghar. If we remember that the average number of days for caravans to traverse that distance normally took thirty-five days at that time, we can get some idea about how fast the Qing army moved and how little resistance it must have encountered.

What these facts tell us is that the success of the Qing expedition owed more to the disarray of the enemy than the strength of the Qing force. This disarray was caused not only by Ya'qūb Beg's critically miscalculated strategy and his sudden death, but also by the longstanding internal discontent so widespread among the Muslims. This popular discontent resulted from the political domination by the Khoqandians and their abuses of power as well as from the worsening of the economic condition in the country. Nevertheless, even when these negative factors are considered, if Ya'qūb Beg had responded more actively to the Qing advance by defending the cities and harassing the long Chinese supply line over the desert caravan routes, we cannot completely rule out the possibility that the Qing expedition might have ended as one of the most disastrous military undertakings in modern Chinese history.

Conclusion

The latter half of the nineteenth century was the period when the force of worldwide modern transformation began to be felt in Central Asia. During that period, the Russian expansion reached its final stage by crossing the Syr Darya; the British empire threw off its "masterly inactivity" and strove to respond to the Russian pressure in Central Asia; and China was going through the painful process of adapting herself to the modern age. The changes in the outer world had always been reflected in Chinese Central Asia throughout its history and this period was no exception. The 1864 Muslim rebellion was a dramatic response to these global changes occurring around Chinese Central Asia.

On June 4, 1864 a revolt erupted in Kucha that produced a shock wave that quickly spread the rebellion to almost every city in Xinjiang. By the end of that year almost the entire area was freed from the control of the Qing empire. However, specific anti-Qing rebel groups neither planned most of these revolts nor were they the products of much close communication or cooperation among the local rebels in different cities. This seemingly paradoxical phenomenon—the rapid and sweeping success of the rebellion and its lack of coordination—can be understood when we look into the direct causes of the rebellion.

As a result of the rebellions in China proper, especially those in Shanxi and Gansu provinces, the Qing could no longer send the subsidies to Xinjiang that were indispensable for maintaining its military force in Xinjiang. The inevitable result was an increase in the tax burden on the local people whose discontent grew deeper. At the same time, the news of the Muslim rebellion in the western part of China was accompanied by frightful stories of massacre. The Tungans, that is, Chinese-speaking Muslims in Xinjiang were extremely perturbed by this news while the Qing officials began to worry about the growing anti-Qing mood among them. Soon rumors were spread all over the cities in Xinjiang that the emperor of China had ordered the Tungans to be massacred. Although the rumor of an imperial decree appears to have no basis in fact, several sources suggest that in some areas localized massacres of Tungans did actually occur on a small scale. It is certainly true that suspicious Qing officials in Xinjiang took precautionary measures to disarm Tungan soldiers, executing ringleaders accused of plotting revolt, and in some cases even slaughtering a number of Tungans. This was the reason it was the Tungans who took up the first arms against the Qing.

The revolt then rapidly developed into full-scale rebellion when the Turkic Muslims who formed the majority of the population in Eastern Turkestan joined it. They had been under Qing domination since the 1750s, ruled by indigenous local officials called *begs* who were closely supervised by Qing officials. While this policy of indirect rule was designed to lessen conflicts with the local people, the dual administrative structure instead merely resulted in an increased level of exploitation by both local and Qing officials. Under these conditions, the Qing found it necessary to increase the number of troops stationed in Xinjiang to prevent and suppress revolts by the Muslim population. The enormous expense required to maintain this ruling structure was a serious burden not only to the Qing but also to the local population.

Popular discontent was expressed by frequent riots that were exploited by the anti-Qing religious group of the Āfāqī khwājas, who had ruled the country before the Qing conquest and then had taken refuge in the neighboring state of Khoqand. The aspiration of these khwājas to regain Kashgharia was in accord with the interests of the Khoqand khanate, which was also looking for a means to put pressure on the Qing court to obtain trade concessions from China. Pursuit of their common interests resulted in the invasions of Kashgharia by Jahāngīr in 1826 and of Yūsuf in 1830. Faced with this crisis, and expecting that the Khoqand rulers would refrain from further hostile actions if China conceded them important commercial privileges, the Qing court granted Khoqand the right to levy a custom tax from foreign merchants in Kashgharia and other benefits in 1832. The agreement seemed to promise the region stability, but this hope crumbled when both countries were thrown into great turmoil: the rebellions of the Taiping and the Nian in China, the intervention of the Qipchaqs and the Qirghizs, and the drastic weakening of central power in Khoqand. China could no longer bear the financial burden for Xinjiang and Khoqand was in no position to restrain the khwājas. As a result, from the end of the 1840s we see a drastic increase in the number of incursions by the khwājas and riots by local people. Social and economic conditions of the Muslim population became more and more unbearable and ominous signs of discontent began to appear everywhere.

It was at this juncture that the revolt of Kucha erupted and, as the news of its success spread throughout Xinjiang, virtually every major city rose in rebellion with it. After the expulsion of Qing power six different centers of rebellion emerged: Kucha, Kashghar, Yarkand, Khotan, Urumchi, and Ili. Because the rebellion broke out without any coordination among the rebel groups involved, there was no agreement on which one should have supreme power. Serious fighting therefore erupted between rival rebel groups representing each region as well as internal conflicts within each region. Ethnic differences between the Tungans and the Turks aggravated the situation. Yet in spite of all these internal conflicts, we can find one common feature shared by them all: the emergence of religious figures as the formal leaders of the rebellion. Although it was not the men of religion, except in Urumchi and Khotan, who initially started the anti-Qing movement, the diverse groups participating in the rebellion found it in their best interest to make established religious figures the official leaders of their regimes. Some of these religious leaders then succeeded in transforming themselves from nominal leaders to actual rulers, but others remained mere titular figureheads.

This feature reflects one of the most conspicuous dynamics of the 1864 Muslim rebellion in Xinjiang. People with various ethnic and social backgrounds filled the rank and file even when their aspirations were not in accord with one another. They joined the rebellion for their own reasons: the danger of massacre for the Tungans, the unbearable tax burdens for the peasants, the unjust infidel rule for religious people, the prospect of taking leadership from beg officials and the opportunity to get spoils for hooligans. However, what they all cried for together was the holy war against the infidel rulers. Although the 1864 rebellion is not a religious war and religion was not its prime motivation either, it was the religion of Islam that all the diverse groups of people shared in common. Nothing but Islam could bridge the conflicts of the class interest, the ethnic animosities, and regional rivalries. The consciousness of holy war therefore became the driving force rallying almost all the Muslim population in Xinjiang. The persistence and tenacity of Islamic ideals had always been the Achilles' heel of Qing imperial ideology in Chinese Central Asia and the 1864 rebellion demonstrated how badly the Qing had failed in inculcating a non-Islamic model of political legitimacy.

Thus, the religious figures with the charisma of saintly lineages emerged because they could best represent the ideal of the holy war. Many of them styled themselves holy warriors (*ghāzī*) and a rebel government established in Urumchi was named Kingdom of Islam (*Qingzhenguo*). However, the slogan of holy war which had been so powerful against the Qing rulers lost its dynamic force once the infidels disappeared. Fighting broke out between and within the rebel groups and the situation turned more and more chaotic. Although the Kuchean regime under the leadership of Rāshidīn Khwāja took the lead sending armies to subdue other areas, it failed to create a unified power. This historical task was achieved by Ya'qūb Beg, a latecomer on the scene.

Ya'qūb Beg, probably an Uzbek in origin, was born in 1820 in Piskent, a small town 50 km to the south of Tashkent. His early career in the Khoqand khanate is cloudy, but it is apparent that he was neither an adventurous soldier of fortune nor a fanatic holy warrior as has been generally depicted. He had started as a minor official and gradually raised his position serving several different khans and powerful figures. Before he came to Kashgharia, he was under 'Ālim Quli, a Qipchaq leader, who was busy preparing for the defense of Tashkent against the Russians. When 'Ālim Quli received a request from Ṣiddīq Beg, a Qirghiz rebel leader in Kashghar, for the dispatch of an Āfāqī khwāja, he decided to send Buzurg, accompanied by Ya'qūb Beg, in order to protect the vested interests of the khanate by manipulating the situation there. This was the pattern repeated in the past, and, in that sense, Ya'qūb Beg was a mere tool of Khoqand's traditional Kashgharian policy.

His obligation to the khanate, however, was suddenly annulled in the middle of 1865 as a result of 'Ālim Quli's death and his incorporation of the political refugees opposing a new ruler of the khanate, Khudāyār, whom he himself had opposed. He became free to act on his own. Almost seven thousand Khoqandian refugees, many of them seasoned warriors and military officers, provided him a firm military basis for the conquest of Eastern Turkestan. Based on these troops, he organized one cavalry and four infantry divisions whose total number reached fifteen thousand. By June 1867 Ya'qūb Beg became the sole ruler of Kashgharia by eliminating rival powers in Yarkand, Khotan, and Kucha, and during 1870–1872 he succeeded in unifying the entire Eastern Turkestan and Urumchi areas.

His task was then how to rule this vast territory as a foreigner who lacked sufficient secular or religious charisma. What he needed first of all was a strong army loyal to him, and so he built a non-tribal standing army of more than forty thousand in strength. To insure their loyalty he gave highest posts to the Khoqandians who came from his own country and shared the same destiny with him. Careful studies show that the majority of the commanders of division and the captains of five hundred were recruited from the Khoqandians. At the same time, in order to check the danger of opposition from army commanders, he took measures to prevent them from establishing an independent military power. He also retained the right to appoint and dismiss army officers above the rank of captain of one hundred.

The monopoly of the Khoqandians was also found in the provincial government. The largest unit of local administration, *vilāyat*, was under the governor called *ḥākim*. The exact number of provinces varies according to sources, but it appears to have fluctuated between seven and ten, which roughly corresponds to the Eight Cities of the Southern Circuit under the Qing rule. The governor took control of civil, financial, military, and judicial branches of the provincial government, but only nominally. This was because Ya'qūb Beg frequently exercised his personal power to appoint the military officers stationed in important areas, and financial officials were also directly responsible to him. This division was a measure aimed at preventing regional officials from consolidating too much power in their own hands.

Although the ruling structure of the Muslim state under Ya'qūb Beg was extremely centralized, it seems that there was no well-structured central government. What we can find is a group of people called *mīrzā*s under the direction of *mīrzābashi* (chief secretary). They took responsibility for the revenue and expenditures of the government and provided advice at the request of Ya'qūb Beg. The power of *mīrzābashi*s was so great that one local historian wrote that they were only next to Ya'qūb Beg. The background of these *mīrzābashi*s shows that they were neither high officials nor religious figures. They were mere professional scribes or accountants, and because they did not have an independent source of influence, they could not but entirely rely upon the favor of Ya'qūb Beg.

However, the military buildup and the centralization of power were not sufficient to secure his rule. What he was conspicuously lacking was legitimacy. He had started as a mere deputy of the Khoqand khanate and had no source of charisma to justify his rule. He himself knew this problem very well and it was why he never called himself khan. What he chose to do to overcome this handicap was to promote Islam and to enforce the regime of *sharī'ah*. He himself showed the model by a frugal way of life as if he were a dervish and he promoted the construction of religious facilities, especially saintly mausoleums. The popular titles like Badaulat and Ataliq Ghāzī by which he was addressed show his inclination to present himself as the image of a holy warrior endowed with divine blessing.

One of the aims for him to open the diplomatic relation with foreign countries was to give an aura of legitimacy to his rule in the eyes of the local population. At the same time, he used diplomacy to enhance his political status in the international community and to find channels for acquiring military armaments. At first, Russia not only ignored the legitimacy of Ya'qūb Beg's rule but also was prepared to use military means to protect her trade rights in Eastern Turkestan and to eliminate the danger posed by him. His strenuous effort to neutralize the threat finally resulted in a commercial agreement with the Russian government in 1872. He also approached England and succeeded in bringing her to signing a commercial treaty in 1874. While trying to maintain the balance of power around his country in this way, he entered into a diplomatic relationship with the Ottoman Empire. His relation with the Ottomans, initiated and propelled by the effort of Sayyid Ya'qūb Khān, bore especially fruitful results. In 1873 he acknowledged the suzerainty of the sultan who reciprocated by bestowing on him the title of *amīr* and massive military support through the dispatch of armaments and military instructors.

However, the Muslim state under Ya'qūb Beg had critical weaknesses, including the widespread discontent of the local population due to economic hardship and the Khoqandian domination. This problem was an inevitable result of his centralization and military buildup. Ya'qūb Beg's army of forty thousand was equivalent in size to the number of Qing troops that had previously been stationed in Xinjiang. But while the Qing court had drawn on the resources from China as a whole to offset the huge costs of maintaining these troops, Ya'qūb Beg could only rely on the tax income from the local population of Xinjiang itself. He attempted to alleviate their discontent by ideological indoctrination stressing the puritanical spirit of Islam and by an iron rule that inculcated fear into various sectors of the society. The discontent, however, was not obliterated but simply suppressed, only to reemerge at the moment of critical weakness.

More important, Ya'qūb Beg had no sure means by which to forestall China's intention to reconquer Xinjiang. He had first attempted employing direct diplomatic means to persuade the Qing rulers to acknowledge the *status quo*. When these negotiations with China failed, he urged Britain to wield its influence upon the Qing court. The British effort to advise the futility of the reconquest seemed to be listened to seriously among some of the high Qing officials like Li Hongzhang and Prince Gong. Probably this news may have given Ya'qūb Beg hope that he might solve the problem by diplomacy.

However, in the middle of 1876 the Qing army under the command of Zuo Zongtang already began its move into Zungharia. Ya'qūb Beg, while having concentrated more than twenty thousand troops in the areas of Toqsun and Kurla preparing for a possible showdown, ignored the request of assistance from the Tungans in Zungharia and ordered his troops not to open fire against the Qing army. This strange order stemmed from his expectation for diplomatic settlement with China. He sent his envoy to London for negotiations with the representative of China and was prepared to accept even the term of submission to China only if he could keep the country. His decision was, however, a critical strategic mistake because the Qing court, under the urgings of Zuo Zongtang and several other Manchu hardliners, was not willing to accept the diplomatic solution.

Ya'qūb Beg's passive policy toward China, especially his order not to open fire, gave a devastating blow to the morale of his army. Many officials and soldiers began to desert to the Chinese side. In the middle of the defection and the confusion he suddenly died around the end of May 1877 in Kurla. This was instantly followed by a massive defection of the Muslim soldiers to the Chinese and by an intense succession struggle within the Muslim camp, which made it impossible for them to fight the Chinese. They never offered any substantial resistance to the Qing troops who conquered the entire area of Eastern Turkestan in just two months. We may well say that the collapse of the Muslim state was self-destruction rather than the result of armed clashes.

The political events in Chinese Central Asia during the period between 1864 and 1877 left enduring marks upon later historical developments in this region. The first, and the most conspicuous change, was its incorporation into the provincial system. As a result of the bitter experience during the period of the rebellion, China now clearly realized that the old way of domination of Xinjiang through Qing military officials and local Muslim begs was no longer adequate. A long history of debates surrounding the plausibility of the establishment of provinces in Xinjiang finally reached its end.[1]

With the introduction of a new provincial system which was followed by extensive immigration of Chinese, sinicization of Xinjiang really began to take place. After the creation of the People's Republic of China this process continued through the colonization by the Military Corps for Production and Construction, which accelerated the massive influx of Han population. At present, the Uyghurs maintain a precarious plurality in numbers over the Han Chinese,[2] but there is no doubt that soon the pendulum will be tilted toward the Han.

It was not only the Chinese attitude that was changed. This turbulent era left an indelible imprint upon the local Muslims as well. During about ten years of Ya'qūb Beg's rule, religious leaders, especially khwājas, who had exercised enormous influence in the past, were executed or lost their political influence. After the Qing entered again in 1877, they ceased to be a predominant social group to be reckoned with. Ḥākim Khān's attempt was virtually the last page of their long history of dominance over the Kashgharian people. Instead, a group of new intellectuals began to emerge who were deeply imbued with the ideas of Jadidism in Russian Turkestan and Turkey. They were critical of religious obscurantism and began to urge the reform of traditional Muslim society. Since then the guiding principle of the popular movements in Xinjiang was nationalism, and holy war no longer could be the sole slogan.[3]

After the great upheaval in the later half of the nineteenth century Chinese Central Asia could no longer stay as it had been. The changes that it brought about in the spheres of the political and social structures, ethnic composition, and foreign relations began to operate as powerful forces in molding the modern history of this region in the twentieth century.

APPENDIX A

Treaty Between Russia and Kashghar (1872)[1]

The following conditions of free trade were proposed and agreed upon between General Aide-de-Camp von Kaufman and Yakoob Beg, ruler of Djety-Shahr.

ARTICLE I

All Russian subjects, of whatsoever religion, shall have the right to proceed for purposes of trade to Djety-Shahr, and to all the localities and towns subjected to the ruler[2] of Djety-Shahr, which they may desire to visit in the same way as the inhabitants of Djety-Shahr have hitherto been, and shall be in the future, entitled to prosecute trade throughout the entire extent of the Russian Empire. The honourable ruler of Djety-Shahr undertakes to keep a vigilant guard over the complete safety of Russian subjects, within the limits of his territorial possessions, and also over that of their caravans, and in general over everything that may belong to them.

ARTICLE II

Russian merchants shall be entitled to have caravanserais, in which they alone shall be able to store their merchandise, in all the towns of Djety-Shahr in which they may desire to have them. The merchants of Djety-Shahr shall enjoy the same privilege in the Russian villages.

ARTICLE III

Russian merchants shall, if they desire it, have the right to have commercial agents (caravanbashis) in all the towns of Djety-Shahr, whose business it is to watch over the regular courts of trade, and over the legal imposition of custom dues. The merchants of Djety-Shahr shall enjoy the same privilege in the towns of Turkestan.

ARTICLE IV

All merchandise transported from Russia to Djety-Shahr, or from that province into Russia, shall be liable to a tax of 2 1/2 percent, *ad valorem*. In every case this tax shall not exceed the rate of the tax taken from Mussulmans being subject to Djety-Shahr.

ARTICLE V

Russian merchants and their caravans shall be at liberty, with all freedom and security, to traverse the territories of Djety-Shahr in proceeding to countries coterminous with that province. Caravans from Djety-Shahr shall enjoy the same advantages for passing through territories belonging to Russia.

These conditions were sent from Tashkent on the 9th of April, 1872.

General Von Kaufman I., Governor-General of Turkestan, signed the treaty and attached his seal to it.

In proof of his assent to these conditions, Mahomed Yakoob, ruler of Djety-Shahr, attached his seal to them at Yangy-Shahr, on the 8th of June, 1872.

This treaty was negotiated by Baron Kaul'bars.

APPENDIX **B**

Treaty Between England and Kashghar (1874)[1]

Treaty between the British Government and His Highness the Ameer Mahomed Yakoob Khan, Ruler of the territory of Kashgar and Yarkund, his heirs and successor, executed on the one part by Thomas Douglas Forsyth, C. B., in virtue of full powers conferred on him in that behalf by His Excellency the Right Honourable Thomas George Baring, Baron Northbrook, of Stratton, and a Baronet, Member of the Privy Council of Her Most Gracious Majesty the Queen of Great Britain and Ireland, Grand Master of the Most Exalted Order of the Star of India, Viceroy and Governor General of India in Council, and on the other part by Syud Mahomed Khan Toorah, Member of the First Class of the Order of Medjedie, &c., in virtue of full powers conferred on him by His Highness.

Whereas it is deemed desirable to confirm and strengthen the good understanding which now subsists between the high contracting parties, and to promote commercial intercourse between their respective subjects, the following Articles have been agreed upon: —

ARTICLE I

The high contracting parties engage that the subjects of each shall be at liberty to enter, reside in, trade with, and pass with their merchandise and property into and through all parts of the dominions of the other, and shall enjoy in such dominions all the privileges and advantages with respect to commerce, protection, or otherwise, which are or may be accorded to the subjects of such dominions, or to the subjects or citizens of the most favoured nation.

ARTICLE II

Merchants of whatever nationality shall be at liberty to pass from the territories of the one contracting party to the territories of the other with their merchandise and property at all times and by any route they please; no restriction shall be placed by either contracting party upon such freedom of transit, unless for urgent political reasons to be previously communicated to the other; and such restriction shall be withdrawn as soon as the necessity for it is over.

ARTICLE III

European British subjects entering the dominions of his Highness the Ameer for purposes of trade or otherwise must be provided with passports certifying to their nationality. Unless provided with such passports they shall not be deemed entitled to the benefit of this Treaty.

ARTICLE IV

On goods imported into British India from territories of his Highness the Ameer by any route over the Himalayan passes which lie to the south of his Highness's dominions, the British Government engages to levy no import duties. On goods imported from India into the territories of his Highness the Ameer, no import duty exceeding 21/2 percent. *ad valorem* shall be levied. Goods imported as above into the dominions of the contracting parties may, subject only to such excise regulations and duties and to such municipal or town regulations and duties, as may be applicable to such classes of goods generally, be freely sold by wholesale or retail, and transported from one place to another within British India, and within the dominions of his Highness the Ameer respectively.

ARTICLE V

Merchandise imported from India into the territories of his Highness the Ameer will not be opened for examination till arrival at the place of consignment. If any disputes should arise as to the value of such goods the Customs officer or other officer acting on the part of his Highness the Ameer shall be entitled to demand part of the goods at the rate of one in 40, in lieu of the payment of duty. If the aforesaid officer should object to levy the duty by taking a portion of the goods, or if the goods should not admit of being so divided, then the point in dispute shall be referred to two competent persons, one chosen by the aforesaid officer and the other by the importer, and a valuation of the goods shall be made, and if the referees shall differ in opinion, they shall appoint an arbitrator, whose decision shall be final, and the duty shall be levied according to the value thus established.

ARTICLE VI

The British Government shall be at liberty to appoint a representative at the Court of his Highness the Ameer, and to appoint commercial agents subordinate to him in any towns or places considered suitable within his Highness's territories. His Highness the Ameer shall be at liberty to appoint a representative with the Viceroy and Governor General of India, and to station commercial agents at any places in British India considered suitable. Such representatives shall be entitled to the rank and privileges accorded to ambassadors by the law of nations, and the agents shall be entitled to the privileges of consuls of the most favoured nation.

ARTICLE VII

British subjects shall be at liberty to purchase, sell, or hire land or houses or depôts for merchandise in the dominions of his Highness the Ameer, and the houses, depôts, or other premises of British subjects shall not be forcibly entered or searched without the consent of the occupier, unless with the cognisance of the British representative or agent, and in presence of a person deputed by him.

ARTICLE VIII

The following arrangements are agreed to for the decision of civil suits and criminal cases within the territories of his Highness the Ameer in which British subjects are concerned: —

(*a.*) Civil suits in which both plaintiff and defendant are British subjects, and criminal cases in which both prosecutor and accused are British subjects or in which the accused is a European British subject mentioned in the 3rd Article of this Treaty, shall be tried by the British representative, or one of his agents, in the presence of an agent appointed by his Highness the Ameer.

(*b.*) Civil suits in which one party is a subject of his Highness the Ameer and the other party a British subject, shall be tried by the courts of his Highness in the presence of the British representative, or one of his agents, or of a person appointed in that behalf by such representative or agent.

(*c.*) Criminal cases in which either prosecutor or accused is a subject of his Highness the Ameer shall, except as above otherwise provided, be tried by the courts of his Highness in presence of the British representatives, or of one of his agents, or of a person deputed by the British representatives, or by one of his agents.

(*d.*) Except as above otherwise provided, civil and criminal cases in which one party is a British subject and the other the subject of a foreign power, shall, if either of the parties is a Mahomedan, be tried in the courts of his Highness; if neither party is a Mahomedan, the case may, with consent of the parties, be tried by the British representative, or one of his agents: in the absence of such consent, by the courts of his Highness;

(*e.*) In any case disposed of by the courts of his Highness the Ameer to which a British subject is party, it shall be competent to the British representative, if he considers that justice has not been done, to represent the matter to his Highness the Ameer, who may cause the case to be retried in some other court, in the presence of the British representative, or of one of his agents, or of a person appointed in that behalf by such representative or agent.

ARTICLE IX

The rights and privileges enjoyed within the dominions of his Highness the Ameer by British subjects under this Treaty shall extend to the subjects of all princes and states in India in alliance with Her Majesty the Queen; and if, with respect to any such prince or state, any other provisions relating to this Treaty, or to other matters, should be considered desirable, they shall be negotiated through the British Government.

ARTICLE X

Every affidavit and other legal document filed or deposited in any court established in the respective dominions of the high contracting parties, or in the Court of the Joint Commissioners in Ladakh, may be proved by an authenticated copy, purporting either to be sealed with the seal of the court to which the original document belongs, or in the event of such court having no seal, to be signed by the judge, or by one of the judges of the said court.

ARTICLE XI

When a British subject dies in the territory of his Highness the Ameer, his movable and immovable property situate therein shall be vested in his heir, executor, administrator, or other representative in interest, or (in the absence of such representative) in the representative of the British Government in the aforesaid territory. The person in whom such charge shall be so vested shall satisfy the claims outstanding against the deceased, and shall hold the surplus (if any) for distribution among those interested. The above provisions, *mutatis mutandis*, shall apply to the subjects of his Highness the Ameer who may die in British India.

ARTICLE XII

If a British subject residing in the territories of his Highness the Ameer becomes unable to pay his debts, or fails to pay any debt within a reasonable time after being ordered to do so by any court of justice, the creditors of such insolvent shall be paid out of his goods and effects; but the British representative shall not refuse his good offices, if needs be, to ascertain if the insolvent has not left in India disposable property which might serve to satisfy the said creditors. The friendly stipulations in the present Article shall be reciprocally observed with regard to his Highness's subjects who trade in India under the protection of the laws.

This Treaty having this day been executed in duplicate, and confirmed by his Highness the Ameer, one copy shall, for the present, be left in the possession of his Highness, and the other, after confirmation by the Viceroy and Governor General of India, shall be delivered to His Highness within twelve months in exchange for the copy now retained by his Highness.

Signed and sealed at Kashgar on the 2nd day of Februray, in the year of our Lord 1874, corresponding with the 15th day of Zilhijj, 1290 Hijri.

(Signed) T. Douglas Forsyth
Envoy and Plenipotentiary.

Whereas a Treaty for strengthening the good understanding that now exists between the British Government and the ruler of the territory of Kashgar and Yarkund, and for promoting commercial intercourse between the two countries, was agreed upon and concluded at Kashgar on the 2nd day of February, in the year of our Lord 1874, corresponding with the 15th day of Zilhijj, 1290 Hijree, by the respective plenipotentiaries of the Government of India and his Highness the Ameer of Kashgar and Yarkund duly accredited and empowered for that purpose: I, the Right Honourable Thomas George Baring, Baron Northbrook, of Stratton, &c., &c., Viceroy and Governor General of India, do hereby ratify and confirm the Treaty aforesaid.

Given under my hand and seal at Government House in Calcutta, this 13th day of April, in the year of our Lord 1874.

(Signed) Northbrook.

APPENDIX **C**

Table of Contents in TAs and THs

This table shows the epitomized title and its starting page (or folio) of each chapter in five different manuscripts and editions of TA and TH which are available to me. The five copies listed below do not exactly match with each other, and it was because Sayrāmī continuously revised his work throughout his life. It is important for researchers to compare and find the changes found in these copies.

Titles of Chapters	TH/ *Enver*	TH/ *Jarring*	TA/ *Pelliot*	TA/ *Jarring*	TA/ *Pantusov*
Preface	27	1r	1v	7r	2
Introduction					
1 History after Noah	41	3r	3v	9r	7
2 Chinggis Khan and his descendants	67	8v			
3 Dughlat tribe and its amīrs	98	15r	10r		
4 Tughluq Temür Khan and his descendants	117	19r	17r	21v	
5 Holy war of Jahāngīr	148	26r	26r	30v	28
6 Muslim under the Chinese rule	158	28r	29v	34v	34
Part 1: Rāshidīn Khwāja					
1 Holy war of Rāshidīn Khwāja	181	33v	38v	44r	44
2 Genealogy of Rāshidīn Khwāja	187	35r	40v	46v	48
3 Failure of Aqsu campaign	190	35v	42r	47v	50
4 Success of Aqsu campaign	197	37v	44r	50r	54
5 Expedition to Ush Turfan	202	38v	46v	52v	57
6 Kashghar campaign	210	40v	49v	55v	62
7 Yarkand campaign	213	41r	51r	57r	65
8 Campaign to Kashghar and Yarkand	220	42v	53r	59r	69
9 Rule of Maḥmūdīn	230	44v	57r	63r	76
10 Isḥāq Khwāja; Ili and Khotan	246	48r	63r	69v	86
11 Conquest of Qarashahr	254	50r	66r	73r	92
12 Conquest of Turfan	271	53v	71v	78v	100
13 Failure of campaign to Murkhu	282	56r	76v	83r	107
14 Submission of Hami and Return of Isḥāq Khwāja	288	57v	78v	85r	111
15 Isḥāq Khwāja's western campaign and its failure	299	60r	82v	89v	116
16 Dissension and demise of Kuchean khwājas	307	62r	85v	93r	121
Part 2: Ya'qūb Beg					
1 Arrival of Ya'qūb Beg and Buzurg	326	66v	91r	99r	131
2 Refugees from Khoqand	340	69v	96v	105r	141

3	Ya‘qūb Beg's rise to power	352	72v	101v	110r	149
4	Khotan campaign	360	74r	104v	113v	155
5	Ḥabīb Allāh's virtue and his rule	377	78r	104v	113v	167
6	Conquest of Aqsu and Kucha	388	80r	115r	124v	174
7	Unification of Yättishahr	399	83r	119r	129v	182
8	The Ottoman empire	417				
9	Battles with the Urumchi Tungans	431	86v	126r	135v	193
10	Conquest of Urumchi	447	90r	132v	141v	202
11	Ḥākim Khān's campaign to Urumchi	459	93r	137v	146r	211
12	Second expedition to Turfan	476	96v	144r	150v	219
13	Merits and demerits of Ya‘qūb Beg's rule	495	100r	151r	157r	231
14	Ḥākim Khān's enthronement	526	104v	160v	165v	245
15	Rise and fall of Beg Quli	533	106v	163v	168v	251
16	Niyāz Ḥākim Beg	546	109v	168v	173r	259
17	Notables during Ya‘qūb Beg's era	563	113r	175v	lacking	270
18	Carreer of the author, Sayrāmī	587	116v	183v	183r	284
19	Reconquest of Chinese emperor	600	120v	187v	187r	291
20	Virtues of Chinese emperor	617	lacking			
Conclusion						
	Description of Yättishahr, and Conclusion	636	lacking	196r	195r	304

Glossary

Āfāqī	followers of Khwāja Āfāq, "Black Mountaineers"
akhūnd (*akhūn)*	title given to Muslim religious leaders
a'lam	scholar
alban (*alvan)*	tributary tax
Altishahr	"Six Cities," that is, Kashgharia
amban	Qing high official (Ma.)
amīr al-mū'minīn	"Commander of the Faithful"
amīr al-umarā	commander-in-chief
amīr	chief, commander
amīr-i lashkar	commander-in-chief
aqsaqal	elder ("white beard")
ataliq	title of a high ranking official (lit., fatherly)
bacha	"dancing boy"
badaulat	"fortunate one"
bashi	low governmental funtionary (lit., head)
batman	unit of measure for crop land
bai	the well-to-do
beg	local Muslim official title
bī (*bīī*)	title for tribal chief (etymologically same as *beg*)
caravanbashi	commercial agent (lit., head of caravan)
dādkhwāh	governor (synonim of *ḥākim*)
dahbashi	"head of ten"
darugha	petty functionary
darvīsh	ascetic, dervish
dayanshay	commander-in-chief (Ch. *dayuanshuai*)
dīvān (*dīvānbegi)*	village headman
elligbashi	"head of fifty"
farsakh	unit of measure for distance (4.5–5 miles)
fatva	legal opinion based on the Islamic law
ghazāt	holy war
ghāzī	holy warrior
ḥājj	pilgrimage (to Mecca)
ḥājjī	one who performed *ḥājj*
ḥākim	governor
huda-i da	head of merchants (Ma.)

imām	preacher, religious title
īshān	high religious title (lit., they)
ishikagha	deputy governor
jigit (yigit)	cavalry
jizyā	poll tax
khalīfa	caliph (lit., deputy)
khānaqāh	prayer house, retreat
kharāj	land tax
khazānachi	treasurer
khitay	China, Chinese
khuṭba	Friday sermon
khwāja	high Muslim religious title
kuhnashahr	"old city"
kuruş	Ottoman monetary unit
langar	halting place
lashkarbashi	commander-in-chief
madrassa	Islamic college
Makhdūmzāda	descendant of Makhdūm-i A'ẓam
masjid	mosque
mazār	holy tomb
mihtar	court official ("keeper of the wardrobe")
miltiq	rifle
mingbashi	"miliarch"
mīr	govenor ("lord")
mīrāb	supervisor of irrigation
mīrzā	secretary (from *amīrzāda*)
mīrzābashi	chief secretary
mu'azzin	the caller of prayer
muftī	religious prosecutor
mullā	teacher (from *mawlā*)
murīd	disciple
musulmān	Muslim
namāz	daily prayer
pādishāh	king, emperor
pādishāhzāda	descendant of king
panjāhbashi	"captain of fifty"
pānṣad (pānṣadbashi)	"captain of five hundred"
parvānachi	court official ("keeper of the royal seal")
pīr (pīrī)	religious master
pul	smallest monetary unit
qāḍī	judge
qāḍī kalān	chief judge

qarawul	frontier guard-post
qonalgha	irregular levy ("quartering")
qushbegi	high official title in Bukhara and Khoqand
samāʾ	listening to music
saman-pul	irregular tax on grains
sarbāz	infantry
sarkār	treasurer
sayyid	high religious title
sekke	coinage
shahīd	martyr
shāngyū	elder of merchants (Ch. *shangye*)
sharīʿah	religious law of Islam
shaykh al-Islām	head of *ʿulamā*
shaykh	lord; leader of Sufi order
soyurghal	fief
Sufi	Islamic mystics (*ṣūfī*)
sulṭān	king, ruler
tängä	silver coin (equal to 50 *puls*)
taranchi (*tariyachi*)	Eastern Turkestanis in Zungharia (lit., cultivator)
top	cannon
tungchi	interpreter (Ch. *tongshi*)
ṭanāb	tax on orchards; unit of measure for non-crop land
ṭillā	gold coin
ʿulamā	Muslim scholars ("the learned")
urda	residence of governor or ruler (from *orda* or *ordu*)
ʿushr	land tax; tithe
vaqf	endowment
vilāyat	province
vizīr	minister
wayshang	suburban market (Ch. *waishang*)
yāmbū	silver ingot (Ch. *yuanbao*)
yangishahr	new city
yanshay	commander (Ch. *yuanshuai*)
yasawul	aide-de-camp
Yättishahr	"Seven Cities," that is, Kashgharia
Yeniçeri	cavalry army in the Ottoman empire (Janissary)
yüzbashi	centurion
zakāt	alms tax, or tax on livestock or commodities
zakātchi	collector of *zakāt*

List of Chinese Characters

ahong 阿訇
ahun 阿渾
*Atuwai (Atuoai) 阿托愛
Bai Su 白素
Bai Yanhu 白彥虎
bangban dachen 幫辦大臣
banshi dachen 辦事大臣
bazong 把總
Beilu 北路
bingtun 兵屯
bo 伯
cang 倉
Cangcing (Changqing) 常清
Cangling (Changling) 長齡
canjiang 參將
canzan dachen 參贊大臣
Cenglu (Chenglu) 成祿
Changji 昌吉
changmaozi 長毛子
chantou hui 纏頭回
Chen Tai 陳泰
chitun 旗屯
chou 丑
Cui Wei 崔偉
Dahu 大虎
dangshi 當十
dangwu 當五
dapao 大砲
daqian 大錢
dayuanshuai 大元帥
dazhuang 大莊
Dian Manla 田滿拉
Dihua 迪化
Dong Fuxiang 董福祥
Dongcheng 東城

donggan	東干
Donglu	東路
Dongzhiyuan	董志原
dou	斗
duguan	都觀 (都官)
duguan-beg	都官伯克
Dorongga (Duolonga)	多隆阿
dutong	都統
Edui	鄂對
Elute	額魯特
fangbing	防兵
Fujuri (Fuzhuli)	富珠哩
Fukang	阜康
Ganzhou	甘州
Gedimu	格的木
Gongchen Cheng	拱宸城
Gongning Cheng	鞏寧城
gongshi	公示
guanbi minfan	官逼民反
Guangren Cheng	廣仁城
Guanzhong	關中
Gucheng	古城
Gumadi (Gumudi)	古牧地
Gumu	古牧
Guo Songdao	郭嵩燾
haifang	海防
hancheng	漢城
hanhui	漢回
hanren	漢人
He Buyun	何步雲
Heilongjiang	黑龍江
heiqian	黑錢
Hesi	河西
Hongmiao	紅廟
hongqian	紅錢
Hongshanzui	紅山嘴
hou	侯
huanfang	換防
Huang Hezhuo	黃和卓
Huang Wanpeng	黃萬鵬
huangdi	皇帝
Huangdian	黃田

hubu	户部
Hufuye	虎夫耶
Huibu	回部
huicheng	回城
huimin	回民
Huining Cheng	惠寧城
huitun	回屯
Huiyuan Cheng	惠遠城
Hunasi	胡那斯
hutun	户屯
jasaq junwang	札薩克郡王
Jehol	熱河
Jiadilinye	戛的林耶
jiaofang	教坊
jiaohui	剿回
jiaopai	教派
Jiayuguan	嘉峪關
Jibuku	吉布庫
jihai	已亥
Jimsa	吉木薩
Jin Laosan	金老三
Jin Liang	金良
Jin Shun	金順
Jin Xiangyin	金相印
jin	斤
Jinghe	精河
Jinjibao	金積堡
Jinxing	錦性
jiucheng	舊城
jiujiao	舊教
junfu	軍府
junxian	郡縣
Kong Cai	孔才
kouliang	口糧
koutou	叩頭
Kuburenye	庫不忍耶
Kuiying	奎英
Lan Fachun	藍發春
laorenjia	老人家
laotaiye	老太爺
Li Hongzhang	李鴻章
Li Shi	李十

Li Yunlin	李雲麟
lianghui	良回
liangru weichu	量入為出
liang	兩
lingdui dachen	領隊大臣
Liu Jintang	劉錦棠
Liu Songshan	劉松山
lu	路
luying	綠營
Ma Chungliang	馬忠良
Ma Duosan	馬朵三
Ma Guan	馬官
Ma Guiyuan	馬貴原
Ma Hualong	馬化漋 (馬化龍)
Ma Jingui	馬金貴
Ma Long	馬隆
Ma Quan	馬全
Ma Rende	馬人得
Ma Sheng	馬升
Ma Si	馬四
Ma Tai	馬太 (馬泰)
Ma Tuzi	馬禿子
Ma Wenlu	馬文祿
Ma Yanlong	馬彥龍
Ma Yuan	馬元
Ma Zhanao	馬占鰲
Ma Zhong	馬仲
Maimaitieli	邁買铁里
Maizimuzate	邁孜木雜特
Manas	瑪納斯
mancheng	滿城
Ma Zhenhe	馬振和
menhuan	門宦
miehui	滅回
Mingsioi (Mingxu)	明緒
Muhanmode Zhairifu	穆罕默德·翟日夫
Mulei	木壘
Muleihe	木壘河
Nanguan	南關
Nanlu bacheng	南路八城
Nanlu	南路
Nanshan	南山

Nayanceng (Nayancheng)	那彥成
Ningyuan Cheng	寧遠城
Paxia	怕夏
Pichang	璧昌
Pingliang	平涼
Pingžui (Pingrui)	平瑞
pinji	品級
Prince Chun	醇親王
Prince Gong	恭親王
puerqian	普爾錢
qianfan	遣犯
qiantun	遣屯
Qidaowan	七道灣
Qieshi	伽師
qingzhen guo	清真國
qingzhen wang	清真王
Qitai	奇台
Qur Qarausu	庫爾喀喇烏蘇
Qutubi	呼圖壁
renyin	壬寅
saifang	塞防
Salingga (Salinga)	薩靈阿
Sandaohezi	三道河子
shalu jingjin	殺戮淨盡
shangye	商爺
Shashanzi	沙山子
Shen Baozhen	沈葆楨
Shengjing	盛京
shen	申
shiba daying	十八大營
shi	石
Su Manla	蘇滿拉
Su Yude	蘇玉得
Suiding Cheng	綏定城
Suilai	綏來
Suo Dalaoye	索大老爺
Suo Huanzhang	索煥章
Suo Wen	索文
Suzhou	肅州
taizhan	臺站
Taleqi Cheng	塔勒奇城
tianming	天命

Tianshan Beilu	天山北路
Tianshan Nanlu	天山南路
tidu	提督
Tongguan	潼關
tongling	統領
tongshi	通事
tuanlian	團練
tuhui	屠回
tuntian	屯田
Tuo Delin	妥得璘
Tuo Ming	妥明
Ulongge (Wulonge)	武隆額
Urcingga (Wuerchinga)	烏爾清阿
Urenbu (Wurenbu)	武人布
waifei	外匪
waixiang	外廂
Wang Dechun	王得春
wang	王
Wei Guangdao	魏光燾
Weigan	渭干
Wenxiang	文祥
Wenyi	文藝
Wu Sangui	吳三桂
xiaozhuang	小莊
Xichun Cheng	熙春城
Xidaotang	西道堂
xiexiang	協餉
xincheng	新城
Xining	西寧
xinjiao	新教
Xintan	新灘
Xu Xhuedi	徐學第
Xu Xuegong	徐學功
Xu Zhanbiao	徐占彪
yancai	鹽菜
yancaiyin	鹽菜銀
Yang Chun	楊春
Yang Ziying	楊子英
yanglian	養廉
yanqi	燕齊
Yebcongge (Yebuchonge)	業布沖額
Yiheiwani	依黑瓦尼

Yili jiangjun	伊犁將軍
Yu Deyan	禹得彥
Yu Huen	余虎恩
Yu Xiaohu	于小虎
yuanbao	元寶
yuanshuai	元師
Yumen	玉門
Yusupi	玉素皮
Jaohūi (Zhaohui)	兆惠
Zhande Cheng	瞻德城
Zhang Yao	張曜
Zhang Yue	張越
Zhangjiakou	長家口
zhangjiao	掌教
Zheherenye	哲赫忍耶
Zhili	直隸
zhufang	駐防
Zhunbu	準部
Zhungaer	準噶爾
zhongtang daren	中堂大人
zhuxing huiren	著姓回人
zongli yamen	總理衙門

REFERENCE MATTER

Notes

INTRODUCTION

1. *Zhongguo tongji nianjian: 2000*, comp. Guojia Tongji Ju (Peking: Guojia Tongji Chubanshe, 2000), p. 96. As of 1999 the number of the population reached 17,179,000.

2. For example, see Liu Yingsheng, *Xibei minzushi yu Chahetai hanguoshi yanjiu* (Nanjing: Nanjing Daxue Chubanshe, 1994); Michal Biran, *Qaidu and the Rise of the Independent Mongol State in Central Asia* (Surrey: Curzon Press, 1997); Wei Liangdao, *Yeerjiang hanguoshigang* (Haerbin: Heilongjiang Jiaoyu Chubanshe, 1994).

3. See Saguchi Tōru's trilogy: *Jūhachi-jūkyū seiki Higashi Torukisutan shakaishi kenkyū* (Tokyo: Yoshikawa Kōbunkan, 1963); *Shinkyō minzokushi kenkyū* (Tokyo: Yoshikawa Kōbunkan, 1986); *Shinkyō Musurimu kenkyū* (Tokyo: Yoshikawa Kōbunkan, 1995). Hori Sunao also published a number of articles dealing with social and economic aspects of Xinjiang during the Qing period (see Bibliography). In Russia we have two good studies: L. I. Duman, *Agrarnaia politika Tsinskogo provitel'stva v Sin'tsiane v kontse XVIII veka* (Moscow: Izd-vo Akademii Nauk SSSR, 1936); V. S. Kuznetsov, *Ekonomicheskaia politika Tsinskogo pravitel'stva v Sin'tsiane v pervoi polovine XIX veka* (Moscow: Nauka, 1973). Pan Zhiping published *Zhongya Haohanguo yu Qingdai Xinjiang* (Zhongguo Shehui Kexue Chubanshe, 1991) in which he used important archival documents preserved in Peking. In English there is an excellent study published by James A. Millward, *Beyond the Pass: Economy, Ethnicity, and Empire in Qing Central Asia, 1759–1864* (Stanford: Stanford University Press, 1998).

4. Nonetheless, there are a couple of good surveys showing the persistence of the continental trade in the post-Mongol period. See Morris Rossabi, *China and Inner Asia: From 1368 to the Present Day* (London: Thames and Hudson, 1975); Saguchi Tōru, *Roshia to Ajia sōgen* (Tokyo: Yoshikawa Kōbunkan, 1967). Several Japanese scholars have strongly criticized the so-called "Silk Road" perspective and put more emphasis on the importance of the relationship between the nomads in the north and the sedentaries in the south, which they regard as the real dynamics of Inner Asian history. See, for example, Mano Eiji, *Chūō Ajia no rekishi* (Tokyo: Kōdansha, 1977); Komatsu Hisao ed., *Chūō Yūrasiashi* (Tokyo: Yamakawa Shubbansha, 2000).

5. *The Life of Yakoob Beg; Athalik Ghazi, and Badaulet; Ameer of Kashgar* (London: W. H. Allen, 1878).

6. D. Tikhonov, "Vosstanie 1864 g. v Vostochnom Turkestane," *Sovetskoe vostokovedenie*, no. 5 (1948); "Uigurskie istoricheskie rukopisi kontsa XIX i nachala XX v.," *Uchenye zapiski Instituta Vostokovedeniia*, no. 9 (1954); A. Khodzhaev,

Tsinskaia imperiia, Dzhungariia i Vostochnyi Turkestan (Moscow: Izd-vo 'Fan' Uzbekskoi SSR, 1979); D. I. Isiev, *Uigurskoe gosudarstvo Iettishar* (Moscow: Izd-vo 'Nauka,' Glav. red. vostochnoi lit-ry, 1981).

7. Burhan Shahidi (Baoerhan), "Lun Agubo zhengquan," *Lishi yanjiu*, 1958, no. 3; "Zailun Agubo zhengquan," *Lishi yanjiu*, 1979, no. 8; Ji Dachun, "Shilun yibaliusi nian Xinjiang nongmin qiyi," *Minzu yanjiu*, 1979, no. 2.

8. In this respect, we learn much from the works by Japanese scholar Hamada Masami. Among others, see his "Murrā Birāru no *Seisenki* ni tsuite," *Tōyō gakuhō*, vol. 55, no. 4 (1973); "L'Histoire de Ḫotan de Muḥammad A'lam" (1–3), *Zinbun*, no. 15 (1979); no. 16 (1980); no. 18 (1982); "Jūkyū seiki Uiguru rekishi bunken jōsetsu," *Tōhō gakuho*, no. 55 (1983).

9. The printed edition of this work is *Taarikh-i emenie. Istoriia vladetelei Kashgarii* (Kazan: Tabkhane-i Medresse-i Ulum, 1905). For a brief introduction to Sayrāmī's work, see V. Bartol'd, "Taarikh-i Emenie," *Sochineniia*, vol. 8 (Moscow: Nauka, 1973), 213–19; V. P. Iudin, "Ta'rikh-i amniia," *Materialy po istorii Kazakhskikh khanstv XV–XVIII vekov* (Alma-Ata: "Nauka," 1969), 476–86; Enver Baytur (Anwaer Bayituer), "Maola Musha Shayiranmi he *Yimideshi*," *Minzu yanjiu*, 1984, no. 3: 26–33.

10. According to Enver Baytur, a Qirghiz scholar in Xinjiang, there is an autographed copy of this work in Peking (Institute of Nationalities, Academy of Social Sciences). I failed to get access to this manuscript and I had to rely on Enver's translation in Modern Uyghur (*Tarikhi hämidi*, Peking: Millätlär Näshriyati, 1986). Fortunately, however, there is a copy of this work in Gunnar Jarring Collection, Lund, Sweden (Prov. no. 163). Although this copy lacks the final pages, it enables us to check most of Enver's translation.

11. *Voina musul'man protiv Kitaitsev* (Kazan: Universitetskaia tipografiia, 1880–81), 2 vols. Cf. M. Hamrajev, "Bilal Nazim: ein Klassker der uigurischer Literatur," *Ungarische Jahrbücher*, no. 42 (1970): 77–99; M. Hamada, "Murrā Birāru no *Seisenki* ni tsuite."

12. For the manuscripts in Russia and their contents, consult L. V. Dmitrieva et al., comp., *Opisanie Tiurkskikh rukopisei Instituta Narodov Azii*, vol. 1: Istoriia (Moscow: Izd-vo 'Nauka,' Glav. red. vostochnoi lit-ry, 1965); A. M. Muginov, comp., *Opisanie Uigurskikh rukopisei Instituta Narodov Azii* (Moscow: Izd-vo vostochnoi literatury, 1962); D. I. Tikhonov, "Uigurskie istoricheskie rukopisi kontsa XIX i nachala XX v.," pp. 146–74; V. P. Iudin, "Nekotorye istochniki po istorii vosstaniia v Sin'tsziane v 1864 godu," *Trudy Instituta istorii, arkheologii i etnografii im. Ch. Ch. Valikhanov Akademii Nauk Kazakskoi SSR*, no. 15 (1962): 171–96; K. Usmanov, "Uigurskie istochniki o vosstanii v Sin'tsziane 1864 goda," *Voprosy istorii*, no. 2 (1947): 87–89. We do not know yet the full scope of the manuscript collection in China, but see Yusuf Beg Mukhlisov, comp., *Uigur klassik edibiyat qol yazmiliri katalogi* (Xinjiang, 1957). Cf. Iudin's review of Mukhlisov's work in *Trudy Instituta istorii, arkheologii i etnografii im. Ch. Ch. Valikhanov Akademii Nauk Kazakskoi SSR*, no. 15 (1962): 197–206. Many of the manuscripts available in the West are well explained in Hamada's "Jūkyū seiki Uiguru rekishi bunken jōsetsu," *Tōhō gaku*, no. 55 (1983): 353–401. The extant sources, the locations, the date of compilation, the authors or copyists, and other related information can be found in the Bibliography in this book.

13. *Visits to High Tartary, Yarkand, and Kashghar* (London: J. Murray, 1871).

14. "Report on His Journey to Ilchi, the Capital of Khotan, in Chinese Tartary," *Journal of the Royal Geographical Society*, no. 37 (1867).

15. *Turkistan: Notes of a Journey in Russian Turkistan, Khokand, Bukhara and Kuldja*, 2 vols. (New York: Sampson Low, 1877).

16. *J.-L. Dutreuil de Rhins. Mission scientifique dans la haute Asie, 1890–1895* (Paris: E. Leroux, 1897–98).

17. Among others *Qinding Pingding Shan-Gan Xinjiang huifei fanglue*, Yi Xin et al., comp., 320 chs. (Taipei; Chengwen Chupanshe repr., 1968).

18. T. D. Forsyth, *Report of a Mission to Yarkund, 1873–1874* (Calcutta: Foreign Department Press, 1875).

19. A. N. Kuropatkin, *Kashgariia* (St. Petersburg: Izd. imp. Russkago geograficheskago obshchestva, 1879). Fortunately we have an English translation of this important work, *Kashgaria: Eastern or Chinese Turkestan*, W. E. Gowan, trans. (Calcutta: Thacker, Spink and Co., 1882). The English translation omits the Appendix on the routes and the trade items between Russia and Kashgharia in 1876, which is found at the end of the original.

20. *Kāşgar tārīhī* (Istanbul: Mihran Matbaası, 1300/1882–83). Modern Turkish translation by İsmail Aka et. al., *Kaşgar Tarihi: Bāis-i Hayret Ahvāl-i Garibesi* (Kırıkkale: Eysi, 1998).

CHAPTER I

1. *Xiyu congzhi* (also called *Xiyu jianwenlu*), Chunyuan, comp. (Qiangshutang edition in 1818; Taipei, Wenhai Chubanshe repr., 1966), 26r.

2. Forsyth, *Report of a Mission to Yarkund*, p. 44.

3. *Huijiang tongzhi* (1925 jiaoyinben; Taipei: Wenhai Chubanshe repr., 1966), q. 10, 3r–3v. This number probably increased later as the political situation in Kashgharia worsened. As will be related later, a Muslim writer (Ḥājjī Yūsuf) wrote that in the Kucha rebellion of 1864 more than a thousand garrison soldiers were killed.

4. *Huijiang tongzhi*, q. 10, 2v; q. 7, 2r; q. 8, 3r. This was slightly larger than the walls of Khotan (1.3 km) or Kahsghar (1.4 km) although the wall of Yarkand, the former capital of Moghul Khanate, was exceptionally long (about 4.8 km).

5. Thus the Muslim town was variously called *huicheng* (Muslim city), *jiucheng*, (Old city), or *kuhnashahr* ("Old city" in Turkic) while the Manchu fort was called *mancheng* (Manchu city), *xincheng* (New city), or *yangishahr* ("New city" in Turkic). According to a recent study by James A. Millward (*Beyond the Pass*, pp. 149–52), from the 1840s a new term *hancheng* (Chinese city; or its equivalent in Turkic, *khitayshahri*. See TH/Jarring, 38v [see Note 8 below]; TH/Enver, p. 203; TA/Pantusov, p. 58) began to be used designating the Manchu fort because of influx of a considerable number of Chinese merchants into the fort.

6. *Report of a Mission to Yarkund*, p. 44.

7. *Waishiang* means "suburban areas" in Chinese.

8. A manuscript of *Tārīkh-i ḥamīdī* (hereafter abbreviated as TH) in the Gunnar Jarring Collection, Lund, Sweden (TH/Jarring), 33v–34r. TH is a revised version of Sayrāmī's *Tārīkh-i amniyya* (TA). In this book I used two different manuscripts

(TA/Pelliot and TA/Jarring) and one printed edition (TA/Pantusov) of TA, one manuscript (TH/Jarring) and one modern Uyghur translation (TH/Enver) of TH. For more detailed information on these manuscript and editions, see Appendix B and the Bibliography. *Jawzā* is one of the twelve seasons based on the solar calendar, and it corresponds to the period from May 22 to June 21. Compare the quoted text with TH/Enver, pp. 182–83; TA/Pantusov, p. 45.

9. There are several hypotheses on the etymology of this term. See M. Hartmann, *Chinesische-Turkistan: Geschichte, Verwaltung, Geistesleben und Wirtschaft* (Halle a.S.: Gebauer-Schwetschke Druckerei und Verlag, 1908), pp. 104–105; S. R. Dyer, "Soviet Dungan Nationalism: A Few Comments on Their Origin and Language," *Monumenta Serica*, no. 33 (1977–1978): 349–62.

10. The term "Uyghur" was introduced as a designation for nationality for the first time in the 1930s. In the Muslim materials of the nineteenth and the twentieth centuries we can find terms like "Qirghiz" and "Qazaq." These were employed not as an ethnic nomenclature but as names of tribal people whose nomadic way of life was sharply distinguished from the sedentary Turkic Muslims. On the emergence of national consciousness among the Uyghurs in the modern period, see Dru C. Gladney, "Ethonogenesis of the Uighur," *Central Asian Survey* 9, no. 1 (1990): 1–28.

11. *Qinding Pingding Shan-Gan Xinjiang huifei fanglue*, comp. Yi Xin et al. (Taipei: Chengwen Chubanshe repr., 1968), q. 68, 1r–2r; *Xinjiang tuzhi*, comp. Yuan Dahua (Taipei: Wenhai Chubanshe repr., 1965), q. 116, 1r. These Chinese sources should be given more credit because they are based on the contemporary military reports written on the spot. Sayrāmī, relying on his memory, seems to have made a mistake. The first day of Muḥarram, 1281 (June 6, 1864), is not Saturday as he asserts but Monday. The date given in the Chinese sources, June 4, is Saturday.

12. TH/Jarring, 28r. Also see TA/Pelliot, 29v; TA/Pantusov, p. 34; TA/Jarring, 34v; TH/Enver, p. 158. Some of the manuscripts have "Mā Shūr Akhūnd Mā Lūng Shams al-Dīn Khalīfa." It is possible to regard Mā Lūng Shams al-Dīn Khalīfa as one person.

13. *Hanren* literally means "Han people" and *huimin* "Muslim population," but Saling, with these two terms, seems to have in mind the Chinese (Tungans) and the (Turkic) Muslims. According to Qing terminology, the Tungans were called *hanhui* or *donggan* and distinguished from the Turkic Muslims who were usually called *chantouhui* ("Muslim with turban"). The term *huimin* was often used to designate both groups.

14. The manuscript of this work, now at the Institut Narodov Azii in St. Petersburg, was not available to me. However, the résumé of its contents can be found in D. Tikhonov, "Vosstanie 1864 g. v Vostochnom Turkestane." Ḥājjī Yūsuf provides more interesting details about the initial stage of the revolts. According to him, there was a conspiracy by several Kuchean Muslims (Ibrāhīm Tura, Yolbars Tura, Ṣādiq Beg, Qāsim Beg, Rūza Beg, Bahādur Tukhta, and so on), but somehow it was not realized, and after this aborted attempt the three Tungan leaders started the action on their own initiative. In the meantime, Chinese scholars believe that the Kucha revolt broke out at first by the laborers working near the Weigan river under the worst condition. See Ji Dachun, "Shilun yibaliusi nian Xinjiang nongmin qiyi," p. 39; *Xinjiang jianshi* (Urumqi: Xinjiang Renmin Chubanshe, 1980), vol. 2, p. 110. This argument

is based on a report of field research done in Kucha in 1975 which has not been published.

15. *Daqing lichao shilu*, Tongzhi-3–6–*yiyou* (the date is in the order of the reign: title, year, month, and day).

16. *Kanding Xinjiangji*, comp. Wei Guangdao et al. (Taipei: Shangwu Yinshuguan, 1963; *Xinjiang Yanjiu Congshu*, vol. 10, ed. Yuan Dongli), q. 1, 1r.

17. *Manla* is Chinese transcription of *mullā*, a title for a Muslim religious leader.

18. *Xinjiang tuzhi*, q. 116, 1r. There can be no doubt that Ma Long in the Chinese sources is Mā Lūng Akhūnd in the works of Sayrāmī and Ḥājjī Yūsuf. Huang Hezhuo is the transcription of Khān Khwāja, which was later the title of Rāshidīn Khwāja who became the ruler (khan) of the Kuchean regime. However, as will be explained later, he was not the one who started the revolt at first, so the assertion of *Xinjiang tuzhi* is certainly misleading.

19. *Chanmūzā* is the transcription of *changmaozi* (Long Hairs), a pejorative appellation applied to the Taipings. But it is not clear what *Ūsūnggūī* means. It looks like the transcription of Wu Sangui who had rebelled during Kangxi's reign. Although the rebellion of Wu Sangui had taken place much ealier, because of its notoriety his rebellion may have been called together with the Taiping rebellion.

20. TH/Jarring, 30r–30v; TH/Enver, pp. 165–167; TA/Pantusov, pp. 39–40.

21. In Chinese, *taizhan.*

22. TH/Jarring, 30v.

23. *Ẓafar-nāma,* 20r–20v. This manuscript is in the India Office Library (Ms. Turki 5).

24. *Daqing lichao shilu*, Tongzhi-3–8–*guisi.*

25. On the Muslim massacre in Shanxi and Gansu, see the recent study by Wu Wanshan, *Qingdai xibei huimin qiyi yanjiu* (Lanzhou: Lanzhou Daxue Chubanshe, 1991), pp. 137–40.

26. *Pinghuizhi*, comp. Yang Yuxiu (Jiannan Wangshi, ed., 1889), q. 7, 1v–2r.

27. Philip A. Kuhn, *Rebellion and Its Enemies in Late Imperial China: Militarization and Social Structure, 1769–1864* (Cambridge, Mass.: Harvard University Press, 1970; 2nd ed., 1980), pp. vi–vii.

28. *Pinghuizhi*, q. 7, 1v–2r.

29. *Sobranie sochinenii*, vol. 3 (Alma-Ata: Glavnaia red. Kazakhskoi Sovetskoi entsiklopedii, 1985), pp. 159–60.

30. Haneda Akira *Chūō Ajiashi kenkyū* (Kyoto: Rinsen Shōten, 1982), p. 76; Saguchi Tōru, *Shinkyō minzokushi kenkyū*, pp. 301–306.

31. Valikhanov, *Sobranie sochinenii*, vol. 3, p. 161. According to his estimation there were 5,500 in Kashghar; 2,200 in Yarkand; 1,400 in Khotan; 600 in Aqsu; 800 in Turfan; 300 in Barchuq; and 300 in Sayram. Besides these, there were soldiers stationed at front posts (*qarawul*) and postal stations (*örtäng*) as well as merchants and other individual Tungans. Adding all these together, he surmised the total number of Khitays did not exceed 15,000.

32. Millward, *Beyond the Pass*, pp. 168–175.

33. E. Schuyler, *Turkistan: Notes of a Journey in Russian Turkistan, Khokand, Bukhara and Kuldja*, vol. 2 (London: Sampson Low, 1877), pp. 174, 197.

34. *Qinding Pingding Shan-Gan Xinjiang Fanglue*, q. 95, 23v–24r.

35. Shaw, *Visits to High Tartary*, pp. 47–48.

36. Cf. J. Fletcher, "Ch'ing Inner Asia *c.* 1800," in *The Cambridge History of China*, vol. 10, pt. 1, ed. J. K. Fairbank (Cambridge: Cambridge University Press, 1978), pp. 35–36.

37. Thomas J. Barfield, *Perilous Frontier: Nomadic Empires and China* (Cambridge, Mass.: Basil Blackwell, 1989), pp. 266–95; Miyawaki Junko. *Saigō no yuboku teikoku* (Tokyo: Kōdansha, 1995).

38. B. P. Gurevich, *Mezhdunarodnye otnosheniia v Tsentral'noi Azii v XVII–pervoi polovine XIX v.* (Moscow: Nauka, 1979), p. 120.

39. Wei Yuan, *Shengwuji*, vol. 1 (Peking: Zhonghua Shuju, 1984 repr.), p. 156. For a more detailed account of the Qing conquest of the Zunghars, see I. Ia. Zlatkin, *Istoriia Dzhungarskogo khanstva (1635–1758)* (Moscow: Nauka, 1964), pp. 425ff; M. Courant, *L'Asie centrale aux XVIIe et XVIIIe siécle: Empire kalmouk ou empire mantchou?* (Lyon: A. Rey imprimeur-editeur, 1912), pp. 97ff; P. Pelliot, *Notes critiques d'histoire Kalmouke (Texte)* (Paris: Librairie d'Amerique et d'Orient, 1960), pp. 8–14; C. R. Bawden, *The Modern History of Mongolia* (London: Weidenfeld and Nicholson, 1968), pp. 115ff.

40. Thus Makhdūmzāda means "offsprings of the great master." His original name was Aḥmad Khwājagi-yi Kasanī.

41. On the activities of Khwāja Isḥāq in Eastern Turkestan, see Sawada Minoru's "Hōjā Ishaqqu no shūkyō kattō," *Seinan Ajia kenkyū*, no. 27 (1987).

42. At present scholars in Xinjiang call the descendants of Isḥāq "Isḥāqiyya" and the descendants of Yūsuf "Ishqiyya." However, I have not yet found the term "Ishqiyya" in contemporary Muslim sources. The term "Āfāqiyya" is not attested in the sources either, but here I adopted it to designate the followers of Khwāja Āfāq and his descendants because it is widely accepted by Western scholars and easily brings that group to mind.

43. There are a number of Muslim works on the history of the Makhdūmzāda khwājas and the conflicts between the two branches of this family. The best known work among them is *Tadhkira-i 'azīzān* (or, *Tadhkira-i khwājagān*) written by Muḥammad Ṣādiq Kāshgharī around 1768. For epitomized translations, see Martin Hartmann, "Ein Heiligenstaat im Islam: Das Ende der Caghataiden und die Herrschaft der Choğas in Kašgarien," *Der islamische Orient: Berichte und Forschungen*, pts. 6–10 (Berlin: W. Peiser, 1905); R. B. Shaw, "The History of the Khōjas of Eastern-Turkistan," edited and supplemented by N. Elias, *Journal of the Asiatic Society of Bengal*, no. 66, pt. 1, extra number (Calcutta, 1897). There are dozens of copies of this famous work. The text on which Hartmann based his translation is Ms. Or. Oct. 3292 (Staatsbibliotek zu Berlin, Preussischer Kulturbesitz, Orientalabteilung), and the one that Shaw used for his translation is Or. 5378 (British Library). Cf. Hartmann, "Die osttürkischen Handschriften der Sammlung Hartmann," *Mitteilungen des Seminars für orientalische Sprachen zu Berlin*, vol. 7, no. 2 (1904): 1–21; note of N. Elias in Shaw's "The History of the Khōjas," pp. i–iii; H. Beveridge, "The Khojas of Eastern Turkistan," *Journal of the Asiatic Society of Bengal*, no. 71 (1902): 45–46. For the scope of the existing copies of *Tadhkira-i 'azīzān*, consult H. F. Hofman, *Turkish Literature: A Bio-Bibliographical Survey*, sec. 3, pt. 1, vol. 4 (Utrecht: University of Utrecht, 1969), pp. 25–30. On the conflict between these two khwāja

families see the following studies. Saguchi Tōru, "Higashi Torukisutan hōken shakaishi jōsetsu: Hoja jidai no ichi kōsatsu," *Rekishigaku kenkyū*, no. 134 (1948): 1–18; H. G. Schwarz, "The Khwajas of Eastern Turkestan," *Central Asiatic Journal* 20, no. 4 (1976): 266–296; Pan Zhiping, "Hezhuo chongbai de xingshuai," *Minzu yanjiu*, 1992, no. 2: 61–67; Liu Zhengyin, "Hezhuo jiazu xingqi qian Yisilanjiao zai Xiyu de huodong ji qi zhengzhi beijing," *Shijie zongjiao yanjiu*, 1991, no. 4: 57–64.

44. On the date of this event, see *Khronika*, critical text, translation, commentaries and study by O. F. Akimushkin (Moscow: Nauka, 1976), pp. 323–24. This work was written in Persian by Shāh Maḥmūd ibn Mīrzā Fāḍil Churās.

45. *Tadhkira-i 'azīzān* (Bodleian: d. 20), 26r.

46. For the Qing conquest of Kashgharia and the fate of the khwājas, see Saguchi's *Shakaishi kenkyū*, chs. 1 and 2. Also cf. a good survey in L. I. Duman's "Zavoevanie Tsinskoi imperiei Dzhungarii i Vostochnogo Turkestana," in *Man'chzhurskoe vladychestvo v Kitae* (ed. S. L. Tikhvinskii, Moscow: Nauka, 1966), pp. 264–88.

47. Saguchi, *Shakaishi kenkyū*, pp. 197–199.

48. Hori Sunao, "Jūhachi-nijū seiki Uiguru joku jinko shiron," *Shirin* 60, no. 4 (1977): 123.

49. Fletcher, "Ch'ing Inner Asia *c.* 1800," p. 74.

50. See Shimada Jōhei's article, "Hōja jidai no beku tachi," *Tōhō gaku* 3 (1952): 1–9. He called this change the transformation "from the age of *amīr* to the age of *beg*." However, it seems to me that there was no fundamental difference between the terms *amīr* and *beg*, except that one is Persian and the other is Turkic. Both of them were actually equivalent to a Monglian word *noyan*. See K. A. Pishchulina, *Iugo-vostochnyi Kazakhstan v seredine XIV–nachale XVI vekov* (Alma-Ata: Nauka, 1977), pp. 156–57. G. Clauson regards the title of "beg" as originating from the Chinese word *bo*. See his *An Etymological Dictionary of Pre-Thirteenth-Century Turkish* (Oxford: Oxford University Press, 1972), p. 322.

51. Saguchi, *Shakaishi kenkyū*, pp. 104–105.

52. One *batman* is the cultivated land on which one could sow 5 *shi* and 3 *dou* of grain. On the measurements used in Xinjiang, see Ji Dachun's "Weiwuerzu duliangheng jiuzhi kaosuo," *Xiyu yanjiu*, 1991, no. 1.

53. Saguchi, *Shakaishi kenkyū*, pp. 109–24. The term *shang* is not from the Chinese word meaning present but from *cang*, treasury. See Fletcher, "The Biography of Khwush Kipäk Beg (d. 1781) in the *Wai-fan Mêng-ku Hui-pu wang-kung piao chuan*," *Acta Orientalia* 36, nos. 1–3 (1982): 171.

54. I would like to express my gratitude to the late professor Joseph Fletcher Jr. who kindly lent me a copy of this important source preserved at the Ōki Bunko, the Institute of Tōyo Bunka Kenkyūsho in Tokyo University. The full title of this document is *Yeerqiang cheng zhuanglishu huihu zhengfu ge xiangce* (A register of the itemized taxes of the Muslim households and of the names and the distances of the villages in Yarkand). For a more detailed study see Hori Sunao, "Tōkyō Daigaku Tōyo Bunka Kenkyūsho shōjō *Yeerqiang cheng zhuanglishu huihu zhengfu ge xiangce*," *Kōnan Daigaku Kiyō* (Bungakuhen), no. 51 (1983).

55. As Hori Sunao's study has shown, this change was the result of the reform taken as a remedy after the invasion of Jahāngīr in the late 1820s. See his "Shinchō no kaikyō tōji ni tsuite ni-san mondai," *Shigaku zasshi* 88, no. 3 (1979): 15–19.

56. The term *taranchi* came from the Mongol word *tariyachi(n)* meaning "cultivator" and they were those who had been forcefully moved to the Ili valley for cultivating land in the late seventeenth century by the Zunghars. See Saguchi, *Shinkyō minzokushi kenkyū*, pp. 281–84.

57. It is worth mentioning here about the confusion of the terms *yüzbashi* and *yüzbegi*. According to *Xiyu tuzhi* (q. 29, 19r) there was only one *yüzbeg* in Ili, but later sources prove the existence of 60–80 *yüzbeg*s in the same area. See *Xinjiang shilue*, q. 5, 32v; W. Radloff, *Proben der Volksliteratur der nordlichen türkischen Stämme*, vol. 1, pt. 6: Dialekt der Tarantschi (St. Petersburg, 1886), p. 27 (text) and p. 35 (translation). It seems to me that *yüzbashi* found in the Yarkand register corresponds to *yüzbeg* in Ili. Valikhanov shows that the term *yüzbegi* was also used in Kashgharia. See *Sobranie sochinenii*, vol. 3, p. 124.

58. See Hori's "Tōkyō Daigaku Tōyo Bunka Kenkyūsho shōjō."

59. TH/Jarring, 31r–31v; TH/Enver, pp. 169–70; TA/Pelliot, 35r–35v.

60. Radloff, *Proben der Volksliteratur*, vol. 1, pt. 6, p. 27 (text), p. 35 (translation).

61. One such edict was published by G. Raquette, *Eine kaschgarische Waqf-Urkunde aus der Khodscha-Zeit Ost-Turkestans* (Lund: C. W. K. Gleerup, 1930). The copies of several edicts preserved in the Gunnar Jarring Collection also contain mentions of these titles.

62. This incident will be explained in detail later in this book.

63. Valikhanov, *Sobranie sochinenii*, vol. 3, p. 172.

64. Akimushkin, *Khronika*, 49r (text).

65. *Sobranie sochinenii*, vol. 3, pp. 172–73, 181.

66. *Sobranie sochinenii*, vol. 3, p. 162.

67. *Sobranie sochinenii*, vol. 3, p. 184.

68. The Qing conquest of the Zunghars not only physically exterminated these nomads but also intended to erase the memory of their existence by banning the use of the word Zunghar (in Chinese *Zhungaer*). Instead, an old term Elute (i.e., Ölöt) was introduced. Ölöt is a shortened form of Ögöled and should be distinguished from Oyirad or Oyirod. On these terms, see Okada Hidehiro's "Doruben Oiratto no kigen," *Shigaku zasshi* 83, no. 6 (1974).

69. The names Zhunbu and Huibu were also used to designate Zungharia and Kashgharia.

70. For detailed accounts of the administration in Xinjiang, see Zeng Wenwu, *Zhongguo jingying Xiyushi* (Shanghai: Shangwu Yinshuguan, 1936), pp. 264–65; Haneda Akira, *Chūō Ajiashi kenkyū* (Kyoto: Rinsen Shoten, 1982), pp. 73–75; A. Khodzhaev, "Zakhvat Tsinskim Kitaem Dzhungarii i Vostochnogo Turkestana. Bor'ba protiv zavoevatelei," in *Kitai i sosedi v novoe i noveishee vremia* (ed. S. L. Tikhvinskii, Moscow: Izd-vo Nauka, 1982), pp. 171–72; Lo Yunzhi, *Qing Gaozong tongzhi Xinjiang zhengce de tantao* (Taipei: Liren Shuju, 1983), pp. 51–64.

71. Haneda, *Chūō Ajiashi kenkyū*, p. 74.

72. Zeng Wenwu, *Zhongguo jingying Xiyushi*, pp. 301–302.

73. *The Moslem Rebellion in Northwest China 1862–1878: A Study of Government Minority Policy* (The Hague: Mouton, 1966), pp. 178–81.

74. Lin Enxian, *Qingzhao zai Xinjiang de Han-Hui geli zhengce* (Taipei: Shang-

wu Yinshuguan, 1988), p. 128. For the names and terms of officials in Xinjiang, see Hu Zhenghua ed., *Xinjiang zhiguanzhi: 1762–1949* (Urumchi: Xinjiang Weiwuer Zizhiqu Renmin Zhengfu Bangongting, 1992).

75. Wei Yuan, *Shengwuji*, vol. 1, pp. 159–60.

76. Lin Enxian, *Qingzhao zai Xinjiang de Han-Hui geli zhengce*, pp. 129–31.

77. On these colonies consult L. I. Duman's study, *Agrarnaia politika Tsinskogo provitel'stva v Sin'tsiane*, pp. 128–75. Also cf. V. S. Kuznetsov, *Ekonomicheskaia politika Tsinskogo pravitel'stva v Sin'tsiane*, pp. 29–42. On the exiles in Xinjiang see Joanna Waley-Cohen's *Exile in Mid-Qing China: Banishment to Xinjiang, 1758–1820* (New Haven: Yale University Press, 1991); Qi Qingshun, "Qingdai Xinjiang qianfan yanjiu," *Zhongguoshi yanjiu*, 1988, no. 2.

78. *Sobranie sochinenii*, vol. 3, p. 176.

79. *Daqing lichao shilu*, Daoguang-12–2–*yisi*.

80. Wei Yuan, *Shengwuji*, vol. 1, p. 195.

81. *Sobranie sochinenii*, vol. 3, p. 175. In another place (p. 161) he enumerated the number of Chinese garrison (*Kitaiskie garnizony*) soldiers in the "Southern Circuit" (*Nanlu*): 5,500 in Kashghar; 2,200 in Yarkand; 1,400 in Khotan; 600 in Aqsu; and 800 in Turfan (10,500 in total). However, Turfan did not belong to the "Southern circuit," and he omitted Yangihissar, Ush, Kucha, and Qarashahr.

82. *Daqing lichao shilu*, Xianfeng-3–4–*guisi*.

83. *Qinding pingding Zhungaer fanglue*, comp. Fuheng et al. (Yingyin Wenyuange Sikuquanshu, vols. 357–359; reprint in Taipei: Shangwu Yinshuguan, 1983–1986) (xubian), q. 15, 1r–2r.

84. *Daqing lichao shilu*, Xianfeng-3–4–*guisi*.

85. *Shengwuji*, vol. 1, p. 487.

86. Millward, *Beyond the Pass*, pp. 60–61.

87. *Daqing lichao shilu*, Daoguang-12–2–*yisi*.

88. Saguchi, *Shakaishi kenkyū*, pp. 233–60; Kuznetsov, *Ekonomicheskaia politika Tsinskogo pravitel'stva v Sin'tsiane*, pp. 42–88.

89. V. P. Nalivkin, *Kratkaia istoriia Kokandskago Khanstva* (Kazan, 1886), pp. 4–6: French translation by A. Dozon, *Histoire du Khanat de Khokand* (Paris: E. Ledoux, 1889), pp. 61–64. *Bī* or *bīī* has the same etymology as *beg*; all mean "chief."

90. Nalivkin, *Kratkaia istoriia*, p. 59.

91. Cf. L. Lockhart, *Nadir Shah: A Critical Study Based Mainly upon Contemporary Sources* (London: Luzac, 1938), pp. 187ff.

92. Pan Zhiping, *Zhongya Haohanguo yu Qingdai Xinjiang* (Zhongguo Shehui Kexue Chubanshe, 1991), pp. 41–42.

93. *Daqing lichao shilu*, Qianlong-24-9-*gengshen*; *Qinding Pingding Zhungaer fanglue* (zhengbian), q. 78, 10v–13v and q. 82, 5r–6r.

94. The difference between the concepts of the "tributary relation" between China and Central Asian states is well illustrated by J. Fletcher. See his "China and Central Asia. 1368–1884," in *The Chinese World Order: Traditional China's Foreign Relations*, ed. J. K. Fairbank (Cambridge, Mass.: Harvard University Press, 1968), pp. 206–224.

95. *Zhungaer fanglue* (xubian), q. 7, 13r–15v.

96. Op. cit., q. 19, 22r–22v.

97. For the details about this aborted Muslim alliance, see Gurevich, *Mezhdunarodnye otnosheniia*, pp. 187–98.

98. *Sobranie sochinenii*, vol. 3, p. 137. Cf. V. C. Kuznetsov, "Imperiia Tsin' i musul'manskii mir," in *Tsentral'naia Aziia i sosednie territorii v srednie veka* (ed. V. E. Larichev, Novosibirsk: Nauka, 1990), pp. 107–108.

99. Gurevich, *Mezhdunarodnye otnosheniia*, pp. 194–96.

100. Pan Zhiping, *Zhongya Haohanguo*, pp. 52–53.

101. V. Gregorian, *The Emergence of Modern Afghanistan* (Stanford: Stanford University Press, 1969), p. 49.

102. A. Ahmad, *Studies in Islamic Culture in the Indian Environment* (Oxford: Oxford University Press, 1964), pp. 208–209.

103. For example, see Nalivkin, *Kratkaia istoriia Kokandskago khanstva*, p. 76; V. A. Romodin, "Some Sources on the History of the Farghānah and the Khōqand Khānate (16th to 19th cc.) in the Leningrad Mss. Collection," *XXV International Congress of Orientalists: Papers Presented by the USSR Delegation* (Moscow, 1960), p. 18.

104. *Tavārīkh-i shahrukhiyya*, pp. 34–35. This is a history of Khoqand written by Mullā Niyāz b. Mullā 'Ashūr Muḥammad Khōqandī, and its printed edition was published by N. N. Pantusov (*Taarikh shakhrokhi. Istoriia vladetelei Fergany*, Kazan: Tip. Imperatorskago Univ., 1885). He regards the title of this work as *Tā'rīkh-i shahrukhī*, but the correct title appears on p. 24 (*Tavārīkh-i shahrukhiyya nām nihāda*). For the descriptions on Eastern Turkestan in this work, see T. K. Beisembiev, "Ta'rikh-i Shakhrukhi o Vostochnom Turkestane," in *Iz istorii Srednei Azii i Vostochnogo Turkestana XV–XIX vv.*, ed. B. A. Akhmedov (Tashkent: Izdatel'stvo 'Fan' Uzbekskoi SSR, 1987); *"Tarikh-i Shakhrukh" kak istoricheskii istochnik* (Alma-Ata: Izd-vo 'Nauka' Kazakhskoi SSR, 1987).

105. Saguchi, *Shakaishi kenkyū*, pp. 97–98.

106. V. S. Kuznetsov, *Tsinskaia imperiia na rubezhakh Tsentral'noi Azii* (Novosibirsk: Izd-vo 'Nauka,' 1983), p. 60.

107. Ibid.

108. For the Khoqand expansion during this period, consult *Istoriia Kirgizskoi SSR*, vol. 1 (Frunze: 'Kyrgyzstan,' 1984), pp. 490–99; A. Kh. Khasanov, *Narodnye dvizheniia v Kirgizii v period Kokandskogo khanstva* (Moscow: Nauka, 1977), pp. 25–31.

109. Saguchi, *Shakaishi kenkyū*, p. 350.

110. The "Seven Cities" is a synonym of Kashgharia. Words like *haft kishvar* and *haft shahr* are Persian equivalents of the Turkic word *yättishahr*.

111. *Tavārīkh-i shahrukhiyya*, p. 75. Also see Saguchi, *Shakaishi kenkyū*, p. 410.

112. This is a Manchu word meaning "head of merchants." See Fletcher, "Ch'ing Inner Asia," p. 89.

113. *Na Wenyigong zouyi*, comp. Nayanceng (1834; Taipei: Wenhai Chubanshe repr., 1968), ch. 19, 2r–3r.

114. Pan Zhiping, *Zhongya Haohanguo*, pp. 83–84.

115. Fletcher, "Ch'ing Inner Asia," p. 89.

116. Saguchi, *Shakaishi kenkyū*, pp. 389–92.

117. Nalivkin, *Kratkaia istoriia*, p. 109.

118. *Qinding pingding huijiang chiaojin niyi fanglue*, comp. Chao Zhenyong (1830; Taipei: Wenhai Chubanshe repr., 1972), q. 1, 1r–2r. Valikhanov confuses this, known as the "revolt of the Qirghiz Suranchi," with the later invasion of Jahāngīr. See *Sobranie sochinenii*, vol. 3, p. 141, and compare with Saguchi's *Shakaishi kenkyū*, pp. 411ff.

119. *Muntakhab al-tavārīkh*, 340r–340v; Nalivkin, *Kratkaia istoriia*, p. 126. The author of *Muntakhab al-tavārīkh* is Ḥājjī Muḥammad Ḥākim valad-i Ma'ṣūm Khān and I used the manuscript at the Academy of Social Science in St. Petersburg. I would like to thank Beatrice Forbes Manz, at Tufts University, who kindly loaned me her microfilm copy of this manuscript.

120. Valikhanov, *Sobranie sochinenii*, vol. 3, p. 142.

121. *Qinding pingding niyi fanglue*, q. 3, 5r–5v.

122. According to *Report of a Mission to Yarkund* (p. 182) Muḥammad 'Alī Khān sent 'Īsa Dādkhwāh as his commander, but in *Muntakhab al-tavārīkh* (340r) it is stated that 'Īsa Dādkhwāh, escaping from Muḥammad 'Alī Khān, fled to Tashqurghan in the mountain areas of Alai where he stayed about a year and that there he collected followers of Jahāngīr. A Chinese record called the brothers of 'Īsa and Mūsa "rebel subjects of Khoqand" (*Qinding pingding niyi fanglue*, q. 12, 20v–23r). *Tavārīkh-i Shahrukhiyya* (p. 114) states erroneously that Buzurg, not Jahāngīr, invaded Kashghar.

123. *Muntakhab al-tavārīkh*, 340v–341r. In *Qinding pingding niyi fanglue* (q. 12, 20v–23r) this shrine is called *Payghambar Mazār* (prophet's shrine). *Muntakhab* mistook it as the shrine of Āfāq Khwāja, and one of the Chinese sources also calls it "his ancestral khwāja's tomb" (*Shengwuji*, vol. 1, p. 183).

124. The events from Jahāngīr's arrival at Artush and the occupation of the Muslim town are described in relative detail in *Muntakhab al-tavārīkh*, 340v–342v, and its description is corroborated by Qing sources.

125. *Tavārīkh-i shahrukhiyya*, p. 113; Nalivkin, *Kratkaia istoriia*, pp. 122–26.

126. *Tavārīkh-i shahrukhiyya*, p. 114; Nalivkin, *Kratkaia istoriia*, p. 127. Also see TH/Jarring, 26r–26v; TA/Pantusov, pp. 28–30. Although the author of *Tavārīkh-i shahrukhiyya* mistakenly writes that Buzurg, Jahāngīr's son, invaded in 1831, his narration of the event is correct in general. Sayrāmī's description of the Jahāngīr invasion (TH/Jarring, 26r–26v; TA/Pantusov, pp. 28–30) is almost a verbatim translation of *Tavārīkh-i shahrukhiyya* (pp. 114–16) except for the change of Buzurg into Jahāngīr. He made it clear (TA/Pantusov, p. 7) that *Tavārīkh-i shahrukhiyya* was one of his sources.

127. *Muntakhab al-tavārīkh*, 342v.

128. *Muntakhab al-tavārīkh*, 343v–345r.

129. For the detailed description of the invasion and the Qing expedition, see Saguchi, *Shakaishi kenkyū*, pp. 405–67; Zeng Wenwu, *Zhongguo jingying Xiyushi*, pp. 302–308.

130. Kuznetsov, *Ekonomicheskaia politika*, p. 126.

131. Pan Zhiping, *Zhongya Haohanguo*, pp. 101–111.

132. On the internal reform see Saguchi, *Shakaishi kenkyū*, pp. 185–188, 239–241.

133. *Muntakhab al-tavārīkh*, 416r.

134. *Muntakhab al-tavārīkh*, 416r; *Tavārīkh-i shahrukhiyya*, pp. 117–21. Valikhanov reports that forty thousand troops and ten artillery guns were mobilized (*Sobranie sochinenii*, vol. 3, p. 146). *Qushbegi* was one of the top military titles in Khoqand mostly bestowed on highest commanders.

135. Mīrzā Shams Bukhārī erroneously regards that Yūsuf took Yarkand. See his *Nekotorye sobytiiakh v Bukhare, Khokande, i Kashgare* (Kazan: Univ. tipografiia, 1861), p. 39.

136. Valikhanov, *Sobranie sochinenii*, vol. 3, pp. 146–47; Pan Zhiping, *Zhongya Haohanguo*, pp. 121–22.

137. This remark of Pichang, who defended Yarkand during the invasion of Yūsuf, is quoted in Wei Yuan's *Shengwuji*, vol. 1, pp. 196–97.

138. The original of this document written in Turkic is now preserved at the First Historical Archives of China (Zhongguo Diyi Lishi Danganguan) in Peking and its facsimile is published in Pan Zhiping's *Zhongya Haohanguo*, p. 141. Although in the original text the last item of the four points (*tört qismi ish*) is not clearly shown, the Chinese translation of the text made at that time includes the fourth point.

139. *Daqing lichao shilu*, Daoguang-12–3–*gengshen*.

140. *Sobranie sochinenii*, vol. 3, p. 147, Also cf. a partial English translation by John and Robert Michell, *The Russians in Central Asia* (London: E. Stanford, 1865), p. 215. A British report drawn up by the Forsyth Mission in 1873 records the same contents based on the testimony of Valikhanov, *Report of a Mission to Yarkund*, pp. 185, 192.

141. *Daqing lichao shilu*, Daoguang-16–5–*guiwei*.

142. I quote this passage from an anonymous British report entitled "Eastern Turkestan, 1874" (p. 4) in FO 65/902 which includes the translation of the article "Kokand as it is at present," *Russian Imperial Geographical Society*, no. 3 (1849): 195. This British report adds that "According to the same authority (p. 196) after the deportation of 70,000 families from Kashghar by Mahommed Ali Khan, of Kokand, the Chinese, in addition to above subsidy, paid the latter 10,000 tillahs (=R.128,000, or 16,000 *l*) per annum for the single city of Kashghar, which amount was collected on the spot by resident Kokand Ak-sakal. This is, I think, sufficient to show that the Kokand Government did more than merely tax its own subjects in Kashghar."

143. Mehmet Saray, *Rus işgali devrinde Osmanlı develeti ile Türkistan Hanlıklarlı arasındaki siyasi münasebetler (1775–1875)* (Istanbul: Istanbul Matbaası, 1984), p. 46.

144. "The Heyday of the Ch'ing Order in Mongolia, Sinkiang and Tibet," in *The Cambridge History of China*, ed. J.K. Fairbank, vol. 10, pt. 1 (Cambridge: Cambridge University Press, 1978), pp. 375ff. He regards the agreement as being made in 1831, but the final sanction by Daoguang was made in 1832. In the meantime Chinese scholars do not accept Fletcher's assertion that it was "an unequal treaty." See Pan Zhiping and Jiang Lili, "1832–nian Qing yu Haohan yihekao," *Xibei shidi*, 1989, no. 1.

145. *Sobranie sochinenii*, vol. 3, p. 185. On *aqsaqal* there is a brief account by Chen Ching-lung, "Aksakals in the Moslem Region of Eastern Turkistan," *Ural-Al-*

taische Jahrbücher, no. 47 (1975): 41–46, but the historical role of *aqsaqal* needs a fuller examination.

146. Khasanov, *Narodnye dvizheniia v Kirgizii*, pp. 18–42.

147. *Sobranie sochinenii*, vol. 3, pp. 148, 185–86.

148. *Daqing lichao shilu*, Daoguang-16–5–*guiwei*, 16–6–*jiyou*.

149. Nalivkin, *Kratkaia istoriia*, pp. 132–143.

150. Nalivkin, *Kratkaia istoriia*, pp. 145–163; *Istoriia narodov Uzbekistana*, vol. 2 (Tashkent: Izd-vo AN UzSSR, 1947), p. 171.

151. *Ocherki po istorii Srednei Azii* (Moscow: Izd-vo Vostochnyi Literatury, 1958), pp. 209–10.

152. Cf. Kato, "'Shichinin no hōja tachi' no seisen," *Shigaku zasshi* 86, no. 1 (1977): 60–72.

153. For example, see Kuznetsov, *Tsinskaia imperiia*, p. 103.

154. Valikhanov, *Sobranie sochinenii*, vol. 3, p. 148.

155. On these invasions see Saguchi, *Shakaishi kenkyū*, pp. 511–30; Pan Zhiping, *Zhongya Haohanguo*, pp. 156–63.

156. *Report of a Mission to Yarkund*, p. 186. Similar descriptions are found in Nalivkin, *Kratkaia istoriia*, p. 168; Saguchi, *Shakaishi kenkyū*, pp. 514–15.

157. Saguchi, *Shakaishi kenkyū*, pp. 516–17.

158. Valikhanov, *Sobranie sochinenii*, vol. 3, p. 150.

159. Op. cit., p. 156.

160. Op. cit., p. 150.

161. Op. cit., p. 190.

162. *Report of a Mission to Yarkund*, p. 186.

163. These exiles were employed for this purpose from the early nineteenth century, and those who made contributions to the suppression got redemptions. For the exile system in Xinjiang, see Waley-Cohen's *Exile in Mid-Qing China*; N. J. Chou's "Frontier Studies and Changing Frontier Administration in Late Ch'ing China; The Case of Sinkiang, 1759–1911" (Ph.D. dissertation: University of Washington, 1976), pp. 52–80. Muslims' hatred of these exiles is well reflected in Radloff, *Proben*, vol. 1, pt. 6, pp. 31–33 (text) and pp. 41–44 (translation).

164. Valikhanov, *Sobranie sochinenii*, vol. 3, p. 195. The Kashgharians used to visit and gather at this mausoleum during the festival of Bar'āt, the fifteenth day of Sha'bān.

165. *Daqing lichao shilu*, Xianfeng-11–8–*jiwei*; 11–11–*bingshen*.

166. Boulger, *The Life of Yakoob Beg*, p. 214.

167. TH/Jarring, 28r; TH/Enver, p. 156; TH/Pantusov, p. 33 (6 towers).

168. This story is found both in Sayrāmī and Valikhanov, which proves that this story was quite widespread among the people. See TH/Jarring, 28r; Valikhanov, *Sobranie sochinenii*, vol. 3, p. 153.

169. Although it is not clear what this word stands for, it seems to be the transcription of *Huibu* (Muslim region) rather than Gobi (the Desert).

170. *Kawlan* is the transcription of the Chinese word *kouliang* (provisions), while *vaẓīfa* has the same meaning in Arabic.

171. TH/Jarring, 32r–32v; TH/Enver, pp. 173–75; TA/Pantusov, pp. 41–42. The indication that the Qing emperor considered abandoning Xinjiang because of

financial difficulty can also be found in *Ghazāt-i mūslimīn*, in *Three Turki Manuscripts from Kashghar*, ed. E. D. Ross (Lahore, 1908?), pp. 22–23. Cf. Haneda Akira, "Ghazāt-i Mūslimin no yakukō: Ya'qūb-bäg hanran no isshiryō," *Nairiku Ajiashi ronshū*, vol. 1 (Tokyo: Kokusho Kankokai, 1964), pp. 326–27.

172. TH/Jarring, 31r; TH/Enver, pp. 170, 617–23.

173. *Daqing lichao shilu*, Xianfeng-11–2–*xinyou*.

174. *Daqing lichao shilu*, Xianfeng-11–3–*dingwei*.

175. TH/Enver, pp. 617–23. It is interesting to note that Sayrāmī highly praised the Chinese emperor's justice (*'adālätlik*) and sympathy for people (*puqrā-pärwärlik*) which he had displayed during the investigation of this incident. Cf. Hamada, "Shio no gimu to seisen no maede," pp. 133–34.

176. *Kūngshī* seems to be the transcription of *gongshi* (promulgation), and *khaṭṭ* is an Arabic word meaning letter, note, word, and so on.

177. TH/Jarring, 32v; TH/Enver, pp. 175–76 (*kūshī khaṭṭ*); TA/Pantusov, p. 42 (*kūsī*).

178. TH/Jarring, 32v–33r; TH/Enver, pp. 176–77; TA/Pantusov, pp. 41–42.

179. *Report of a Mission to Yarkund*, p. 202.

180. *Tadhkirat al-najāt*, 15v. This is a work by Dāūd of Kurla written in 1282/1865–66 whose manuscript is found in the India Office Library, London (Ms. Turki 4).

181. Grenard, *Mission scientifique dans la haute Asie*, pp. 52–53.

182. *Tadhkira-i Ḥājjī Pādishāh Ḥabīb Allāh vä Rāshidīn Khān vä Ya'qūb Beg*, 2r. This work, whose title was also known as *Tārīkh-i Kāshghar*, was written by Muḥammad A'lam on the 18th of Sha'bān, 1311/Dec. 17, 1894. The manuscript in L'Institut de France (Ms. 3348–8) was translated and annotated by M. Hamada. See his "L'Histoire de Ḫotan de Muḥammad A'lam," *Zinbun*, no. 15 (1979); no. 16 (1980), and no. 18 (1982). Another manuscript is in St. Petersburg. On this manuscript see D.I. Tikhonov, "Uigurskie istoricheskie rukopisi," pp. 150–55; G.M. Ibragimova, "Rukopis' Mukhammada Aliama," *Istoriografiia i istochnikovedenie istorii Azii*, vol. 1 (1965): 50–55.

183. In the Chinese source it is written Hunasi. This village is located to the southwest of Kucha. See *Han-Wei Xinjiang diming cidian* (Urumchi, 1993), p. 260.

184. *Daqing lichao shilu*, Xianfeng-7–*yun* 5–*yisi*, 7–6–*qiwei*.

185. TH/Jarring, 31r–31v; TH/Enver, pp. 169–70; TA/Jarring, 39v–40r; TA/Pelliot, 35r–35v. There is a slight difference in the names of Muslim leaders. According to Valikhanov's explanation, '*tynza*,' that is, *dingza*, probably the transcription of a Chinese word, was a kind of police station where a Qing official called *pādishah* and several local officials were working. See his *Sobranie sochinenii*, vol. 3, pp. 118 and 172. For the description on the punishment of cutting heels—actually crushing ankles—see Philip A. Kuhn, *Soulstealers: The Chinese Sorcery Scare of 1768* (Cambridge, Mass.: Harvard University Press, 1990), pp. 15–17.

186. Cf. Fletcher, "The Heyday of the Ch'ing Order," pp. 385–95.

187. D.I. Tikhonov, "Vosstanie 1864 g. v Vostochnom Turkestane," *Sovetskoe vostokovedenie*, no. 5 (1948): 157.

188. A.E. Madzhi, "Novyi istochnik po istorii Kokanda, Kashgara i Bukhary," *Izvestiia otdeleniia obshchestvennykh nauk Akademii Nauk Tadzhikskoi SSR*, vol.

35, no. 1 (1958): 40–41. Similar epidemics in Western Turkestan are recorded. See *Ibid.*, pp. 38–39; E. Schuyler, vol. 1, pp. 148–49; Mehmet Ātif, *Kāşgar tārīhī*, p. 353. *Kāşgar tārīhī* was written in Istanbul right after the fall of Ya'qūb Beg's regime. The author gives us very detailed and fairly accurate reports on the events in Kashgharia during these turbulent years. His work is invaluable to modern researchers because it put together all the information available to the Ottomans at that time. His work was recently translated into modern Turkish. See *Kaşgar Tarihi: Bāis-i Hayret Ahvāl-i Garibesi*, tr. İsmail Aka et. al. (Kırıkkale: Eysi, 1998).

189. These two words represent Chinese *yancai* and *kouliang*.

190. "Vospominaniia Iliiskago Sibinitsa o Dungansko-Taranchinskom vozstanii v 1864–1871 godakh v Iliiskom krae," *Zapiski Vostochnogo otdeleniia Russkogo Arkheologicheskogo Obshchestva* 18 (1907–1908), p. 249. This is the testimony of a Sibo who lived in Ili at the time of the rebellion, written in Manchu and translated by A. D'iakov.

191. Op. cit., pp. 250–51.

192. TH/Jarring, 33r; TH/Enver, pp. 177–178; TA/Pantusov, p. 43.

CHAPTER 2

1. V. P. Iudin, "Nekotorye istochniki po istorii vosstaniia v Sin'tsiane v 1864 godu," *Trudy Instituta istorii, arkheologii i etnografii im Ch. Ch. Valikhanov Akademii Nauk Kazakhskoi SSR*, no. 15 (1962): 180, 192; Isiev, *Uigurskoe gosudarstvo Iettishar*, p. 13 and a note on page 15.

2. This is the report of Ḥājjī Yūsuf (*Jamī' al-tavārīkh*, f. 60), quoted from Isiev's "Nachalo natsional'no-osvoboditel'nogo vosstaniia Uigurov vo vtoroi polivine XIX v. (1864–1866 gg.)," in *Materialy po istorii i kul'ture Uigurskogo naroda* (Alma-Ata: Nauka, 1978), p. 64.

3. E. D. Ross, tr., *A History of the Moghuls in Central Asia* (1895; London: Curzon Press, 1972 repr.), p. 58. Cf. a new translation by W. M. Thackston, *Tarikh-i-Rashidi. A History of the Khans of Moghulistan* (Department of Near Eastern Languages and Civilization, Harvard University, 1996), p. 31.

4. His name is also known as Odui based on Edui in Chinese sources. Sayrāmī named Aḥmad Wang Beg's ancestors as follows: Mīrzā Aḥmad Wang Beg b. Mīrzā Isḥāq Wang Beg b. Mīrzā 'Uthmān Beyse Beg b. Mīrzā Hādī Beg. *Tadhkira-i khwājagān* also writes his name Mīrzā Hādī (Staatsbibliothek, ms. Or. 3292, p. 3).

5. *Daqing lichao shilu*, Xianfeng-2-7-*wuwu* and *guihai*; 3-1-*bingshen*.

6. *Daqing lichao shilu*, Xianfeng-10-2-*yimao*; 10-6-*xinwei*.

7. *Daqing lichao shilu*, Xianfeng-10-9-*yisi*.

8. *Daqing lichao shilu*, Xianfeng-10-2-*yimao*; 10-6-*xinwei*.

9. Cf. Saguchi, *Shakaishi kenkyū*, p. 189.

10. TH/Jarring, 18r–18v; TH/Jarring, pp. 110–15.

11. TH/Jarring, 34r; TH/Enver, p. 183; TA/Pantusov, p. 45.

12. TH/Jarring, 34r; TH/Enver, pp. 183–84; TA/Pantusov, pp. 45–46.

13. "'En no gimu' to 'seisen' tono maede," *Tōyōshi kenkyū*, vol. 52, no. 2 (1993).

14. TH/Jarring, 18r–18v; TH/Jarring, pp. 110–115.

15. TH/Jarring, 34r–34v; TH/Enver, p. 184; TA/Pantusov, p. 46.

16. Muslim sources wrote his name in several different ways: Rāshidīn, Rāsh al-Dīn, Rashīd al-Dīn, and so on. Considering the fact that all his brothers' names end with al-Dīn—Naẓīr al-Dīn, Jamāl al-Dīn, Fakhr al-Dīn, and Jalāl al-Dīn—we can assume that his name also had the same component of al-Dīn. The Turkic-speaking people in Kashgharia at that time had a tendency of reducing certain phonetic elements: for instance, Jamāl al-Dīn to Jamāldīn, and Hām al-Dīn to Hāmdīn. Cf. TH/Jarring, 35v; TA/Pantusov, p. 46.

17. I do not think Rāsh al-Dīn was his original name. Rāsh (a feather or a heap of winnowed corn) does not make proper sense when it combined with al-Dīn (of religion). Cf. F. Steingass, *A Comprehensive Persian–English Dictionary* (London: Ruoutledge, 1892), pp. 563–64.

18. A. A. Bykov, "Monety Rashaddina, Uigurskogo povstantsa," *Strany i narody Vostoka*, no. 15 (1973): 288–302. The inscriptions on the coins found in Zhu Zhuopeng and Zhu Shengwei's *Xinjiang hongqian* (Shanghai: Xuelin Chubanshe, 1991, pp. 168–170) should be read Sayyid Ghāzī Rāshidīn Khān instead of Sayyid Rāshidīn Khān.

19. TH/Jarring, 37r; TH/Enver, p. 197; TA/Pantusov, p. 54.

20. The contents of the first two works can be found in V. P. Iudin's "Nekotorye istochniki," and the manuscript of the third is in India Office Library (Ms. Turki 4). Cf. Isiev, *Uigurskoe gosudarstvo Iettishar*, p. 13 and note 10 on p. 52.

21. *Ẓafar-nāma*, 20v.

22. *Xiyu congzhi*, q. 3, 5r–6r.

23. On the garrison farm in the Urumchi region during the Qing period, see Wang Xilong's "Qingdai Wulumuqi tundian shulun," *Xinjiang Shehui Kexue*, 1989, no. 5: 101–8.

24. *Pinghuizhi*, q. 7, 1v–2r.

25. He received this title as a reward for his service rendered during the Jahāngīr rebellion. See Ma Xiaoshi, *Xibei huizu geming jianshi* (Shanghai: Dongfang Shushe, 1951), p. 59.

26. Ibid.

27. G. G. Stratanovich, "K voprosu o kharaktere administrativnogo ustroistva i sotsial'noi otnoshenii v Dunganskom Soiuze gorodov (1863–1872 gg.)," *Izvestiia Akademii Nauk Kirgizskoi SSR* (SON), vol. 2, no. 2 (1960): 61.

28. A. N. Geins, "O vosstanii musul'manskogo naseleniia ili Dunganei v zapadnom Kitae," *Voennyi sbornik*, 1866, no. 8: 192 (quoted from A. Khodzhaev's *Tsinskaia imperiia*, p. 109, note 8).

29. *Pinghuizhi*, q. 7, 2r–2v.

30. *Daqing lichao shilu*, Tongzhi-3–6–*yiyou*; 3–7–*dingsi*; *Pinghuizhi*, q. 7, 2v–3r. About the battle of Ushaq Tal we can find a detailed description in TH/Jarring (50v–51r), but the size of the Qing army is exaggerated as 18,000 or 24,000.

31. *Qinding Pingding Shan-Gan Xinjiang fanglue*, q. 70, 1r–1v; *Kanding Xinjiangji*, q. 1, 1r–1v.

32. *Qinding Pingding Shan-Gan Xinjiang fanglue*, q. 73, 10r–10v; q. 81, 1r–2v; *Kanding Xinjiangji*, q. 1, 2r. The latter source dates the beginning of the uprising on July 15, but in the reports by field officials was written as June 26.

33. G. G. Stratanovich, "K voprosu o kharaktere," p. 62.

34. *Qingzhen* literally means "pure and true," but it was used almost synonymously with Islam. On the concept of *qingzhen* as a mark of Muslim identity in modern days, see Dru Gladney's *Muslim Chinese: Ethnic Nationalism in the People's Republic* (Cambridge, Mass.: Harvard University Press, 1991), pp. 7–15.

35. For the eruption of the Urumchi rebellion, see *Qinding Pingding Shan-Gan Xinjiang fanglue*, q. 70, 1r–1v; q. 72, 21r–23r; q. 73, 6r–12v; *Pinghuizhi*, q. 7, 1v–3v. Dāūd proclaimed the beginning of the new era as the year of 2893 of *qingzhen*, but I have no knowledge about the meaning of this number.

36. *Qinding Pingding Shan-Gan Xinjiang fanglue*, q. 86, 9v–10r.

37. TH/Jarring, 55r; TH/Enver, p. 277; TA/Pantusov, pp. 100–107; *Qinding Pingding Shan-Gan Xinjiang fanglue*, q. 80, 19v; q. 81, 2r–2v.

38. *Qinding Pingding Shan-Gan Xinjiang Fanglue*, q. 75, 9v–10r; q. 93, 12v–13r; q. 98, 11r.

39. Khodzahev, *Tsinskaia imperiia*, pp. 28–29.

40. *Pinghuizhi*, q. 7, 4r. Cf. Khodzhaev, *Tsinskaia imperiia*, pp. 28–29.

41. *Kanding Xinjiangji*, q. 1, 12r–13v.

42. Stratanovich, "K voprosu," p. 61.

43. *Huijiang tongzhi*, comp., Hening (Taipei: Wenhai Chubanshe repr., 1966), q. 8, 3r.

44. On this city under the rule of the Qing and Ya'qūb Beg, see Hori Sunao's "Kaikyō toshi Yarukando," *Kōnan Daigaku kiyō* (Bungakuhen), no. 63 (1987).

45. *Qinding Pingding Shan-Gan Xinjiang fanglue*, q. 77, 18v.

46. *Kanding Xinjiangji*, q. 1, 2r.

47. *Report of a Mission to Yarkund*, pp. 202–203; Kuropatkin, *Kashgaria*, p. 157.

48. *Ẓafar-nāma*, 7v–28v.

49. *Ghazāt-i Muslimīn* in E.D. Ross, ed., *Three Turki Manuscripts* (Lahore: Mufid-i-Am Press, 1908?), pp. 39–40.

50. *Ẓafar-nāma*, 7v–28v.

51. *Ẓafar-nāma*, 28v.

52. *Ẓafar-nāma*, 29v. Sayrāmī (TH/Jarring, 41v; TH/Enver, p. 214) writes that when the Kuchean army led by Naẓīr al-Dīn, elder brother of Rāshidīn, arrived in Yarkand, the city was divided into three parts: the Muslim town was partitioned between 'Abd al-Raḥmān and Tungan *imāms*, while the Chinese fort was still held by the Qing army. However, according to *Ghazāt-i Muslimīn*, Ghulām Ḥusayn had been the ruler when the Kuchean army appeared in Yarkand and only after they had left was his elder brother 'Abd al-Raḥmān enthroned as the new ruler (E. D. Ross ed., *Three Turki Manuscripts*, p. 40). Comparing the two sources, we can find that *Ghazāt-i Muslimīn* contains far more detailed and accurate information than Sayrāmī's work. Therefore, we can conclude that right after the revolt Yarkand was not divided into three parts as Sayrāmī asserts but partitioned into two parts, that is, the Manchu fort guarded by the Qing army and the Muslim town taken by the Tungans with a nominal ruler Ghulām Ḥusayn.

53. *Ẓafar-nāma*, 28v–29v.

54. *Sobranie sochinenii*, vol. 3, p. 161.

55. *Report of a Mission to Yarkund*, pp. 35–36.

56. Ibid.

57. *Report of a Mission to Yarkund*, p. 39 and a map facing p. 249.

58. *Sobranie sochinenii*, vol. 3, p. 161.

59. *Report of a Mission to Yarkund*, p. 37.

60. *Qinding Pingding Shan-Gan Xinjiang fanglue*, q. 77, 19r.

61. Ibid.

62. *Jamī' al-tavārīkh*, quoted from Tikhonov's "Uigurskie istoricheskie rukopisi," p. 168.

63. *Tārīkh-i nāma-i Ya'qūb Khān* (INA AN, B 772), 36r–36v, quoted from A. Khodzhaev, *Tsinskaia imperiia*, p. 30 and note 13 on page 110.

64. "Uigurskie istoricheski rukopisi," p. 168.

65. *Visits to High Tartary*, pp. 47–48.

66. According to Valikhanov, one of Ṣiddīq's ancestors, a certain Akim (probably from *ḥākim*), helped the Qing during its conquest of Xinjiang and that Akim was appointed to the *ḥākim* of Tashmaliq for his contribution. He adds that Ṣiddīq was the leader of the Turaygir tribe of the Qirghiz and helped the Qing government end the rebellion of Walī Khān in 1857. For this service he received a hat decorated with red gems and was well received by Qing officials. See *Sobranie sochnenii*, vol. 3, pp. 160, 188.

67. Tikhonov, "Uigurskie istoricheskie rukopisi," pp. 168–69. As he pointed out, Ḥājjī Yūsuf's statement that Qutluq Beg invited Ṣiddīq Beg in October of 1863 is wrong. He seems to have been confused because he wrote his work in 1907–8, more than forty years after the incident.

68. *Kanding Xinjiangji*, q. 1, 2v.

69. *Report of a Mission to Yarkund*, pp. 203–204.

70. See *Xinjiang jianshi*, vol. 2, pp. 127–128. This work also suggests, based on a Muslim source, that the two Tungans, Jin Laosan and Ma Tuzi, were farmers at a *tundian* in Fayzābād (Qieshi).

71. See TH/Jarring, 68r–68v; TH/Enver, p. 333; *Report of a Mission to Yarkund*, p. 204; Kuropatkin, *Kashgaria*, p. 159.

72. *Report of a Mission to Yarkund*, p. 33.

73. Valikhanov, *Sobranie sochinenii*, p. 122. Ḥabīb Allāh built a new wall measuring 25 feet high and 20 feet thick. See W. H. Johnson, "Report on his Journey to Ilchi, the Capital of Khotan, in Chinese Tartary," *Journal of the Royal Geographic Society*, vol. 37 (1867): 14.

74. *Report of a Mission to Yarkund*, p. 33; Valikhanov, *Sobranie sochinenii*, vol. 3, pp. 122–23.

75. *Tadhkira-i Ḥājjī Pādishāh*, 19r–20r.

76. *Tārīkh-i ṣigharī*, 28v–29r.

77. *Tadhkira-i Ḥājjī Pādishāh*, 4r.

78. Johnson, "Journey to Ilchi," p. 4.

79. *Mission scientifique*, vol. 3, p. 54.

80. Ibid.

81. *Tadhkira-i Ḥājjī Pādishāh*, 2r–8v.

82. *Tadhkira-i Ḥājjī Pādishāh*, 2r–2v.

83. TH/Jarring, 78v; TH/Enver, pp. 379–80; TA/Pantusov, pp. 168–69.

84. *Tadhkira-i Ḥājjī Pādishāh*, 3r–8v.
85. *Tadhkira-i Ḥājjī Pādishāh*, 19r–20r.
86. *Tadhkira-i Ḥājjī Pādishāh*, 8v–9r.
87. *Tadhkira-i Ḥājjī Pādishāh*, 9r–10r.
88. Lo Yunzhi, *Qing Gaozong tongzhi Xinjiang zhengce de tantao*, pp. 72–74.
89. Mullā Bīlāl, *Ghazāt dar mulk-i Chīn* (printed edition by N. N. Pantusov, *Voina musul'man protiv Kitaitsev*), p. 11. On this work, see M. Hamrajev, "Bilal Nazim: ein Klassiker der uigurischen Literatur," *Ungarische Jahrbücher*, no. 42 (1970): 77–99; Hamada Masami, "Murrā Birāru no *Seisenki* ni tsuite," *Tōyō gakuhō*, 55, no. 4 (1973): 31–59.
90. "Vospominaiia Iliiskogo Sibintsa o Dungansko-Taranchinskom vozstanii v 1864–1877 godakh v Iliiskom krae," *Zapiski Vostochnogo otdeleniia Russkogo arkheologicheskogo obshchestva*, no. 18 (1907–1908), introduction by A. D'iakov, p. 234.
91. *Daqing lichao shilu*, Tongzhi-4–1–*yimao*.
92. *Ghazāt dar mulk-i Chīn*, p. 11.
93. *Qinding Pingding Shan-Gan Xinjiang fanglue*, q. 44, 10v–11v.
94. According to the recollection of a Sibo, 8,000 Sibos, Oirats and Han Chinese, in addition to 3,000 exiled criminals, were dispatched at that time ("Vospominaniia Iliiskogo Sibintsa," p. 239). But in the memorial of Cangcing, the total number of troops was 5,200 including 3,000 Torghuts, 500 exiled criminals, and some other government forces. *Qinding Pingding Shan-Gan Xinjiang fanglue*, q. 76, 7v–8r.
95. "Vospominaniia Iliiskogo Sibintsa," pp. 239–42; Schuyler, *Turkistan*, vol. 2, p. 178; Grum-Grzhimailo, *Opisanie puteshestviia v Zapadnyi Kitai* (St. Petersburg, 1896), vol. 1, p. 7.
96. The Ili General's headquaters were placed here. This was one of the so-called "Nine Forts of Ili" and the other eight were Huining Cheng (Bayandai), Suiding Cheng (Ukharliq), Guangren Cheng (Ukurborosuk), Zhande Cheng (Chaghan Usu), Gongchen Cheng (Khorgos), Xichun Cheng (Khara Bulaq), Taleqi Cheng (Tarchi), and Ningyuan Cheng (Kulja). The names in parentheses are the Turkic appellations.
97. The word *khānjā* in the Taranchi dialect corresponds to *ḥājjī*. See *Ghazāt dar mulk-i Chīn*, vol. 2 (Pantusov's note), p. 42. Mullā Bīlāl uses the form of *akhūn* (in Chinese transcribed either as *ahong* or *ahun*) rather than *akhūnd*, so I followed him in the case of Ili.
98. Properly it should be 'Abd al-Rasūl, but I followed the spelling of Mullā Bilāl.
99. *Ghazāt dar mulk-i Chīn*, pp. 12–13.
100. Ibid. The fact that the Kulja revolt occurred on November 10, 1864 is confirmed by a memorial of Cangcing and Mingsioi. Cf. "Vospominaniia Iliiskogo Sibintsa," 243 (October 12 in the Julian calendar). Mullā Bīlāl writes that it happened on 12 Jumāda I, 1280 which corresponds to October 25, 1863, but this is obviously wrong. His year 1280 must be a mistake for 1281.
101. *Ghazāt dar mulk-i Chīn*, pp. 17–19. For the locations of Taranchi villages to the south of the Ili river, see Saguchi Tōru's "Taranchi jin no shakai—Iri keikoku no Uiguru buzokushi, 1760–1860," *Shigaku zasshi* 73, no. 11 (1964): 25–33.
102. *Ghazāt dar mulk-i Chīn*, p. 21.

103. *Shāngyū* is a transcription of the Chinese word *shangye*, meaning "head of merchants."

104. *Ghazāt dar mulk-i Chīn*, p. 22. According to "Vospominaniia Iliiskogo Sibintsa" (p. 246), Yākūr Akhūn's Chinese name was Ma I.

105. Chinese sources write his name as Maizimuzate (i.e., Ma'ẓūmzāda) which probably reflects the local pronunciation.

106. *Qinding Pingding Shan-Gan-Xinjiang Fanglue*, q. 92, 4r–4v.

107. *Ghazāt dar mulk-i Chīn*, pp. 24–28.

108. *Ghazāt dar mulk-i Chīn*, pp. 24–28, 34, 40. Bilāl, who had high respect for 'Abd Rasul, called them "the two shāhs."

109. *Qinding Pingding Shan-Gan Xinjiang Fanglue* (q. 106, 29v–30r), *Ghazāt dar mulk-i Chīn* (p. 73) and "Vospominaniia" (p. 251), all agree on the date of the fall of Bayandai. However, there are slight differences in other details. For example, *Ghazāt* records that the Muslims entered the fortress after they had exploded its walls, while "Vospominaniia" writes that they crossed the bridge at midnight when the garrison soldiers were sleeping. Also cf. *Kanding Xinjiangji*, q. 1, 4r.

110. *Ghazāt dar mulk-i Chīn*, pp. 82–96. This *fuchi* is no other than "an adventurer from Andijan named Patcha Hodja" in E. Schuyler's *Turkistan* (vol. 2, p. 183), and "Kaira-khodzha" in "Vospominaniia" (note 2 on page 253). There existed a Bukharan group called *puchin* in the Ili valley under the Zunghar rule (see Haneda, *Chūō Ajiashi kenkyū*, pp. 262–66).

111. *Ghazāt dar mulk-i Chīn*, pp. 82–107. Obul and Abil seem to be variants of Abū al-.

112. *Ghazāt dar mulk-i Chīn*, pp. 118–36; "Vospominaniia," pp. 265–66.

113. *Ghazāt dar mulk-i Chīn*, pp. 99–100 and 136–37.

114. *Ghazāt dar mulk-i Chīn*, pp. 152–62; Schuyler, *Turkistan*, vol. 2, pp. 182–83; "Vospominaniia," pp. 269–70.

115. *Qinding Pingding Shan-Gan Xinjiang fanglue*, q. 107, 1r–2r.

116. Qurbān 'Alī Ayāghūzī, *Kitāb-i tārīkh-i jarīda-i jadīda* (Kazan, 1889), p. 66.

117. *Qinding Pingding Shan-Gan Xinjiang fanglue*, q. 16, 18r, 20v–21r; *Xinjiang Tuzhi*, q. 116, 5v.

118. *Xinjiang jianshi*, vol. 2, p. 114.

119. According to TA/Pantusov (p. 103), he was *sayyid* and "one of the *khwājas* in Sayram." He was assisted by Qāsim Jangī, Āīd Khalīfa, Khwāja Zāīd Khalīfa, and Ḥājjī Bāqī Khalīfa. Here "the *khwājas* in Sayram" seems to denote one of the three major clans (*urugh*, *qabīla*) in Sayram, that is, *khwāja*, *shāh*, and *amīr*.

120. For a detailed account see Tikhonov, "Vosstanie 1864 g. v Vostochnom Turkestane," *Sovetskoe vostokovedenie*, no. 5 (1948): 155–72, and a recent article by Sugawara Jūn, "Kūchā Hōjā no 'seisen' to Muslimu shoseiryoku," *Nairiku Ajiashi kenkyū*, no. 11 (1996): 17–40.

121. TH/Jarring, 34v; TH/Enver, p. 185; TA/Pantusov, pp. 46–47.

122. *Qinding Pingding Shan-Gan Xinjiang fanglue*, q. 70, 4r–5r.

123. *Qinding Pingding Shan-Gan Xinjiang fanglue*, q. 69, 16r–16v.

124. *Qinding Pingding Shan-Gan Xinjiang fanglue*, q. 70, 14v–15v and 20r, mentions two battles around Ushaq Tal on July 5 and July 16 as the author of *Tadhkirat al-najāt* (27r–33v) does (he joined the eastern expedition). Sayrāmī says that

the total number of Qing troops defeated by Isḥāq was 42,000 (TA/Pantusov, pp. 93–94), but this is a highly exaggerated statement. There were about a hundred soldiers in Qarashahr (*Qinding Pingding Shan-Gan Xinjiang fanglue*, q. 68, 3r) and the total number of the assistance army sent from Urumchi and Turfan was only 600 (op cit., q. 69, 17r–17v). An eyewitness gives much more moderate numbers. See *Tadhkirat al-najāt*, 28v and 31v.

125. *Qinding Pingding Shan-Gan Xinjiang fanglue*, q. 68, 3r.

126. The date when they departed Qarashahr is recorded as the 18th of Rabī' II, 1281 (September 20, 1864) in TA/Pantusov (p. 101). However, in TA/Pelliot (72r) they encamped at Tāwilghū and prepared for an expedition on the 12th of Rabī' II, 1281 (September 14, 1864). In TH the date was erased (TH/Jarring, 54r; TH/Enver, p. 273).

127. TH/Jarring, 55r–55v; TA/Enver, pp. 277–79; TH/Pantusov, pp. 104–106. Sayrāmī seems to have exaggerated the number of infidels killed in these areas.

128. Sayrāmī (TH/Jarring, 55v, 56v; TH/Enver, p. 278; TA/Pantusov, p. 105) writes the name of the town as Mūray or Mūrkhū. Mūray apparently corresponds to Mulei, but Mūrkhū seem to transcribe to Muleihe (Mulei River).

129. TH/Jarring, 56r; TH/Enver, pp. 280–81; TA/Pantusov, pp. 106–107. Sayrāmī, at first, wrote the duration of the siege as 5 months, but later he changed it to 6 months and finally to 7–8 months. The second campaign to Mulei was in the spring of 1865 and the fall of Turfan occurred after that. Therefore, it seems that the siege of Turfan began around August of 1864 and, after 7–8 months of fighting, ended in March of 1865.

130. In all the manuscripts of TA (TA/Pantusov, p. 111), the date of their departure to Hami is recorded as the 18th of Dhū al-Ḥijja, 1282 (May 4, 1866). However, TH (TH/Jarring, 57v; TH/Enver, p. 288) changed it to the 18th of Muḥarram, 1282 (June 13, 1865).

131. *Qinding Pingding Shan-Gan Xinjiang fanglue*, q. 76, 19v–20r and q. 86, 11r.

132. *Qinding Pingding Shan-Gan Xinjiang fanglue*, q. 106, 4r; q. 114, 12v; TH/Jarring, 57v–58r; TH/Enver, pp. 288–90; TA/Pantusov, pp. 111–12.

133. Khodzhaev, *Tsinkaia imperiia*, pp. 45–46; Zeng Wenwu, *Zhonguo jingying xiyushi*, p. 322.

134. TH/Jarring, 36r; TH/Enver, pp. 190–92; TA/Pantusov, pp. 50–51.

135. TH/Jarring, 36r–36v; TH/Enver, pp. 193–94; TA/Pantusov, pp. 51–52; *Qinding Pingding Shan-Gan Xinjiang fanglue*, q. 70, 10r.

136. TH/Jarring, 37r–38r; TH/Enver, pp. 198–202; TA/Pantusov, p. 56.

137. *Kanding Xinjiangji*, q. 1, 1v; TH/Jarring, 38v; TH/Enver, p. 201.

138. TH/Jarring, 38v–39r; TH/Enver, pp. 202–204; TA/Pantusov, pp. 57–58.

139. TH/Jarring, 40v–41r; TH/Enver, pp. 210–13; TA/Pantusov, pp. 62–64. Sayrāmī does not mention where the khwājas were imprisoned, but only in TH/Jarring he writes that they were taken to Kashghar. If this is true, the Muslim town of Kashghar may have been taken by Ṣiddīq before the Kuchean army came to Artush. Moreover, Sayrāmī notes that the Qirghiz, after concluding a truce with the Kucheans, conducted the khwājas to Kashghar "with friendship and respect." They made an agreement (*ṣulḥ vä mudārā*) that the Qirghiz would not intervene in the

matters of Ush Turfan and Aqsu while the Kucheans would not interfere with the matters of Kashghar. This description gives us an impression that the two sides were on equal terms. It is possible that Sayrāmī, who had intimate relations with the Kuchean khwājas, tried to keep their honor by this kind of ambiguous statement.

140. TH/Jarring, 41r–41v; TH/Enver, pp. 213–14; TA/Pantusov, p. 65.

141. TH/Jarring, 41v–42r; TH/Enver, pp. 216–17; TA/Pantusov, pp. 65–66.

142. TH/Jarring, 78v; TH/Enver, pp. 380–81; TA/Pantusov, p. 169.

143. On the first Kuchean expedition of Yarkand and its failure, see TH/Jarring, 41r–42v; TH/Enver, pp. 213–19; TA/Pantusov, pp. 65–68. It is not clear when the Kuchean army came back to Kucha. According to Sayrāmī the expedition had started in 1865 and the siege of Yarkand continued about eight months. However, the famous battle of Khan Ariq between Ya'qūb Beg and the second expeditionary army from Kucha occurred at the end of July, so the return of the first expeditionary army should be at least earlier than that date.

144. On this group see Hamada Masami, "Islamic Saints and Their Mausoleums," *Acta Asiatica*, no. 34 (1978): 79–98.

145. *Tārīkh-i rashīdī* (tr. by E. D. Ross), pp. 10–15.

146. On the process of the conflicts between these two groups, see my "Muslim Saints in the 14th to the 16th Centuries of Eastern Turkestan," *International Journal of Central Asian Studies*, vol. 1 (1996): 285–322.

147. TH/Jarring, 34r; TH/Enver, p. 184; TA/Pantusov, p. 46.

148. Ibid.

149. *Report of a Mission to Yarkund*, p. 44.

150. Hamada Masami, "De l'autorité religieuse au pouvoir politique: la révolte de Kūčā et Khwāja Rāshidīn," *Naqshbandis: cheminements et situation actuelle d'un ordre mystique musulman*, ed. M. Gaborieau, A. Popovic and T. Zarcone (Istanbul-Paris: Isis, 1990), pp. 455–89.

151. On various forms of miracles performed by saints, see R. Gramlich, *Die Wunder der Freunde Gottes* (Wiesbaden: Franz Steiner, 1987).

152. "Les <voies> (ṭuruq) soufies en Chine," in *Les ordres mystiques dans l'Islam*, ed. A. Popovic and G. Veinstein (Paris: Ecole des hautes etudes en sciences sociales, 1986), p. 23.

153. Stratanovich, "K voprosu o kharatere," p. 61.

154. *Pinghuizhi*, q. 7, 1v–2r.

155. Ma Xiaoshi, *Xibei huizu geming jianshi*, p. 59.

156. A. N. Geins, "O vosstanii musul'manskogo naseleniia ili Dunganei v zapadnom Kitae," *Voennyi sbornik*, no. 8 (1866): 192 (quoted from A. Khodzhaev's *Tsinskaia imperiia*, p. 109, note 8).

157. *Pinghuizhi*, q. 2, 19r–19v.

158. See Fletcher, "Les <voies> (ṭuruq) soufies en Chine."

159. *Sharqī Turkistān Tārīkhī* (Srinagar, Kashmir: Bruka Parlis Basmakhanesi, 1366/1946–47), p. 391.

160. "Les <voies> (ṭuruq) soufies en Chine." On Aḥmad Sirhindī see A. Ahmad's *Studies in Islamic Culture in the Indian Environment* (Oxford, 1964), pp. 182–90 and Y. Friedman's *Shaykh Ahmad Sirhindi* (Montreal, 1971).

161. H. Einzmann, *Religiöses Volksbrauchtum in Afghanistan: Islamische Heili-*

genverehrung und Wallfartswesen im Raum Kabul (Wiesbaden: Franz Steiner, 1977), p. 24. Thomas J. Barfield, in his private communication with me, pointed out that they were active in the anti-Soviet war and are still very influential.

162. *Yāqūb Begdin ilgäri Kāshqarnī alghan Ṣiddīq Begning Dāstān tadhkirasi*, 1v–5v. This manuscript is found in the India Office Library (Ms. Turki 3), London. This is a copy made by Mīrzā Jalāl al-Dīn Akhūn on the 13th of Jumāda I, 1282 (October 4, 1865). Also cf. Hamada, "Uiguru rekishi bunken," 362–63.

163. According to Ṭālib Akhūnd (Prov. 115, 3v–5v), the person who led Kashgharian begs and expelled Qutluq Beg was a certain Naẓar Shāng Beg. In this respect, his statement agrees with 'Abd al-Bāqī's (*Yāqūb Begdin ilgäri*, 9v). Naẓar Shāng Beg sent Sanā' Allāh Shaykh as an envoy to Ṣiddīq Beg for negotiation, but Ṣiddīq refused to accept his terms. So Naẓar sent an envoy to 'Alīm Quli in Khoqand. In response to this, 'Ālīm Quli dispatched his emissary to Kashghar, whom Naẓar did not trust because he thought that it might be Ṣiddīq's plot.

164. TH/Jarring, 78r–78v; TH/Enver, pp. 378–79; TA/Pantusov, pp. 155–56.

165. See his biography entitled *Khwāja Muḥammad Sharīfning tadhkirasi* (Gunnar Jarring Collection, Prov. 10), 3r–9r. Several copies of this work exist (particularly in Russia) three of which I have seen at the collection of Gunnar Jarring. A partial translation is found in *Materialy po istorii Kazakhskikh khanstv XV–XVIII vekov*, pp. 232–36. Also cf. Akimushkin's *Khronika*, p. 265.

166. There is an important work called *Tadhkira-i Satūq Boghrā Khān*. This is a collection of numerous short biographies of the so-called Uwaysī saints including Satugh Boghra Khan. It was translated and studied by Julian Baldick, *Imaginary Muslims: The Uwaysi Sufis of Central Asia* (London: I. B. Tauris & Co. Ltd., 1993). In one of the manuscripts in Russia the name of Khwāja Muḥammad Sharīf is written as author, which led many scholars including myself to regard him an Uwaysī Sufi. However, recently Devin DeWeese raised a serious doubt about his real authorship of this work. See his *An "Uvaysī" Sufi in Timurid Mawarannahr* (Papers on Inner Asia, no. 22; Bloomington, Indiana: Indiana University, 1993).

167. The competition between these two Sufi orders is most vividly described in the two works of Shāh Maḥmūd ibn Mīrzā Fāḍil Churās. One was translated with excellent annotations by Akimushkin (*Khronika*) and the other titled *Anīs al-ṭālibīn* is in the Bodleian Library (Ms. Ind. Inst. Pers. 45). A part of the latter is printed also in Akimushkin's book, pp. 331–44.

168. For example, see *Xinjiang jianshi*, vol. 2, pp. 91ff; Ji Dachun, "Shilun."

169. See, for example, D. Isiev, "Nachalo," pp. 59–63 and 71–72.

170 Cf. Fletcher, "Ch'ing Inner Asia," p. 69.

171. For the related secondary materials, see Evelyn S. Rawski, "Re-envisioning the Qing: The Significance of the Qing Period in Chinese History," *Journal of Asian Studies*, vol. 55, no. 4 (1990): 829–50.

172. Robert Lee, *The Manchurian Frontier in Ch'ing History* (Cambridge, Mass.: Harvard University Press, 1970). Cf. C. R. Bawden's description of the Qing policy toward Mongolia in *The Modern History of Mongolia* (London: Weidenfeld and Nicholson, 1968, pp. 81–86) tends to emphasize its negative side. This tendency seems to be related to his reliance on the works of Mongol scholars.

173. Suzuki Chūsei, "China's Relation with Inner Asia: The Hsiung-nu, Tibet,"

in *The Chinese World Order: Traditional China's Foreign Relations*, ed. John K. Fairbank (Cambridge, Mass.: Harvard University Press, 1968), pp. 180–197.

174. Sayrāmī (TH/Jarring, 11; TH/Enver, pp. 30, 204, 625) employs sometimes a rather archaic form, *Faghfūr-i Chīn* (Chinese emperor). On the term *faghfūr*, see Paul Pelliot's "Facfur" in *Notes on Marco Polo* (Paris: A. Maisonneuve, 1959–73), pp. 652–661

175. In order to circumvent the inevitable result of perpetual warfare, some jurists, notably belonging to the Shafi'īs, recognized a third status called *Dār al-Ṣulḥ* (Abode of Truce). However, the jurists of the Hanafī school did not acknowledge this third status. See M. Parvin and M. Sommer, "Dar al-Islam: The Evolution of Muslim Territoriality and Its Implication for Conflict Resolution in the Middle East," *International Journal of Middle East Studies*, no. 2 (1980): 4. For the accounts of the above-mentioned three zones, see the articles of "Dār al-Ḥarb," "Dār al-Islām" and "Dār al-Ṣulḥ" in *Encyclopaedia of Islam* (the 2nd ed., Leiden: Brill), vol. 2, fascs. 24 and 25 (1961).

176. Shāh Maḥmūd Churās, *Anīs al-ṭālibīn*, 106r (see printed text in Akimushkin, *Khronika*, p. 342).

177. "Ein Heiligenstaat im Islam: Das Ende der Caghataiden und die Herrschaft der Choğas in Kašgarien," *Der islamische Orient: Berichte und Forschungen*, pts. 6–10 (Berlin: W. Peiser, 1905).

178. Saguchi, *Shinkyō minzokushi kenkyū*, pp. 225–28.

179. See my "The Cult of Saints in Eastern Turkestan: The Case of Alp Ata in Turfan," *Proceedings of the 35th Permanent International Altaistic Conference* (Taipei, 1992), pp. 199–226.

180. It is interesting to note that *jihād*, a more popular Arabic word for holy war, was hardly ever used in the Muslim literature of the nineteenth century Xinjiang.

CHAPTER 3

1. I have seen only the Russian translation, *Magomet-Iakub, Emir Kashgarskii* (St. Petersburg, 1903), tr. I. G.

2. Kuropatkin, *Kashagria*, pp. 159–60.

3. "Badaulet," pp. 94–95.

4. *Turkistan*, vol. 1, pp. 132–36.

5. *Buried Treasures of Chinese Turkestan* (1928; Oxford University Press, 1985 repr.), p. 24.

6. *The Life of Yakoob Beg*, pp. vii–viii.

7. See his *Pivot of Asia* (Boston: Little, Brown, 1950), p. 32.

8. "Badaulet," p. 94. His memoir tends to overstate his role as an early patron of Ya'qūb Beg, but it contains some details, not found in other sources, on Ya'qūb Beg's career in the Khoqand khanate.

9. TA/Pantusov, p. 131.

10. *Kashgaria*, p. 159. He also reported that Ya'qūb Beg's father was "Ismet-Oola" and that he married a woman in Piskent and got Ya'qūb Beg from her. However, there is no other evidence to support his assertion that Ya'qūb Beg's parents

had divorced right after his birth and, because his mother remarried a butcher in Piskent and he grew up in his house, he was sometimes called the son of a butcher.

11. *Report of a Mission to Yarkund*, pp. 97–98.

12. *The Life of Yakoob Beg*, pp. 77–78. His claim that Ya'qūb Beg is Amīr Temür's descendant seems to be based on the report in *Mission to Yarkund* (p. 97). The part in this report was written by H. Bellew.

13. *Kashmir and Kashghar* (London: Trübner & Co., Ludgate Hill, 1875), p. 300.

14. *Report of a Mission to Yarkund*, p. 55.

15. *Visits to High Tartary*, pp. 373, 357–58.

16. For example, see TH/Enver, pp. 504–13; TA/Pantusov, pp. 237–39.

17. "Badaulet," p. 94.

18. The word *sart* which originally came from the Sanskrit *sartha*, meaning merchant, retained its original meaning up to the eleventh century. The earliest occurrence of the term in Turkic texts goes back to the eighth century in the Manichean texts from Turfan. Cf. Clauson, *An Etymological Dictionary*, p. 846. From the late twelfth and the thirteenth centuries the word *sarta'ul* among the Mongols meant the Muslims in general. See, P. Pelliot, *Notes sur l'histoire de la Horde d'Or* (Paris: Adrien-Maisonneuve, 1949), p. 34. Later it came to mean town dwellers. The actual usages in the nineteenth century are found in Shaw's *Visits to High Tartary*, pp. 25–26 and Schuyler's *Turkistan*, vol. 1, pp. 104–105.

19. *Kashgaria*, pp. 159–60.

20. "Badaulet," pp. 94–95.

21. Nalivkin, *Histoire du Khanat de Khokand*, pp. 174–99.

22. "Badaulet," p. 95.

23. On this event see Nalivkin, *Kratkaia istoriia*, pp. 167–68; *Istoriia Kirgizskoi SSR*, vol. 1 (Frunze, 1984), p. 559. The author of *Tavārīkh-i shahrukhiyya* (p. 182) puts the date of 'Azīz's death as 1266/1849–50. Cf. Bartol'd, "Izvlechenie iz *Ta'rīkh-i shāhrukhī*," in *Sochineniia*, vol. 2, pt. 2 (1964), p. 351.

24. "Badaulet," p. 95. Bellew writes incorrectly (*Report of a Mission to Yarkund*, p. 98) that Ya'qūb Beg was promoted from *mahram* to *qushbegi* when he was made the governor of Aq Masjid. Aq Masjid was governed by a beg subject to Tashkent *ḥākim*, not by *qushbegi* which was one of the highest military ranks in the khanate. Also see Maksheev's correction in Kuropatkin's *Kashgariia*, pp. 183–84.

25. "Badaulet," pp. 95–96; TH/Jarring, 66v; TA/Pantusov, pp. 131–32; FO 65/902, "Eastern Turkistan, 1874," p. 2; a memoir by a certain Mullā Mīrzā which was translated by M. F. Gavrilov, "Stranichka iz istorii Iakub-beka Badauleta—pravitelia Kashgarii," in *V. V. Bartol'du. Turkestanskie druz'ia ucheniki i pochitateli* (Tashkent: Tipo-lit. No.2 Kazgiza, 1927), p. 126.

26. Maksheev's accounts quoted in *Kashgaria*, p. 183.

27. This was witnessed by a Russian merchant, S. Ia. Kliucharev, who stayed at that time in Tashkent. See Appendix in Vel'iaminov-Zernov's "Istoricheskiia izvestiia o Kokanskom khanstve ot Mukhammeda-Ali do Khudaiar-Khana," *Trudy Vostochnogo otdeleniia Russkogo Arkhelogogicheskogo Obshchestva*, no. 2 (1856): 363–64.

28. See *Report of a Mission to Yarkund*, p. 98; H. Rawlinson, *England and Rus-*

sia in the East (London: J. Murray, 1875), p. 166; Boulger, *The Life of Yakoob Beg*, pp. 79–81; Schuyler, *Turkistan*, vol. 1, p. 64. All these sources repeat the same mistake. A. N. Kuropatkin who had argued the same story rectified the mistake by inserting Maksheev's report (cf. *Kashgaria*, p. 161, note 1). For a more detailed description about the fall of Aq Masjid, see A. I. Maksheev, *Istoricheskii obzor Turkestana i nastupatel'nago dvizheniia v nego Russkikh* (St. Petersburg, 1890), pp. 179 ff.

29. Nalivkin, *Kratkaia istoriia*, pp. 169–71; Vel'iaminov-Zernov, "Istoricheskiia izvestiia," pp. 347–52.

30. On this title, also called *bahādurbashi* in the khanate, see A. L. Troitskaia, "'Zopovedniki'—kurūk Kokandskogo Khana Khudaiara," *Sbornik Gosudarstvennoi Publichnoi Biblioteki imeni M. E. Saltykova-Shchedrina* 3 (Leningrad, 1955), p. 138, note 3.

31. Mīrzā Aḥmad ("Badaulet," p. 96) clearly writes that Nār Muḥammad was killed six months after he had been taken to Khoqand. *Report of a Mission to Yarkund* makes a strange mistake on page 197 by writing that 'Ālim Quli killed "Suliman Khoja" and made Nār Muḥammad, "the brother-in-law of Yákúb Beg," Tashkent governor. But the original text of *Tavārīkh-i shahrukhiyya* (22r–23r) reads that 'Ālim Quli killed Shādmān Khwāja Qushbegi, Tashkent governor, and made Nār Muḥammad Parvānachi who was his own father-in-law (*pidār-i 'arūs-i khūd*) a new governor. Note that *Report of a Mission to Yarkund* has a correct translation on page 99.

32. Nalivkin, *Kratkaia istoriia*, p. 173.

33. *Report of a Mission to Yarkund*, pp. 98, 195.

34. "Badaulet," p. 96.

35. *Tavārīkh-i shahrukhiyya*, 13r–15r.

36. Nalivkin also writes this in his *Kratkaia istoriia*, p. 194.

37. *Tavārīkh-i shahrukhiyya*, 15r–22r.

38. On this rebellion see Nalivkin, *Kratkaia istoriia*, pp. 185–86.

39. "Badaulet," p. 97.

40. Isiev follows the statements in *Report of a Mission to Yarkund* and "Badaulet." See his *Uigurskoe gosudarstvo*, pp. 53–54, note 6.

41. TH/Jarring, 67r–68r; TH/Enver, pp. 328–31; TA/Pantusov, pp. 133–35.

42. Kuropatkin, *Kashgaria*, pp. 182–87.

43. Boulger, *The Life of Yakoob Beg*, p. 86.

44. *Kashgaria*, p. 162.

45. Valikhanov, *Sobranie sochinenii*, vol. 3, pp. 142–47; cf. English translation by John and Robert Michell, *The Russians in Central Asia* (London: E. Stanford, 1865), pp. 202–12.

46. "Badaulet," p. 98.

47. *Xinjiang jianshi*, vol. 2, p. 133, quotes this from the biography of Yūnus Jān, Yarkand governor, entitled *History of Ferghana and Kashghar*, written by 'Muhanmode Zhairifu.'

48. *Report of a Mission to Yarkund*, p. 198.

49. Bellew states that the number of people who left Tashkent was only 66 (*Kashmir and Kashghar*, p. 323; 68 in *Report of a Mission to Yarkund*, p. 204), and

according to an Ottoman source it was about. 40–50 (Mehmet Ātif, *Kāşgar tārīhī*, pp. 344–345).

50. Shaw, *Visits to High Tartary*, p. 48.

51. Shaw, *Visits to High Tartary*, pp. 48–49.

52. *Tavārīkh-i shahrukhiyya*, 26r–27r. Ṭālib Akhūnd (Prov. 115, 11v) exaggerates the numbers of Ṣiddīq's army (30,000) and of Ya'qūb Beg's (40,000). *Tavārīkh-i shahrukhiyya* (27r) has a more reasonable number for Ṣiddīq's army (3,000). TA/Pantusov (p. 138) writes that Ṣiddīq went to Farrash, his original base, and gathered 6,000–7,000 Qirghizs. Both shrines were located by the Qizil river which flows between the two parts of Kashghar. See *Report of a Mission to Yarkund*, p. 39.

53. *Tavārīkh-i shahrukhiyya*, 27r–28v.

54. He received this title from 'Ālim Quli. The holder of this title in Bukhara supervised the *vaqf* economy. See A. A. Semenov, "Bukharskii traktat o chinakh i zvaniiakh i ob obiazannostiakh nositelei ikh v srednevekovoi Bukhare," *Sovetskoe vostokovedenie*, no. 5 (1948): 141.

55. This is not Ya'qūb Beg's brother-in-law who was executed but 'Ālim Quli's father-in-law, former Tashkent governor.

56. *Tārīkh-i ṣigharī*, 28v–29r and 31r. Sayrāmī writes (TA/Pantusov, p. 170; TH/Enver, pp. 381–82) that the embassy to Khudāyār sent by Ḥabīb Allāh was headed by his son 'Abd al-Raḥmān and the return embassy was headed by Mīr Baba Dādkhwāh (in TH, Nār Muḥammad Parvānachi) and Mīrzā Baba Beg Ḥiṣṣārī with 250 cavalry, and that when they reached Yarkand they encountered Ya'qūb Beg who was fighting with Hām al-Dīn Khwāja. And he continues that Ya'qūb Beg, after holding most of the Khoqandian soldiers, sent 'Abd al-Raḥmān to Khotan. Considering that 'Ālim Quli died on May 21, 1865 (Maksheev, *Istoricheskii obzor*, p. 231), the Khotan party must have reached Khoqand while he was alive. It is unthinkable that they had an audience with Khudāyār who was in Bukhara at that time. And his claim that the Khotanese embassy was headed by 'Abd al-Raḥmān is also misleading. I am more inclined to believe the accounts of *Tārīkh-i ṣigharī* whose author escorted the return embassy to Yarkand. On the title of *parvānachi* and *hudāīchi* in the Khoqand khanate, see A. L. Troitskaia, *Katalog arkhiva Kokandskikh khanov* (Moscow: Izd-vo 'Nauka,' Glav. red. vostochnoi lit-ry, 1968), pp. 557, 569.

57. Sayrāmī mentions a secret communication between Niyāz Beg of Yarkand and Ya'qūb Beg. See TH/Jarring, 69r; TH/Enver, pp. 386–87; TA/Pantusov, pp. 138–39.

58. *Tārīkh-i ṣigharī*, 29r–30v.

59. *Visits to High Tartary*, p. 53. Also see TH/Jarring, 41v; TH/Enver, pp. 215–16; TA/Pantusov, p. 66.

60. *Kanding Xinjiangji*, q. 1, 5r. The author of *Tārīkh-i ṣigharī*, 'Abd Allāh, apparently gives a wrong date for the fall of Yangihissar as "a Wednesday of the month of 'Āshūr in the year of ox" (32r), which corresponds, according to the Ferghana system of the twelve animal cycle as 'Abd Allāh uses, to May 27–June 25 of 1865. Because 'Ālim Quli died on May 21, this is contradictory to his later remarks that Mīr Baba whom Ya'qūb Beg sent to Khoqand after the fall of Yangihissar met 'Ālim Quli.

61. On his origin there is a difference of opinion. 'Abd Allāh regards him as a Yangihissari (*Tārīkh-i ṣigharī*, 32v) while Sayrāmī includes his name in the list of the people who joined Ya'qūb Beg in Osh (TH/Jarring, 68v; TH/Enver, p. 334; TA/Pantusov, p. 137).

62. TH/Jarring, 69v; TH/Enver, p. 339; TA/Pantusov, p. 140; *Tārīkh-i ṣigharī*, 32v. The number nine had a symbolic meaning to the Central Asian Turks. Schuyler notes (*Turkistan*, vol. 1, p. 143) that "The wedding presents are usually given by nines, which is looked upon as a sacred number, nine times nine being usually the largest number that is given. The number nine is used with regard to other presents, as those given to guests or in exchange of hospitality." Cf. Kuropatkin, *Kashgaria*, p. 42. The Mongols also had a similar custom, as being testified by the term *yisun chaghan-u alban* (the tribute of the nine whites), which comprised eight white horses and one white camel. Cf. Bawden, *The Modern History of Mongolia*, p. 59.

63. *Tārīkh-i ṣigharī*, 28v–33v. Kuropatkin, however, reports (*Kashgaria*, p. 165) that Mīr Baba did not see 'Ālim Quli.

64. *Tārīkh-i ṣigharī*, 38r–40v and Ṭālib Akhūnd (Prov. 115), 13v–17v. The accounts of *Tārīkh-i ṣigharī* is taken here, even though there is a significant disagreement between these two sources. Ṭālib Akhūnd says that the terms of the conciliation were to raise Kichik Khān Tura to *pādishāh* and to make Ṣiddīq *lashkarbashi*. The two armies, he continues, then marched against Kashghar led by Ya'qūb Beg, Ṣiddīq Beg, 'Abd Allāh, Ghāzī Beg and 'Azīz Beg, who were opposed by an army sent by Buzurg and commanded by Muqarrab Shāh, Ghaffār Beg and Gänjä Beg. Buzurg's army is said to have lost the battle and Buzurg himself to have lost the rulership. It is interesting that Ṭālib Akhūnd claims the early clash between Ya'qūb Beg and Buzurg, and its relation with the later opposition of Muqarrab Shāh. Sayrāmī notes that Muqarrab Shāh Beg, Ghāzī Pānṣad, 'Azīz Jilād and Mullā Ibrāhīm tried to persuade Buzurg to get rid of Ya'qūb Beg (TH/Jarring, 70r; TH/Enver, p. 341; TA/Pantusov, pp. 141–42). We cannot say what exactly happened. The signs of the antagonism between Ya'qūb Beg and Buzurg may have appeared from this early period.

65. Muqarrab Shāh was from a place Mughal Tarim in the vicinity of Khan Ariq. Ṭālib Akhūnd gives a detailed description of this incident (Prov. 115, 20v–30r).

66. TH/Jarring, 43v; TH/Enver, p. 223; TA/Pantusov, p. 71. This number may be a considerably inflated one. *Tārīkh-i ṣigharī* (42r) estimates the number to have been about 40,000, and Ṭālib Akhūnd (Prov. 115, 32v–33r) 50,000.

67. *Tārīkh-i ṣigharī*, 42v; TH/Jarring, 70r; TH/Enver, p. 342; TA/Pantusov, p. 142. Ṭālib Akhūnd extremely exaggerates the numbers (total 30,000 in Prov. 115, 33v–34r).

68. See *Tārīkh-i ṣigharī*, 31v–32r and 42r.

69. TH/Jarring, 44r; TH/Enver, p. 226; TA/Pantusov, p. 73.

70. For detailed accounts of the battle, see TH/Jarring, 43v–44v; TH/Enver, pp. 224–28; TA/Pantusov, pp. 69–75; *Tārīkh-i ṣigharī*, 41v–44r; *Report of a Mission to Yarkund*, pp. 208–209; Ṭālib Akhūnd (Prov. 115), 32r–38v. Kuropatkin mistakes this battle as having taken place before the capture of Yangihissar (*Kashgharia*, p. 164), and the same mistake appears in Isiev's *Uigurskoe gosudarstvo*, pp. 20–21. Also consult Tikhonov's "Vosstanie 1864 g.," pp. 168–69, which is largely based on Sayrāmī's work.

71. TH/Jarring, 44r; TH/Enver, p. 227; TA/Pantusov, p. 74.

72. Ibid.

73. Sayrāmī states in his *Tārīkh-i ḥamīdī* that Jamāl al-Dīn's army left Yarkand on the second of Jumāda II, 1282 (October 23, 1865) and the battle took place on the 22nd day of the same month (November 12) (see, TH/Jarring, 43v, 70v; TH/ Enver, pp. 224, 344; TA/Pantusov, p. 144). In TH/Enver (p. 344) the departure of the Kuchean khwājas from Yarkand is dated on the third of Jumāda I, 1283 (Sept. 13, 1866), which is apparently wrong. We know from Chinese sources that after the battle of Khan Ariq Ya'qūb Beg took Kashghar's Manchu fort on September 1, therefore, the date of the battle should be before that, and thus we cannot accept Sayrāmī's claim that it happened in November. We should also note that Mīr Baba Hudāīchī (whom Ya'qūb Beg had dispatched to Khoqand) returned after 'Ālim Quli had died on May 21 and that his return was just after Ya'qūb Beg's arrival at Kashghar from Khan Ariq (*Tārīkh-i ṣigharī*, 44r).

74. TH/Jarring, 44v; TH/Enver, pp. 228–29; TA/Pantusov, p. 75.

75. *Tārīkh-i ṣigharī*, 44v.

76. TH/Jarring, 71v; TH/Enver, p. 348; TA/Pantusov, p. 147.

77. *Tārīkh-i ṣighārī*, 45r; Kuropatkin, *Kashgaria*, p. 167. On the date of the occupation, see *Kanding Xinjiangji*, q. 1, 6r;

78. *Tārīkh-i ṣigharī*, 47v; TA/Pantusov, p. 145.

79. For a fuller list of names see *Tārīkh-i ṣigharī*, 46r–46v; TH/Jarring, 71r; TA/Pantusov, p. 145.

80. See Aḥmad Quli Andijānī, *Janāb-i Badaulatni ḥikāyatlari* (Houghton Library, Harvard University: uncatalogued), 5v. This was a common phrase used for proclamation of a new ruler to the people in the streets. Cf. *Tadhkira-i 'azīzān* (Bodleian: d. 20), 87v and 88v ("*dūr dūr-i Islām dūr dūr-i Ḥaḍrāt-i Khwāja-i Jahān*").

81. *Janāb-i Badaulatni ḥikāyatlari*, 11r. Sayrāmī writes that Buzurg left the country 60 days after the end of the season of Capricorn, that is, between February and March (TA/Pantusov, pp. 147–48). 'Abd Allāh gives the date of Buzurg's departure as the end of Ramaḍān, 1281 (probably a mistake of 1282), that is, February of 1865 (1866). Shaw's assertion that Buzurg left in 1868 (*Visits to High Tartary*, p. 55) is probably wrong. For more detailed accounts of the struggle between Ya'qūb Beg and Buzurg, see *Tārīkh-i ṣigharī*, 48v–56r; *Report of a Mission to Yarkund*, pp. 210–13; TH/Jarring, 71v–72r; TH/Enver, pp. 348–51; TA/Pantusov, pp. 147–49; Ṭālib Akhūnd (Prov. 115), 46r–55r; Kāmil Khān Īshān, "Risale-i-Iakubi; Vospominaniia o Iakub-beke Kashgarskom Kamil'-Khana-Ishana," *Istorik-Marksist*, no. 3 (1940): 131.

82. The second of Barat, 1282/ Dec. 21, 1865 in TH/Jarring (60r) and TH/Enver (p. 299). The date in TA/Pantusov (p. 116) is wrong.

83. TH/Jarring 73r; TH/Enver, pp. 354–55 (the second of Rabī' I, 1283/July 15, 1865).

84. According to *Tārīkh-i ṣigharī* (58r), Ya'qūb Beg entrusted the city to Mīr Baba. Muḥammad Yūnus Jān Shaghawul wrote a history of Ferghana and Kashghar, *Ḥadīqat al-ḥaqā'iq* (Garden of Truths), or *Ḥadā'iq al-anvār* (Gardens of Lights). Two defective manuscripts exist in Russia. See C. A. Storey, *Persidskaia literatura; Bibliograficheskii obzor*, trans. by Iu. E. Bregel' (Moscow: 'Nauka,' 1972), vol. 2, p. 1196.

85. TH/Jarring, 74r; TH/Enver, p. 359 (25th day of Rabīʻ II, 1283/Sep. 6, 1866). Cf. TA/Pantusov, p. 155.

86. W. H. Johnson, "Report on His Journey to Ilchi, the Capital of Khotan, in Chinese Tartary," *Journal of the Royal Geographical Society*, no. 37 (1867): 9.

87. TH/Jarring , 73r; TH/Enver, p. 362; TA/Pantusov, p. 157.

88. According to Sayrāmī, Niʻmat Allāh, but in *Tārīkh-i ṣigharī* Ibrāhīm ṣudūr.

89. TH/Jarring, 81r; TH/Enver, p. 392; TA/Pantusov, p. 177.

90. According to Sayrāmī (TH/Enver, p. 373), on his seal was inscribed the phrase of "The Beloved of Allāh to whom the intercession is directed" (*Huwa al-Ḥabīb Allāh dhī turjāʻ shifāʻathu*).

91. *Tadhkira-i Ḥājjī Pādishāh* (24r–28r) does not mention Ḥabīb Allāh's visit to Zava. According to it, he and his son, Maʻṣūm Khān, were arrested in Khotan and taken to Yarkand where they were killed later. TA/Pantusov (p. 163) and *Sharqī Turkistān Tārīkhī* by Mehmet Emin Bughra (p. 386) write that 40,000 people were killed, but this may be an exaggerated number.

92. TH/Jarring, 76v; TH/Enver, p. 371; TA/Pantusov, pp. 162–63.

93. TA/Pantusov, p. 166; *Tadhkira-i Ḥājjī Pādishāh*, 24r. As I pointed out, *Tārīkh-i ṣigharī* usually gives dates one year earlier and the capture of Khotan is not an exception: Ramaḍān, 1282/January–February, 1866 (60r). It should be Ramaḍān, 1283. Cf. Hamada, "L'Histoire," pt. 3, p. 77. R. B. Shaw who usually gives wrong dates correctly writes that Khotan fell in January, 1867. See his *Visits to High Tartary*, p. 56. According to Sayrāmī, Yaʻqūb Beg returned to Kashghar on Shawwāl 18, 1283 (Feb. 23, 1867). Cf. TH/Jarring, 77v; TA/Pantusov, p. 166; Shawwāl 28 (March 5) in TH/Enver, p. 376.

94. The poem of Muḥammad Aʻlam in his *Tadhkira-i Ḥājjī Pādishāh* (48r–49v). Cf. *Mission scientifique*, vol. 3, 58 and Hamada, "L'Histoire," pt. 2, pp. 206–207.

95. Ḥabīb Allāh had three sons: ʻAbd al-Raḥmān, Ibrāhīm and Maʻṣūm. The first son was killed in the battle of Piyalma, and the other two were killed by Yaʻqūb Beg.

96. Like Khotan some other cities in Eastern Turkestan had epithets: Kashghar, the City of Nobles (*ʻAzīzān-i Kāshghar*); Aqsu, the City of Holy Warriors (*Ghāzīyān-i Aqsū*); Yarkand, the City of Elders (*Pīrān-i Yārkand*); Turfan, the City of Foreigners (*Gharībān-i Turfān*), and so on. See *Tārīkh-i jarīda-i jadīda* (India Office Library, Ms. Turki 2), 8r–8v; Katanov, "Volkskundliche Texte," pp. 1220–21.

97. TH/Jarring, 45v–46v; TH/Enver, pp. 234–39; TA/Pantusov, pp. 78–82. Mīrzā Jān came from Yarkand and was Īshān Mīr Ghiyāth al-Dīn's grandson (TA/Pantusov, p. 67).

98. Kubrawiyya started from Najm al-Dīn Kubra (d. 1221); Isḥāqiyya was the group following Khwāja Isḥāq (d. 1599); Ni'matiyya was stemmed from Ni'mat Allāh Walī (d. 1430) from Mahan; Rabūdiyya is believed to have originated from Rabīʻa (d. 801) who had lived in Basra; and Davāniyya came from Davānī (d. 1502) of Iran. On a brief explanation on these sects, see TH/Enver, pp. 743–44.

99. Many of the inhabitants in Ush Turfan were called by this name because they were immigrants from other cities of Eastern Turkestan, especially (Kuhna) Turfan, which caused the change of name of the city from Ush to Ush Turfan. They were moved here after the suppression of the Ush Turfan rebellion and the following massacre. On this appellation, see TH/Jarring, 39v–40r; TH/Enver, p. 207; TA/Pantusov, pp. 60–61.

100. TH/Jarring, 47r–47v; TH/Enver, pp. 240–46; TA/Pantusov, pp. 82–86.

101. TH/Jarring, 61v–62v; TH/Enver, pp. 305–10; TA/Pantusov, pp. 120–23.

102. TH/Jarring, 62v; TH/Enver, p. 310; TA/Pantusov, p. 123.

103. TH/Jarring, 62v–63r; TH/Enver, pp. 310–11; TA/Pantusov, pp. 123–24.

104. TH/Jarring, 80v–81r; TH/Enver, pp. 390–92; TA/Pantusov, pp. 175–76. On Jamāl al-Dīn's execution, see TH/Jarring, 65v, 82r; TH/Enver, pp. 322–23, 392.

105. On the conquest of Kucha, also cf. TH/Jarring, 80r–83r; TH/Enver, pp. 388–99; TA/Pantusov, pp. 174–82.

106. TH/Jarring, 65v–66r; TH/Enver, pp. 315–25; TA/Pantusov, pp. 127–31. Muḥammad Khwāja Ḥaḍrat was a famous religious man in Ya'qūb Beg's time (see TH/Jarring, 113v).

107. TH/Jarring, 82v; TA/Pantusov, pp. 128–30 and 178–80; *Tārīkh-i ṣigharī*, 61v–65r.

108. TH/Jarring, 65v–66r; TH/Enver, pp. 323–25.

109. *Pinghuizhi*, q. 7, 4r. On Ma Duosan (or, Ma Wenyi), see Ma Xiaoshi, *Xibei huizu geming jianshi*, pp. 47–52. On Ma Yanlong and Ma Si (or, Ma Chungliang, Ma Wenlu) see *Pinghuizhi*, q. 3, 1r and 19r–19v. There are several studies on Ma Hualong and his Jahriyya branch. See, for example, Mian Weilin's *Ningxia Yisilan jiaopai gaiyao* (Yinchuan: Ningxia Renmin Chubanshe, 1981), pp. 58–100.

110. This is not to be confused with the one in the Gansu-Qinghai border. It is located around Manas and Urumchi in Zungharia. See *Pinghuizhi*, q. 7, 5v.

111. *Kanding Xinjiangji*, q. 1, 13r. According to TH/Jarring (90r), almost 10,000 families of Han Chinese had fled to Nanshan mountain escaping Isḥāq's attack and most of them came under the command of Xu Xuegong.

112. TH/Jarring, 42r–42v, 85r–85v; TH/Enver, pp. 218, 406–409; TA/Pantusov, pp. 67–68, 188–89.

113. Sayrāmī suggests (TH/Jarring, 86v; TH/Enver, p. 432; TA/Pantusov, p. 193; TA/Pelliot, 126v) that this happened in the spring of 1870, or the season of *thawr* (between April 22–May 21 of 1870). *Kanding Xinjiangji* (q. 1, 13r) writes that a large number of Tungans attacked Qitai in March 1870, and that in April they invaded the territory of the "Andijanis" up to the border of the fort at Yar and were defeated by Ya'qūb Beg. In spite of the fact that these two sources indicate the date of the border incident taking place in April–May, we cannot accept this date because there is a piece of evidence that Ya'qūb Beg undoubtedly left Kashghar on March 11 for the counterattack. The date of March 11 is found in Ya'qūb Beg's letter addressed to the viceroy of British India, dated Rajab, 1258 A.H. Though Ya'qūb Beg writes in one place Dhū al-Ḥijja 8, 1287 (Enclosure 10), in all circumstances Dhū al-Ḥijja 8, 1286/March 11, 1870 is correct as it appears in Enclosure 11. See FO 65/874, Enclosures 10 and 11.

114. TH/Jarring, 86v–90v; TH/Enver, pp. 431–49; TA/Pantusov, pp. 193–204; *Kāşgar tārīhī*, pp. 373–75. Sayrāmī writes that Ya'qūb Beg dispatched his army to Urumchi on Rajab 4, 1287/September 30, 1870, after he had taken Turfan. This is contradictory to his remarks that the Tungans had attacked Kurla in the season of *thawr* and that the siege of Tufan by Ya'qūb Beg's army lasted nine months. Here the date of the fall of Turfan was taken from *Kanding Xinjiangji*, q. 1, 13v. Schuyler (*Turkistan*, vol. 2, p. 319) regards the fall of Turfan as July of 1870. At the same

time, there is a discrepancy in TA, TH and *Kanding Xinjiangji* on the question of who the Tungan commander in Turfan was. Sayrāmī writes that it was Sō Yanshay (Suo Huanzhang) while in the latter (q. 1, 13r–13v) is found Ma Zhong. Another source (see Stratanovich, "K voprosu," p. 63) confirms Sayrāmī's opinion. *Xinjiang jianshi* (vol. 2, p. 140) writes that the fall of Turfan was on the 9th day of the 10th month (November 11) and the Tungan leaders were Ma Zhong and Ma Rende, but it does not clarify the source.

115. However, according to *Kanding Xinjiangji* (q. 2, 13v), Ya'qūb Beg made Ma Zhong *ḥākim* and let him administer the city.

116. The name of this place derived from the Roman emperor Decius (r. 249–251) who was related with the legend of the "Seven Sleepers of Ephesus" (*Aṣḥāb al-Kahf* in Islamic literature). This legend was also quite popular in Eastern Turkestan, and it is reported that there was a cave of the Seven Sleepers at a place called Tuyuq near Daqiyanus. See Qurbān 'Alī's *Tārīkh-i jarīda-i jadīda* (India Office Library: Ms. Turki 2), 17rff; A. v. Le Coq, *Volkskundliches aus Ost-Turkistan* (Berlin: D. Reimer, 1916), p. 3. Also cf. printed edition of Qurbān 'Alī's work, *Kitāb-i jarīda-i jadīda* (Kazan, 1884), pp. 18ff. On the legend of the Aṣḥāb al-Kahf see a long treatise in TH/Enver, pp. 661ff; R. Paret, "Ashāb al-Kahf" in *Encyclopaedia of Islam* (the second edition, vol. 1, fasc. 11, 1958).

117. Sources disagree about who was made the leader of the Urumchi Tungans: Ma Zhong in *Kanding Xinjiangji* (q. 1, 13v); Dāūd Khalīfa in Ṭālib Akhūnd (Prov. 116, 28v–30v); Sō Dālūyā in TH (Jarring, 91v; Enver, p. 454); and in Stratanovich ("K voprosu," p. 63).

118. According to Sayrāmī, Xu Xuegong's brother's name is Māshūye (TH/Jarring, 90v; TH/Enver, p. 448; TA/Pelliot, p. 133r). However, *Kangding Xinjiangji* (q. 1, 14r) writes his name as Xu Xuedi, which is probably correct.

119. Qarā Mōdūn in TH/Jarring (92r) and TA/Pantusov (p. 207), but Qara Murun in TH/Enver (p. 456) which is incorrect. On the map of Aurel Stein (Serial no. 23) in his *Innermost Asia* (Oxford: Clarendon Press, 1928) we can find Qara Mudu.

120. This date is confirmed by Ya'qūb Beg's letter found in FO 65/874, Enclosures 10 and 11.

121. TH/Jarring, 92r–92v; TH/Enver, p. 460; TA/Pantusov, p. 211; Stratanovich, "K voprosu," p. 63. However, *Kanding Xinjiangji* (q. 1, 13v) writes that it was Ma Zhong who was killed and that the incident happened in the 4th month of 1871.

122. TH/Jarring, 93r; TH/Enver, p. 461; TA/Pantusov, pp. 212, 216. But according to *Xinjiang jianshi* (vol. 2, p. 176), it was Ma Rende, the son of Ma Zhong.

123. TH/Jarring, 93v; TH/Enver, pp. 462–63; TA/Pantusov, p. 213. According to *Kanding Xinjiangji* (q. 1, 14r), Ya'qūb Beg's army took Urumchi and expelled Dāūd Khalīfa in the 10th month of 1871 (Nov. 13–Dec. 11), and in the first month (Feb. 9–March 8) of the next year Xu Xuegong began to attack the city. This record agrees with Sayrāmī's statement.

124. Cf. Stratanovich, "K voprosu," pp. 63–64. It was during this time that the Russian merchant I. Somov visited Manas (January–May 1872) with a huge caravan. He left us a vivid description of the situation in Manas on the eve of its con-

quest by Beg Quli. A Chinese source also mentions Somov's caravan (*Pinghuizhi*, q. 7, 5v–6r).

125. TH/Jarring, 93v–94r; TH/Enver, pp. 466–68; TA/Pantusov, pp. 213–14. *Kanding Xinjiangji* (q. 1, 14r) wrongly states that Paxia (i.e., *pādishāh*, that is, Ya'qūb Beg) led the second expeditionary army for himself. *Xinjiang jianshi* (vol. 2, pp. 177–78) seems to repeat this mistake.

126. *Kanding Xinjiangji*, q. 1, 14r–14v; TH/Jarring, 94r–94v; TH/Enver, pp. 467–68; TA/Pantusov, p. 214.

127. Sayrāmī writes that the Tungan leader called Lawrīnjā (i.e., Dāūd) in Manas killed himself when the city fell to Beg Quli (TA/Pantusov, p. 215). *Pinghuizhi* (q. 7, 5r–5v) erroneously reports that both Dāūd and Ma Guan died during the first Urumchi expedition led by Ya'qūb Beg himself in 1870–71.

128. TH/Jarring, 96v; TH/Enver, p. 477; TA/Pantusov, p. 220.

CHAPTER 4

1. TH/Jarring, 103r; TH/Enver, 516; TA/Pantusov, p. 240.
2. TH/Jarring, 100v; TH/Enver, pp. 496–97.
3. R. B. Shaw, "A Grammar of the Language of Eastern Turkestan," *Royal Asiatic Society of Bengal*, no. 3 (1877): 322–23, 349.
4. TH/Jarring, 100v; TH/Enver, p. 497.
5. "Kāşgar iqlīmin hākim-i sāhib al-i'tibār Ya'qūb Hān." See Nāme-i Hümāyūn, no. 13 (cf. *Kāşgar tārīhī*, pp. 388–89).
6. "Kāşgar amīrī şahāmetlū Ya'qūb Hān." See Yıldız tasnif, 33–11279–73–91.
7. FO 65/879, Enclosures no. 3 and no. 4.
8. See Appendix A.
9. On the assumption of *amīr* title, see Bellew's *Kashmir and Kashghar*, p. 304; T. E. Gordon, *The Roof of the World* (Edinburgh: Edmonston and Douglas, 1876), p. 87.
10. *Kashmir and Kashghar*, pp. 299–300.
11. *Report of a Mission to Yarkund*, p. 40.
12. *Report of a Mission to Yarkund*, p. 99.
13. For example, see *Report of a Mission to Yarkund*, p. 99; *Kashgaria*, pp. 47–48. Boulger did not even mention this post. Tikhonov's "Nekotorye voprosy" is the same case.
14. A. Kuhn puts it as the twelfth rank in the military hierarchy, and the ninth in the court. See his *The Province of Ferghana, formerly Khanate of Kokand*, tr. from German by F. Henvey (Simla, 1876), pp. 27–28. Also see Troitskaia, *Katalog*, p. 554.
15. Like *mīrzā*, this was the official who conducted scribal works.
16. TH/Jarring (115v) has a long lacuna from this point. However, it is found in TH/Enver, pp. 576ff; TA/Pantusov, pp. 277ff.
17. TH/Enver, pp. 575–76; TA/Pantusov, p. 277.
18. *Kashgaria*, p. 47; *Report of a Mission to Yarkund*, p. 99.
19. It was also called *tash* or *sang*, both meaning "stone." There is no doubt that these terms were originated from the custom of putting stones to indicate the distance. It is interesting to note that another term, *yighachi* (wood), was used for the

same purpose. One *tash* theoretically corresponds to 12,000 camel paces, but in Kashgharia it was approximately 4.5 miles. Also cf. Grenard, "Spécimens de la littérature moderne du Turkestan chinois," *Journal asiatique*, 9e sér., tom. 13 (1899), 339–44; *Report of a Mission to Yarkund*, pp. 241, 436.

20. Sayrāmī lists the names of seven *mīrzās*, which contradicts Kuropatkin's assertion that Ya'qūb Beg's chancellery consisted of four *mīrzās*.

21. TH/Jarring, 88v; TH/Enver, pp. 440, 576; TA/Pantusov, pp. 277–78.

22. TH/Jarring, 88v; TH/Enver, p. 440.

23. *Visits to High Tartary*, p. 247.

24. *Kashgaria*, p. 47.

25. TH/Enver, p. 577; TA/Pantusov, p. 278. Zūngtūng Dārīn seems to be a transcription of "zhongtang daren," a respected appellation for commander-in-chief. This does not necessarily mean that he met with Zuo Zongtang who did not set foot in Xinjiang at that time.

26. *Report of a Mission to Yarkund*, pp. 226–32, 422–33.

27. Op. cit., pp. 214–15, 251, 431.

28. Op. cit., pp. 453–54.

29. Its literal meaning is "Seven Cities," but it was used almost synonymously with Altishahr (Six Cities), that is, Kashgharia.

30. TH/Jarring, 100v; TH/Enver, p. 496.

31. TH/Jarring, 80v; TH/Enver, p. 388; TA/Pantusov, p. 174.

32. TH/Jarring, 81v; TH/Enver, p. 393; TA/Pantusov, 177–78.

33. *Visits to High Tartary*, p. 245, 378.

34. On the number of *ḥākim beg*, see Saguchi's *Shakaishi kenkyū*, pp. 126–27.

35. TH/Enver, pp. 435, 467, 540; *Report of a Mission to Yarkund*, pp. 219, 224, 254; Shaw, *Visits to High Tartary*, p. 246.

36. Saguchi's *Sinkyō minzokushi kenkyū*, pp. 293–300.

37. TH/Enver, p. 414.

38. *Report of a Mission to Yarkund* (p. 55) writes that up to Sariqol was Ya'qūb Beg's territory and, beyond that, the Wakhan valley belonged to the Afghan territory.

39. TH/Jarring, 74r, 77r; TH/Enver, pp. 359, 374.

40. TH/Jarring, 72v; TH/Enver, p. 352; TA/Pantusov, p. 150.

41. TH/Jarring, 80v; TH/Enver, p. 388: TA/Pantusov, p. 174.

42. TH/Jarring, 77r; TH/Enver, p. 374; TA/Pantusov, p. 165.

43. V. Minorsky and I. P. Petrushevskii concur in these points. See *Tadhkirat al-Mulūk: A Manual of Ṣafavid Administration* (London: Printed for the Trustees of the "E. J. W. Gibb memorial," 1943; repr. in 1980), p. 27; "K istorii instituta soiurgala," *Sovetskoe vostokovedenie*, no. 6 (1949): 233–34, 245.

44. A detailed analysis of the *soyurghal* practice in Central Asia is found in Abduraimov's *Ocherki agrarnykh otnoshenii v Bukharskom khanstve v XVI–pervoi polovine XIX veka* (Tashkent: Izd-vo 'Fan' Uzbekskoi SSR, 1966–70), vol. 2, pp. 100–112. Also cf. his discussion of *tankhwāh* in the same book, pp. 112–24.

45. This opinion was first raised by D. Tikhonov (see "Nekotorye voprosy," p. 113) and later was accepted by some other scholars. See Isiev's *Uigurskoe gosudarstvo*, p. 27; *Xinjiang jianshi*, vol. 2, p. 170.

46. On the usage of *soyurghal* in Shāh Maḥmūd Churās, see *Khronika*, 52v, 53r, 55v, 56v, 61v, 64v, 69r, 70v, 71r, 75r, 77r, 79r, 79v, 80r, and 84v.

47. These data were drawn from various sources such as TH; TA; *Tadhkira-i Ḥājjī Pādishāh*; *Tārīkh-i ṣigharī*; Ṭālib Akhūnd's work; *Dāstān-i Muḥammad Ya'qūb Beg*; *Report of a Mission to Yarkund*; N. F. Petrovskii's "Kratkaia svedeniia o litsakh, imevshikh otnosheniia ko vremeni Kashgarskago vladetelia Bek-Kuli Beka" (Published by N. Ostroumov. *Protokoly zasedanii i soobshcheniia chlenov Turkestanskago kruzhka liubitelei arkheologi*, no. 21 [1917]: 89–101), and so on.

48. *Uigurskoe gosudarstvo*, p. 27. He does not provide any evidence, either.

49. "Yakūbu Begu seiken no seikaku ni kansuru ichi kōsatsu," *Shigaku Zasshi* 96, no. 4 (1987): 1–42.

50. For example, Sayrāmī shows a sample of a document in which Guma was called *vilāyat*. See TA/Pantusov, p. 247. Also cf. Shaw, *Visits to High Tartary*, p. 246; *Report of a Mission to Yarkund*, pp. 219, 440.

51. Kuropatkin, *Kashgaria*, pp. 41–42.

52. *Report of a Mission to Yarkund*, pp. 6, 104; Bellew, *Kashmir and Kashghar*, pp. 281–82.

53. Kuropatkin, *Kashgaria*, p. 46; TA/Pantusov, pp. 155, 166, 178.

54. TA/Pantusov, p. 150.

55. Op. cit., p. 175.

56. Op. cit., pp. 155, 166, 178, 181, 202, 217.

57. For example, see *Tadhkira-i Ḥājjī Pādishāh*, 34r (52,000); TA/Pantusov, p. 185 (more than 50,000); Gavrilov, "Stranichka," 131 (60,000); *Sharqī Turkistān Tārīkhī*, pp. 401–402 (80,000).

58. Gordon, *The Roof of the World*, p. 92.

59. *Dāstān-i Muḥammad Yā'qūb*, 1v–2r, 3r; *Report of a Mission to Yarkund*, pp. 13–14; Kuropatkin, *Kashgaria*, pp. 225–30.

60. "Report of the Mirza's Exploration," *Proceedings of the Royal Geographical Society* 15, no. 3 (1871): 194.

61. Ṭālib Akhūnd (Prov. 116), 9r.

62. *Kashgaria*, p. 200.

63. Their names are found in the list of *Tārīkh-i ṣigharī*, 46r. And for the background of Mīrzā Aḥmad, see his "Badaulet," pp. 90–94. On 'Umar Quli, see TA/Pantusov, pp. 145, 175, 282; Petrovskii, "Kratkiia svedeniia," p. 96. Jāmadār, or "Nubbi Buksh" in Gordon's *The Roof of the World* (pp. 90–92), was an Afghan, born in Punjab, and served for a long time in the Sikh army and, later, in the Khoqand army. See Kuropatin, *Kashgaria*, pp. 175, 221–22; TA/Pantusov, pp. 145, 147, 282; Petrovskii, "Kratkiia svedeniia," p. 92; Shaw, *Visits to High Tartary*, p. 347.

64. TH/Enver, 584–85; TA/Pantusov, pp. 282–84. Also see Shinmen's article, "Yakūbu Begu seiken no seikaku ni kansuru ichi kōsatsu."

65. Ivanov, *Ocherki po istorii Srednei Azii*, p. 190.

66. See Khanykov, *Opisanie Bukharskago khanstva* (St. Petersburg: 1843) pp. 53ff; S. S. Gubaeva, *Etnicheskii sostav naseleniia Fergany v kontse XIX-nachale XX v* (Tashkent: Izd-vo 'Fan' Uzbekskoi SSR, 1983).

67. Hartmann, "Ein Heiligenstaat," pp. 347–60.

68. TH/Jarring, 101r; TH/Enver, p. 499; TA/Pantusov, p. 233; Gordon, *The Roof of the World*, p. 76.

69. Kuropatkin, *Kashgaria*, p. 197.

70. Op. cit., p. 208.

71. *Visits to High Tartary*, p. 255.

72. Kuropatkin, *Kashgaria*, p. 208. According to Shaw (*Visits to High Tartary*, p. 228), in 1868–69 one gold *ṭillā* (Khoqand-made) was worth between 32–35 and a large silver *yambu* equal to 1,100 *tängäs*. If Kuropatkin is correct, one *yambu* had the value of the same 1,100 *tängäs* in 1876–77. However, there seems to have been a slight depreciation of silver value after the end of the Urumchi expeditions.

73. Kuropatkin, *Kashgaria*, p. 213.

74. Op. cit., p. 66.

75. Op. cit., pp. 208–209.

76. *Dāstān-i Muḥammad Yā'qūb*, 2v.

77. Kuropatkin, *Kashgaria*, pp. 209–10; *Dāstān-i Muḥammad Yā'qūb*, 2v.

78. We can cull many cases of mentioning these arms in Sayrāmī's work. If I just list the mention of cannons, see TH/Enver, pp. 185, 198, 203, 214, 236, 238, 256, 258, 261, 263, 265, 272, 281, 283, and so forth.

79. *Visits to High Tartary*, p. 267.

80. *Kashgaria*, p. 191.

81. FO 65/874, no. 50 (St. Petersburg, March 26, 1872; from Loftus to Granville).

82. See Kuropatkin, *Kashgaria*, pp. 191–94. Also cf. an account in the Russian newspaper *Golos*, June 9, 1874, which was translated and included in FO 65/902, from Loftus to the Earl of Derby. Sayrāmī also mentions a workshop (*ishkhāna*), but only rudimentary arms and cloths were made there (TH/Jarring, 83r; TH/Enver, p. 400; TA/Pantusov, p. 183).

83. Kuropatkin, *Kashgaria*, pp. 205–206.

84. Op. cit., p. 205.

85. Op. cit., p. 214

86. Bellew remarks that the uniform was made of a yellow leather coat and a conical leather cap attached with fur around it (*Kashmir and Kashghar*, p. 289). Kuropatkin who visited there a few yeas after Bellew mentions about the leather cap of the same shape and reddish *kaftan* (*Kashgaria*, p. 201).

87. Gordon, *The Roof of the World*, pp. 94–95.

88. Ibid.

89. Yıldız tasnif, no. 33–1481–73–91.

90. *Kāşgar tārīhī*, p. 390.

91. *Kāşgar tārīhī*, pp. 390–93.

92. Ibid.

93. Ibid.

94. *Kāşgar tārīhī*, p. 405.

95. *Kāşgar tārīhī*, p. 196.

96. TH/Jarring, 96r; TH/Enver, p. 473; TA/Pantusov, p. 218.

97. *Visits to High Tartary*, p. 272.

98. Kuropatkin, *Kashgaria*, p. 212.

99. *Turkistan*, vol. 2, p. 162.

100. Op. cit., p. 158.

101. Op. cit., p. 164.

102. Op. cit., p. 197.

103. Pantusov, *Svedenie o Kul'dzhinskom raione*, p. 9. According to the report of H. Landsdell who traveled the Ili region in 1882, the Tungan population in 1862 in this area was about 60,000, but after the Qing reconquest the number shrank to 3,000 (2,100 males and 900 females). See his *Russian Central Asia including Kuldja, Bokhara, Khiva and Merv*, vol. 1 (London: Searle and Livington, 1885), pp. 208–209.

104. *Xinjiang tuzhi*, q. 43.

105. TH/Jarring, 94v, 96r; TH/Enver, pp. 467–68, 474; TA/Pantusov, pp. 214, 215, 218. According to I. Somov, the residents in Manas were no more than 6,000, and the male population in Urumchi, Turfan, Sanju, Gumadi, and Qutupi was about 40,000 (the female population being much more than the male, at least two or three times). See Stratanovich, "K voprosu," p. 61.

106. Zeng Wenwu, *Zhongguo jingying Xiyu shi*, p. 353.

107. *Buried Treasures of Chinese Turkestan* (1928; Hong Kong, Oxford: Oxford University Press, 1985 repr.), p. 49.

108. *Report of a Mission to Yarkund*, p. 45.

109. *Xinjiang tuzhi*, q. 97, p. 26r.

110. *Report of a Mission to Yarkund*, p. 50.

111. For example, see *Report of a Mission to Yarkund*, p. 35.

112. *Visits to High Tartary*, p. 248.

113. *Report of a Mission to Yarkund*, p. 253.

114. Op. cit., pp. 254, 464.

115. See *Xinjiang tuzhi*, q. 97, 25v–26r.

116. Mehmet Emin Bughra (*Sharqī Turkistān Tārīkhī*, p. 386) states that forty thousand (probably an exaggerated figure) were killed in Khotan. *Tadhkira-i Ḥājjī Pādishāh* (27r) writes that three thousand died in Qaraqash alone.

117. See *Report of a Mission to Yarkund*, pp. 62–63; *Kashgaria*, pp. 34, 126.

118. Ṭālib Akhūnd (Prov. 117), 21v–23r; TH/Enver, p. 470; TA/Pantusov, pp. 215–16.

119. TH/Jarring, 101r; TH/Enver, p. 499; TA/Pantusov, p. 233.

120. This is what Sayyid Aḥrār, an envoy to British India in 1871–72, told British officials. See FO 65/874.

121. *Sobranie sochinenii*, vol. 3, pp. 161–162.

122. TH/Jarring, 84r; TH/Enver, pp. 400–401; TA/Pantusov, p. 183; TA/Jarring, p. 131v; TA/Pelliot, 121v–122r. Tikhonov mistranslates the text as "The infantry and the cavalry soldiers, more than fifty thousand, were obliged to work in workshops." See his "Nekotorye voprosy vnutrennei politiki Iakub-Beka," *Uchenye zapiski Instituta Vostokovedenie*, no. 14 (1958): 136. However, the text reads: "The number of the infantry and the cavalry soldiers exceeded fifty thousand. And [*sic*] artisans and craftsmen who were obliged to work in workshops were near to fifty thousand."

123. TH/Jarring, 84r; TH/Enver, pp. 400–401; TA/Pantusov, p. 183.

124. Ibid; *Report of a Mission to Yarkund* (p. 478) calls master *aqsaqal* and mentions the existence of some 200 recognized carpet-weaving masters in Khotan.

125. TH/Jarring, 84r; TH/Enver, pp. 400–401.

126. *Report of a Mission to Yarkund*, p. 478.

127. *Report of a Mission to Yarkund*, p. 476. Cf. the testimony of Vasilii Nikitin quoted in Tikhonov's "Nekotorye voprosy," pp. 133–34. Compare the practice during the Qing rule in Aḥmad Shāh Naqshbandī's "Narrative of the Travels of Khwajah Ahmud Shah Nukshbundee Syud," *Journal of the Asiatic Society of Great Britain and Ireland* 25, no. 4 (1856): 350.

128. Bellew, *Kashmir and Kashghar*, pp. 289–90.

129. On the characteristics of commercial transactions in Kashgharian markets, see Sanada Yasushi's "Oasisu bazaru no seidai kenkyū," *Chūō Daigaku Daigakuin kenkyū nenbō*, no. 6 (1977): 207–20.

130. *Report of a Mission to Yarkund*, p. 482.

131. One of the best studies on the financial, especially monetary, system in Xinjiang during the Qing period was done by Kuznetsov. See his *Ekonomicheskaia politika*, pp. 146–62; cf. Wang Zhaowu, "Jindai Xinjiang huobi shulue," *Minzu yanjiu*, 1992, no. 3.

132. Bykov, "Monety Rashaddina," pp. 288–96. Also see Du Jianyi and Gu Peiyu, *Xinjiang Hongqian daquan tushuo* (Peking: Zhonghua Shuju, 1996), pp. 400–407, where 28 *puls* were listed.

133. TH/Jarring, 79r; TH/Enver, p. 383; TA/Pantusov, pp. 170–71.

134. TH/Enver, p. 401. It is curious that TH/Jarring (83r) and TA/Pantusov (p. 183) writes as if Ya'qūb Beg minted copper coins in the name of Daoguang Emperor (r. 1821–50) of China ("*Khāqān-i Chīn Dawāng Khānning nāmidä mīth pūl qoydurdi*"). Cf. TA/Jarring, 130r; TA/Pelliot, 120v.

135. Gavrilov, "Stranichka," p. 132.

136. Istanbul Arkeologi Müzesi has at least three such coins, two *qizil ṭillā*s and one *aq tängä* (nos. 2064, 2065, and 2066) minted in 1290/1873–74 and 1291/1874–75, bearing "*Sulṭān 'Abdülazīz*" with the date on the obverse side, and "*ḍarb-i dār al-salṭānat-i Kāshghar*" (no. 2064), "*ḍarb-i maḥrūsa-i Kāshghar*" (no. 2065), or "*ḍarb-i laṭīf-i Kāshghar*" (no. 2066) on the reverse. Also see *Report of a Mission to Yarkund*, p. 494; cf. the photos of nos. 2065 and 2066 in A. R. Bekin's "Yakup Beg'in Doğu Türkistan'ı eğemenligi altına alması," in *Doğu Dilleri* 2, no. 1 (1971), p. 117.

137. *Report of a Mission to Yarkund*, p. 494.

138. FO 65/874, "Strictly confidential; Memorandum of an Interview with the Envoy of Yarkand," p. 4 (Dec. 25, 1871).

139. "Journey to Ilchi," p. 5 and the note in page 13. Also see *Journal de St. Peterburg*, March, 1872 (a copy included in FO 65/874, no. 50), and Kuropatkin's *Kashgaria*, p. 71.

140. Quoted from E. Schuyler, *Turkistan*, vol. 2, p. 318.

141. Schuyler, *Turkistan*, vol. 1, p. 217.

142. Kuropatkin, *Kashgaria*, p. 88.

143. Cf. *Kashgaria*, pp. 68–69, 76–77.

144. See G. J. Alder, *British India's Northern Frontier 1865–95: A Study in Imperial Policy* (London: Published for the Royal Commonwealth Society by Longmans, 1963), pp. 318–319 (all the numbers are reduced to half for the reason he explains).

145. Shaw, *Visits to High Tartary*, pp. 226, 312.

146. *Report of a Mission to Yarkund*, p. 269.
147. Bellew, *Kashmir and Kashghar*, p. 302.
148. Boulger, *The Life of Yakoob Beg*, p. 120.
149. Valikhanov, *Sobranie sochinenii*, vol. 3, p. 157.
150. TH/Enver, p. 516; TA/Pantusov, pp. 240–41.
151. TH/Jarring, 101v; TH/Enver, p. 502.
152. For example, see *Report of a Mission to Yarkund*, p. 17.
153. TH/Jarring, 101v; TH/Enver, pp. 502–503; TA/Pantusov, p. 235.
154. Bellew, *Kashmir and Kashghar*, pp. 308–309, 324, 344–45; Stein, *Ruins of Khotan*, p. 143.
155. This episode is recorded only in TA/Enver, pp. 409–412.
156. TH/Jarring, 100v; TH/Enver, p. 497; TA/Pantusov, p. 232.
157. TH/Jarring, 100v–101r; TH/Enver, pp. 497–99.
158. TA/Pantusov, p. 234.
159. *Report of a Mission to Yarkund*, p. 104.
160. Ibid. For a specimen of the passport, see Shaw, "A Grammar of the Language of Eastern Turkistan," *Royal Asiatic Society of Bengal*, no. 3 (1877): 322–23, 349.
161. TH/Jarring, 101r; TH/Enver, p. 499; TA/Pantusov, p. 233. However, according to Bellew's observation, there was a military band, and at some special occasions music was played within individuals' houses. See his *Kashmir and Kashghar*, p. 286.
162. *Kashgaria*, p. 39.
163. Kuropatkin (*Kashgaria*, p. 43) says *kharāj* while Sayrāmī (TA/Pantusov, p. 242) and the British embassy (*Report of a Mission to Yarkund*, p. 103) have *'ushr*. For the same confusion in Western Turkestan see Schuyler, *Turkistan*, vol. 1, pp. 298–99, 303. It seems that there was a tendency in Western Turkestan to use *'ushr* for the collection of one tenth from the land produce while *kharāj* for the collection of more than one tenth, such as one fifth or sometimes even higher. Cf. A. A. Semenov, "Ocherk pozemel'no-podatnogo i nologovogo ustroistva v Bukharskogo khanstva," *Trudy Sredne-Aziatskogo Gosudarstvennogo Universiteta* 2, no. 1 (1929): 22.
164. *Report of a Mission to Yarkund*, p. 103. This kind of exaction was not unique only to Kashgharia at that time, but had been a widespread practice for a long period of time in Western Turkestan too. For example, see Troitskaia (*Katalog*, p. 567) for the case in Khoqand during the reign of Khudāyār, and *Istoriia Uzbekskoi SSR* (Tashkent: Izd-vo AN Uzbekskoi SSR, 1956–57), vol. 1, pp. 355–56 for the case during the Timurids.
165. Right after the Qing conquest 1 *batman* was the same as 4 *shi* and 5 *dou*, but from 1761 it changed to 5 *shi* 3 *dou*. One *batman* equals in weight 640 *jin*, that is, 382.08kg. See Ji Dachun, "Weiwuerzu duliangheng jiuzhi kaosuo," pp. 60–61. For a survey on the units of measurement in Xinjiang, see Hori Sunao, "Jūhachi-nijū seiki Uiguru zoku no doryōkō ni tsuite," *Otemae Joshi Daigaku ronshū*, no. 12 (1978): 57–67.
166. Valikhanov, *Sobranie sochinenii*, vol. 3, p. 186.
167. Ibid.
168. *Report of a Mission to Yarkund*, p. 103.

169. "A Sketch of the Turki Language," p. 136. On the eve of the Russian conquest of Western Turkestan, one *ṭanāb* was about 2,700–2,800 m^2 in Samarqand and Tashkent while it was about 4,100 m^2 in Khiva. See Abduraimov, *Ocherki agrarnykh otnoshenii*, vol. 1, p. 215, note 94. Also cf. Budagov, *Sravnitel'nyi slavar,'* vol. 1, p. 741; Troitskaia, "Arkhiv Kokandskikh khanov XIX veka; Predvaritel'nyi obzor," *Trudy Gosudarstvennoi Publichnoi Biblioteki imeni M. E. Saltykova-Shchedrina*, no. 2 (5) (1957): 187.

170. *Report of a Mission to Yarkund*, p. 103.

171. Kuropatkin, *Kashgaria*, p. 43.

172. A Muslim source relates that the Zunghars levied "100,000 *tängä*s from 100,000 people in the cities of Moghulistan" as the annual *jizya*. See *Tadhkira-i 'azīzān* (Bodleian: d. 20), 37r–38v and 96v; Hartmann, "Ein Heiligenstaat," pp. 17, 32–33, 59. But according to a report of a Chinese general who conquered Kashgharia, from Kashghar alone the amount of 67,000 *tängä*s (in cash as well as in kind) were taken at the time of Galdan Tsering. See *Zhungaerh fanglue* (zhengpian), q. 75, pp. 30v–31r.

173. On this subject see Shimada's "Shindai kaikyō no jintozei," *Shigaku zasshi* 61, no. 11 (1952): 25–40; Haneda, *Chūō Ajiashi kenkyū*, pp. 117–21.

174. *Report of a Mission to Yarkund*, p. 103.

175. Ibid.

176. Schuyler, *Turkistan*, vol. 1, p. 304.

177. *Report of a Mission to Yarkund*, p. 77.

178. Troitskaia, *Katalog*, p. 553. Also cf. *Istoriia Uzbekskoi SSR*, vol. 1, p. 356.

179. *Kashgaria* (p. 43) has a wrong translation. See the Russian original (p. 33). The word *saman* means "straw." See Clauson, *An Etymological Dictionary*, p. 829.

180. *Report of a Mission to Yarkund*, pp. 504–505.

181. *Kashgaria*, p. 43. But his transcription, *tari-kara*, is wrong. Sayrāmī writes this as *tärkä* (TH/Jarring, 103v; TH/Enver, p. 520). As for the similar custom in Khoqand, see Troitskaia, *Katalog*, p. 564.

182. The text of TA/Pantusov (pp. 242–43) is misleading. See TH/Jarring, 103v–104r; TH/Enver, pp. 519–20; TA/Jarring, 164r; TA/Pelliot, 159r.

183. Sayrāmī and Ḥājjī Yūsuf have mentioned this. See Tikhonov, "Nekotorye voprosy," p. 130. Also see *Xinjiang jianshi*, vol. 2, p. 171. On the etymology and other examples of the same custom, see Radloff, *Versuch*, vol. 2, pp. 538–39; Bartol'd, "Otchet o kamandirovke v Turkestan," in *Sochinenie*, vol. 8, p. 203.

184. TH/Enver, p. 415.

185. Kuropatkin, *Kashgaria*, p. 42.

186. Shaw, *Visits to High Tartary*, pp. 307, 276, 320.

187. TH/Jarring, 103v; TH/Enver, p. 518; TA/Pantusov, p. 241.

188. "A Sketch of the Turki Language," p. 122.

189. *Visits to High Tartary*, p. 265.

190. He adds that "one *principal Sirkar* and several *Mirzas*" were attached to the governor. See *Kashgaria*, p. 44.

191. TH/Jarring, 82v; TH/Enver, p. 397; TA/Pantusov, p. 181.

192. *Report of a Mission to Yarkund*, pp. 504, 509.

193. A.A. Semenov, "Bukharskii traktat," p. 149, note 72; M.A. Abduraimov,

Ocherki agrarnykh otnoshenii, vol. 1 (Tashkent: Izd-vo 'Fan' Uzbekskoi SSR, 1966), p. 83.

194. Troitskaia, *Katalog*, p. 562.

195. TH/Enver, p. 579; TA/Pantusov, pp. 279–80, 194.

196. TH/Enver, pp. 579, 589; TA/Pantusov, p. 285. Sayrāmī worked eleven years (1867–1877) as *mīrzā*. Also cf. *Materialy po istorii Kazakhskikh khanstv XV–XVIII vekov*, ed. S. K. Ibragimov et al. (Alma-Ata: 'Nauka,' 1969), pp. 478–80.

197. Gordon, *The Roof of the World*, p. 98.

198. Shaw, *Visits to High Tartary*, pp. 217, 259; *Report of a Mission to Yarkund*, p. 103; Boulger, *The Life of Yakoob Beg*, pp. 148–49. Also see, TH/Jarring, 84r; TH/Enver, pp. 403–404; TA/Pantusov, p. 185.

199. TH/Enver, pp. 518–19; TA/Pantusov, p. 242; TA/Jarring, 163v.

200. *Report of a Mission to Yarkund*, p. 509. Also cf. Hayward, "Journey from Leh to Yarkand," p. 133.

201. In the Khoqand and the Bukharan khanates the *dīvānbegi* was one of the highest officials in the court, in charge of collecting revenue. Troitskaia, *Katalog*, p. 542; Abduraimov, *Ocherki agrarnykh otnoshenii*, vol. 1, pp. 72–74.

202. TH/Enver, pp. 518–19; TA/Pantusov, p. 242.

203. This was also written in different characters with the same pronunciation. Cf. Saguchi, *Shakashi kenkyū*, pp. 116–17.

204. *Kashgaria*, p. 64; also see the note on page 63.

205. TH/Enver, p. 517; TA/Pantusov, p. 241.

206. TH/Enver, pp. 522–23; TA/Pantusov, p. 248.

207. *Kashmir and Kashghar*, pp. 354–55. About Bellew's own observation, see pp. 382–83.

CHAPTER 5

1. R. Pipes, *Russia Under the Old Regime* (New York: Scribner, 1974), p. 83.

2. H. C. Rawlinson, *England and Russia in the East* (London: J. Murray, 1875), pp. 141–42.

3. Op. cit., p. 331.

4. As for the settlement between Russia and England on the questions of the Afghan boundaries and for the different attitudes toward the responsibility of the British government, see Schuyler, *Turkistan*, vol. 2, pp. 266–69.

5. E. Hertslet, ed., *Treaties, &c., Between Great Britain and China; and Between China and Foreign Powers* (London: Harrison, 1896), vol. 1, pp. 449–54, 461–72.

6. FO 65/868, nos. 19 and 27 (from Lumley to Russell).

7. *Tārīkh-i ṣigharī*, 65v–66r; TA/Pantusov, p. 182; Schuyler, *Turkistan*, vol. 2, p. 317. Also cf. M. A. Terent'ev, *Russia and England in Central Asia* (Calcutta: Foreign Dept. Press, 1876), vol. 1, 263; Alder, *British India's Northern Frontier*, p. 35.

8. *Turkistan*, vol. 2, p. 317. Also see Boulger, *The Life of Yakoob Beg*, pp. 182–84. He later died in Guma during Ya'qūb Beg's reign. See Petrovskii, "Kratkiia svedeniia," p. 95.

9. See N. Aristov, "Nashi otnosheniia k Dunganam, Kashgaru i Kul'dzhe," *Ezhegodnik: Materialy dlia statistiki Turkestanskago kraia*, no. 2 (1873), p. 181.

10. FO 65/871, no. 16, Oct. 25, 1869 (from Cayley to Thornton).

11. B. P. Gurevich, "Istoriia 'Iliiskogo voprosa' i ee Kitaiskie fal'sifikatory," *Dokumenty oprovergaiut protiv fal'sifikatsii istorii Russko-Kitaiskikh otnoshenii* (Moscow: 'Mysl,' 1982), p. 434.

12. Op. cit., pp. 434–35.

13. Terent'ev, *Russia and England*, vol. 1, pp. 272–73.

14. Gurevich, "Istoriia 'Iliiskogo voprosa,'" pp. 436–38.

15. Terent'ev, *Russia and England*, vol. 1, p. 272.

16. Op. cit., pp. 266–77.

17. Op. cit., p. 281.

18. See Boulger's *The Life of Yakoob Beg*, pp. 320–21; his text is reproduced in Alder's *British India's Northern Frontier*, p. 323.

19. FO 65/874, no. 288, Oct. 16, 1872 (from Loftus to Granville).

20. Kuropatkin, *Kashgaria*, p. 62.

21. Boulger, *The Life of Yakoob Beg*, pp. 199–211.

22. Kuropatkin, *Kashgaria*, pp. 12–17.

23. The British relation with Kashghar is well analyzed by G. J. Alder in his *British India's Northern Frontier*, pp. 15–99.

24. Op, cit., pp. 39–40.

25. On their visit see G. Henderson and A. O. Hume, *Lahore to Yarkand* (London: L. Reeve, 1873).

26. FO 65/874 contains detailed reports on his arrival and the interview with the viceroy.

27. Shaw, *Visits to High Tartary*, p. 68.

28. Alder, *British India's Northern Frontier*, pp. 48–49.

29. English translation of the letter is in FO 65/877, enclosure no. 3.

30. FO 65/877, enclosure 5.

31. The text of the treaty is also found in Boulger's *The Life of Yakoob Beg*, pp. 322–29 and in Alder's *British India's Northern Frontier*, pp. 324–28.

32. On the background of Shaw's return see Alder, *British India's Northern Frontier*, pp. 52–53. The Russians appointed Reintal' as the first commercial agent. See Terent'ev, *Russia and England*, vol. 1, p. 291.

33. Alder, *British India's Northern Frontier*, p. 55. For example, see how wildly the population was estimated by various authorities in R. Michell's "Eastern Turkestan and Dzungaria and the Rebellion of the Tungans and Taranchis, 1862 to 1866," n.p., n.d., pp. 5–7.

34. Alder, *British India's Northern Frontier*, p. 54.

35. This section is based on my article, "1870–nyondae Kashgharia-Osman jeguk gan oegyo gyoseop eui jeonmal gua teugjing," *Jungang Asia Yeongu*, no. 1 (Seoul, 1996), in which I expanded and revised the earlier version on the Kashghar-Ottoman relations in my dissertation. On this topic we have now a very detailed study by Rana von Mende-Altaylı, *Die Beziehungen des osmanischen Reiches zu Kashghar und seinem Herrscher Ya'qub Beg, 1873–1877* (Bloomington, Indiana: Papers on Inner Asia No. 31, 1999). Especially we can find in this work the German translation of several important Ottoman documents related to our topic.

36. Boulger, *The Life of Yakoob Beg*, pp. 169–170. However, there are some

conflicting reports about his birth and parents. See Mende-Altaylı, *Die Beziehungen*, p. 29.

37. T. D. Forsyth, *Autobiography and Reminiscences of Sir Douglas Forsyth* (ed. by his daughter; London: R. Bentley and Son, 1887), pp. 60ff.

38. TH/Jarring, 86r; TH/Enver, p. 418.

39. İrāde Hāriciye, no. 13785. This document is in *Osmalı devleti ile Kafkasya, Türkistan ve Kırım Hanlıkları arasındaki münasebetlere dāir arşiv belgeleri (1687–1908)* (Ankara: Başbakanlık Develet Arşivleri Genel Müdürlügü, 1992). Also cf. Saray, *Rus işgali devrinde*, pp. 70–71.

40. See Saray, *Rus işgali devrinde*, p. 70.

41. TH/Enver, pp. 418–419. In TH/Jarring (86r) this part is omitted.

42. FO 65/957, June 6, 1876, (from Loftus to Derby).

43. Alder, *British India's Northern Frontier*, p. 63.

44. Shaw, *Visits to High Tartary*, p. 327.

45. For more details, see Saray, *Rus işgali deverinde*, pp. 28–98.

46. B. Lewis, *The Emergence of Modern Turkey* (1961; 2nd ed. Oxford: Oxford University Press, 1968; 1979 repr.), pp. 123–24.

47. The activities of Jamāl al-Dīn Afghānī, who stayed in Istanbul in 1869–71, do not seem to have given much influence on the formation of the Pan-Islamic mood during this period. Afghānī's Pan-Islamic appeal came somewhat later, probably from circa 1877, when he wrote in one of his letters that he would "send missionaries of sharp tongue to Kashghar and Yarkand to call the believers of those lands to the unity of the people of the faith." See N. R. Keddie's *Sayyid Jamāl ad-Dīn "al-Afghānī." A Political Biography* (Berkeley: University of California Press, 1972), p. 137. Keddie thinks (pp. 129–33) the letter was composed around 1877–78.

48. Mehmet Atif, *Kāşgar tārīhī*, p. 366.

49. Quoted from Ş. Mardin, *The Genesis of Young Ottoman Thought* (Princeton, N.J.: Princeton University Press, 1962), p. 60, note 110.

50. FO 65/877, Enclosure no. 4.

51. FO 65/877, Enclosure no. 5.

52. İrāde Dahiliye, No. 46454.

53. İrāde Dahiliye, No. 15524. According to İrāde Dahiliye, No. 46685, in July a new decision was made to the effect that the first-class of the Mecīdī order, instead of the first-class Ottoman order, should be given to Sayyid Ya'qūb Khān.

54. İrāde Dahiliye, No. 15546. Cf. *Kenan Bey asarı* (transcription in *Kaşgar tārīhī*, pp. 371–72); Mende-Altaylı, *Die Beziehungen*, pp. 41–42.

55. İrāde Dahiliye, No. 46753.

56. İrāde Dahiliye, No. 49054.

57. *Kashmir and Kashghar*, p. 188.

58. *Kāşgar tārīhī*, p. 363. On the career of Zamān Bey, see Kuropatkin, *Kashgaria*, pp. 10–11. However, 'Alī Kāzim, one of the military instructors who returned from Kashghar after the fall of Ya'qūb Beg's regime, recollects that 2,000 rifles, 6 cannons, and some other military equipment were sent (Yıldız tasnif, 33–1481–73–91). On the other hand Mehmet Yūsuf, one of the four above-mentioned officers, recalls that 3,000 rifles and 30 cannons together with three instructors (Mehmet Yūsuf himself, Yūsuf Ismā'īl, and Ismā'īl Ḥaqq Efendi for drilling cavalry, infantry,

and artillery respectively) were dispatched. See FO 17/826 ("Translation of statement made by Muḥammad Yusaf, Effendi, late in the service of the Amīr of Kāshghar"). The difference in the numbers of armaments found in various sources can be attributed to the blurring of memories after the lapse of a long time and also to the additional purchase of arms in Egypt where Sayyid Ya'qūb Khān stopped on his way back to Kashghar. Therefore, the list found in Ya'qūb Beg's letter—1,200 rifles of old and new types, 6 cannons, and 4 instructors (with one additional civilian)—should be accepted to be most authentic.

59. Ignatiev's report dated June 14, 1873, Constantinople. Quoted from FO 65/903, St. Petersburg, June 14, 1873 (from Loftus to Derby).

60. *İslam Ansiklopedisi*, vol. 2 (Istanbul: Türkiye Diyanet Vakfı, 1989), pp. 143–57; Mardin, *The Genesis*, pp. 67, 249.

61. FO 65/903; Sarary, *Rus işgali devrinde*, p. 86.

62. T. E. Gordon, *The Roof of the World*, pp. 29–30; Bellew, *Kashmir and Kashghar*, pp. 187–88.

63. İrāde Dahiliye, No. 49054.

64. *Kāşgar tārīhī*, p. 384.

65. Bellew, *Kashmir and Kashghar*, p. 304.

66. According to T. E. Gordon, another eyewitness, this order was issued at the Qurbān festival on January 28, 1874 (*The Roof of the World*, p. 87). Sayrāmī's assertion (TH/Enver, p. 420) that he received from the sultan the title of *mīrākhōr* is not found in any other source.

67. Between 1873 and 1875 there was no remarkable event to note. But Sayyid Ya'qūb Khān's letter, informing what Ya'qūb Beg did after he had received the presents from the sultan, was delivered to the Ottoman consul in Bombay, and the consul reported it to the sultan with the translation of that letter (İrāde Dahiliye, No. 15817). One more episode to mention is that Ya'qūb Beg's sister, Ay Bibi, visited Istanbul on her way back from the pilgrimage to Mecca and received a cordial reception (*Kāşgar tārīhī*, p. 386).

68. İrāde Dahiliye, No. 49016 and No. 49054.

69. İrāde Dahiliye, No. 49054. Cf. *Kenan Bey asarı (Kāşgar tārihi*, pp. 373–74); Mende-Altaylı, *Die Beziehungen*, pp. 50–51.

70. *Kāşgar tārīhī*, pp. 386–87.

71. İrāde Dahiliye, No. 49145, No. 49220 and No. 49338.

72. Saray, *Rus işgali devrinde*, p. 105. Cf. The text of this is found in İrāde Dahiliye, No. 49426. Cf. *Kenan Bey asari*, pp. 9–12 (*Kāşgar tārihi*, pp. 378–79); Mende-Altaylı, *Die Beziehungen*, pp. 52–53.

73. In *Kāşgar tārīhī* (p. 387) we can find a complete list of these additional items.

74. Op. cit., pp. 387–90.

75. Op. cit., p. 387.

76. S. J. Shaw and E. K. Shaw, *History of the Ottoman Empire*, p. 156.

77. F.O. 65/930, no. 323, St. Petersburg, Oct. 27, 1875 (from Loftus to Derby).

78. F.O.65/929, no. 292, St. Petersburg, Sep. 27, 1875 (from Doria to Derby). Cf. *Kāşgar tārīhī*, pp. 388–89.

79. Many of the nineteenth century writers, including H. Rawlinson and M. A. Terent'ev, were the advocates of the Great Game theory, and this approach is very

popular even today. Among others, see L. E. Fretchling, "Anglo–Russian Rivalry in Eastern Turkistan, 1863–1881," *Royal Central Asian Journal*, no. 26, pt. 3 (1939); V. G. Kiernan, "Kashghar and the Politics of Central Asia, 1868–1878," *The Cambridge Historical Journal*, vol. 11, no. 3 (1955); O. E. Clubb, *China and Russia: The "Great Game"*(New York: Columbia University Press, 1971); E. Ingram, *The Beginning of the Great Game in Asia 1828–1834* (Oxford: Clarendon Press, 1979); P. B. Henze, "The Great Game in Kashgaria: British and Russian Missions to Yakub Beg," *Central Asian Survey*, vol. 8, no. 2 (1989); P. Hopkirk, *The Great Game: The Struggle for Empire in Central Asia* (1990; New York: Kodansha America, 1994 repr.); K. E. Meyer and S. B. Brysac, *Tournament of Shadows: The Great Game and the Race for Empire in Central Asia* (Washington: A Cornelia and Michael Bessie Book, 1999).

80. FO 65/957, no. 444 (secret), St. Petersburg, Sep. 26, 1876 (from Loftus to Derby).

81. FO 65/989, quoting the *Turkestan Gazette*, no. 1, Jan. 5/17, 1877.

CHAPTER 6

1. On the operations and the failure of the Qing government to suppress the Shanxi-Gansu Muslim rebellion before the arrival of Zuo Zongtang, see Wen-djang Chu, *Moslem Rebellion in Northwest China*, pp. 23–88.

2. *Shan-Gan jieyulu* in *Huimin qiyi*, comp. Bai Shouyi, vol. 4 (Shanghai: Shengzhou Guoguangshe, 1952), p. 311; Feng Zenglie and Feng Junping, "Yisilanjiao zai Tongzhi nianjian Shanxi huimin fanqing qiyi zhong suoqide zuoyong," in *Yisilanjiao zai Zhongguo* (Ningxia: Ningxia Renmin Chubanshe, 1982), pp. 205–207. On the Muslim rebellion in Shanxi and Gansu, the traditional view by scholars like Lin Gan and Ma Changshou who regarded it as a peasant revolution has been criticized recently by those who understand it from the viewpoint of national struggle. However, even one such critic, Wu Wanshan, emphasizes the important role of religious leaders. See his "Qingzhao Tongzhi nianjian huimin qiyi xingzhi de zaijiantao," *Xibei Minzu Xueyuan xuebao* (Zhesheban), 1985, no. 1: 62–69; Lin Ji, "Qingdai Shan-Gan huimin qiyi yanjiu gaishu," *Minzu yanjiu*, 1988, no. 5.

3. For this topic, see Ma Tong, *Zhongguo Yisilanjiao jiaopai menhuan zhidu shilue* (Ningxia Renmin Chubanshe, 1983) and his *Zhongguo Yisilanjiao jiaopai menhuan suyuan* (Ningxia Renmin Chubanshe, 1987).

4. The most important source for the study of Zuo Zongtang is the collection of his memorials, letters and literary works, entitled *Zuo Wenxianggong quanji* (repr. Taipei: Wenhai Chubanshe, 1964). Based on this, not a few biographies were written. Among others, see *Zuo Wenxianggong nianpu*, compiled by Lo Zhengjun (reprinted as *Zuo Zongtang nianpu*, Changsha, 1982, with additional notes) and W. L. Bales, *Tso Tsungt'ang. Soldier and Statesman of Old China* (Shanghai: Kelly and Walsh, 1937). Especially on Zuo's northwestern campaign, see Lu Fengge's *Zuo Wenxianggong Zhengxi shilue* (1947; repr. Taipei, 1972); Qin Hancai's *Zuo Wenxianggong cai Xibei* (1945; reprinted in Shanghai, 1946); L. B. Fields, *Tso Tsung-t'ang and the Muslims.* (Kingston, Ontario: Limestone Press, 1978). For more recent studies, see Yang Dongliang, *Zuo Zongtang pingchuan* (Changsha: Hunan

Renmin Chubanshe, 1985); Dong Caishi, *Zuo Zongtang pingchuan* (Peking: Zhongguo Shehui Kexue Chubanshe, 1984).

5. Wen-djang Chu, *The Moslem Rebellion*, p. 132; Yang Dongliang, *Zuo Zongtang pingchuan*, pp. 155–56.

6. O. V. Poiarkov, *Poslednii epizod Dunganskago vozstaniia* (Vernoe, 1901), p. 11. According to *Tārīkh-i jarīda-i jadīda* (pp. 64–65 of the Kazan edition), his other name was Nūr al-Dīn. On the historical evaluation of his role, see Chang Dezhong, "Bai Yanhu de yingxiong xingxiang burong waiqu" (*Huizu Wenxue luncong*, Ningxia Renmin Chubanshe, 1990) no. 1, pp. 264–71. According to Ma Xiaoshi (*Xibei Huizu geming jianshi*, p. 41), the leaders of these "four big battalions" were Bai Yanhu, Cui Wei, Yu Deyan, and Ma Zhenhe.

7. Yiang Dongliang, *Zuo Zongtang pingchuan*, p. 157. See also the map in Bales, *Tso Tsungt'ang*, p. 240.

8. Ma Xiaoshi, *Xibei Huizu geming jianshi*, pp. 38–41.

9. K. C. Liu and R. J. Smith, "The Military Challenge: The North-west and the Coast," in *Cambridge History of China* (Cambridge: Cambridge University Press, 1980), vol. 2, pt. 2, ed. by J. K. Fairbank and K. C. Liu, pp. 230–31.

10. See Feng and Feng, "Yisilanjiao," p. 220.

11. Poiarkov, *Poslednii epizod*, p. 22.

12. There was a claim that Ma was not executed by the order of Zuo Zongtang but by a Qing army officer named Yang Ziying who had defected in disguise to the Muslims during the siege of Jinjibao. But there seems to be no evidence to support such a claim. See Guan Lianji, "Guanyu Ma Hualong zhi si de lishi zhenxiang," *Minzu yanjiu*, 1984, no. 5: 74–76.

13. *Zuo Wenxianggong quanji* (zougao), q. 41, 9r; Ma Xiaoshi, *Xibei Huizu geming jianshi*, pp. 44–47; Bales, *Tso Tsungt'ang*, pp. 276–78.

14. Ma Zhanao supposedly said that "To surrender after the victory would bring more profit than to surrender after the defeat." His remark, if it is true, appears to support our assumption. See Ma Xiaoshi, *Xibei Huizu geming jianshi*, p. 47.

15. Ma Tong, *Yisilanjiao Jiaopai menhuan zhidu shilue*, p. 234.

16. I. Hsü, "The Great Policy Debate in China, 1874: Maritime Defense vs. Frontier Defense," *Harvard Journal of Asiatic Studies*, no. 25 (1964–65): 213.

17. Chu, *The Moslem Rebellion*, pp. 113–14.

18. J. L. Rawlinson, *China's Struggle for Naval Development, 1839–1895* (Cambridge, Mass.: Harvard University Press, 1967), p. 56.

19. *Qinding Pingding Shan-Gan Xinjiang fanglue*, q. 137, 18r–20v.

20. See Khodzhaev, *Tsinskaia imperiia*, pp. 46–47.

21. Hsü, "The Great Policy Debate," p. 217.

22. *Zuo Wenxianggong quanji* (zougao), q. 46, 32r–41r.

23. Khodzhaev, *Tsinskaia imperiia*, p. 71.

24. Hsü, "The Great Policy Debate," p. 227.

25. Chu, *The Moslem Rebellion*, pp. 121–22.

26. Khodzhaev, *Tsinskaia imperiia*, p. 80.

27. Ibid.

28. FO 65/957, no. 240, St. Petersburg, May 30, 1876 (from Loftus to Derby). The parentheses and the brackets are in the text, and the date of the *Turkestan Gazette* is not given.

29. It is not easy to calculate the total number of the Qing troops advancing to the north of Tianshan. According to Yang Dongliang's study (*Zuo Zongtang pingchuan*, p. 242), the total number was about thirty to forty thousand. Khodzhaev points out that Zuo's army consisted of 141 battalions (about 75,000 soldiers), but it probably included the rear troops. See also Zeng Wenwu, *Zhongguo jingying Xiyushi*, p. 334; Bales, *Tso Tsungt'ang*, pp. 350–51.

30. Very often they are mentioned together in Zuo Zongtang's memorials. For example, see *Zuo Wenxianggong quanji* (zougao), q. 49, 25r–26r. According to *Tārīkh-i jarīda-i jadīda* (the Kazan edition, p. 64), Yu Xiaohu's Muslim name was 'Alī Qanbar (or, 'Alī Qambar).

31. *Kanding Xinjiangji*, q. 1, 16r–16v. For the Tungan raid of Hami, cf. A. von Le Coq, "Osttürkische Gedichte und Erzählungen," *Keleti Szemle*, no. 18 (1918–19): 83, 89.

32. See *Tadhkira-i Ḥājjī Pādishāh*, 34v; TA/Pantusov, p. 220; *Tārīkh-i ṣighārī*, 102v.

33. *Tārīkh-i ṣighārī* 102v–104r.

34. Zuo Zongtang wrote that "Bai Yanhu took fierce Tungans of Shanxi and Gansu, and they settled separately in Hongmiao, Gumu, and Manas." See *Kanding Xinjiangji*, q. 2, 8v. It seems that the base of Bai's group was at Hongmiaozi and that of Yu's in Manas. Cf. *Zuo Wenxianggong quanji* (zougao), q. 49, 35r; *Pinghuizhi*, q. 7, 13r; Poiarkov, *Poslednii epizod*, p. 35.

35. Forsyth, *Report of a Mission to Yarkund*, p. 19.

36. TH/Enver, pp. 482–484; TH/Jarring, 97v–98r; TA/Pantusov, pp. 222–24. One Chinese source (*Kanding Xinjiangji*, q. 2, 14r) writes that Ya'qūb Beg "sent Atuoai (*Atuwai), an enemy commander, with several thousand cavalry for assistance," while another source (*Zuo Wenxianggong quanji*, zougao, q. 49, 3r and 5r) points out that 358 "Andijani" soldiers commanded by one *pānṣad* and one *yüzbashi* were all killed when the fort was taken.

37. Yıldız tasnif, 33–1481–73–91.

38. Later he was taken as a prisoner by the Qing army and, after being released, he went to Peshawar where he wrote a short recollection at the request of British officials. His memoir is found in FO 17/826, No. 1621.

39. *Zuo Wenxianggong quanji* (zougao), q. 49,1r–3r; *Qinding Pingding Shangan Xinjiang fanglue*, q. 300, 6v–10v; *Pinghuizhi*, q. 7, 13r–14r; *Kanding Xinjiangji*, q. 2, 13r–14v; TH/Jarring, 98r; TH/Enver, pp. 483–84; TA/Pantusov, p. 224. Also note an interesting episode in *Kāşgar tārīhī*, pp. 409–11.

40. *Zuo Wenxianggong quanji* (zougao), q. 49, 3v–4r.

41. TH/Jarring, 98r; TH/Enver, pp. 483–84; TA/Pantusov, p. 224. According to *Kāşgar tārīhī* (pp. 411–12), at first the cavalry under the command of Muḥammad Sa'īd and the artillery under Mā Dālūya fought with the Qing army. Initially they overpowered the enemy but, soon being exhausted, had to retreat. It does not mention Ya'qūb Beg's order of retreat.

42. Yang Dongliang, *Zuo Zongtang pingchuan*, p. 215.

43. *Kashgaria*, pp. 241–42.

44. *Zuo Wenxianggong quanji* (zougao), q. 50, 34v.

45. Op. cit., 36r–36v.

46. Op. cit., 17r–19v.

47. Boulger, *The Life of Yakoob Beg*, pp. 250–52.

48. According to Sayrāmī (TA/Pantusov, p. 278), he was a Bukharan and served as a *mīrzā* under Mahī al-Dīn Makhdūm.

49. TH/Jarring, 99v; TH/Batyur, pp. 490–91; TA/Pantusov, p. 228.

50. *Tadhkira-i Ḥājjī Pādishāh*, 38r; Tālib Akhūnd (Prov. 117), 92r–93r. Several Soviet scholars like Khodzhaev and Baranova accept this theory. See *Tsinskaia imperiia*, p. 99; "Svedeniia Uigurskoi," p. 93.

51. *Zuo Wenxianggong quanji* (shudu), q. 19, 30r–31v.

52. Kuropatkin, *Kashgaria*, p. 249.

53. *Zuo Wenxianggong quanji* (zougao), q. 50, 71r–71v.

54. See the Russian text in Kuropatkin's *Kashgariia*, p. 211, which reads "V eto vremia s nim sdelalsia udar, lishiushii ego pamiati i iazyka." However, its English translation (*Kashgaria*, pp. 248–49)—"In the struggle with him [i.e., Sabīr Akhūnd] he received a blow which deprived him of his senses"—is somewhat ambiguous and could be misunderstood, as if Ya'qūb Beg was hit by Sabīr Akhūnd and died. As a matter of fact, the assertion by Takakuwa and Ji Dachun, claiming that he was beaten to death, was misguided by this vague translation. See "Yakub Beg no shiin ni tsuite," *Shigaku zasshi* 30, no. 4 (1919): 107–11, and "Guanyu Agubo zhi si," *Xinjiang Daxue xuebao* (shekeban), 1970, no. 2: 149–51. Also note the same mistake in *Xinjiang jianshi* (vol. 2, p. 190).

55. Hamada, "L'Histoire," pt. 3, pp. 83–84.

56. Cf. Baranova, "Svedeniia Uigurskoi," p. 93, note 76.

57. See TH/Jarring, 99v; TH/Enver, p. 490; TA/Pantusov, p. 228; Boulger, *The Life of Yakoob Beg*, pp. 250–52; Kuropatkin, *Kashgariia*, p. 249; Baranova, "Svedeniia Uigurskoi," p. 92, note 74.

58. *Ot Kul'dzhi za Tian'-Shan' i na Lob-Nor* (Moscow: Gos. izd-vo geogr. litry, 1947), pp. 92–93; an English translation by E. D. Morgan, *From Kulja, Across the Tian Shan to Lob-Nor* (London: S. Low, Marston, Searle, & Rivington, 1879), pp. 127–29.

59. See *Zuo Wenxianggong quanji* (zougao), q. 50, 71r–71v.

60. For example, see Mehmet Yūsuf (in FO 17/826) and Zamān Khān (in *Kashgaria*, p. 250).

61. TH/Jarring, 98r–98v; TH/Enver, p. 485; TA/Pantusov, p. 225.

62. See Khodzhaev, *Tsinskaia imperiia*, p. 54.

63. P. Potagos, *Dix années de voyages dans l'Asie Centrale et l'Afrique équatoriale*, vol. 1 (Paris: Librairie Fischbacher, 1885), tr. from Greek by A. Meyer, J. Blancard and L. Labadie, and ed. by E. Burnouf, pp. 91–92 (cited from J. Fletcher, "China and Central Asia," p. 223 and note 121 on pp. 367–78).

64. FO 17/825, April 9, 1876 (from Forsyth to Wade).

65. FO 17/825, no. 219, Dec. 10, 1876 (from Fraser to Derby).

66. Ibid.

67. He was also known as 'Īshān Khān' whom Mīrzā Aḥmad erroneously considered to have been sent to the Chinese emperor. Khodzhaev repeats this error (*Tsinskaia imperiia*, p. 68 and note 2 on p. 116).

68. İrāde Dahiliye, No. 60621.

69. İrāde Hāriciye, No. 16526.

70. İrāde Dahiliye, No. 60710 and No. 60716.

71. This is what Sayyid Ya'qūb Khān secretly told to D. Forsyth. Quoted from I. Hsü, "British Mediation of China's War with Yaqub Beg, 1877," *Central Asiatic Journal* 9, no. 2 (1964), p. 145.

72. Hsü, "British Mediation," pp. 146–47.

73. See TA/Pantusov, p. 225; *Tadhkira-i Ḥājjī Pādishāh*, 35r; Ṭālib Akhūnd (Prov. 117), 78v; Qurbān 'Alī's *Tārīkh-i ḥamsa-i sharqī*, p. 119 (quoted from Khodzhaev, *Tsinskaia imperiia*, p. 91).

74. TH/Jarring, 98r; TH/Enver, p. 485; TA/Pantusov, p. 225.

75. Ibid.

76. Ṭālib Akhūnd (Prov. 117), 79v.

77. Sayrāmī writes that there were thirty thousand troops and provisions that could feed these troops for ten years in Toqsun and Turfan (TH/Jarring, 99r; TH/Enver, p. 488; "thirty years" in TA/Pantusov, p. 227).

78. FO 65/95, no. 444 (secret), St. Petersburg, Sep. 26, 1876 (from Loftus to Derby).

79. FO 65/989, quoting the *Turkestan Gazette*, no. 1, Jan. 5/17, 1877.

80. *Tadhkira-i Ḥājjī Pādishāh*, 37r. Also cf. Baranova, "Svedeniia," p. 91.

81. For example, see Tālib Akhūnd (Prov. 117), 71r–73r and *Tadhkira-i Ḥājjī Pādishāh*, 35r–36v.

82. *Zuo Wenxianggong quanji* (zougao), q. 50, 35r–36v and 71r; *Pinghuizhi*, q. 7, 19v–22r; *Qinding Pingding Shan-Gan Xinjiang fanglue*, q. 303, 17v–18r.

83. See TH/Jarring, 97v; TH/Enver, p. 485; TA/Pantusov, pp. 225–26.

84. Grenard "Spécimen," p. 31.

85. TA/Pantusov, p. 226.

86. On this topic see Immanuel Hsü, "British Mediation of China's War with Yakub Beg."

87. *Kāşgar tārīhī*, p. 406. Later he went to India and died in Delhi in 1317/1899 (Mende-Altaylı, *Die Beziehungen*, p. 29).

88. The statement of Mehmet Yūsuf, an Ottoman officer, is in FO 17/825. On the political development in Kashgharia after Ya'qūb Beg's death, two other Ottoman officers' reports are useful. One is by Zamān Khān found in Kuropatkin's *Kashgaria* (pp. 249ff) and the other by 'Alī Kāzim in Yıldız tasnif (33–1481–73–91). The facsimile and the transcription of the latter are found in A. R. Bekin, "Sultan 'Abdülhamid'e sunulan Doğu Türkistan ile ilgili bir rapor," *Doğu Dilleri*, vol. 3, no. 4 (1983): 39–66. Also Mehmet Ātif, in his *Kāşgar tārīhī*, gives quite detailed accounts which are useful if we read them carefully.

89. Sayrāmī erroneously regards Ḥākim Khān as having been chosen *khan* while Ḥaqq Quli was in Kurla (TH/Jarring, 105r; TH/Enver, p. 527; TA/Pantusov, p. 246). Mehmet Ātif's assertion that Ḥaqq Quli went to Kashghar with an intention to kill his brother, is also doubtful (*Kāşgar tārīhī*, pp. 431–32). Why would he attempt such a thing with only a small number of soldiers, or why, in the first place, would he go himself?

90. Kuropatkin, *Kashgaria*, p. 251. Also cf. Mehmet Ātif, *Kāşgar tārīhī*, pp. 433–36; TA/Pantusov, pp. 246–48.

91. Mehmet Ātif, *Kāşgar tārīhī*, pp. 436–37.

92. Kuropatkin, *Kashgaria*, p. 251; Mehmet Ātif, *Kāşgar tārīhī*, pp. 437–40.

93. TH/Jarring, 111r; TH/Enver, pp. 553–54; TA/Pantusov, pp. 252–54.

94. *Zuo Zongtang nianbu*, p. 334; *Zuo Wenxianggong quanji* (zougao), q. 51, 28r.

95. Dong Caishi, *Zuo Zongtang pingchuan*, p. 167.

96. TH/Jarring, 107r–108v; TH/Enver, pp. 537–42; TA/Pantusov, pp. 254–57.

97. Poiarkov, "Poslednii epizod," p. 6.

98. See FO 17/826, no. 1621. Passing through Sariqol and Wakhan and crossing the Pamir, he arrived in Badakhshan, and then he went to Peshawar via Kabul.

99. See his report in Yıldız tasnif, 33–1481–73–91. They first went to Ladakh and, thence, with the help of the British reached Bombay. There they could take the ship heading to their country.

100. On the Ming Yol monument, see Liu Yongneng, "Agubo zuihou fumieh de lishi jianzheng," *Xinjiang Daxue xuebao* (Shekeban), 1979, no. 3: 51–59.

101. FO 17/826, no. 127.

102. Yıldız tasnif, 33–1638 (pp. 148–51). Kemal H. Karpat regards this Ya'qūb as "representative" of the Kashghar regime stationed in Istanbul. See his article, "Yakub Bey's Relations with the Ottoman Sultans: A Reinterpretation," *Cahiers du Monde russe et sovietique*, vol. 32, no. 1 (1991): 26. The petition was delivered by a Kashgharian "infantry commander" named Mehmet Khān who came to Istanbul. It is highly possible that this Mehmet Khān was the same person to whom Henvey referred, erroneously as "Ahmed."

103. The Russian proposal is also confirmed not only by the aforementioned report of Henvey but also by a Qing document. General Kaufman is reported to have told Beg Quli as follows: since the Qing and Russia are "opposed against each other because of the Ili question, this is a good opportunity for you to recover your country. If you send a declaration to the Kashgharians urging them to expel the Chinese, many cities will transmit your declaration amongst themselves and [your aim] shall be achieved." See *Shae qinhuashi*, vol. 3 (Peking: Zhongguo Shehui Kexueyuan Jindaishi Yanjiusuo, 1981), p. 263.

104. Yıldız tasnif, 14–382. Cf. Mende-Altaylı, *Die Beziehungen*, pp. 63–65.

105. *Kāşgar tārīhī*, pp. 457–58.

106. For the negotiation and the return of Ili, consult I. Hsü, *The Ili Crisis* (Oxford: Clarendon Press, 1965).

107. Bales, *Tso Tsungt'ang*, p. 376.

108. "The Late Ch'ing Reconquest of Sinkiang: A Reappraisal of Tso Tsung-t'ang's Role," *Central Asiatic Journal* 12, no. 1 (1968): 50.

CONCLUSION

1. Cf. Enoki Kazuo, "Shinkyō no kenshō" (1–5), *Kindai Chūgoku*, no. 15 (1984): 158–90; no. 16 (1884): 36–69; no. 17 (1985): 75–90; no. 18 (1986): 44–59; no. 19 (1987): 48–82; Kazutada Kataoka, *Shinchō Shinkyō tōji kenkyū* (Tokyo: Yuzankaku, 1991): pp. 61–199.

2. According to the most recent statistics in *Xinjiang nianjian 1999* (Urumchi: Xinjiang Nianjianshe, 1999, pp. 11–22), the Uyghurs are 8,139,458 and the Han Chinese are 6,741,116.

3. On the nationalist movement prior to the Communist takeover, see Andrew D. Forbes, *Warlords and Muslims in Chinese Central Asia: A Political History of Republican Sinkiang 1911–1949* (Cambridge: Cambridge University Press, 1986); Wang Ke, *Higashi Torukisutan Kyōwakuni kenkyū: Chukoku to Isuramu minzoku mondai* (Tokyo: Tokyō Daikagu Shupankai, 1995); Hamada Masami, "La trasmission du mouvement nationaliste au Turkestan oriental (Xinjiang)," *Central Asian Survey* 9, no.1 (1990): 29–48.

APPENDIX A

1. I reproduced this text, with modifications, from Boulger's *The Life of Yakoob Beg*, pp. 320–321. The Russian original text can be found in Kuropatkin's *Kashgariia*, pp. 49–50 (cf. English translation in *Kashgaria*, pp. 61–62).

2. "Chief" in Boulger's text. As I mentioned earlier, the Russian word *vladetel'* should be translated as "ruler." For the original Russian text, see Kuropatkin's *Kashgariia*, pp. 49–50. The translator of his book renders this word correctly (*Kashgharia*, pp. 61–62).

APPENDIX B

1. I reproduced this text from a document in the Public Record Office (ZHC 1/3920), entitled "Kashgar Treaty. Copy of the Treaty of Commerce lately concluded with the Amir of Kashgar. Ordered, by the House of Commons, to be printed, 15 June 1874." Also cf. Boulger, *The Life of Yakoob Beg*, pp. 322–29; Alder, *British India's Northern Frontier*, pp. 324–28.

Bibliography

MANUSCRIPTS AND DOCUMENTS

Since this study heavily relies on Muslim sources most of which are still in manuscript form, it seems necessary to list them in this separate section to show the amount of existing Islamic literature on the topic. Each Muslim source is supplied with the title, its author, the date of writing, the location(s) of the manuscript(s), the printed edition if any, the name of the copyist and the date of copying if known, folios, and other bibliographical information. The items to which I do not have access are indicated with an asterisk. Diplomatic documents stored in archives in Turkey and England are also listed here.

MUSLIM SOURCES

*Amīr 'Alī** (Sublime Leader). 'Ashūr Akhūnd b. Ismā'īl b. Muḥammad; Institut Narodov Azii Akademii Nauk in Russia (hereafter INA AN): C 759, C 580; 1280/1863–64; maybe an autograph: cf. Muginov, nos. 19 and 20, and Dmitrieva, nos. 134 and 135.

Anīs al-ṭālibīn (Companion of the Seekers). Shāh Maḥmūd ibn Mīrzā Fāḍil Churās; Bodleian Library (Oxford): Ms. Ind. Inst. Pers. 45; ms. of Turkī translation, *Rafīq al-ṭālibīn*, INA AN: B 771; cf. Akimushkin, *Khronika*, pp. 331–44.

Äsirlär sadasi (Voice of the Era). Alma-Ata, 1963.

*Badaulat-nāma** (Book of the Fortunate). Muḥammad 'Umar Marghinānī (the author of *Jang-nāma*); INA AN: C 587; 1308/1890; an autograph by the request of N. F. Petrovskii; 61f; cf. Muginov, no. 25; Dmitrieva, no. 141.

*Buzkhan Tūram bilän Yāqūb Begni vaqī'asi** (Events on Buzkhan Tūram and Yāqūb Beg). Anonymous; L'Institut de France: Ms. 3398–7; 6f; cf. Hamada, "Uiguru rekishi bunken."

Dāstān-i Muḥammad Yā'qūb Beg (Story of Muḥammad Ya'qūb Beg). Mīrzā Bī; India Office Library: Ms. Turki 6; 1294/1877–78; Jumāda I, 1311/Nov. 10–Dec. 9 of 1898; 20f.

Ghazāt-i muslimīn (Holy War of Muslims). Anonymous; in E. D. Ross, *Three Turki Manuscripts from Kashghar*; cf. Haneda's Japanese translation, "Wari Han" and "Ghazāt-i-Müslimin."

*Ghazāt al-muslimīn** (Holy War of Muslims). Muḥammad Ṣāliḥ Yārkandī; INA AN: B 3980; probably 1281/1864–65; copied in 1912, Kashghar; cf. Dmitrieva, no. 136.

Ghazāt dar mulk-i Chīn (Holy War in China). Mullā Bilāl; 1293/1876–77; Pantusov's printed text *Voina musul'man protiv Kitaitsev*; cf. Hamada, "Murrā Birāru."

*Ghuljaning vaqī'atlarining bäyāni** (Story of the Events in Kulja). Qāsim Beg; INA AN: B 4018; copied at the end of the nineteenth century; 01+15+001f; cf. Dmitrieva, no. 139, and Tikhonov's "Uigurskie," pp. 173–74.

Jalāl al-Dīn Katakīning tadhkirasi (Biography of Jalāl al-Dīn Katakī). Anonymous; G. Jarring Collection: uncatalogued; 40f; cf. Muginov, nos. 134–140.

*Jamī' al-tavārīkh** (Collection of Histories) (or, *Tārīkh-i Ya'qūb Badaulat* (History of Ya'qūb Badaulat]). Ḥājjī Yūsuf b. Mullā 'Ashūr b. Qurbān Ṣūfī b. Ṣafar Bāy; INA AN: D 124; Ṣafar Bāy; Jumāda I, 1325—Muḥarram, 1326/June 1907–March 1908; 352f; cf. Muginov, no. 157, Dmitrieva, no. 145; and Tikhonov, "Uigurskie," pp. 166–72.

Janāb-i Badaulatni ḥikāyatlari (Stories of His Highness Badaulat). Aḥmad Quli Andijānī; The Houghton Library, Harvard University: uncatalogued; 1322/1904–05 in Kashghar; 56p.

*Jang-nāma** (Book of War). Muḥammad 'Umar Marghinānī (*nom de plume*: Umīdī); INA AN: B 292; 1305/1888; 5v–46r; cf. Muginov, no. 335, and Dmitrieva, no. 138.

Kāşgar tārīhī (History of Kashghar). Mehmet Ātif. Istanbul: Mihran Matbaası, 1300/1882–83. Modern Turkish translation by İsmail Aka et al., *Kaşgar Tarihi: Bāis-i Hayret Ahvāl-i Garibesi*. Kırıkkale: Eysi, 1998.

Khronika (Chronicle). Shāh Maḥmūd ibn Fāḍil Churās; critical text, translation, commentaries and study by O. F. Akimushkin, Moscow: Nauka, 1976; *Säydiyä Khandanliq tärikhigä dair materiyallar* (modern Uyghur translation) Qäshqär: Qäshqär Uyghur Näshriyäti, 1988.

Kitāb-i tārīkh-i jarīda-i jadīda. See *Tārīkh-i jarīda-i jadīda*.

Muntakhab al-tavārīkh (Selection from histories). Ḥājjī Muḥammad Ḥākim valad-i Ma'ṣūm Khān; INA AN: D 90.

Osmalı devleti ile Kafkasya, Türkistan ve Kırım Hanlıkları arasındaki münasebetlere dāir arşiv belgeleri (1687–1908) (Archival documents on the relations between the Ottoman state and Caucasus, Turkestan, and Crimean khanates). Ankara: T.C. Başbakanlık, Devlet Arşivleri Genel Müdürlüğu, Osmanlı Arşivi Daire Başkanlığı, 1992.

*Qānūn nāma-i 'asākir** (Canon book of the army). Anonymous; INA AN: B 1022; probably 1879–80; 45f; cf. Muginov, no. 273.

*Risāla-i khāqān ichidä Tunganlari qilghan ishi** (Treatise on the activities of Tungans in the realm of Emperor). Anonymous; INA AN: C 579; at the end of the nineteenth century; cf. Muginov, no. 213; Dmitrieva, no. 142; Tikhonov, "Uigurskie," pp. 155–57.

*Shajārat al-anṣāb-i Sayyid Muḥammad Ḥākim Khān Khwājam** (Genealogical tree of Sayyid Muḥammad Ḥākim Khān Khwājam). Anonymous, but may be Qārī 'Umar Muḥammad; INA AN: B 292; 1v–5r; copied in 1305/1888; cf. Muginov, no. 343.

Sharqī Turkistān Tārīkhī [History of Eastern Turkestan]. Mehmet Emin Bughra. Srinagar, Kashmir: Bruka Parlis Basmakhanesi, 1366/1946–47. A new printed edition was published in Ankara: Fatma Bugra, 1987.

*Shi'ār dar na't-i Ḥaḍrat-i Khān Khwājam Pādishāh** (Verses in eulogy of His Highness Khān Khwājam Pādishāh). A collection of four different works: (1) *Rashīd al-Dīn nāma* by Qārī Najm al-Dīn (2r–37v); (2) a work by Ghiyāth (38r–47r);

(3) *Risāla-i maktūb* by Muḥammad Ṣāliḥ Yārkandī (48r–87v); (4) an anonymous work of no title (88r–97r); INA AN: C 584; written shortly before the fall of Kuchean regime; cf. Iudin, "Nekotorye istochniki."

Tadhkira-i Ḥājjī Pādishāh Ḥabīb Allāh vä Rāshidīn Khān vä Ya'qūb Beg [Biography of Ḥājjī Pādishāh Ḥabīb Allāh, Rāshidīn Khān and Ya'qūb Beg] (also known as *Tārīkh-i Kāshghar*). Muḥammad A'lam; the 18th of Sha'bān, 1311/Dec. 17, 1894. The two extant manuscripts are (1) L'Institut de France: ms. 3348–8; for translation in French by Hamada, cf. his "L'Histoire de Ḫotan de Muḥammad A'lam" in 3 parts; and (2)* INA AN: B 2332; 61f; cf. Muginov, no. 40a; Dmitrieva, no. 143; Tikhonov, "Uigurskie," pp. 150–55; and Ibragimova's article "Rukopis' Mukhammeda Aliama."

Tadhkira-i 'azīzān [Biography of nobles] (or, *Tadhkira-i khwājagān* [Biography of khwājas]. Muḥammad Ṣādiq Kāshgharī; written ca. 1768; for available copies, see Hofman, *Turkish Literature*, section 3, pt. 1, vol. 4, pp. 25–30; there are two epitomized translations (see Hartmann and Shaw); a copy in the Bodleian Library, Oxford (Ind. Inst. Pers. d. 20), was also used in this book.

Tadhkira-i Satūq Boghrā Khān (Biography of Satūq Boghrā Khān). Khwāja Muḥammad Sharīf; Bibliothèque Nationale, Paris: Suppl. Turc 1286; 375f; the same work in Leningrad; cf. Muginov, nos. 81 and 82; for a summarized translation, see Baldick.

Tadhkira-i irshād (Record of guidance). Anonymous; Bibliothèque Nationale, Paris: Suppl. Turc 1006 which was wrongly titled *Kitāb-i Tughluq Timur Khaning qiṣaṣlari.*

Tadhkira-i Khwāja Muḥammad Sharīf (Biography of Khwāja Muḥammad Sharīf). Anonymous; three copies in G. Jarring Collection: Prov. 10, Prov. 73, and one uncatalogued; for other copies in Leningrad, cf. Muginov, nos. 105–106. Also cf. Hartmann, "Die osttürkischen Handschriften," p. 7; and Ross, *Three Turki Manuscripts*, p. 4.

Tadhkirat al-najāt (Record of salvation). Dāūd of Kurla; India Office Library: Ms. Turki 4; 1282/1865–66; 73f.

(Ṭālib Akhūnd's *History of Yaq'qūb Beg*). Ṭālib Akhūnd b. Mullā Ni'mat Mingbegi of Khotan; Gunnar Jarring Collection: Provs. 115, 116, and 117; the first day of Jumāda II, 1317/Oct. 6, 1899; no title in the text: author's name appears only in Prov. 117, but it is apparent that the three mss. are written by the same hand and that they form one coherent history of Ya'qūb Beg.

Tārīkh-i amniyya (History of Peace). Mullā Mūsa Sayrāmī; 1321/1903. There is one printed edition and several manuscripts. (1) Pantusov's printed edition (TA/Pantusov): see Pantusov, (2) Bibliothèque Nationale, Paris: Collection Pelliot B 1740 (TA/Pelliot); copied in 1325/1907–08; autograph(?); 208f, (3) Gunnar Jarring Collection (TA/Jarring): uncatalogued; 210f, (4)* INA AN: C 335; 302f; cf. Muginov, no. 27 and Dmitrieva, no. 144, (5)* in PRC; 166f; autograph; cf. Mukhlisov, p. 45 (no. 69) and Iudin's "Review," p. 200, (6)* in PRC; copied in 1907 by Ḥājjī Yūsuf of Tashmaliq (probably the author of *Jamī' al-tavārīkh* of INA AN D 124); 162f; discovered in Kashghar; cf. Mukhlisov, p. 46 (no. 70) and Iudin's "Review," p. 200. Also consult Tikhonov, "Uigurskie," pp. 159–66; Iudin, "Tarikh-i amniia;" Bartol'd, "Taarikh-i Emenie;" Baranova, "Svedeniia." There is a modern Uyghur translation, *Tärikhi äminiyä* (Urumchi: Shinjang Khälq Näshriyäti, 1988).

Tārīkh-i ḥamīdī (History of Ḥamīd). Mullā Mūsa Sayrāmī; this is a revision of the preceding work. Two copies are known to exist. (1) Gunnar Jarring Collection, Lund: Prov. no. 163 (TH/Jarring); probably written in 1326/1908–09 (see 124r); copied not prior to 1345/1927 probably by Ḥājjī Ghulām Muḥammad Khān Khwājam. (2)* PRC, Institute of Nationalities in Pekin; written in July 10, 1908; copied on July 7, 1911 by author; 399 pp.; modern Uyghur translation by Enver Baytur, *Tārīkh-i hämīdī* (TH/Enver; Peking: Millätlär Näshriyäti, 1986).

Tārīkh-i jarīda-i jadīda (A new little history). Qurbān ʿAlī valad-i Khālid Ḥājjī Ayaghūzī; 1306/1886–87. (1) India Office Library: Ms. Turki 2; copied on May 14, 1893; 74f, (2)* INA AN: C 578; 78f; cf. Muginov, no. 28, and Dmitrieva, no. 137, (3) a printed edition, *Kitāb-i tārīkh-i jarīda-i jadīda* (Kazan, 1889), 71pp.; (4) Staatsbibliothek in Berlin: Ms. Orient. Oct. 1670.

*Tārīkh-i nāma-i Yaʿqūb Khān** (History of Yaʿqūb Khān). Maḥmūd valad-i Mīr Aḥmad Shaykh Gharīb; INA AN: B 772; 1316/1898; 78f; cf. Muginov, no. 41, and Tikhonov, "Uigurskie," pp. 157–59.

Tārīkh-i rashīdī (History of Rashīd). Mīrzā Muḥammad Ḥaydar (Dughlāt); for more information about the locations of the available mss., cf. Storey's *Persidskaia*, vol. 2, pp. 1202–1206; English translation, see Ross, Thackston.

Tārīkh-i ṣigharī (Little history). ʿAbd Allāh Pānṣad; British Library: Or. 8156; in Persian; the 15th of Muḥarram, 1291/March 4, 1874; 107f; cf. the chapter on the history of Eastern Turkestan by H. W. Bellew in *Report of a Mission to Yarkund in 1873*.

*Tavārīkh-i ḥamsa-i sharqī** (Histories of five Eastern countries). Imām Qurbān ʿAlī Ḥājjī Ḥamīd Oghli; Kazan, 1910.

Tavārīkh-i shahrukhiyya (Histories of Shahrukh) (or, *Tārīkh-i shahrukhī*). See Pantusov.

Yāqūb Begdin ilgäri Kāshqarnī alghan Ṣiddīq Begning dāstān tadhkirasi [Story of Ṣiddīq Beg who took Kashghar prior to Yaʿqūb Beg]. Qāḍī ʿAbd al-Bāqī Kāshgharī; India Office Library: Ms. Turki 3; copied by Mīrzā Jalāl al-Dīn Akhūnd on Jumāda I 13, 1282/Oct.4, 1865; 28f.

Ẓafar-nāma (Book of victory). Muḥammad ʿAlī Khān Kashmīrī; India Office Library: Ms. Turki 5; 1284/1867–68; 95f.

*Ẓafar-nāma** (Book of victory). Mullā Shaqīr; in PRC, see Mukhlisov, pp. 16–17; cf. partial transcription in *Äsirlär sadasi*, pp. 310–32; Aitbaev, "<Zafar-name> mulla Shakira."

OTTOMAN DOCUMENTS

Başbakanlık arşivi in Istanbul has a number of Ottoman documents related to the Kashgharian state. Many of these contain useful information on the activities of envoys from Kashgharia and the response of the Ottoman government to their requests. The archival numbers are as follows.

(1) Yıldız tasnif (kısm, evrak, zarf, and karton): 33–1211–73–91, 33–1279–73–91, 33–1481–73–91, 33–1638–73–91, 14–382–126–9.

(2) İrāde tasnif:
———Dahiliye; 15524, 15546, 46454, 46685, 46753, 47768, 47978, 49016, 49054, 49145, 49220, 49338, 49343, 49426, 49650, 50480, 60621, 60710, 60716.
———Majlis-i Mahsus; 1992.
———Hāriciye; 15817, 15837, 16299, 16353, 16500, 16526.
———Nāme-i Hümāyūn; defter no. 13.

BRITISH DOCUMENTS

The Public Record Office in London keeps many diplomatic correspondences between the British Indian government, the British embassy in St. Petersburg, the British embassy in Peking, and the Foreign Ministry in London. Most of them are found in FO 65 (Russia) and FO 17 (China). Especially valuable are summarized translations from the contemporary Russian journals and newspapers in FO 65. Besides these, "Parliamentary Papers: House of Common Report" has several documents related to our topic.

ADDITIONAL SOURCES AND STUDIES

Fbduraimov, M. A. *Ocherki agrarnykh otnoshenii v Bukharskom khanstve v XVI–pervoi polovine XIX veka* (Study of the agrarian relations in the Bukharan khanate in the sixteenth through the first half of the nineteenth centuries). 2 vols. Tashkent: Tashkent: Izd-vo 'Fan' Uzbekskoi SSR, 1966–70.

Ahmad, A. *Studies in Islamic Culture in the Indian Environment*. Oxford: Oxford University Press, 1964.

Aḥmad Shāh Naqshabandī. "Route from Kashmir, viâ Ladakh, to Yarkand." Translated from the Persian ms. by J. Dowson. *Journal of the Royal Asiatic Society of Great Britain and Ireland*, no. 12 (1850): 344–58.

———. "Narrative of the travels of Khwajah Ahmud Shah Nukshbundee Syud." *Journal of the Asiatic Society of Bengal* 25, no. 4 (1856): 372–85.

Aitbaev, A. "<Zafar-name> mulla Shakira—vazhnyi istochnik po istorii Kucharskogo vosstaniia 1864 g. (*Ẓafar-nāma* by Mullā Shaqīr—an important source on the history of the 1864 Kuchean rebellion). *Iz istorii Srednei Azii i Vostochnogo Turkestana XV–XIX vv*. Taskent: Izd-vo 'Fan' Uzbekskoi SSR, 1987.

Akabirov, S. F., et al., comps. *Uzbeksko-russkii slovar'* (Uzbek–Russian dictionary). Moscow: Gos. Izd-vo inostrannykh i natsionalnykh slovarei, 1959.

Alder, G. J. *British India's Northern Frontier 1865–95: A Study in Imperial Policy*. London: Published for the Royal Commonwealth Society by Longmans, 1963.

Aristov, N. "Nashi otnosheniia k Dunganam, Kashgaru i Kul'dzhe" (Our relations with Tungans, Kashghar and Kulja). *Edzhegodnik: Materialy dlia statistiki Turkestanskago kraia*, no. 2 (1873).

Baikova, N. B. "Anglo-Kashgarskii torgovyi dogovor 1874 goda." (The Anglo–Kashgharian trade agreement of 1874). *Kratkie soobshcheniia Instituta Vostokovedeniia*, no. 4 (1952): 52–55.

Baldick, Julian. *Imaginary Muslims: The Uwaysi Sufis of Central Asia*. London: I. B. Tauris and Co. Ltd., 1993.

Bales, W. L. *Tso Tsungt'ang: Soldier and Statesman of Old China*. Shanghai: Kelly and Walsh, 1937.

Baranova, Iu. G. "Svedeniia Uigurskoi khroniki Ta'rikh-i amniia o vosstanovlenii Tsinskogo gospodstva v Sin'tsziane v 1875–1878 gg." (Reports of an Uyghur chronicle *Tārīkh-i amniyya* on the reestablishment of the Qing rule in Xinjiang in 1875–1878). *Materialy po istorii i kul'ture uigurskogo naroda* (Materials for the history and the culture of the Uyghur people). Alma-Ata, 1978: 73–133.

Barfield, Thomas J. *Perilous Frontier: Nomadic Empires and China*. Cambridge, Mass.: Basil Blackwell, 1989.

Bartol'd, V. V. *Sochineniia* (Collected works). 9 vols., vol. 2 in 2 parts. Moscow: Nauka, 1963–1977.

———. "Izvlechenie iz Ta'rīkhi Shākhrukhī" (Extract from *Tārīkh-i shahrukhī*). *Ibid.*, vol. 2, pt. 2: 350–58.

———. "Otchet o komandirovke v Turkestan" (An account of a mission to Turkestan). *Ibid.*, vol. 8: 119–210.

———. "Taarikh-i Emenie." vol. 8: 213–19.

Bawden, C. R. *The Modern History of Mongolia*. London: Weidenfeld and Nicholson, 1968.

Becker, S. *Russia's Protectorate in Central Asia: Bukhara and Khiva, 1865–1924*. Cambridge, Mass.: Harvard University Press, 1968.

Beisembiev, T. K. "Ta'rikh-i Shakhrukhi o Vostochnom Turkestane" (*Tārīkh-i shahrukhi* on Eastern Turkestan). *Iz istorii Srednei Azii i Vostochnogo Turkestana XV–XIX vv.* Ed. B. A. Akhmedov, Tashkent: Izd-vo 'Fan' Uzbekskoi SSR, 1987: 162–74.

———. *"Tarikh-i shahrukh" kak istoricheskii istochnik* (*Tārīkh-i Shahrukhi* as a historical source). Alma Ata: Izd-vo 'Nauka' Kazakhskoi SSR, 1987.

Bekin, A. R. "Yakub Beğ zamanında Doğu Türkistan'ın dış ilişkileri" (Foreign relations of Eastern Turkestan during the period Ya'qūb Beg). *Doğu Dilleri* 2, no. 1 (1971): 31–43.

———. "Yakup Beğ'in Doğu Türkistan'ı eğemenliği altına alması" (Ya'qūb Beg's seizure of Eastern Turkestan under his sovereignty). *Ibid.* 2, no. 2 (1975): 99–119.

———. "Yakup Beğ'den önce Doğu Türkistan'daki ayaklanmalar" (Rebellions in Eastern Turkestan prior to Ya'qūb Beg). *Ibid.* 2, no. 4 (1981): 17–37.

———. "Sultan 'Abdülhamid'e sunulan Doğu Türkistan ile ilgili bir rapor" (A report sent to Sultan 'Abdülhamid on relations with Eastern Turkestan). *Ibid.* 3, no. 4 (1983): 39–66.

Bellew, H. W. *Kashmir and Kashgar: A Narrative of the Embassy to Kashgar in 1873–74*. London: Trübner and Co., Ludgate Hill, 1875.

Beveridge, H. "The Khojas of Eastern Turkistan." *Journal of the Asiatic Soceity of Bengal*, no. 71 (1902): 45–46.

Biran, Michal. *Qaidu and the Rise of the Independent Mongol State in Central Asia*. Surrey: Curzon Press, 1997.

Boulger, D. C. *The Life of Yakoob Beg; Athalik Ghazi, and Badaulet; Ameer of Kashgar*. London: W. H. Allen, 1878.

Brunnert, H. S., and V. V. Hagelstrom. *Present Day Political Organization of China*.

Revised by N. Th. Kolessoff and translated by A. Beltchenko from the Russian. Shanghai: Kelly and Walsh, 1912.

Budagov, L., comp. *Sravnitel'nyi slovar' Turetsko-Tatarskikh narechii*. 2 vols. St. Petersburg: Tip. Imp. Akademii nauk, 1869–71.

Burhan Shahidi (Baoerhan 包爾漢). "Lun Agubo zhengquan" 論阿古柏政權(On Ya'qūb Beg's regime). *Lishi yanjiu*, 1958, no. 3: 1–7.

———. "Guanyu Xinjiang lishi de ruogan wenti" 關於新疆歷史的若干問題(On the several questions on the history of Xinjiang). *Minzu yanjiu*, 1979, no. 1: 18–24.

———. "Zailun Agubo zhengquan" 再論阿古柏政權(Again on Ya'qūb Beg's regime). *Lishi yanjiu*, 1979, no. 8: 68–80.

———, comp. *Wei-Han-E zidian* 維漢俄字典 (Uyghur-Chinese-Russian dictionary). Peking: Minzu Chubanshe, 1953.

Bykov, A. A. "Monety Rashaddina, Uigurskogo povstantsa." (Money of Rāshidīn, an Uyghur rebel). *Strany i narody Vostoka*, no. 15 (1973): 288–302.

Chang, Dezhong 常德忠. "Bai Yanhu de yingxiong xingxiang burong waiqu 白彥虎的英雄形象不容歪曲" (Heroic image of Bai Yanhu should not be distorted). *Huizu wenxue luncong* 回族文學論叢. no. 1, Yinchuan: Ningxia Renmin Chubanshe, 1990.

Chen, Ching-lung. "Aksakals in the Moslem Region of Eastern Turkistan." *Ural-Altaische Jahrbücher*, no. 47 (1975): 41–46.

Chen, Yuan 陳垣., comp. *Zhong-Xi-Hui shi rili* 中西回史日曆 (Daily calendar of Chinese, Western and Islamic history). Peking: Zhonghua Shuju repr., 1962.

Chou, N. J. "Frontier Studies and Changing Frontier Administration in the Late Ch'ing China: The Case of Sinkiang 1759–1911." Ph. D. dissertation: University of Washington, 1976.

Chu, Wen-djang. *The Moslem Rebellion in Northwest China 1862–1878: A Study of Government Minority Policy*. The Hague: Mouton, 1966.

Clauson, G. *An Etymological Dictionary of Pre-Thirteenth-Century Turkish*. Oxford: Oxford University Press, 1972.

Clubb, O. E. *China and Russia: The "Great Game."* New York: Columbia University Press, 1971.

Courant, M. *L'Asie centrale aux XVIIe et XVIII siècles: Empire kalmouck ou empire mantchou?* Lyon: A. Rey imprimeur-editeur, 1912.

Courteille, Pavet de., comp. *Dictionnaire turk-oriental*. Paris: Impr. imperiale, 1870.

Dabbs, J. A. *History of Discovery and Exploration of Chinese Turkestan*. The Hague: Mouton, 1963.

Daqing lichao shilu 大清歷朝實錄 (The veritable records of the great Qing dynasty). 1220 quans. Taipei; Huawen Chubanshe repr., 1964.

Davies, R. H., comp. *Report on the Trade and Resources of the Countries on the Northwestern Boundary of British India*. Lahore: Printed at the Government Press, 1862.

DeWeese, Devin. *An "Uvaysī" Sufi in Timurid Mawarannahr*. Papers on Inner Asia, no. 22 (1993). Bloomington: Research Institute for Inner Asia Studies.

Dmitrieva, L. V., comp., *Opisanie Tiurkskikh rukopisei Instituta Narodov Azii* (Description of Turkic manuscripts in INA). vol. 1 (Istoriia). Moscow: Izd-vo 'Nauka,' Glav. red. vostochnoi lit-ry, 1965.

Doerfer, G. *Türkische und mongolische Elemente im Neupersischen.* 4 vols., Wiesbaden: F. Steiner, 1963–1975.

Dong, Caishi 董蔡時. *Zuo Zongtang pingchuan* 左宗棠評傳(Biographical Study of Zuo Zongtang). Peking: Zhongguo Shehui Kexue Chubanshe, 1984.

Dryer, June. *China's Forty Millions: Minority Nationalities and National Integration in the People's Republic of China.* Cambridge, Mass.: Harvard University Press, 1976.

Du, Jianyi 杜堅毅 and Gu Peiyu 顧佩玉. *Xinjiang Hongqian daquan tushuo* 新疆紅錢大全圖説 (Complete collection of Xinjiang *hongqian* with illustrations and explanations). Peking: Zhonghua Shuju, 1996.

Duman, L. I. *Agrarnaia politika Tsin'skogo pravitel'stva v Sin'tsiane v kontse XVIII veka* (Agrarian policy of the Qing government in Xinjiang at the end of the eighteenth century). Moscow: Izd-vo AN SSSR, 1936.

———. "Zavoevanie Tsinskoi imperiei Dzhungarii i Vostochnogo Turkestana" (The Qing conquest of Zungharia and Eastern Turkestan). In *Man'chzhurskoe vladychestvo v Kitae* (The Manchu rule in China). Moscow: 'Nauka,' 1966. English translation by D. Skvirsky, *Manzhou Rule in China*, Moscow: Progress Publishers, 1983: 264–68.

Dyer, S. R. "Soviet Dungan Nationalism: A Few Comments on Their Origin and Language." *Monumenta Serica*, no. 33 (1977–1978).

"Eastern Toorkistan." *The Edinburgh Review*, no. 284 (1874).

Einzmann, H. *Religiöses Volksbrauchtum in Afghanistan: Islamische Heiligenverehrung und Wallfartswesen im Raum Kabul.* Wiesbaden: Franz Steiner, 1977.

Encyclopaedia of Islam. The 1st ed., Leiden, 1913–36. The 2nd ed., Leiden, 1960–in progress.

Enoki, Kazuo 榎一雄. "Shinkyō no kenshō" 新疆の建省 (Establishment of province in Xinjiang). *Kindai Chūgoku* 近代中國, no. 15 (1984): 158–90; no. 16 (1984): 36–69; no. 17 (1985): 75–90; no. 18 (1986): 44–59; no. 19 (1987): 48–82.

Enver Baytur (Anwaer Bayituer 安瓦爾·巴依圖爾). "Maola Musha Shayiranmi he *Yimideshi*" 毛拉穆莎·莎依然米和<伊米德史> (Mullā Mūsa Sayrāmī and *Tārīkh-i ḥamīdī*). *Minzu yanjiu*, 1984, no. 3: 26–33.

Fan, Xiao 樊嘯. "Duiyu Agubo zhe yi renwu pingjia de shangque" 對於阿古柏這一人物評價的商榷(Discussion on the evaluation of Ya'qūb Beg). *Xinhua yuebao* 新華月報, 1955, no. 3: 208–210.

Fairbank, John K., ed. *The Chinese World Order: Traditional China's Foreign Relations.* Cambridge, Mass.: Harvard University Press, 1968.

Fei, Xiaotong 費孝通. *Zhonghua minzu duoyuan iti geju* 中華民族多元一體格局 (The unified structure of Chinese nationalities). Peking: Zhongyang Minzu Xueyuan Chubanshe, 1989.

Feng, Zenglie 馮增烈 and Feng Jun 馮鈞. "Yisilanjiao cai Dongzhi nianjian Shanxi huimin fan Qing qiyi zhong suoqi de zuoyong" 伊斯蘭教在同治年間陝西回民反清起義中所起的作用(The role of Islam in the anti-Qing uprising of the Shanxi Muslims during the period of the Dongzhi reign). *Yisilanjiao cai Zhongguo* 伊斯蘭教在中國(Islam in China). Ningxia: Ningxia Renmin Chubanshe, 1982: 199–227.

Fields, L. B. *Tso Tsung-t'ang and the Muslims*. Kingston, Ontario: Limestone Press, 1978.

Fletcher, J. Jr. "China and Central Asia. 1368–1884." *The Chinese World Order: Traditional China's Foreign Relations*. Ed. by J. K. Fairbank. Cambridge, Mass.: Harvard University Press, 1968: 206–224.

———. "Ch'ing Inner Asia c. 1800." *The Cambridge History of China*. Ed. by D. Twitchett and J. K. Fairbank. vol. 10, pt. 1. Cambridge: Cambridge University Press, 1978: 35–106.

———. "The Heyday of the Ch'ing Order in Mongolia, Sinkiang and Tibet." Ibid. 351–408.

———. "The Biography of Khwush Kipäk Beg (d. 1781) in *Wai-fan Mêng-ku Hui-pu wang-kung piao chuan*." *Acta Orientalia* 35, no. 1–3 (1982): 167–72.

———. "Les <voies> (ṭuruq) soufies en Chine." *Les ordres mystiques dans l'Islam*. ed. by A. Popovic and G. Veinstein. Paris: Ecole des hautes etudes en sciences sociales, 1985: 13–26.

———. "The Naqshbandiyya in Northwest China." Unpublished work.

———. *Studies on Chinese and Islamic Inner Asia*. Ed. by B. F. Manz. Brookfield, VT: Variorum, 1995.

Forbes, Andrew D. *Warlords and Muslims in Chinese Central Asia: A Political History of Republican Sinkiang 1911–1949*. Cambridge: Cambridge University Press, 1986.

Forsyth, T. D. *Report of a Mission to Yarkund in 1873*. Calcutta: Foreign Department Press, 1875.

———. *Autobiography and Reminiscences of Sir Douglas Forsyth*. Ed. by his daughter. London: R. Bentley and Son, 1887.

Freeman-Grenville, G. S. P. *The Muslim and Christian Calendars*. London: R. Collings, 1977.

Fretchling, L. E. "Anglo–Russian Rivalry in Eastern Turkistan, 1863–1881." *Royal Central Asian Journal*, pt. 3, no. 26 (1939): 471–89.

Friedman, Y. *Shaykh Ahmad Sirhindi*. Montreal: McGill University, Institute of Islamic Studies, 1971.

Gavrilov, M. F. "Stranichka iz istorii Iakub-Beka Badauleta—pravitelia Kashgarii" (A page from the history of Ya'qūb Beg Badaulat—the ruler of Kashgharia). In *V. V. Bartol'du. Turkestanskie druz'ia ucheniki i pochitateli*. Tashkent: Tipo-lit, 1927: 125–32.

Geins, A. N. "O vosstanii musul'manskogo naseleniia ili Dunganei v zapadnom Kitae" (On the rebellion of Muslim people or Tungans in western China). *Voennyi sbornik*, 1866, no. 8.

Gladney, Dru C. "Ethonogenesis of the Uighur." *Central Asian Survey* 9, no. 1 (1990): 1–28.

———. *Muslim Chinese: Ethnic Nationalism in the People's Republic*. Cambridge, Mass.: Harvard University Press, 1991.

Gordon, T. E. *The Roof of the World*. Edinburgh: Edmonston and Douglas, 1876.

Gramlich, R. *Die Wunder der Freunde Gottes*. Wiesbaden: Franz Steiner, 1987.

Gregorian, V. *The Emergence of Modern Afghanistan*. Stanford: Stanford University Press, 1969.

Grenard, M. F. *J.-L. Dutreuil de Rhins. Mission scientifique dans la haute Asie, 1890–1895*. Paris: E. Leroux, 1897–98.

———. "Spécimens de la littérature moderne du Turkestan chinois." *Journal asiatique* 9 sér., tom. 13 (1899): 304–346.

Grigor'ev, V. V. *Zemlevedenie K. Rittera* (Physical geography of K. Ritter). 2 vols. St. Petersburg, 1869–1873.

Grum-Grzhimailo, G. E. *Opisanie puteshestviia v Zapadnyi Kitai* (Description of the travel in the western China). 3 vols. St. Petersburg, 1896.

Guan, Lianji 關連吉. "Guanyu Ma Hualong zhi si de lishi zhenxiang" 關于馬化龍之死的歷史真象. *Minzu yanjiu,* 1984, no. 5.

Gubaeva, S. S. *Etnicheskii sostav naseleniia Fergany v kontse XIX–nachale XX v.* (Ethnic composition of the population of Ferghana at the end of the nineteenth and the beginning of the 20th centuries). Tashkent: Izd-vo 'Fan' Uzbekskoi SSR, 1983.

Gurevich, B. P. "Velikokhan'skii shovinizm i nekotorye voprosy istorii narodov Tsentral'noi Azii v XVIII–XIX vekakh" (The Great Han chauvinism and several questions on the history of the Central Asian peoples in the eighteenth to nineteenth centuries). *Voprosy istorii*, 1974, no. 9: 45–63.

———. *Mezhdunarodnye otnosheniia v Tsentral'noi Azii v XVII-pervoi polovine XIX v.* (International relations in Central Asia in the seventeenth through the first half of the nineteenth centuries). Moscow: Nauka, 1979.

———. "Istoriia 'Iliiskogo voprosa' i ee Kitaiskie fal'sifikatory" (History of 'Ili Question' and Chinese falsifiers). In *Dokumenty oprovergaiut protiv fal'sifikatsii istorii Russko-Kitaiskikh otnoshenii* (Documents refute the falsification of the history of the Russo–Chinese relations). Moscow: 'Mysl,' 1982: 423–59.

Habibzade, Ahmet Kemal. *Çin-Türkistan hatıraları* (Recollection on Chinese Turkestan). Izmir: Marifet Matbaası, 1341/1922–23. Translated into Modern Turkish by N. Ahmet Ozalp, Istabul: Kitabevi, 1996.

Hamada, Masami. 濱田正美 "Murrā Birāru no *Seisenki* ni tsuite" ムッラ-ビラ-ルの<聖戰記>について(On *Ghazāt dar mulk-i Chīn* by Mullā Bilāl). *Tōyō gakuhō* 55, no. 4 (1973): 31–59.

———. "Islamic Saints and Their Mausoleums." *Acta Asiatica*, no. 34 (1978): 79–98.

———. "L'Histoire de Ḫotan de Muḥammad A'lam." In 3 parts. *Zinbun*, no. 15 (1979): 1–45; no. 16 (1980): 172–208; no. 18 (1982): 65–93.

———. "Jūkyū seiki Uiguru rekishi bunken jōsetsu" 十九世紀ウィグル歷史文獻序説 (Introduction to the Uyghur historical works of the 19th century). *Tōhō gakuho*, no. 55 (1983): 353–401.

———. "De l'autorité religieuse au pouvoir politique: la révolte de Kūčā et Khwāja Rāshidīn." *Naqshbandis: cheminements et situation actuelle d'un ordre mystique musulman*. Ed. M. Gaborieau, A. Popovic, and T. Zarcone, Istanbul-Paris: Isis, 1990: 455–89.

———. "La trasmission du mouvement nationaliste au Turkestan oriental (Xinjiang)." *Central Asian Survey* 9, no.1 (1990): 29–48.

———. "'Shio no gimu' to 'seisen' no maede" '鹽の義務'と'聖戰'の間て (Between the "obligation of salt" and "holy war"). *Tōyōshi kenkyū*, no. 2 (1993): 122–48.

Hamrajev, M. "Bilal Nazim: ein Klassiker der uigurischen Literatur." *Ungarische Jahrbücher*, no. 42 (1970): 77–99.

Han-Wei Xinjiang diming cidian 漢維新疆地名辭典 (Dictionary of Chinese-Uyghur geographical names in Xinjiang). Urumchi, 1993.

Haneda, Akira. 羽田明 "Minmatsu Shinshō no Higashi Torukisutan" 明末清初の東トルキスタン(Eastern Turkestan in the late Ming and the early Qing period). *Tōyōshi kenkyū* 7, no. 5 (1942): 1–37.

———. "Wari Han no ran no isshiryō" ワリ汗の亂の一史料 (A source on the rebellion of Walī Khān). In *Tsukamoto Hakushi shōju kinen Bukkyō shigaku ronshū* 塚本博士頌壽記念佛教史學論集. Kyoto Tsukamoto Hakushi shōju Kinenkai, 1961: 62–78.

———. "Ghazāt-i-Müslimin no yakukō—Ya'qūb-bäg hanran no isshiryō" Ghazāt-i Müslimin の譯稿: Ya'qūb-bäg 反亂の一史料 (Draft translation of *Ghazāt-i muslimīn*: A source for the rebellion of Ya'qūb Beg). Nairiku Ajia shi ronshū 内陸アジア史論集. Vol. 1. Tokyo: Kokusho Kankokai, 1964: 324–39.

———. *Chūō Ajiashi kenkyū* 中央アジア史研究 (Study on Central Asian history). Kyoto: Rinsen Shōten, 1982.

Hartmann, Martin. *Chinesisch-Turkestan: Geschichte, Verwaltung, Geistesleben und Wirtschaft*. Halle a. S.: Gebauer-Schwetschke Druckerei und Verlag, 1908.

———. "Die osttürkischen Handschriften der Sammlung Hartmann," *Mitteilungen des Seminars für orientalische Sprachen zu Berlin* 7, no. 2 (1904): 1–21.

———. "Ein Heiligenstaat im Islam: Das Ende der Caghataiden und die Herrschaft der Choğas in Kašgarien." *Der islamische Orient: Berichte und Forschungen*, pts. 6–10. Berlin: W. Peiser, 1905: 197–374.

Hayward, G. "Journey from Leh to Jarkand and Kashgar and Exploration of the Sources of the Jarkand river." *Journal of the Royal Geographical Society*, no. 40 (1870): 33–166.

Hedin, Sven. *Scientific Results of a Journey in Central Asia, 1899–1902*. 2 vols. Stockholm: Lithographic Institute of the General Staff of the Swedish Army, 1904–07.

Henderson, G., and A. O. Hume. *Lahore to Yarkand*. London: L. Reeve, 1873.

Henze, Paul B. "The Great Game in Kashgaria: British and Russian Missions to Yakub Beg." *Central Asian Survey* 8, no. 2 (1989): 61–95.

Hertslet, E. *Treaties, &c., Between Great Britain and China; and Between China and Foreign Powers*. 2 vols. London: Harrison, 1896.

Hofman, H. F. *Turkish Literature. A Bio-Bibliographical Survey*. Section 3, pt. 1, vols. 1–6. Utrecht: University of Utrecht, 1969.

Hong, Yuan. 洪源 "Agubo zhengquan de benzhi he Qingbing xizheng de yiyi" 阿古柏政權的本質和清兵西征的意義(The basic features of Ya'qūb Beg's regime and the significance of the Qing expedition to the west). *Xinhua yuebao*, 1955, no. 3: 206–208.

Hopkirk, Peter. *The Great Game: The Struggle for Empire in Central Asia*. New York: Kodansha America, 1990; 1994 repr.

Hori, Sunao. 堀直 "Jūhachi-nijū seiki Uiguru joku jinkō shiron" 十八-二十世紀ウイグル族人口試論 (A preliminary discussion of the Uyghur population in the eighteenth to the twentieth centuries). *Shirin* 60, no. 4 (1997): 111–28.

———. "Jūhachi-nijū seiki Uiguru zoku no doryōkō ni tsuite" 十八-二十世紀ウィグル族の度量衡について (On the measurements of the Uyghurs in the eighteenth to twentieth centuries). *Otemae Joshi Daigaku ronshū*, no. 12 (1978): 57–67.

———. "Shinchō no kaikyō tōji ni tsuite ni-san mondai" 清朝の回疆統治についての二三問題 (A couple of questions on the Qing rule in the Muslim region). *Shigaku zasshi* 88, no. 3 (1979): 1–35.

———. "Shindai kaykyō no kaihe seido"清代回疆の貨幣制度 (Currency system in the Muslim region of Xinjiang). *Nakajima Satoshi Sensei kōki kinen ronshū* 中嶋敏先生古稀紀念論集 (Tokyo: Kyūko Shoin, 1980): 581–602.

———. "Tōkyō Daigaku Tōyo Bunka Kenkyūsho shōjō *Yeerqiang cheng zhuanglishu huihu zhengfu ge xiangce*" 東京大學東洋文化研究所所藏葉爾羌城莊里數回户正賦各項冊. *Kōnan Daigaku kiyō* (Bungakuhen), vol. 51 (1983): 21–56.

———. "Kaikyō toshi Yarukando" 回疆都市ヤルカンド. (Yarkand: A city of the Muslim region). *Kōnan Daigaku kiyō* (Bungakuhen), no. 63 (1987): 39–51.

Hsiao, Ch'i-ch'ing. *The Military Establishment of the Yuan Dynasty*. Cambridge, Mass.: Harvard University Press, 1978.

Hsü, I. "British Mediation of China's War with Yaqub Beg, 1877." *Central Asiatic Journal* 9, no. 2 (1964): 142–49.

———. "The Great Policy Debate in China, 1874; Maritime Defense vs. Frontier Defense." *Harvard Journal of Asiatic Studies*, no. 25 (1964–65): 212–28.

———. *The Ili Crisis*. Oxford: Clarendon Press, 1965.

———. "The Late Ch'ing Reconquest of Sinkiang: A Reappraisal of Tso Tsung-t'ang's Role." *Central Asiatic Journal* 12, no. 1 (1968): 50–63.

Hu, Zhenghua 胡正華, ed. *Xinjiang zhiguanzhi: 1762–1949*. 新疆職官志 (List of officials in Xinjiang). Urumchi: Xinjiang Weiwuer Zizhiqu Renmin Zhengfu Bangongting, 1992.

Huijiangzhi 回疆志 (Gazeteer of Muslim region). Taipei: Chengwen Chubanshe repr., 1968.

Huijiang tongzhi 回疆通志 (General gazeteer of Muslim region). Compiled by Hening 和寧. 1925 jiaoyinben; Taipei: Wenhai Chubanshe repr., 1966.

Huimin qiyi 回民起義 (The Muslim uprising). Compiled by Bai Shouyi 白壽義. 4 vols. Shanghai: Shengzhou Guoguangshe, 1952.

Ibragimova, G. M. "Kratkaia kharakteristika nekotorykh istochnikov o Man'chzhurskikh zavoevaniakh Sin'tsziana" (A brief characteristic of several sources on the Manchu conquest of Xinjiang). *Uchenye zapiski Instituta Vostokovedeniia*, no. 16 (1958): 404–24.

———. "Rukopis' Mukhammeda Aliama" (Muḥammad A'lam's manuscript). *Istoriografiia i istochnikovedenie istorii Azii* (Historiography and source study of Asian history), vol. 1 (1965): 50–55.

Imanaga, Seiji. 今英清二 *Chūgoku kaikyōshi jōsetsu* 中國回教史序説(Introduction to the history of Chinese Islam). Tokyo: Kobundo, 1966.

Ingram, E. *The Beginning of the Great Game in Asia 1828–1834*. Oxford: Clarendon Press, 1979.

Isiev, D. A. "Nachalo natsional'no-osvoboditel'nogo vosstaniia Uigurov vo vtoroi polovine XIX v. (1864–1866 gg.)" (The beginning of the national-liberation insurrection of the Uyghurs in the second half of the nineteenth century). In *Materialy po istorii i kul'ture Uigurskogo naroda*. Alma-Ata: Nauka, 1978: 59–72.

———. *Uigurskoe gosudarstvo Iettishar* (The Uyghur government Yättishahr). Moscow: Izd-vo 'Nauka,' Glav. red. vostochnoi lit-ry, 1981.

İslam Ansikopedisi (Encyclopaedia of Islam). Istanbul: Türkiye Diyanet Vakfı, 1988–.

Israeli, Raphael. *Muslims in China: A Study in Cultural Confrontation*. London: Curzon Press, 1980.

Istoriografiia i istochnikovedenie istorii stran Azii (Historiography and the source study on the history of Asian countries). Vyp. 1, Leningrad: Izd-vo Leningradskogo Universiteta, 1965.

Istoriia Kirgizskoi SSR (History of Kirgiz SSR). Vol. 1. Frunze: 'Kyrgyzstan,' 1984.

Istoriia Uzbekskoi SSR (History of Uzbek SSR). Vol. 1. Tashkent: AN Uzbekskoi SSR, 1955–56.

Iudin, V. P. "Nekotorye istochniki po istorii vosstaniia v Sin'tsiane v 1864 godu" (Several sources on the history of the insurrection in Xinjiang in 1864). *Trudy Instituta istorii, arkheologii i etnografii im. Ch. Ch. Valikhanova Akademii Nauk Kazakhskoi SSR*, no. 15 (1962): 171–96.

———. "Review" of Yusuf Beg Mukhlisov's *Uigur klassik edibiyati qol yazmiliri katalogi. Ibid.* no. 15 (1962): 197–206.

———. "Tarikh-i amniia." *Materialy po istorii Kazakhskikh Khanstv XV–XVIII vekov* (Materials on the history of Kazakh khanate in the fifteenth through eighteenth centuries). Alma-Ata, 1969: 476–90.

Ivanov, P. P. *Ocherki po istorii Srednei Azii (XVI–sredina XIX v)* (Study on the history of Middle Asia, from the sixteenth through the middle of the nineteenth centuries). Moscow: Izd-vo Vostochnyi Literatury, 1958.

'Izzat Allāh, Mīr. "Travels beyond the Himalaya." *Journal of the Royal Asiatic Society of Great Britain and Ireland*, no. 7 (1843): 283–342.

———. *Travels in Central Asia*. Translated by Captain Henderson. Calcutta: Printed at the Foreign Dept. Press, 1872.

Jarring, G. *An Eastern Turki-English Dialect Dictionary*. Lund: C. W. K. Gleerup, 1964.

Ji, Dachun 紀大椿. "Guanyu Agubo zhi si" 關於阿古柏之死(On the death of Ya'qūb Beg). *Xinjiang Daxue xuebao* (Shekeban), 1970, no. 2: 149–51.

———. "Shilun yibaliusi nian Xinjiang nongmin qiyi" 試論一八六四年新疆農民起義(A preliminary discussion of the 1864 peasant uprising in Xinjiang). *Minzu yanjiu*, 1979, no. 2: 37–45.

———. "Agubo dui Xinjiang de ruqin ji qi fumie 阿古柏對新疆的入侵及其覆滅 (Ya'qūb Beg's invasion of Xinjiang and his downfall). *Lishi yanjiu*, 1979, no. 3: 86–96.

———. "Weiwuerzu duliangheng jiuzhi kaosuo" 維吾爾族度量衡舊制考索(Research on the old system of measurements of the Uyghur people). *Xiyu yanjiu*, 1991, no. 1: 59–66.

Johnson, W. H. "Report on His Journey to Ilchi, the Capital of Khotan, in Chinese Tartary." *Journal of the Royal Geographical Society*, no. 37 (1867): 1–47.

Kāmil Khān Īshān. "Risale-i-Iakubi; Vospominaniia o Iakub-beke Kashgarskom Kamil'-Khana-Ishana" (Kāmil Khān Īshān's recollection on Ya'qūb Beg of Kashghar). *Istorik-Marksist*. 1940, no. 3: 129–35.

Kanding Xinjiangji 勘定新疆記 (Records of the pacification of Xinjiang). Compiled by Wei Guangtao 魏光燾 et al. 8 quans. Taipei: Taiwan Shangwu Yinshuguan, 1966 (*Xinjiang Yanjiu Congkan*, vol. 10, ed. by Yuan Dongli).

Karpat, Kemal H. "Yakub Bey's Relations with the Ottoman Sultans: A Reinterpretation." *Cahiers du monde russe et sovietique* 32, no. 1 (1991).

Katanov, N. Th. "Volkskundliche Texte aus Ost-Türkistan." Published by K. Menges. *Sitzungsberichte der preussischen Akademie der Wissenschaften* (Sitzung der phil.-hist. Klasse), no. 30 (1933): 1173–1293.

Kataoka, Kazutada 片岡一忠. *Shinchō Shinkyō tōchi kenkyū* 清朝新疆統治研究 (Study on the Qing rule in Xinjiang). Tokyo: Yūzankaku, 1991.

Kato, Naoto 加藤直人. "Shichinin no hōja tachi no seisen" 七人のホージャたちの聖戰 (The holy war of the Seven Khwājas). *Shigaku zasshi* 86, no. 1 (1977): 60–72.

Keddie, N. R. *Sayyid Jamāl ad-Dīn "al-Afghānī." A Political Biography*. Berkeley: University of California Press, 1972.

Kenan, Yūsuf, comp. *Kenan Bey asarı* (Work of Kenan Bey). Istanbul: Mekteb-i Sanayi Matbaası, 1874.

Khanykov, N. *Opisanie Bukharskago khanstva* (Description of the Bukharan khanate). St. Petersburg, 1843.

Khasanov, A. Kh. *Narodnye dvizheniia v Kirgizii v period Kokandskogo khanstva* (Popular movements in Kirgizia during the period of the Khoqand khanate). Moscow: Nauka, 1977.

Khodzhaev, A. *Tsinskaia imperiia, Dzhungariia i Vostochnyi Turkestan* (The Qing empire, Zungharia and Eastern Turkestan). Moscow: Izd-vo 'Fan' Uzbekskoi SSR, 1979.

———. "Zakhvat Tsinskim Kitaem Dzhungarii i Vostochnogo Turkestana. Bor'ba protiv zavoevatelei" (The occupation of Zungharia and Eastern Turkestan by Qing Chin. The struggle against the conquerors). In *Kitai i sosedi v novoe i noveishee vremia* (China and its neighbors in the modern and the contemporary periods). Moscow: Izd-vo 'Nauka,' Glav. red. vostochnoi lit-ry, 1982: 153–202.

Kiernan. V. G. "Kashghar and the Politics of Central Asia, 1868–1878." *The Cambridge Historical Journal* 11, no. 3 (1955): 317–42.

Kim, Hodong 金浩東. "The Muslim Rebellion and the Kashghar Emirate in Chinese Central Asia, 1864–1877." Ph. D. dissertation, Harvard University, 1986.

———. "The Cult of Saints in Eastern Turkestan: The Case of Alp Ata in Turfan." *Proceedings of the 35th Permanent International Altaistic Conference*. Taipei, 1992: 199–226.

———. "Muslim Saints in the 14th to the 16th Centuries of Eastern Turkestan." *International Journal of Central Asian Studies*, vol. 1 (1996): 285–322.

———. "1870–nyondae Kashgharia-Osman jeguk gan oegyo gyoseop eui jeonmal gua teugjing" (Characteristics and development of diplomatic Relations between Kashgharia and the Ottoman empire). *Jungang Asia Yeongu*, no. 1 (Seoul, 1996): 37–64.

Kitai i sosedi v novoe i noveishee vremia (China and her neighbors in the modern and contemporary periods). Ed. S. L. Tikhvinskii, Moscow: Izd-vo 'Nauka,' Glav. red. vostochnoi lit-ry, 1982.

Komatsu, Hisao 小松久男, ed., *Chūō Yūrasiashi* 中央ユ-ラシア史 (History of Central Eurasia). Tokyo: Yamakawa Shubbansha, 2000.

Kornilov, N. *Kashgariia, ili Vostochnyi Turkestan* (Kashgharia, or Eastern Turkestan). Tashkent, 1903.

Kuhn, A. von. *The Province of Ferghana, formerly Khanate of Kokand*. Translated from German by F. Henvey. Simla, 1876.

Kuhn, Philip A. *Rebellion and Its Enemies in Late Imperial China: Militarization and Social Structure, 1769–1864*. Cambridge, Mass.: Harvard University Press, 1970; 2nd ed., 1980.

———. *Soulstealers: The Chinese Sorcery Scare of 1768*. Cambridge, Mass.: Harvard University Press, 1990.

Kuropatkin, A. N. *Kashgariia*. St. Petersburg: Izd. imp. Russkago geograficheskago obshchestva, 1879. Partial translation into English by W. E. Gowan, *Kashgaria: Eastern or Chinese Turkestan*. Calcutta: Thacker, Spink and Co., 1882.

Kutlukov, M. "Vzaimootnosheniia Tsinskogo Kitaia s Kokandskim Khanstvom" (The interrelations between Qing China and the Khoqand khanate). In *Kitai i sosedi v novoe i noveishee vremia*. Moscow, 1982: 203–16.

———. "Tsinskoe zovoevanie Dzhungarii i Vostochnogo Turkestana v 1755–1759 gg. i osveshchenie v trudakh mestnykh Kashgariskikh istorikov" (The Qing conquest of Zungharia and Eastern Turkestan in 1755–1759 and its description in the works of local Kashgharian historians). *Iz istorii Srednei Azii i Vostochnogo-Turkestana XV–XIX vv.*: 59–82.

Kuznetsov, V. S. *Ekonomicheskiaia politika Tsinskogo pravitel'stva v Sin'tsiane v pervoi polivine XIX veka* (The economic policy of the Qing government in Xinjiang in the first half of the nineteenth century). Moscow: Nauka, 1973.

———. *Tsinskaia imperiia na rubezhakh Tsentral'noi Azii* (The Qing empire on the borders of Central Asia). Novosibirsk: Izd-vo 'Nauka,' Sibirskoe otd-nie, 1983.

———. "Imperiia Tsin i musul'manskii mir" (The Qing empire and the Muslim world). *Tsentral'naia Aziia i sosednie territorii v srednie veka* (Central Asia and the neighboring territories in the medieval period). Ed. V. E. Larichev, Novosibirsk: Nauka, 1990: 106–114.

Landsdell, H. *Russian Central Asia including Kuldja, Bokhara, Khiva and Merv*. London: Searle and Livington, 1885.

Lattimore, O. *Inner Asian Frontiers of China*. New York: American Geographical Society, 1940; Boston repr., 1961.

———. *Pivot of Asia*. Boston: Little, Brown, 1950.

Le Coq, Albert von. *Volkskundliches aus Ost-Turkistan*. Berlin: D. Reimer, 1916.

———. *Buried Treasures of Chinese Turkestan*. 1928; Oxford University Press, repr. 1985.

Lee, Robert H. G. *The Manchurian Frontier in Ch'ing History*. Cambridge, Mass.: Harvard University Press, 1970.

Lewis, B. *The Emergence of Modern Turkey*. 1961; 2nd ed., Oxford: Oxford University Press, 1968; repr. 1979.

Lin, Enxian 林恩顯. *Qingzhao zai Xinjiang de Han-Hui geli zhengce* 清朝在新疆的漢回隔離政策(Segregation policy of the Qing dynasty between the Hans and the Muslims in Xinjiang). Taipei: Shangwu Yinshuguan, 1988.

Lin, Ji 林吉. "Qingdai Shan-Gan huimin qiyi yanjiu gaishu" 清代陝甘回民起義研究

概述(Survey of the Studies on the Shanxi-Gansu Muslim rebellion during the Qing dynasty). *Minzu yanjiu*, 1988, no. 5: 107–112.

Liu, Kwang-ching and R. J. Smith. "The Military Challenge: The North-west and the West." *The Cambridge History of China*, vol. 2, pt. 2. Ed. J. K. Fairbank and K. C. Liu. Cambridge: Cambridge University Press, 1980: 202–273.

Liu, Yingsheng 劉迎胜. *Xibei minzushi yu Chahetai hanguoshi yanjiu* 西北民族史與察合台汗國史研究(Studies on the history of North-western peoples and Chaghatay khanate). Nanjing: Nanjing Daxue Chubanshe, 1994.

Liu, Yongneng 柳用能. "Agubo zuihou fumie de lishi jianzheng" 阿古柏最後覆滅的歷史見證(A historical evidence of the final destruction of Ya'qūb Beg). *Xinjiang Daxue xuebao* (Shekeban), 1979, no. 3: 51–59.

Liu, Zhengyin 劉正寅. "Hezhuo jiazu xingqi qian Yisilanjiao zai Xiyu de huodong ji qi zhengzhi beijing" 和卓家族興起前伊斯蘭教在西域的活動及其政治背景(Islamic missionary activities and its political backgrounds prior to the rise of the Khwāja family in the Western Region). *Shijie zongjiao yanjiu*, 1991, no. 4: 57–64.

Lo, Yunzhi 羅運治. *Qing Gaozong tongzhi Xinjiang zhengce de tantao* 清高宗統治新疆政策的探討(Study on the policy of the Emperor Qianlong in ruling Xinjiang). Taipei: Liren Shuju, 1983.

Lockhart, L. *Nadir Shah: A Critical Study Based Mainly upon Contemporary Sources*. London: Luzac, 1938.

Loewenthal, R., comp., *The Turkic Languages and Literatures of Central Asia: A Bibliography*. The Hague: Mouton, 1957.

Lu, Fengge 盧鳳閣. *Zuo Wenxianggong zhengxi shilue* 左文襄公征西史略(Brief history of Zuo Zongtang's Western campaign). 1947; repr. Taipei: Wenhai Chubanshe, 1972.

Ma, Tong 馬通. *Zhongguo Yisilanjiao jiaopai menhuan zhidu shilue* 中國伊斯蘭教教派門宦制度史略(Brief history of *jiaopai* and *menhuan* in Chinese Islam). Ningxia Renmin Chubanshe, 1983.

———. *Zhongguo Yisilanjiao jiaopai menhuan suyuan* 中國伊斯蘭教教派門宦溯源(Origins of *jiaopai* and *menhuan* of Chinese Islam). Ningxia Renmin Chubanshe, 1987.

Ma, Xiaoshi 馬霄石. *Xibei huizu geming jianshi* 西北回族革命簡史(Short history of the revolution of the Hui people in the Northwest). Shanghai: Dongfang Shushe, 1951.

Madzhi, A. E. "Novyi istochnik po istorii Kokanda, Kashgara i Bukhary" (A new source for the history of Khoqand, Kashghar, and Bukhara). *Izvestiia otdeleniia obshchestvennykh nauk Akademii Nauk Tadzhikskoi SSR* 35, no. 1 (1958): 35–42.

Magomet-Iakub, Emir Kashgarskii. St. Petersburg, 1903. The original novel in French, and translated into Russian by I. G.

Maksheev, A. I. *Istoricheskii obzor Turkestana i nastupatel'nago dvizheniia v nego Russkikh* (Historical survey of Turkestan and the aggresive movements of the Russians into it). St. Petersburg, 1890.

Man'chzhurskoe vladychestvo v Kitae (Manchu domination in China). Ed. S. L. Tikhvinskii, Moscow: Nauka, 1966.

Mano, Eiji 間野英二. *Chūō Ajia no rekishi* 中央アジアの歴史 (History of Central Asia). Tokyo: Kōdansha, 1977.

Manz, B. F. *The Rise and Rule of Tamerlane*. Cambridge, Engl.: Cambridge University Press, 1989.

———. *Central Asia in Perspective*. Boulder: Westview Press, 1994.

Mardin, Ş. *The Genesis of Young Ottoman Thought*. Princeton, NJ: Princeton University Press,1962.

Martynov, A. S. *Status Tibeta v XVII–XVIII vekakh v traditionnoi Kitaiskoi sisteme politicheskikh predstavlenii* (The status of Tibet in the seventeenth through the eighteenth centuries within the traditional Chinese system of political conceptions). Moscow: Nauka, 1978.

Materialy po istorii Kazakhskikh khanstv XV–XVIII vekov (Materials on the history of Qazaq khanates in the fifteenth through eighteenth centuries). Ed. S. K. Ibragimov et al. Alma-Ata: 'Nauka,' 1969.

Mende-Altaylı, Rana von. *Die Beziehungen des osmanischen Reiches zu Kashghar und seinem Herrscher Ya'qub Beg, 1873–1877*. Papers on Inner Asia no. 31, (1999). Boomington: Research Institute for Inner Asia Studies.

Menges, K. "Glossar zu den volkskundlichen Texten aus Ost-Türkistan II." *Akademie der Wissenschaften und der Literatur* (Abhandlungen der geistes- und sozial-wissenschaftlichen Klasse), no. 14 (1954): 679–817.

Meyer, Karl E. and S. B. Brysac. *Tournament of Shadows: The Great Game and the Race for Empire in Central Asia*. Washington, DC: A Cornelia and Michael Bessie Book, 1999.

Mian, Weilin 勉維霖. *Ningxia Yisilan jiaopai gaiyao* 寧夏伊斯蘭教派概要(A survey of the Islamic sects in Ning-hsia). Yinchuan: Ningxia Renmin Chubanshe, 1981.

Michell, John and Robert. *The Russians in Central Asia*. London: E. Stanford, 1865.

Michell, R. "Eastern Turkestan and Dzungaria and Rebellion of the Tungans and Taranchis, 1862 to 1866." n.p., n.d.

Millward, James A. *Beyond the Pass: Economy, Ethnicity, and Empire in Qing Central Asia, 1759–1864*. Stanford: Stanford University Press, 1998.

Minorsky, V. translated and explained. *Tadhkirat al-Mulūk: A Manual of Ṣafavid Administration*. E. J. W. Gibb Memorial Series, New Series 16. London: Luzac, 1943; repr. 1980.

Mīrzā Aḥmad. "Badaulet Iakub-bek, Atalyk Kashgarskii." Published by N. Veselovskii. *Zapiski Vostochnogo otdeleniia Russkogo arkheologicheskogo obshchestva*, no. 11 (1899): 87–103. Ya'qūb beg's photo is found on the page facing p. 87.

Mīrzā Shams Bukhārī. *Nekotorye sobytiia v Bukhare, Khokande i Kashgare* (Some events in Bukhara, Khoqand and Kashghar). Translated with commentaries by V. V. Grigor'ev. Kazan: Univ. tipografiia, 1861.

Miyawaki, Junko. *Saigō no yuboku teikoku* 最後の遊牧帝國 (The last nomadic empire). Tokyo: Kōdansha, 1995.

Morgan, G. *Anglo-Russian Rivalry in Central Asia: 1810–1895*. London: Cass, 1981.

Mu, Yuan 穆淵. *Xinjaing huobishi* 新疆貨幣史 (History of currency in Xinjiang). Urumchi: Xinjiang Daxue Chubanshe, 1994.

Muginov, A. M., comp. *Opisanie uigurskikh rukopisei Instituta Narodov Azii* (Description of the Uyghur manuscripts in INA). Moscow: Izd-vo vostochnoi literatury, 1962.

Mukhlisov, Yusuf Beg., comp., *Uigur klassik edibiyati qol yazmiliri katalogi* (Catalogue of manuscripts on the Uyghur classical literature). Xinjiang, 1957.

Na Wenyigong zouyi 那文毅公奏議 (Memorials of Nayanceng). Compiled by Nayanceng. 80 quans. Taipei; Wenhai Chubanshe repr., 1968.

Nadzhip, E. N., comp., *Uigursko-russkii slovar'* (Uyghur-Russian dictionary). Moscow: Sovetskaia Entsiklopediia, 1968.

Nalivkin, V. P. *Kratkaia istoriia Kokandskago Khanstva* (Short history of Khoqand khanate). Kazan, 1885. French tr. by A. Dozon, *Histoire du Khanate de Khokand*. Paris: E. Ledoux, 1889.

Nishida, Tamotsu 西田保. *Sa Sōdō to Shinkyō mondai* 左宗棠と新疆問題 (Zuo Zongtang and the Xinjiang question). Tokyo: Hakubunkan, 1942.

Nyman, L. E. *Great Britain and Chinese, Russian and Japanese Interests in Sinkiang, 1918–1934*. Stockholm: Esselte Studium, 1977.

Okada, Hidehiro 岡田英弘. "Doruben Oiratto no kigen" トルベン·オイラットの起源 (The origin of Dörben Oyirat). *Shigaku zasshi* 83, no. 6 (1974): 1–43.

Pan, Zhiping 潘志平. *Zhongya Haohanguo yu Qingdai Xinjiang* 中亞浩罕國與清代新疆(The Khoqand khanate in Central Asia and Xinjiang during the Qing period). Zhongguo Shehui Kexue Chubanshe, 1991.

———. "Hezhuo chongbai de xingshuai" 和卓崇拜的興衰 (The rise and decline of the cult of khwājas). *Minzu yanjiu*, 1992, no. 2: 61–67.

Pan, Zhiping, and Jiang Lili 蔣莉莉. "1832–nian Qing yu Haohan yihekao" 1832年清與浩罕議和考(A study on the Qing-Khoqand Agreement in 1832). *Xibei shidi*, 1989, no. 1.

Pantusov, N. N., ed. *Voina musul'man protiv Kitaitsev* (Muslims' war against the Chinese). 2 vols. Kazan: Universitetskaia Tipografiia, 1880–81. See *Ghazāt dar mulk-i Chīn.*

———. *Svedeniia o Kul'dzhinskom raione za 1871–1877 gody* (Information on the Kulja region during 1871–1877). Kazan: Universitetskaia Tipografiia, 1881.

———, ed. *Taarikh Shakhrokhi; Istoriia vladetelei Fergany* (*Tā'rīkh-i Shahrukhī*: history of the rulers of Ferghana). Kazan: Tip. Imperatorskago Univ., 1885.

———. "Taranchinskia pesni" (Taranchi songs). Collected and translated by N. N. Pantusov. *Zapiski Russkago geograficheskago obshchestva po otdeleniiu etnografii* 17, no. 1 (1890).

———. *Materialy po izucheniiu narechiia taranchei Iliiskago okruga* (Materials for the study of the Taranchi dialect in Ili region). Kazan: Tipo-litogr. Imperatorskago Univ., 1901.

———, ed. *Taarikh-i emenie. Istoriia vladetelei Kashgarii.* (*Tārīkh-i amniyya*: History of the ruler of Kashgharia). Kazan: Tabkhane-i Medresse-i Ulum, 1905.

———, ed. and tr. "Obraztsy taranchinskoi narodnoi literatury" (Specimens of Taranchi popular literature). *Izvestiia Obshchestva arkheologii, istorii i etnografii* 25, no. 2–4 (1909); tr. 220 pp., text. 165pp.

Parvin, M., and M. Sommer. "Dar al-Islam: The Evolution of Muslim Territoriality and Its Implication for Conflict Resolution in the Middle East." *International Journal of Middle East Studies*, no. 2 (1980): 1–21.

Pelliot, P. *Notes sur l'histoire de la Horde d'Or*. Paris: Adrien-Maisonneuve, 1949.

———. *Notes critique d'histoire Kalmouke: Texte*. Paris: Adrien-Maisonneuve, 1960.

———. *Notes on Marco Polo*. 3 vols. Paris: Adrien-Maisonneuve, 1959–73.

Petrovskii, N. F. "Kratkaia svedeniia o litsakh, imevshikh otnosheniia ko vremeni Kashgarskago vladetelia Bek-Kuli Beka" (Brief information on the persons related with the time of Kashghar ruler, Beg Quli Beg). Published by N. Ostroumov. *Protokoly zasedanii i soobshcheniia chlenov Turkestanskago kruzhka liubitelei arkheologi*, no. 21 (1917): 89–101.

Petrushevskii, I. P. "K istorii instituta soiurgala" (To the history of soyurghal institution). *Sovetskoe vostokovedenie,* no. 6 (1949): 228–46.

Pevtsov, M. V. *Puteshestvie po Vostochnomu Turkestanu, Kun'-Luniu, severnoi okraine Tibetskogo nagor'ia i Chzhungarii v 1889–m i 1890–m godakh* (Travel to Eastern Turkestan, the northern part of Tibetan mountains and Zungharia in 1889–1890). St. Petersburg, 1895.

Pinghuizhi 平回志 (Record of suppression of the Muslims). Compiled by Yang Yuxiu 楊毓秀. 8 quans. The Jiannan Wangshi edition, 1889.

Pipes, R. *Russia Under the Old Regime*. New York: Scribner, 1974.

Pishchulina, K. A. *Iugo-vostochnyi Kazakhstan v seredine XIV–nachale XVI vekov* (South-eastern Kazakhstan from the middle of the fourteenth to the beginning of the sixteenth century). Alma-Ata: Nauka, 1977.

Poiarkov, O. V. *Poslednii epizod Dunganskago vozstaniia* (The last episode of the Tungan rebellion). Vernoe, 1901.

Potagos (Papagiotis). "Le Pamir." *Bulletin de la Societé de Geographie*, 1866.

——. *Dix années de voyages dans l'Asie centrale et l'Afrique équatoriale*. Translated from Greek by A. Meyer, J. Blancard, and L. Labadie, and edited by E. Burnouf. Only vol. 1 was published. Paris, 1885.

Pritsak, O. "Das Neuuigurische." *Philologiae Turcicae Fundamenta*, vol. 1. Ed. by J. Deny et al. Aquis Mattiacis: Steiner, 1959: 525–63.

Przheval'skii, H. M. *Ot Kul'dzhi za Tian'-Shan' i na Lob-nor*. Moscow: Gos. izd-vo geogr. lit-ry, 1947. English tr. by E. D. Morgan with Introduction by Sir T. D. Forsyth, *From Kulja, across the Tian Shan to Lob-Nor*, London: S. Low, Marston, Searle, & Rivington, 1879.

Qi, Qingshun 齊清順. "Qingdai Xinjiang qianfan yanjiu 清代新疆遣犯研究" (A study on the exiles in Xinjiang during the Qing period). *Zhongguoshi yanjiu*, 1988, no. 2: 83–95.

———. "Qingdai Xinjiang guanli yanglianyin" 清代新疆官吏養廉銀(*Yanglianyin* of the officials in the Qing period). *Xinjiang Daxue xuebao* (Zhesheban), 1990, no. 2: 35–41.

Qin, Hancai 秦翰才. *Zuo Wenxianggong cai Xibei* 左文襄公在西北(Zuo Zongtang in the Northwest). 1945; repr. in Shanghai: Shangwu Yinshuguan, 1946.

Qingdai Zhongguo Yisilanjiao lunji 清代伊斯蘭教論集(Collection of articles on the Chinese Islam during the Qing period). Yinchuan: Ningxia Renmin Chubanshe, 1981.

Qinding Pingding Huijiang chaojin niyi fanglue 欽定平定回疆剿擒逆裔方略(An imperially commissioned military history of the pacification of the Muslim region and the extermination of the rebels' posterity). Compiled by Cao Zhenyong 曹振鏞 et al., 80 quans. Taipei; Wenhai Chubanshe repr., 1972.

Qinding Pingding Shan-Gan Xinjiang huifei fanglue 欽定平定陝甘新疆回匪方略 (An imperially commissioned military history of the pacification of the rebels in

Shanxi, Gansu and Xinjiang). Compiled by Yi Xin 奕訢 et al., 320 quans. Taipei; Chengwen Chubanshe repr., 1968.

Qinding Pingding Zhungaer fanglue 欽定平定準噶爾方略(An imperially commissioned military history of the pacification of the Zunghars). Compiled by Fuheng 傅恒 et al., 54+85+32 quans. Taipei; Shangwu Yinshuguan repr. (Yingyin Wenyuange Sikuquanshu, vols. 357–359).

Radloff, W. *Proben der Volksliteratur der nördlichen türkischen Stämme*. Vol. 1, pt. 6 (Dialect der Tarantschi). St. Petersburg, 1886.

———. *Versuch eines Wörterbuches der Türk-Dialecte* (*Opyt slovaria tiurkskikh narechii*). 4 vols. St. Petersburg: de l'Academie Imperiale des Sciences, 1893–1911.

Rakhimov, T. R. *Kitaiskie elementy v sovremennom Uigurskom iazyke: slovar'* (Chinese elements in the contemporary Uyghur language: Dictionary). Moscow: 'Nauka,' 1970.

Raquette, G. "Eastern Turki Grammar. Practical and Theoretical with Vocabulary." *Mitteilungen des Seminars für orientalische Sprachen* 15–17, no. 2, in three pts. Berlin, 1912–14.

———. *Eine kashgarische Wakf-Urkunde aus der Khodscha-Zeit Ost-Turkestans*. Lund: C. W. K. Gleerup, 1930.

Rawlinson, H. *England and Russia in the East*. London: J. Murray, 1875.

Rawlinson, J. L. *China's Struggle for Naval Development, 1839–1895*. Cambridge, Mass.: Harvard University Press, 1967.

Rawski, Evelyn S. "Re-envisioning the Qing: The Significance of the Qing Period in Chinese History." *Journal of Asian Studies* 55, no. 4 (1990): 829–50.

"Report of the Mirza's Exploration." *Proceedings of the Royal Geographic Society* 15, no. 3 (1871): 175–204.

Romodin, V. A. "Some Sources on the History of the Farghānah and the Khōqand Khānate (16th to 19th cc) in the Leningrad Mss Collection." In *XXV International Congress of Orientalists: Papers Presented by the USSR Delegation*. Moscow, 1960.

Ross, E. D., tr. *A History of the Moghuls of Central Asia: Being the Tarikh-i-Rashidi of Mirza Muhammad Haidar, Dughlāt*. Edited with commentary, notes, and map by N. Elias. 1895; new impression in London: Curzon, 1972.

———, ed. *Three Turki Manuscripts from Kashghar*. Lahore: Mufid-i-Am Press, 1908?. See *Ghazāt-i muslimīn*.

Rossabi, Morris. *China and Inner Asia: From 1368 to the Present Day*. London: Thames and Hudson, 1975.

———, ed. *China among Equals: The Middle Kingdom and Its Neighbors, 10th–14th Centuries*. Berkeley: Unversity of California Press, 1983.

Rostovskii, S. "Tsarskaia Rossiia i Sin'-Tsian v XIX–XX vekakh" (Tsarist Russia and Xinjiang in the nineteenth through the twentieth centuries). *Istorik-Marksist*, 1936, no. 3 (55): 26–53.

Saguchi, Tōru 佐口透. "Higashi Torukisutan hōken shakaishi jōsetsu: Hoja jidai no ichi kōsatsu" 東トルキスタン封建社會史序説:ホージャ時代の一考察(Introduction to the history of the feudal society in Eastern Turkestan: An examination of the Khwāja period). *Rekishigaku kenkyū*, no. 134 (1948): 1–18.

———. *Jūhachi-jūkyū seiki Higashi Torukisutan shakaishi kenkyū* 十七-十八世紀東トルキスタン社會史研究 (Study on the social history of Eastern Turkestan in the eighteenth through the nineteenth centuries). Tokyo: Yoshikawa Kōbunkan, 1963.

———. "Taranchijin no shakai—Iri keikoku no Uiguru buraku shi, 1760–1860" タランチ人の社會—イリ溪谷のウィグル部族史, 1760–1860 (The Taranchi society: the history of the Uyghurs in the Ili valley). *Shigaku zasshi* 73, no. 11 (1964): 1–52.

———. *Roshia to Ajia sōgen* ロシアとアジア草原 (Russia and Asian steppe). Tokyo: Yoshikawa Kōbunkan, 1967.

———. *Shinkyō minzokushi kenkyū* 新疆民族史研究 (Studies on the history of the people in Xinjiang). Tokyo: Yoshikawa Kōbunkan, 1986.

———. *Shinkyō Musurimu kenkyū* 新疆ムスリム研究 (Studies on the Muslims in Xinjiang). Tokyo: Yoshikawa Kōbunkan, 1995.

Sanada, Yasushi 眞田安. "Oasisu bazaru no seidai kenkyū" オアシス.バザルの靜態研究 (A static study on the Oasis bazar). *Chūō Daigaku Daigakuin kenkyū nenbō*, no. 6, (1977): 207–20.

Saray, M. *Rus işgali devrinde Osmanlı devleti ile Türkistan hanlıkları arasındaki siyasi münasebetler [1775–1875]* (The political relations between the Ottoman government and the Turkestan khanates during the period of the Russian conquest (1775–1875)). Istanbul: Istanbul Matbaası, 1984.

Sawada, Minoru 澤田稔. "Hōjā Ishaqqu no shūkyō kattō" ホジャ·イスハックの宗教活動 (Religious activities of Khwāja Isḥāq). *Seinan Ajia kenkyū*, no. 27 (1987).

Schimmel, A. *Mystical Dimensions of Islam*. Chapel Hill: University of North Carolina Press, 1975.

Schuyler, E. *Turkistan: Notes of a Journey in Russian Turkistan, Khokand, Bukhara and Kuldja*. 2 vols., New York: Sampson Low, 1877.

Schwarz, Henry G.. "The Khwajas of Eastern Turkestan." *Central Asiatic Journal* 20, no. 4 (1976): 266–96.

———, comp. *An Uyghur-English Dictionary*. Bellingham: Western Washington, 1992.

Semenov, A. A. "Ocherk pozemel'no-podatnogo i nalogovogo ustroistva v Bukharskogo khanstva" (Study of the land-tax and of the revenue system in the Bukharan khanate). *Trudy Sredne-Aziatskogo Gosudarstvennogo Uniersiteta* 2, no. 1 (1929).

———. "Bukharskii traktat o chinakh i zvaniiakh i ob obiazannostiakh nositelei ikh v srednevekovoi Bukhare" (A Bukharan treatise on the offices and the titles, and their responsibilities in medieval Bukhara). *Sovetskoe vostokovedenie*, no. 5 (1948): 137–53.

Serebrennikov, A. G. *Turkestanskii krai: sbornik materialov dlia istorii ego zavoevaniia* (Turkestan: a collection of materials for the history of its conquest). Especially vols. 21 and 22. Tashkent: Tip. Shtaba Turkestanskago voen. okruga, 19–?.

Shae qinhuashi 沙俄侵華史 (History of the aggression of Imperial Russia). 3 vols. Peking: Zhongguo Shehui Kexueyuan Jindaishi Yanjiusuo, 1981.

Shaw, R. B. *Visits to High Tartary, Yarkand, and Kashghar*. London: J. Murray, 1871.

———. “A Grammar of the Language of Eastern Turkistan.” *Journal of the Asiatic Society of Bengal*, 1877, no. 3: 242–368.

———. “A Sketch of the Turki Language as Spoken in Eastern Turkistan. Part 2 (Vocabulary).” Ibid., extra number to part 1 for 1878: 1–226.

———. “The History of the Khōjas of Eastern-Turkestan. Summarized from the Tazkira-i-khwājagān of Muḥammad Ṣādiq Kāshgharī.” Ed. by N. Elias, and supplement to Ibid. 46, pt. 1 (1897).

Shaw, S. J., and E. K. Shaw. *History of the Ottoman Empire and Modern Turkey*. 2 vols. Cambridge, Engl.: Cambridge University Press, 1976–1977.

Shengwuji 聖武記 (The records of imperial military might). Compiled by Wei Yuan 魏源. Peking: Zhonghua Shuju repr., 1984. 2 vols.

Shimada, Jōhei 嶋田襄平. “Aruti shahuru no wataku to han to” アルティ.シャフルの和卓と汗と (Khwājas and khāns of Altishahr). *Tōyō gakuhō* 34, nos. 1–4 (1952): 103–131.

———. “Shindai kaikyō no nintōzei” 清代回疆の人頭税 (Poll tax in the Muslim region in the Qing period). *Shigaku zasshi* 61, no. 11 (1952): 25–40.

———. “Hōja jidai no beku tachi” ホ-ヂャ時代のベク達 (The begs during the period of the khwāja (domination)). *Tōhō gaku*, no. 3 (1952): 1–9.

Shinmen, Yasushi 新勉康. “Yakūbu Begu seiken no seikaku ni kansuru ichi kōsatsu” ヤ-く-ブ.べぐ政權の性格に關する一考察 (A study on the characteristics of Ya‘qūb Beg’s regime). *Shigaku zasshi* 96, no. 4 (1987): 1–42.

Shorter Encyclopaedia of Islam. Ed. by H. A. R. Gibb and J. H. Kramers. Leiden: E. J. Brill, 1961.

Skrine, C. P. and P. Nightingale. *Macartney at Kashgar: New Light on British, Chinese and Russian Activities in Sinkiang, 1890–1918*. Norfolk: Methuen, 1973.

Stein, Aurel. *Innermost Asia*. Oxford: Clarendon Press, 1928.

Steingass, F. A. *Comprehensive Persian–English Dictionary*. London: Routledge, 1892.

Storey, C. A. *Persidskaia literatura: Bibliograficheskii obzor* (Persian literature: A bibliographical survey). 3 vols. Translated from English with additions by Iu. E. Bregel. Moscow: ‘Nauka,’ 1972.

Stratanovich, G. G. “K voprosu o kharaktere administrativnogo ustroistva i sotsial’noi otnoshenii v Dunganskom Soiuze gorodov (1863–1872 gg.)” (On the question of the characteristics of the administrative structure and the social relations in the Tungan Union of the Zungharian cities [1863–1872]). *Izvestiia Akademii Nauk Kirgizskoi SSR (SON)* 2, no. 2 (1960): 53–65.

Sugawara, Jūn 管原純. “Kūchā Hōjā no ‘seisen’ to Muslimu shoseiryoku” ク-チャ-·ホ-ジャの‘聖戰’とムスリム諸勢力 (“Holy war” of the Kuchean khwājas and Muslim groups). *Nairiku Ajiashi kenkyū*, no. 11 (1996).

Sukhareva, O. A. *Islam v Uzbekistane*. (Islam in Uzbekistan). Tashkent: Izd-vo AN Uzbekskoi SSR, 1960.

Sushanlo, M. *Dunganskoe vosstanie vtoroi poloviny XIX veka i rol’ v nem Bai Ian’khu* (The Tungan rebellion in the second half of the nineteenth century and Bai Yanhu’s role). Frunze: Kirgizskoe gos. Izd-vo, 1959.

Suzuki, Chūsei. “China’s Relation with Inner Asia: The Hsiung-nu, Tibet.” In *The Chinese World Order*: 180–97.

Takakuwa, Komayoshi 高桑駒吉. "Yakub Beg no shiin ni tsuite" 阿古栢伯克(*Yakub Beg*)の死因に就いて(On the cause of Ya'qūb Beg's death). *Shigaku zasshi* 30, no. 4 (1919): 107–111.

Terent'ev, M. A. *Russia and England in Central Asia*. 2 vols., Calcutta: Foreign Dept. Press, 1876. Translation of *Rossiia i Angliia v Srednei Azii*, St. Petersburg, 1875.

Thackston, W. M., tr. *Tarikh-i-Rashidi. A History of the Khans of Moghulistan*. Department of Near Eastern Languages and Civilization, Harvard University, 1996.

Tikhonov, D. "Vosstanie 1864 g. v Vostochnom Turkestane" (The 1864 uprising in Eastern Turkestan). *Sovetskoe vostokovedenie*, no. 5 (1948): 155–72.

———. "Uigurskie istoricheskie rukopisi kontsa XIX i nachala XX v" (The Uyghur historical manuscripts at the end of the nineteenth and the beginning of the twentieth centuries). *Uchenye zapiski Instituta Vostokovedeniia*, no. 9 (1954): 146–74.

———. "Nekotorye voprosy vnutrennei politiki Iakub-beka" (Several questions on Ya'qūb Beg's internal policy). Ibid., vol. 14 (1958): 109–137.

Trimingham, J. S. *The Sufi Orders in Islam*. Oxford: Clarendon Press, 1971.

Troitskaia, A. L. "Voennoe delo v Bukhare v pervoi polovine XIX veka" (Military matters in Bukhara in the first half of the 19th century). *Trudy Akademii Nauk Tadzhikskoi SSR (Institut istorii, arkheologii i etnografii)*, no. 17 (1953): 211–17.

———. "'Zopovedniki'-kurūk Kokandskogo Khana Khudaiara" ("Reserve"-*qurūq* of Khudāyār Khan of the Khoqand khanate). *Sbornik Gosudarstvennoi Publichnoi Biblioteki imeni M. E. Saltykova-Shchedrina,* no. 3 (1955): 122–56.

———. "Arkhiv Kokandskikh khanov XIX veka" (Archive of Khoqand khans in the nineteenth century). Ibid., no. 2 (5) (1957): 185–209.

———. *Katalog arkhiva Kokandskikh khanov XIX veka* (Catalogue of the archive of Khoqand khans in the nineteenth century). Moscow: Izd-vo 'Nauka,' Glav. red. vostochnoi lit-ry, 1968.

Usmanov, K. "Uigurskie istochniki o vosstanii v Sin'tsziane 1864 goda" (Uyghur sources on the uprising in Xinjiang in 1864). *Voprosy istorii*, 1947, no. 2: 87–89.

Vakar, N. "The Annexation of Chinese Turkestan." *The Slavonic and East European Review* 14, no. 40 (1935): 118–23.

Valikhanov, Ch. Ch. *Sobranie sochinenii* (Collected works). 5 vols. Alma-Ata, 1961–1972. A new edition has come out under the same title of *Sobranie sochinenii* (Alma-Ata: Glavnaia red. Kazakhskoi Sovetskoi entsiklopedii, 1984–85). Partial English translation on Kashgharia by John and Robert Michell, *The Russians in Central Asia*, London: E. Stanford, 1865.

Ve'liaminov-Zernov, V. V. "Istoricheskiia izvestiia o Kokanskom khanstve ot Mukhammeda-Ali do Khudaiar-Khana" (Historical informations on the Khoqand khanate from Muḥammad 'Alī to Khudāyār Khan). *Trudy Vostochnogo otdeleniia Russkogo arkheologicheskogo obshchestva*, no. 2 (1856): 329–70.

Veniukov, M. I. *Opyt voennago obozreniia russkikh granits v Azii* (Preliminary military survey of the Russian frontiers in Asia). St. Petersburg, 1873–1876.

"Vospominaniia Illiiskago Sibintsa o Dungansko-Taranchinskom vozstanii v 1864–1871 godakh v Iliiskom krae" (Recollection of an Ili Sibo on the Tungan-Taranchi insurrection in 1864–1871 in the Ili region). Intro. A. D'iakov. *Zapiski*

Vostochnogo otdeleniia Russkogo arkheologicheskogo obshchestva, no. 18 (1907–1908): 233–82.

Waley-Cohen, Joanna. *Exile in Mid-Qing China: Banishment to Xinjiang, 1758–1820*. New Haven: Yale University Press, 1991.

Wang, Ke 王珂. *Higashi Torukisutan Kyōwakuni kenkyū: Chūkoku to Isuramu minzoku mondai* 東トルキスタン共和國研究：中國のイスラムと民族問題 (Study on Eastern Turkestan Republic: Islam in China and the nationality question). Tokyo: Tokyō Daikagu Shupankai, 1995.

Wang, Xilong 王希隆. "Qingdai Wulumuqi tuntian shulun" 清代烏魯木齊屯田述論 (Description of agricultural colony in Urumchi during the Qing period). *Xinjiang Shehui Kexue*, 1989, no. 5: 101–108.

Wang, Zhaowu 王昭武. "Jindai Xinjiang huobi shulue" 近代新疆貨幣述略(Brief Description of monetary units in modern Xinjiang). *Minzu yanjiu*, 1992, no. 3.

Wathen, W. H. "Memoir on the U'sbek State of Kokan, Properly Called Khokend (the Ancient Ferghana) in Central Asia." *Journal of the Asiatic Society of Bengal* 3, no. 32 (1834): 369–78.

———. "Notes of a Pilgrimage Undertaken by an Usbek and His Two Sons from Khokend or Kokan, in Tatary, through Russia, &c. to Mecca. Obtained in Conversation with the Parties." Ibid. 3, no. 32 (1834): 379–82.

———. "Memoir on Chinese Tatary and Khoten." Ibid. 4, no. 48 (1835): 635–64.

Wei-Han zidian 維漢字典(Uyghur-Chinese dictionary). Urumchi: Xinjiang Renmin Chubanshe, 1982.

Wei, Liangdao 魏良韜. *Yeerjiang hanguo shigang* 葉爾羌汗國史綱 (Short history of the Yarkand khanate). Haerbin: Heilongjiang Jiaoyu Chubanshe, 1994.

Weiwuerzu jianshi 維吾爾族簡史 (Brief history of Uyghur people). Urumchi: Xinjiang Renmin Chubanshe, 1991.

"Western China." *The Edinburgh Review*, no. 127 (April, 1868): 357–96.

Whiting, A. S. and Sheng Shih-ts'ai. *Sinkiang: Pawn or Pivot?* East Lansing, Mich.: Michigan State University Press, 1958.

Wu, Wanshan 吳萬善. "Qingzhao Tongzhi nianjian huimin qiyi xingzhi de zaijiantao" 清朝同治年間陝甘回民起義性質的再檢討 (Reexamination of the characteristics of the Muslim uprising in Shanxi and Gansu during the reign of Tongzhi in the Qing period). *Xibei Minzu Xueyuan xuebao* (Zhesheban), 1985, no. 1: 62–69.

———. *Qingdai xibei huimin qiyi yanjiu* 清代西北回民起義研究 (Study on the Muslim uprising in the Northwest during the Qing period). Lanzhou: Lanzhou Daxue Chubanshe, 1991.

Xinjiang nianjian 1999 新疆年鑑 (Xinjiang yearbook 1999). Urumchi: Xinjiang Nianjianshe, 1999.

Xinjiang jianshi 新疆簡史 (A short history of Xinjiang). 2 vols. Xinjiang Renmin Chubanshe, 1979–80.

Xinjiang shihlue 新疆識略 (Brief information on Xinjiang). Compiled by Song Yun 松筠. 12 quans. Taipei; Wenhai Chubanshe repr., 1965.

Xinjiang tuzhi 新疆圖志 (Gazetteer of Xinjiang with maps). Compiled by Yuan Dahua 袁大化 et al., 116 quans. Taipei; Wenhai Chubanshe repr., 1965.

(Huang-yu) Xiyu tuzhi 皇輿西域圖志 (Imperially commissioned gazetteer of the Western Regions with maps). Compiled by Fuheng 傅恆 et al., 4 + 48 quans. Taipei; Wenhai Chubanshe repr., 1970.

Xiyu congzhi 西域總志 (General survey of Western Region) (or, known as *Xiyu wenjianlu* 西域聞見錄 [Record of observation on Western Region]). Chunyuan 椿園. Qiangshutang edition in 1818; Taipei: Wenhai Chubanshe repr., 1966.

Yang, Dongliang 楊東梁. *Zuo Zongtang pingchuan* 左宗棠評傳 (Biographical Study of Zuo Zongtang). Changsha: Hunan Renmin Chubanshe, 1985.

Yeerqiang cheng zhuanglishu huihu zhengfu ge xiangce 葉爾羌城莊里數回户正賦各項冊 (A register of the itemized taxes of the Muslim households and of the names and the distances of the villages in Yarkand). Preserved at the Ōki Bunko, the Institute of Tōyo Bunka Kenkyūsho, Tokyo University.

Yüan, Tsing. "Yaqub Beg (1820–1877) and the Moslem Rebellion in Chinese Turkestan." *Central Asiatic Journal* 6, no. 2 (1961): 136–67.

Zeng, Wenwu 曾問吾. *Zhongguo jingying Xiyushi* 中國經營西域史 (History of Chinese rule of the Western regions). Shanghai: Shangwu Yinshuguan, 1936.

Zenker, J. Th., comp. *Dictionnaire turc-arabe-persan.* 2 vols. Leipzig: W. Engelmann, 1866–76; repr. Hildesheim and New York, 1979.

Zhongguo shaoshu minzu 中國少數民族 (National minorities in China). Peking: Renmin Chubanshe, 1981.

Zhongguo tongji nianjian: 2000 中國統計年鑑 (China statistical yearbook 2000). Compiled by Guojia Tongji Ju. Peking: Guojia Tongji Chubanshe, 2000.

Zhu, Zhuopeng 朱卓鵬 and Zhu Shengwei 朱聖魏. *Xinjiang hongqian* 新疆紅錢 (Red cash in Xinjiang). Shanghai: Xuelin Chubanshe, 1991.

Zlatkin, I. Ia. *Istoriia Dzhungarskogo khanstva (1635–1758)* (History of the Zunghar khanate [1635–1758]). Moscow: Nauka, 1964.

Zuo Wenxianggong nianpu 左文襄公年譜 (The chronology of Zuo Zongtang). Compiled by Lo Zhengjun 羅正鈞. A new edition published in Changsha: Yuelu Shushe, 1983, as *Zuo Zongtang nianpu* 左宗棠年譜.

Zuo Wenxianggong quanji 左文襄公全集 (The collected works of Zuo Zongtang). Compiled by Zuo Zongtang 左宗棠. 100 quans. Taipei; Wenhai Chubanshe repr., 1964.

Index